**Sign Multilingualism**

# Sign Language Typology

Editors
Marie Coppola, Onno Crasborn, Ulrike Zeshan

Editorial board
Sam Lutalo-Kiingi, Ronice Müller de Quadros,
Nick Palfreyman, Roland Pfau, Adam Schembri,
Gladys Tang, Erin Wilkinson, Jun Hui Yang

# Volume 7

# Sign Multilingualism

Edited by
Ulrike Zeshan, Jenny Webster

ISBN 978-1-5015-2494-3
e-ISBN (PDF) 978-1-5015-0352-8
e-ISBN (EPUB) 978-1-5015-0338-2
ISSN 2192-5186
e-ISSN 2192-5194

**Library of Congress Control Number: 2019952836**

**Bibliographic information published by the Deutsche Nationalbibliothek**
The Deutsche Nationalbibliothek lists this publication in the Deutsche Nationalbibliografie; detailed bibliographic data are available on the Internet at http://dnb.dnb.de.

© 2021 Walter de Gruyter Inc., Boston/Berlin and Ishara Press, Lancaster, UK
This volume is text- and page-identical with the hardback published in 2020.
Printing and binding: CPI books GmbH, Leck

www.degruyter.com

# Contents

About this book —— VII

## Part I

1 **Forces shaping sign multilingualism**
   Evangelia Adamou, Onno Crasborn, Jenny Webster and
   Ulrike Zeshan —— 1

2 **Repair in cross-signing: Trouble sources, repair strategies and communicative success**
   Kang-Suk Byun, Connie de Vos, Ulrike Zeshan and
   Stephen Levinson —— 23

3 **Two languages at hand – Code-switching in bilingual deaf signers**
   Ulrike Zeshan and Sibaji Panda —— 81

4 **Stabilisation of the lexicon in an emerging jargon: The development of signs to express animate referents in a sign language contact situation**
   Tashi Bradford, Susanne Michaelis and Ulrike Zeshan —— 127

5 **A minimalist perspective on code blending in TİD – Turkish bimodal bilingualism**
   Selçuk İşsever, Bahtiyar Makaroğlu, İclâl Ergenç and
   Hasan Dikyuva —— 171

6 **Blending languages: Bimodal bilinguals and language synthesis**
   Ronice Müller de Quadros, Diane Lillo-Martin and
   Deborah Chen Pichler —— 201

7 **Methodological innovations in sign multilingualism research**
   Jenny Webster, Kang-Suk Byun, Sibaji Panda and Tashi Bradford —— 227

## Part II

8     Burundi Sign Language-Indian Sign Language bilinguals' community of practice
Sibaji Panda —— 261

9     A community profile of "sign-speakers" at the Indore Deaf Bilingual Academy
Sibaji Panda —— 267

10    Micro-communities of practice: A case study of cross-signing participants in the UK
Tashi Bradford —— 273

11    Micro-communities of practice: A case study of cross-signing participants in India
Tashi Bradford —— 277

12    Community profile of an international group of sign language users: Linguistic and social aspects
Kang-Suk Byun —— 283

**Language Index** —— 293
**Subject Index** —— 295

# About this book

This volume shares findings and innovations from the MULTISIGN project ("Multilingual behaviour in sign language users", European Research Council grant agreement no. 263647). This study encompassed five years of intensive research (2011 to 2016) and laid the groundwork for a new linguistic sub-field, Sign Multilingualism Studies. The project was led by the International Institute for Sign Languages and Deaf Studies (iSLanDS) at the University of Central Lancashire in Preston, UK, in cooperation with partners in the Netherlands, Turkey, India, Germany, and the USA. We are grateful for the European Research Council funding that has made the MULTISIGN study and this volume possible. This includes funding not only for MULTISIGN itself but also for the projects INTERACT (ERC grant agreement 269484, awarded to Professor Stephen Levinson at the Max-Planck Institute for Psycholinguistics) and Grammatical Universals (ERC advanced grant 670985, awarded to Professor Martin Haspelmath at Leipzig University), which facilitated the contribution of two of the volume's chapters.

MULTISIGN contributed toward establishing Sign Multilingualism Studies as a sub-field by demonstrating the array of research questions, methodologies, and findings that scholars can exploit in this area, and collecting large and diverse data sets to examine sign language users' bi- and multilingual behaviours in various situations. The three strands of the project – cross-signing, sign-switching, and sign-speaking – have several overarching findings in common, including the salience of metalinguistic skills and the role of social learning in communities of practice. Moreover, the typological profile of the languages involved, sociolinguistic norms, individual linguistic backgrounds, and the surrounding linguistic environments all play a role in bi- and multilingual outputs. Findings from this project constitute the main content of this volume. By identifying the scope of Sign Multilingualism Studies and its relationships with other areas of linguistics, MULTISIGN paved the way for further research to be integrated into this sub-field.

In addition to sign language linguistics and bi-/multilingualism studies, the MULTISIGN project accessed expertise from other areas of linguistics, including psycholinguistics (Karen Emmorey, San Diego State University), formal grammatical theory (Selçuk İşsever, Ankara University), and pidgin and creole linguistics (Susanne Michaelis, Max Planck Institute for Evolutionary Anthropology and Leipzig University). Moreover, we are particularly grateful to several other colleagues who have greatly enhanced the value of this volume. Stephen Levinson and Connie de Vos supervised PhD student Kang-Suk Byun at the Max Planck Institute for Psycholinguistics, enabling a study on conversational repair to be included in the volume. Evangelia Adamou (National Centre for Scientific Research in France, CNRS) and Onno Crasborn (Radboud University) have contributed their expertise on multilingualism in spoken language and sign language research respectively, adding valuable discussions to the introductory chapter. We also extend our special gratitude to Ronice Müller de Quadros (Federal University of Santa Catarina, Brazil), Diane Lillo-Martin (University of Connecticut), and Deborah Chen Pichler (Gallaudet University), whose vital contribution has enabled us to broaden the scope of this volume to include child language data.

This volume is structured in two main parts. Part 1 contains the main chapters covering key findings and insights related to various bi- and multilingual settings that involve sign language users. Part 2 is about five micro-communities of practice that emerged during the MULTISIGN project work described in Part 1. Three of these communities relate to the rapid emergence of improvised inter-languages in situations of sign language contact (i.e. cross-signing), with communities located in the UK, India, and the Netherlands. The other two communities involve hearing bimodal bilinguals in one group of research participants (i.e. sign-speaking), and deaf signers fluent in two different sign languages in another group (i.e. sign-switching). Most of the Part 1 chapters relate directly to one or more chapters in Part 2, and vice versa. The chapter on bimodal bilingualism in Turkish and Turkish Sign Language in Part 1 does not correspond to a chapter in Part 2, because this group of research participants did not form a sustained community of practice, coming together for data collection sessions only. Conversely, the Indian sign-speakers' community of practice discussed in Part 2 is not represented in Part 1, because the findings from this research were published separately and are not included in this volume.

The high number of deaf multilingual signers in the MULTISIGN team was crucial for the innovative ethics of the project, deaf people's agency in research, and a robust empirical position. With a deaf senior researcher, two deaf research assistants, a deaf PhD student, and a deaf technician, this project contributed toward building research capacity among deaf communities. Various deaf participants from Burundi, India, Germany, Indonesia, Jordan, Nepal, and Turkey worked as fieldwork assistants and ELAN data annotators, giving them first-hand experience of research. Some took part in dedicated capacity-building activities, including a two-week training programme in India undertaken in conjunction with a group of local deaf university students. These factors serve to advance "deaf-led research", which involves how a project operates, its agency, and its team composition.

MULTISIGN's impact extended into linguistics disciplines that have tended to be dominated by spoken languages, and reached beyond academia by illuminating the high-level linguistic skills of international deaf community members. These skills were harnessed in a subsequent applied project called SIGNSPACE

('Multilingual work spaces for sign language users – An online portal driving social innovation', European Research Council grant number 737587). SIGNS-PACE piloted a social innovation by translating the MULTISIGN findings into an online portal with automated sign-to-sign translation, activities that increase meta-linguistic awareness, and tools for setting up multilingual work spaces for transnational groups of deaf signers to collaborate remotely. We hope to continue our work on Sign Multilingualism Studies in both theoretical and applied contexts, and hope to inspire others to undertake further explorations in this area of research.

Part I

# Forces shaping sign multilingualism

Evangelia Adamou, Onno Crasborn, Jenny Webster and Ulrike Zeshan

## 1 Sign multilingualism in context

Sign multilingualism is a field that concentrates on a range of complex multilingual behaviours in sign language users. Although bilingualism and multilingualism is well-entrenched as a domain in spoken language research, these areas have only recently begun to be studied in relation to sign languages, commonly in applied research. For example, bilingualism research in sign language linguistics has investigated deaf people's competence in one signed and one spoken language, usually in its written form. Such studies have often been connected to bilingual-bicultural deaf education, also known as "sign bilingualism", wherein a sign language is used for instruction in order to build competence in a written language (Wilbur 2000). Earlier work had primarily emphasised sign systems like Signed Exact English (e.g. Wilbur 1979), discussing the language contact phenomena inherent in those without taking a broader perspective of language contact.

Psycholinguists have also studied bilingualism involving a sign language, notably in research on "bimodal bilingualism" with hearing children of deaf parents (e.g. Emmorey et al. 2008). However, there are many other complex instantiations of multilingualism involving sign languages, sometimes in the visual-gestural modality only and sometimes in combination with spoken languages.

The need to illuminate these behaviours led to the study "Multilingual Behaviours in Sign Language Users" (MULTISIGN), funded by the European Research Council between 2011 and 2016. MULTISIGN covered occurrences in various settings of three types of phenomena which had previously been sparsely documented or unrecognised, namely: "cross-signing" (the rapid emergence of improvised inter-languages in situations of sign language contact), "sign-speaking" (the structurally mismatched simultaneous use of signing and speaking), and "sign-switching" (codeswitching between sign languages). The majority of contributions in this volume have arisen from the MULTISIGN project, and this first chapter serves as an introduction to the volume and situates it in a wider context.

In the remaining sections, we look at Sign Multilingualism from several perspectives. Section 1.1 compares various branches of bi- and multilingualism research involving sign languages, and equivalent or related phenomena from research on spoken languages, in order to place the study in a wider context of bilingualism research. This section also identifies some interesting phenomena from the sign language modality and from bimodal situations. Section 1.2 explores how the chapters in this volume offer a broader perspective on language contact and the communicative behaviour of signers and speakers. This perspective goes beyond a narrow definition of "linguistics", and includes semiotics, multimodality, translanguaging, and the machinery of multilingual human interaction. Section 2 discusses the main factors that contribute to the communicative settings and outputs described in the volume. These factors include the typological profiles of the languages involved, sociolinguistic norms and social learning, the external linguistic environment, and individual personal factors such as language background and metalinguistic awareness. This section also explores why some of these factors may be facilitative of communication, while others are inhibitive. Finally, section 3 explains how the rest of this volume is structured.

## 1.1 What sign languages teach us about bilingualism

There is currently a boom in research on sign languages contributing not only to a better understanding of how they work but also to a variety of theoretical discussions in linguistics. Indeed, sign languages present several specificities that allow researchers to take a fresh look at a number of research questions, old and new alike. For example, sign languages are generally new languages – most of them with less than 200 years of use – and as such offer a privileged look into language creation which has been addressed mainly through the study of creoles and pidgins. In particular, the study of homesign languages – created by children who do not have access to *any* input – gives us the rare opportunity to observe the fundamentals of human language (Goldin-Meadow et al. 2014). Sign languages are also of special interest because they rely on the visual-gestural modality and therefore offer a window onto cognition beyond what can be observed through the study of co-speech gesture (cf. Zeshan 2015).

In this section, we aim to draw comparisons between various branches of bi- and multilingualism research involving sign languages, such as those represented in this volume, and equivalent or related phenomena from research on spoken languages. This enables us to situate the current research in the wider context of bilingualism research, and to pinpoint particularly interesting phenomena of bi- and multilingualism, either within the sign language modality or in bimodal settings with both signed and spoken languages.

As summarised in Zeshan and Panda (2015), three lines of research can be identified for bilingualism involving a sign language (see Table 1):

a) Research on *sign bilingualism*, targeting bilinguals who use in parallel a sign language A and a spoken language B in its written form.

b) Research on *bimodal bilingualism*, examining the hearing individuals who use a sign language A and a spoken language B.

c) Research on *sign multilingualism*, considering the bilinguals who use more than one sign language.

**Table 1.** Language contact in sign languages

| sign bilingualism | bimodal bilingualism | sign multilingualism |
|---|---|---|
| sign language A & spoken language B in writing | sign language A & spoken language B | sign language A & sign language C |

The chapters in this volume focus on two of the above-mentioned types of bilingualism, i.e., bimodal bilingualism and sign multilingualism.

### 1.1.1 Bimodal bilingualism

Bimodal bilinguals use in parallel a sign language, which relies on manual signs and non-manual behaviours (including head positions, body postures, and facial expressions), and a spoken language. Studies on bimodal bilinguals therefore allow us to observe the *simultaneous* articulation of two languages, a co-articulation that is impossible for spoken languages as they both unfold in the same modality. Interestingly, the sequential use of a sign language and a spoken language, similar to codeswitching observed in spoken languages, is rare (e.g., Bank 2015 on NGT). The two ways of language mixing, simultaneous and consecutive, therefore seem to largely depend on language modality: if simultaneous mixing (blending) is possible, this is what happens. According to Emmorey et al. (2008), the fact that bimodal bilinguals prefer using both languages rather than suppressing one of them indicates that this inhibition mechanism is associated with high cognitive costs. Following on from work by these and subsequent authors, the simultaneous use of signs and spoken words by bimodal bilinguals has been called "code-blending".

Researchers note that the parallel use of a sign language and a spoken language develops naturally among hearing children of deaf parents.[1] Studies show that, despite inter-speaker variation, the spoken language is generally dominant in bimodal bilingual communication among hearing people (see also Müller de Quadros, Lillo-Martin, and Chen Pichler, this volume). The interpretation of this finding is still under debate, with some researchers considering that it is due to the fact that spoken languages are dominant in the broader sociolinguistic context, others suggesting that this preference may reflect a more general human preference for spoken language (Lillo-Martin et al. 2014), and yet others indicating that the focus is likely to depend on the communicative setting. Zeshan and Panda (2017) mention that the bimodal individual may adopt different styles depending on her primary and secondary audiences.

Bimodal bilingual communication should be differentiated from what is termed "sign-supported speech" or "simultaneous communication", a form of bimodal communication which is used in formal settings, such as meetings and lectures, and explicitly targets the parallel use of signed and spoken languages. Bimodal bilinguals, in contrast, do not explicitly aim at the use of the two languages, but this co-articulation arises spontaneously and often becomes the default mode of communication. This indicates that both languages are active for the bimodal bilinguals, a conclusion that is also supported by experimental data (e.g. Morford et al. 2011), and is in accordance with results from unimodal bilingual studies which indicate that both languages are "on" among bilinguals (see Kroll et al. 2015, for a review of the experimental literature on the parallel activation of the bilingual's two languages). Similarly to the well-documented capacity of bilinguals to choose the appropriate code from an early age, current studies also demonstrate that bimodal bilinguals are sensitive to the communicative context and to their interlocutors and can suppress one of the two languages when appropriate.

A widely used method for the study of bimodal bilingualism is the corpus-based analysis of semi-spontaneous interactions, and this is the method that prevails in the MULTISIGN project and in the studies of this volume. These studies cover a substantial range of languages and settings, with the following combinations:
- Turkish Sign Language (TİD) with spoken Turkish (Işsever, Ergenc, Dikyuva, and Makaroglu); adult participants; bilingual setting.

---

[1] The French film *La Famille Bélier* (2014) by Eric Lartigau nicely illustrates such bimodal interactions.

– Brazilian Sign Language (Libras) with Brazilian Portuguese, and American Sign Language with English (Müller de Quadros, Lillo-Martin, and Chen Pichler); young children; two bilingual settings.
– Indian Sign Language (ISL) with Hindi and English (Zeshan and Panda 2017); adult participants; trilingual setting.

The privileged use of corpora for the study of bimodal bilingualism might be due to the fact that many sign languages are not yet well-described, which means that priority is given to the description of the language before turning to the use of other methods, such as grammaticality judgments and experiments. These methodological concerns are similar to those that dominate the study of lesser-described languages more generally.

Analyses of a variety of naturalistic corpora, especially in this volume, indicate that bimodal bilinguals do not *continuously* use the two languages, i.e., the spoken language and the sign language, jointly alongside each other. This may be due to restrictions related to the cognitive load involved in the use of two languages in a single interaction, much like what has been experimentally shown for spoken language alternation. However, we would like to suggest that the systematic use of a sign language and a spoken language in daily communication, as practised by highly proficient bilinguals, most likely attenuates processing costs, in the same way as demonstrated in a study involving bilingual speakers who frequently codeswitch in everyday life (Adamou and Shen 2017). Thus Panda (Chapter 9, this volume) describes a community of highly proficient individuals in India who have developed specific bimodal bilingual skills in the context of a school for deaf children. Such frequent parallel use of the signed and spoken language is reminiscent of the greater cognitive ease that professional interpreters demonstrate with language alternations (Ibáñez, Macizo and Bajo 2010). Memory and processing limitations could therefore be considered as biases, but not necessarily as decisive factors within this bilingual behaviour.

Since parallel use of a sign language and a spoken language is partial, the contexts in which parallel use does occur are of great interest for linguists. For example, while most studies show that there is generally a semantic congruence between the signed and the spoken language, i.e., the same meaning is expressed in the signed and spoken components, it appears that structural congruence is not required. Again, when comparing this with the literature on codeswitching, recent studies show that although structural congruence is a facilitating factor, it is definitely not a prerequisite for codeswitching (Torres Cacoullos and Travis 2015; Adamou 2016). It is of course widely documented for spoken languages that structural congruence can be obtained through calques, and indeed calques are encountered in the bimodal data as well. We present in (1) an example from Müller de Quadros, Lillo-Martin, and Chen Pichler (this volume) that illustrates, on the one hand, the semantic congruence of the two languages, and on the other hand, a syntactic calque in a bimodal utterance where the spoken component, here English, follows the word order of the signed component, in this case ASL.

(1) MOTHER    WHERE                     [ASL]
    Mommy     Where                     [English]
    'Where's Mommy?'

Müller de Quadros, Lillo-Martin, and Chen Pichler (this volume) suggest that the observed semantic congruence in bimodal bilingual interactions indicates that bimodal bilinguals form a single proposition (following Emmorey et al. 2008).

These authors further argue that bimodal bilinguals use a single derivation; i.e., the mental linguistic computational system incorporates elements from the two languages into a single derivation. The study by Işsever, Ergenc, Dikyuva and Makarolu (this volume) supports this approach. The authors show that the elements from the spoken language, Turkish, are not only partly mirrored in the sign language, but that there is a common verb phrase to which the two languages contribute lexically. This can be seen at the level of the verb phrase where 'watch' is expressed in Turkish and 'movie' in TİD, as illustrated in example (2).

(2) Ben   de    gid-ip     izle-me-di-m              [TURKISH]
    I     too   go-CONJ    watch-NEG-PAST-1SG
    I           GO         MOVIE  NOT                [TİD ]
    'I didn't go to watch the movie either.'

However, Zeshan and Panda (2017) provide counter-evidence from Indian Sign Language and Hindi (with minimal English), showing that 48% of the signed and spoken output features syntactic and/or semantic mismatches. What the authors find is that the two propositions share the same communicative intent. To account for the different character of these bimodal bilingual utterances, the authors refer to their data as "sign-speaking". Such differences are reminiscent of the differences between patterns described in "classic codeswitching" (see Myers-Scotton and Jake 2017) and atypical phenomena encountered in mixed languages and in their early stages of formation (Meakins 2013; Adamou and Granqvist 2015; Adamou and Shen 2017).

Based on their bimodal bilingual data, Müller de Quadros, Lillo-Martin, and Chen Pichler (this volume) elaborate the Language Synthesis model and suggest that it can account for all bilingual competence, bimodal and unimodal alike.

More specifically, the Language Synthesis model is a late lexical insertion model; i.e., abstract roots first enter into the computation of a sentence and Vocabulary Insertion takes place once the Syntactic Derivation is accomplished. In contrast, MacSwan (2014) has adapted an early lexical insertion model to account for code-switching; i.e., a Select function draws the Lexical Items from the two lexicons of the bilingual into the Lexical Array, at which stage, Word Order follows the Lexical Items' properties. Then Merge and other operations lead to the Spell Out in the Phonological Component and the Covert Component. Alternative accounts are derived from the psycholinguistic model of speech production in Levelt (1989). This model served as a basis for the Matrix Language Frame model and the 4-M model, which was posited for bilinguals and monolinguals (see Myers-Scotton and Jake 2017, for an updated version), and the model elaborated by Emmorey et al. (2008) for bimodal bilinguals. In future work, the challenge for any model of language production will be to account successfully for both the unimodal bilingual data and the bimodal bilingual data.

### 1.1.2 Complex multilingual settings

A number of interesting findings come from the studies on sign multilingualism, that is, the use of more than one sign language in interactions. Chapters 3 (Panda and Zeshan) and 8 (Panda) report on a study that documents the process of constituting a small bilingual community using two unrelated sign languages, Burundi Sign Language (BuSL) and Indian Sign Language (ISL). It appears that the bilingual signers develop an unmarked way of communicating in a shared mixed variety, independently of the duration of their stay in India and their length of exposure to ISL. This result brings to mind the data from small bilingual communities of spoken languages, which also appear to have patterns of mixing in terms of proportions independent of exposure to the dominant language (Adamou 2016).

In terms of proportions of signs in this Burundi-Indian community, Zeshan and Panda (2015: 112) show that each of the two contributes between 25% and 35%; in other words, 50–70 signs could be clearly identified as being from Burundi or from India. This proportion is more balanced than that found in most bilingual corpora from small communities, in which one language is clearly numerically-dominant and the other at best contributes up to 35% of the word-tokens (Adamou 2016). A possible interpretation of the result from the Burundi-Indian community could be due to the remaining 30–50% of similar signs in the corpus. Indeed, Zeshan and Panda (2015: 111) report that for 40% of the signs used by these signers, the researchers were not able to categorise them as belonging to either BuSL or ISL.

More generally, unrelated sign languages are known to share a relatively large proportion of signs (cf. Meier, Cormier, and Quinto-Pozos 2002; Zeshan and Panda 2015). The shared vocabulary observed in such cases is mainly due to the iconicity of the manual modality, allowing for signs to be understood without prior knowledge of the language. This feature is much less prevalent in spoken languages and constitutes a major difference between the languages that rely on the manual modality and those that rely on the spoken modality.

The Burundi-Indian contact situation exhibits additional complexity due to the presence of shared signs and secondary language contact. The studies in this volume present a particularly rich array of settings, some of which involve more than two languages in contact. Thus, Zeshan and Panda (2017) report that, in a trilingual setting, ISL and Hindi are frequently used in combination in a typologically rare manner, characterised by frequent syntactic and semantic mismatches, whereas English insertions are rarer and follow the more typical patterns of bimodal bilingual communication. This differential treatment in trilingual settings is also found in the interactions of Roma from Greece who exhibit a typologically-rare Romani-Turkish mixing whereas insertions from Greek, the state's official language, follow classic codeswitching patterns (Adamou and Granqvist 2015).

As discussed in this section, the studies that investigate bilingual communication involving sign languages shed new light on the theoretical questions that are at the centre of attention in contemporary linguistics and cognitive science. There is no doubt that this is a research field that will continue to grow and contribute to our understanding of the bilingual mind and the use of two or more languages in society.

## 1.2 Linguistic repertoires of deaf signers

For a long time, one of the central questions in the study of sign languages has been what the effect of the different modality on language structure may be (Klima and Bellugi 1979; Meier 2002; Sandler and Lillo-Martin 2006). Does the fact that sign languages are produced by a different set of articulators, and are perceived visually, impact their structure? If so, how? Which properties of human language transcend modality and can truly be called universal, holding for both spoken and signed languages?

Essentially, these are mono-modal questions: they concern the visual modality in which sign language is produced and perceived, in contrast to the primarily auditory perception of hearing-seeing speakers. But more recently, the field of linguistics has been developing into a multimodal undertaking, accepting that there are many interactions between "verbal" (or spoken) and "nonverbal" (or visual) aspects of communication. For instance, Özyürek et al. (2005) showed that the form of spatial description gestures is influenced by the grammar of the spoken language. Many studies have shown that in perception, people do not just process speech but relate it to information in the speaker's visual behaviour. Swerts and Krahmer (2008) and Krahmer and Swerts (2009) showed that the speech signal has more visual corollaries in the facial behaviour than in the visual perception of the speech articulators ("speech-reading"). Studies on sign languages have started to explore to what extent they also make use of additional, "gestural", components in utterances or even at the level of the sign (Liddell 2003; Hodge and Johnston 2014).

The chapters in this volume demonstrate that unimodality in the sense of a single visual perceptual channel still enables two types of multilingualism: the use of a sign language with a spoken language and the use of two sign languages. There are many ways in which spoken languages impact sign language usage in the visual modality: through visual-manual representations of scripts (fingerspelling, e.g. Branson et al. 1994 on Auslan, and Padden 2002 on ASL); mouthings in sign languages (Boyes Braem and Sutton-Spence 2001); and various forms of more extended code-mixing at the grammatical level, as in sign-supported speech or artificially constructed codes (Wilbur 1979, 1990). All three of these have been extensively studied in the last 50 years. Among them, mouthings have received the most attention. In most sign languages, they appear to be very prominent, especially where signers attend schools that place an important focus on spoken language. Bank (2015) found in a corpus study that in Sign Language of the Netherlands (NGT), mouthings are used in almost every sentence, leading to the conclusion that the "pure" use of NGT or any monolingual concept of what NGT is, is a fiction (Crasborn 2016).

**1.2.1 Challenging the narrow perspective of linguistics**

Some scholars would argue that while it is a positive development that linguists are looking into signed and spoken languages in their multimodal and/or multilingual contexts, there are many more aspects to human interaction. Kusters et al. (2017) phrases this as the need to look not just at the *linguistic* resources that two interlocutors bring to bear, but at the wider semiotic resources that signers or speakers bring to an interaction. This includes not just the interlocutors' knowledge of language, but also the physical environment (Shohamy 2015), for instance. Some of the studies on international interactions between signers, including those in Bradford, Michaelis, and Zeshan in this volume, illustrate how participants make use of nearby objects (such as a signer's T-shirt), and Zeshan (2015: 229) likewise mentions the use of "exophoric pointing to objects and other referents in the vicinity". Pointing to objects or locations visible to interlocutors, however, is often neatly integrated with the rest of the utterance. Liddell (2003) refers to the term "real space" to distinguish it from an imagined or "surrogate" space, and the use of real and surrogate space shows a similar integration of pointing signs in ASL syntax. The fact that "[t]he boundaries between different sign and spoken languages and modalities become fuzzy in sign language contexts" (Kusters et al. 2017: 6) does not relieve us from the task of teasing apart the contributions from the different languages at play and from other non-linguistic resources.

The studies on cross-signing in this volume are especially interesting in this respect. When there are fewer shared linguistic resources to build on, one might expect an intensive use of extra-linguistic resources. In the data analysis for the chapter by Bradford, Michaelis, and Zeshan, the category SPACE is used for 'real space', for instance pointing to objects in the area around the interlocutors. Although not the focus of the study, the examples that are presented do not show a prominent use of real space at all. The authors in addition remark that in the data, this category appears infrequently: in the two rounds of the game that participants played, SPACE accounts for under 4% of all signs. Rather, the interlocutors intensively exploit the part-lexical and non-lexical constructions that are available in each of their sign languages. These include size-and-shape specifiers, classifier constructions, gestures, and constructed action.

Chapter 2 (Byun, de Vos, Zeshan and Levinson) investigates errors in the communication flow, where the addressee signals that he or she has not understood something, i.e. "other-initiated repairs". The cross-signers in this study come from all over the world, all with different language backgrounds. Among the total number of 87 cases of repair identified in the data sets, the large majority (78) consisted of a lexical item that was not understood by the other party. The ways in which these non-understandings were resolved all involved strategies that are also found in regular signed discourse, such as producing a synonym, explaining a concept, giving an example, using constructed action, or articulating complex signs like classifier constructions. The use of (fingerspelled) spoken language also formed part of the strategies, even though this was relatively unsuccessful. The main observation here is that the strategies harnessed by cross-signers are all known methods used by same-language signers, and are amenable to linguistic analysis.

## 1.2.2 Languaging or using language?

Studies on language contact over the last ten years have argued that the purely linguistic take on communication in multilingual contexts is too narrow. There is no sense in which two discrete systems come into contact and "mix" (as in Muysken 2000) to yield multilingual utterances. Garcia and Wei (2015), for example, argue that what children are doing in multilingual settings like a New York school is more a form of "(trans)languaging" than using a rigidly defined language in the traditional sense. Garcia and Cole (2014) discuss the same issue in the context of deaf bilinguals' language use. This especially pertains to the case of the cross-signing interactions like those explored in this volume. The "linguistic repertoires" (Busch 2012) of the people involved are super-diverse, yet they manage to have fruitful interactions based almost exclusively on their regular linguistic competence as multilingual users of primarily signed but also spoken languages.

Nonetheless, in order to understand the way in which signers from different areas combine their native language with forms learned from their interlocutor or newly negotiated forms, we have to assume that there is a way in which we can characterise the communicative patterns a signer would use in his/her native environment, however fluid or variable these patterns might be, both within and across speakers and signers. The fact that "language structure emerges from language use" (Tomasello 2003: 5, as quoted in Zeshan 2015) does not imply that there is no language structure, and this holds as much for monolingual interactions as multilingual interactions.

The need signalled in Kusters et al. (2017) to integrate the multilingual with the multimodal perspective is widely felt in linguistics. Phonetic studies of the type mentioned earlier highlight that we are only beginning to understand how our so-called "non-verbal" behaviour is integrated with our "verbal" behaviour. However, many would argue that it *is* integrated. In his investigation of multimodal interaction among hearing people, Enfield (2009) argues that what he calls a "composite utterance" is in fact an utterance: a unit of multimodal linguistic expression that can be analysed with the tools of linguistics.

The chapters in this volume contribute to a broad view on language contact situations and the communicative behaviour of signers/speakers in such contexts. The studies illustrate that the questions and methodologies are fundamentally linguistic: they concern the units of language(s) and related part-lexical and non-lexical expressions, and how these are combined. Although many additional questions on the use of contextual information could also be posed, the detailed studies in this volume present new findings and taken together contribute substantially to our understanding of the multilingual behaviour of signers.

## 2 Forces shaping multilingual behaviours in sign language users

As mentioned above, when investigating the various bi- and multilingual behaviours that sign language users engage in, it is appropriate to go beyond a narrowly framed linguistic account and include considerations such as other semiotic resources, as well as social and cognitive factors. In fact, the various case studies assembled in this volume show evidence of a range of factors that shape people's communicative behaviours. Some of these factors are briefly explored in this section.

In a study on cross-signing in Zeshan (2019), the relative communicative success of participants in a linguistic elicitation task is captured in terms of the following contributing factors: sociolinguistic norms, external linguistic environment, metalinguistic factors, typological profile of the languages involved, social learning in a community of practice, and individual personal factors such as linguistic background. On the basis of the data, it is hypothesised that some of these factors may have either facilitating effects on the elicitation task (i.e. they make communication easier), or inhibiting effects (i.e. they present an obstacle to communication).

The authors in this volume similarly discuss a number of factors, both linguistic and non-linguistic, that contribute to the communicative settings and outputs. In this section, we briefly discuss the typological profiles of the languages involved (1.3.1), sociolinguistic norms and social learning in communities of practice (1.3.2), and the wider linguistic environment surrounding the bi-/multilingual setting (1.3.3). The impact of all of these factors is evidenced in the contributions to this volume, although not all factors are relevant in all chapters.

### 2.1 Typological profiles in bi- and multilingual situations

One of the hallmarks of this volume is the wide range of languages covered in its contributions. This range of typological diversity adds to the richness of the research findings. For instance, Işsever et al. point out that their work differs from previous work on bimodal bilingualism partly due to the typological characteristics of Turkish and TİD. The authors argue that some of the instances of code-blending between Turkish and TİD in their data involve congruent structures. According to the categorisation in Muysken (2000), congruent lexicalisation applies where two languages happen to have parallel word orders, so that the equivalent lexical sequence is compatible with the grammars of both languages. As Turkish and

TID are both head-final, congruent lexicalisation is regularly observed, as in this example (Işsever et al., this volume):

(3) | Bu | yüzden | Bursa-yı | çok | sev-iyor-um | [TURKISH]
| --- | --- | --- | --- | --- | --- |
| this | reason | Bursa-ACC | VERY | like-PROG-1SG | |
| THIS | REASON | BURSA | VERY | LIKE | [TİD] |

'For this reason, I like Bursa very much'

However, as this example also shows, Turkish and TİD are very divergent morphologically.

The authors compare these patterns of Turkish-TİD congruent lexicalisation with data on code-blending in Italian Sign Language and spoken Italian, where the word orders are incompatible, LIS being an SOV language and Italian an SVO language (Brentari and Donati 2013), and conclude that "the typological features of languages seem to have an impact on the blending patterns".

Where more than two languages are involved in a contact situation, it is relevant to consider the further complexity of their relationships with each other. For example, in the case of ISL-Hindi-English trilinguals, the substantial part of the data where the simultaneous signed and spoken output is syntactically parallel (coded as PAR utterances, see Zeshan and Panda 2017) is facilitated by the fact that Hindi and ISL both have basic verb-final constituent orders and that additionally, word orders in Hindi are quite flexible due to the presence of inflectional morphology. A simultaneous combination of ISL with English, an SVO language with more rigid word order, would pose quite a different challenge. However, the preference for Hindi in the bimodal output, with the use of English as an Embedded Language (in the sense of Myers-Scotton 2001) limited to insertions, also has sociolinguistic reasons in this context.

The typological profile of languages is also important in situations of cross-signing, in particular with respect to typological similarity and dissimilarity. Though recognising that there is currently no methodology for measuring the typological distance between sign languages, Zeshan (2019) argues that cross-signing may present a more difficult challenge if the signer's own language is very divergent from the other sign languages present in the setting. Within the concerned data set, this applies to Japanese Sign Language, which has many particularities not generally shared with other sign languages around the world, including its extensive gender-marking system. This typological distance is a likely inhibiting factor for communicative success in the earliest stages of cross-signing, in comparison with combinations of other languages that have fewer typological particularities setting them apart from each other.

## 2.2 Sociolinguistic norms and social learning

Several chapters address issues in relation to social and sociolinguistic factors that contribute to an understanding of the bi- and multilingual case studies. For the group of trilingual sign-speakers in India, Zeshan and Panda (2017) includes data that show how the primary and secondary audiences that the sign-speaker has in mind determine the degree to which grammatical features from ISL or from Hindi dominate the discourse. Primary deaf audiences cue ISL structures, whereas secondary audiences cue Hindi structures. Interestingly, examples of balanced discourses, where neither of the two languages is grammatically dominant, are also found in the data.

Another example is the use of literacy in the form of a manual alphabet (fingerspelling) and writing (e.g. tracing in the air or on surfaces such as the palm of the hand) that is observed as part of the multimodal repertoire of cross-signers. Partly, this reflects cultural practices and sociolinguistic norms in their country of origin, and the differences in these practices can lead to communicative difficulties (see Zeshan 2015 on the use of written numbers in Arabic, Japanese, and Bahasa Indonesia). On the other hand, if participants share a language of literacy, this can potentially be a bridge that facilitates communication by making manual alphabets and writing-related strategies more available and useful. Chapter 2 by Byun et al. includes literacy as one of the frequent repair strategies used by cross-signers, though this strategy leads to successful repair only some of the time, which underscores both the potential and the difficulties inherent in literacy practices.

In several chapters, it is argued that the small bi- and multilingual communities of sign language users develop shared linguistic characteristics through social learning, and that they constitute communities of practice (CoPs). Though the term "community of practice" (Wenger 1998) has traditionally been applied to larger groups, e.g. professionals in the sphere of law, authors in this volume contend that small groups of individuals – in some cases as small as four to six individuals – can also show characteristics and behaviours suggestive of CoPs. They use the term "micro-community of practice" (MCoP) to recognise that these exist on a reduced scale compared to typical larger CoPs, and to indicate that the emergence of their shared linguistic behaviour may have some interesting differences from their larger counterparts. Each MCoP can be shown to develop its own linguistic characteristics (cf. Lave and Wenger 1991; Eckert and McConnell-Ginet 1992).

Thus Panda (Chapter 8, this volume) notes that the MCoP of bilingual BuSL-ISL users is characterised by their shared background and intensive contact in India (see also Zeshan and Panda 2015). The linguistic variety that emerged from their bilingual signed communication is characterised by consistent contributions of both BuSL and ISL signs, with similar proportions; considerable use of the pool of shared signs in both sign languages; and usually following the source language's patterns in their use of signs from closed grammatical classes, but not open lexical classes (Zeshan and Panda 2015: 126–127).

A particularly clear case of emerging linguistic norms in a MCoP is presented in Chapter 4 by Bradford, Michaelis, and Zeshan. The authors trace the development over time of an inter-language among two groups of cross-signers with respect to the domain of animate referents. The groups start out with a range of variants for signing MALE and FEMALE, and over three to four weeks, the feature pool of variants is greatly reduced to just one or two signs being used for each of the meanings. These two micro-communities of cross-signers are described in the sociolinguistic sketches by Bradford (Chapters 10 and 11, this volume), and it is evident from these sketches that both groups are engaged in social learning, joint endeavours, and group identity formation. For instance, they develop specific in-group jokes and humour.

Such shared social undertakings characterise CoPs in general, and shared linguistic norms are part of the picture. For example, the deaf Burundians arrived in India with the intention of studying at university. As they lived and learned with each other and together with deaf Indians, they developed bilingual linguistic norms alongside their group objectives.

The fact that different sociolinguistic norms lead to different bilingual outputs with regard to linguistic structures is particularly visible when comparing the bimodal bilinguals in India (Zeshan and Panda 2017, and Chapter 9) and in Turkey (Chapter 5 by Işsever et al.). In India, the intention to convey information in a non-disrupted way equally to the deaf and hearing people present in the situation leads to linguistic outputs with mismatched semantic and syntactic structures in the signed and spoken language. In Turkey, on the other hand, we do not find such a pattern, and there is evidence that spoken Turkish is sociolinguistically more dominant.

## 2.3 Linguistic environments surrounding the bi-/multilingual setting

The various settings reported on in this volume are situated in larger linguistic environments. The notion of linguistic ecology (Haugen 1972) is particularly relevant in the more complex cases where multiple languages are involved. In Chapter 4 (Bradford, Michaelis, and Zeshan), the authors argue that the selection of variants for MALE and FEMALE from the feature pool over time is, to a substantial extent, driven by the sign languages used in the environment surrounding the micro-community of cross-signers. For the group located in India, the selection of signs is doubly facilitated not only by the wider Indian Sign Language using setting but also by the fact that the signs MALE and FEMALE are the same in India and Nepal, where two of the signers in the group come from. This in turn is an effect of the geographical and linguistic contact between these adjacent regions. In the UK (see Chapter 10 by Bradford), the linguistic ecology has three layers: the micro-community of cross-signers, the international research institute where the group is embedded and where the main language used is International Sign, and the wider British Sign Language using community. Therefore, the variants selected over time include both IS and BSL signs.

Another similar factor is discussed in Zeshan (2019) in terms of the sign language environment in the home areas of the cross-signing participants. This consideration includes the level of dialectal diversity, which can vary across locations. For instance, Japanese Sign Language is comparatively homogenous and dialectal diversity is decreasing (cf. Sagara 2016), with the Tokyo dialect emerging as a standard variety. At the other end of the spectrum, the sign language environment of Solo in Java, Indonesia, is highly multi-dialectal (Palfreyman 2014, 2015), and multi-dialectalism is characteristic of many areas of Indonesia. Potentially, signers from areas with a greater extent of dialectal variation could be at an advantage in cross-signing situations, because they would have more experience with lexical flexibility, and Zeshan (2019) discusses some preliminary evidence with respect to cross-signers from Japan and Indonesia. The same participants also feature in Chapters 2 and 4 in this volume.

In cross-signing settings, the linguistic ecology includes various sign languages as well as some uses of literacy. By contrast, the cases of bimodal bilingualism include both signing and speaking, and we see evidence of the dominance of spoken languages in some of the chapters, including both settings with children (in Brazil and in the US), and with adults (in Turkey), though the Indian sign-speakers seem to go against this general trend.

## 3 Structure of this volume

With the MULTISIGN project and the present volume as its major output, the intention has been to kick-start a new linguistic sub-discipline of "Sign Multilingualism Studies", developing this area both theoretically and methodologically. The contributions in this volume extend known bi- and multilingual phenomena to the domain of sign languages, going beyond current approaches into novel areas that are specific to the use of sign languages. We hope that MULTISIGN inspires more research in this new field, investigating e.g. the characteristics of International Sign (cf. Rosenstock 2008; Hiddinga and Crasborn 2011; Friedner and Kusters 2015; Whynot 2016), the simultaneous or sequential acquisition of more than one sign language, issues of interpreting between sign languages, and language attitudes in settings where more than one sign language is being used.

This volume is structured in two main parts. Part 1 contains detailed case studies of various multilingual settings involving sign language users. The studies cover a wide variety of locations and theoretical issues, aiming to present to the reader the rich and diverse emerging field of Sign Multilingualism Studies. In addition to individual cases, Part 1 also includes a chapter on methodological innovations (Webster, Byun, Panda, and Bradford) that cuts across several of the research settings. With the emergence of a new field of research, it is only natural that new methodologies need to be found as well.

Part 2 features an exploration of several groups of participants and communities of practice that were formed during the MULTISIGN study. In the two chapters by Panda (Chapters 8 and 9), research conducted with signers in India is brought to life by documenting the Burundi-Indian bilingual signers and the ISL-Hindi-English bimodal bilingual sign-speakers as micro-communities of practice. This is followed by two chapters by Bradford (Chapters 10 and 11) on the micro-communities of cross-signing participants who were recorded in 2012 in the UK and in 2014 in India. Finally, Byun (Chapter 12) examines the cross-signers who met in 2004 at the Max-Planck Institute for Psycholinguistics in the Netherlands.

A separate part with details about each group of participants was deemed necessary so that the case studies in Part 1 can be better understood in relation to the settings, which are, for the most part, highly unusual. Moreover, Part 2 also serves as an explicit reminder that after all, the participant groups are the main actors in these various research undertakings. Their communities of practice, though transitory, are valuable for documentation in their own right. The explicit documentation of the settings also prevents us from seeing linguistic data in isolation from the people who have engaged with us in research and have generously shared their languages, skills, time, and commitment with the research team.

## References

Adamou, Evangelia & Xingjia Rachel Shen. 2017. There are no language switching costs when codeswitching is frequent. *International Journal of Bilingualism* 1–18. doi: 10.1177/1367006917709094.

Adamou, Evangelia & Kimmo Granqvist. 2015. Unevenly mixed Romani languages. *International Journal of Bilingualism* 19. 525–547.

Adamou, Evangelia. 2016. *A corpus-driven approach to language contact. Endangered languages in a comparative perspective*. Boston & Berlin: Mouton de Gruyter.

Akande, Akinmade. 2016. Multilingual practices in Nigerian army barracks. *African Identities* 14(1). 38–58.

Allsop, Lorna, Bencie Woll & John Martin Brauti. 1995. International Sign: The creation of an international deaf community and sign language. In Heleen F. Bos & Gertrude Schermer (eds.), *Sign Language Research 1994: Proceedings of the Fourth European Congress on Sign Language Research*. Munich, September 1–3, 1994.

Bank, Richard. 2015. *The ubiquity of mouthings in NGT: A corpus study*. Nijmegen: Radboud University PhD thesis. Utrecht: LOT.

Boyes Braem, Penny & Rachel Sutton-Spence (eds.). 2001. *The hands are the head of the mouth: The mouth as articulator in sign languages*. Hamburg: Signum Press.

Busch, Brigitta. 2012. The linguistic repertoire revisited. *Applied Linguistics* 33(5). 503–523.

Byun, Kang-Suk, Anastasia Bradford, Ulrike Zeshan, Stephen C. Levinson & Connie de Vos. 2018. First encounters: Repair sequences in cross-signing. *Topics in Cognitive Science* (Special Issue on Miscommunication) 10. 314–334.

Byun, Kang-Suk, Connie De Vos, Stephen C. Levinson & Ulrike Zeshan. 2016. Repair strategies and recursion as evidence of individual differences in metalinguistic skill in cross-signing. Poster presented at the 12th International Conference on Theoretical Issues in Sign Language Research (TISLR12), Melbourne, Australia, 4–7 January.

Byun, Kang-Suk. 2016. *Cross-signing*. Ishara Signed Publications No. 3. Nijmegen: Ishara Press.

Byun, Kang-Suk, Sean Roberts, Connie De Vos, Stephen C. Levinson & Ulrike Zeshan. 2016. Content-biased and coordination-biased selection in the evolution of expressive forms in cross-signing. Paper presented at the 7th Conference of the International Society for Gesture Studies, Université Sorbonne-Nouvelle, Paris, 18–22 July.

Cooper, Audrey. 2014. Signed languages and sociopolitical formation: The case of "contributing to society" through Hồ Chí Minh City Sign Language. *Language in Society* 43. 311–332.

Cormier, Kearsy, Adam Schembri, David Vinson & Eleni Orfanidou. 2012. First language acquisition differs from second language acquisition in prelingually deaf signers: Evidence from sensitivity to grammaticality judgement in British Sign Language. *Cognition* 124. 50–65.

Crasborn, Onno. 2016. What is a sign language? *Linguistic Approaches to Bilingualism* 6(6). 768–771.

Donati, Caterina & Chiara Branchini. 2013. Challenging linearization: Simultaneous mixing in the production of bimodal bilinguals. In Ian Roberts & Theresa Biberauer (eds.), *Challenges to Linearization*, 93–128. Berlin/Boston: Mouton de Gruyter.

Emmorey, Karen, Helsa B. Borinstein, Robin Thompson & Tamar H. Gollan. 2008. Bimodal bilingualism. *Bilingualism: Language and Cognition* 11(1). 43–61.

Enfield, Nick J. 2009. *The anatomy of meaning*. Cambridge: Cambridge University Press.

Friedner, Michelle. 2016. Understanding and not-understanding: What do epistemologies and ontologies do in deaf worlds? *Sign Language Studies* 16(2). 184–203.

Friedner, Michelle & Annelies Kusters (eds.). 2015. *It's a small world: International deaf spaces and encounters*. Washington, DC: Gallaudet University Press.

García, Ofelia & Li Wei. 2015. Translanguaging, bilingualism and bilingual education. In Wayne E. Wright, Sovicheth Boun & Ofelia García (eds.), *The handbook of bilingual and multilingual education*, 223–240. Malden, MA: Wiley Blackwell.

Giezen, Marcel R. & Karen Emmorey. 2016. Semantic integration and age of acquisition effects in code-blend comprehension. *Journal of Deaf Studies and Deaf Education* 21(2). 213–221.

Giezen, Marcel R., Henrike K. Blumenfeld, Anthony Shook, Viorica Marian & Karen Emmorey. 2015. Parallel language activation and inhibitory control in bimodal bilinguals. *Cognition* 141. 9–25.

Goldin-Meadow, Susan, Savithry Namboodiripad, Carolyn Mylander, Asli Ozyurek & Burcu Sancar. 2014. The resilience of structure built around the predicate: Homesign gesture systems in Turkish and American deaf children. *Journal of Cognition and Development* 16(1). 55–80.

Haugen, Einar. 1972. *The ecology of language*. Stanford: Stanford University Press.

Hiddinga, Anja & Onno Crasborn. 2011. Signed languages and globalization. *Language in Society* 40(4). 483–505.

Hodge, Gabrielle & Trevor Johnston. 2014. Points, depictions, gestures and enactment: Partly lexical and non-lexical signs as core elements of single clause-like units in Auslan (Australian Sign Language). *Australian Journal of Linguistics* 34(2). 262–291.

Ibáñez, A., Pedro Macizo & Maria Teresa Bajo. 2010. Language access and language selection in professional translators. *Acta Psychologica* 135. 257–266.

Klima, Edward & Ursula Bellugi. 1979. *The signs of language*. Cambridge, MA: Harvard University Press.

Krahmer, Emiel, & Marc Swerts. 2009. Audiovisual prosody: Introduction to the Special Issue. *Language and Speech* 52(2–3). 129–133.

Kroll, Judith, Paola Dussias, Kinsey Bice & Lauren Perroti. 2015. Bilingualism, mind, and brain. *Annual Review of Linguistics* 1. 377–394.

Kusters, Annelies. 2014. Deaf sociality and the Deaf Lutheran Church in Adamorobe, Ghana. *Sign Language Studies* 14(4). 466–487.

Kusters, Annelies, Massimiliano Spotti, Ruth Swanwick & Elina Tapio. 2017. Beyond languages, beyond modalities: Transforming the study of semiotic repertoires. *International Journal of Multilingualism* 14(3). 219–232.

Levelt, Willem J.M. 1989. *Speaking: From intention to articulation*. Cambridge, MA: MIT Press.

Liddell, Scott. 2003. *Grammar, gesture and meaning in American Sign Language*. Cambridge: Cambridge University Press.

Lillo-Martin, Diane, Ronice Muller de Quadros, Deborah Chen Pichler & Zoe Fieldsteel. 2014. Language choice in bimodal bilingual development. *Frontiers in Psychology* 5. 1163–1178.

MacSwan, Jeff. 2014. Programs and proposals in codeswitching research: Unconstraining theories of bilingual language mixing. In Jeff MacSwan (ed.), *Grammatical theory and bilingual codeswitching*, 1–34. Cambridge, MA: MIT Press.

Meakins, Felicity 2013. Mixed languages. In Peter Bakker & Yaron Matras (eds.), *Contact languages*, 159–228. Boston, MA & Berlin: Walter de Gruyter.

Meier, Richard P. 2002. Why different, why the same? Explaining effects and non-effects of modality upon linguistic structure in sign and speech. In Richard P. Meier, Kearsy Cormier, & David G. Quinto-Pozos (eds.), *Modality and structure*, 1–26. Cambridge: Cambridge University Press.

Meier, Richard P., Kearsy Cormier & David G. Quinto-Pozos (eds.). 2002. *Modality and structure in signed and spoken languages*. Cambridge: Cambridge University Press.

Morford, Jill P., Erin Wilkinson, Agnes Villwock, Pilar Piñar, & Judith F. Kroll. 2011. When deaf signers read English: Do written words activate their sign translations? *Cognition* 118. 286–292.

Muysken, Pieter. 2000. *Bilingual speech: A typology of code mixing*. Cambridge: Cambridge University Press.

Myers-Scotton, Carol & Janice Jake. 2017. Revisiting the 4-M model: Codeswitching and morpheme election at the abstract level. *International Journal of Bilingualism* 21. 340–366.

Özyürek, Asli, Reyhan Furman & Susan Goldin-Meadow. 2015. On the way to language: event segmentation in homesign and gesture. *Journal of Child Language* 42(1). 64–94.

Özyürek, Asli, Sotaro Kita, Shanley E.M. Allen, Reyhan Furman & Amanda Brown. 2005. How does linguistic framing of events influence co-speech gestures? Insights from crosslinguistic variations and similarities. *Gesture* 5(1–2). 219–240.

Palfreyman, Nick. 2014. *Sign language varieties of Indonesia: A linguistic and sociolinguistic investigation*. Preston: University of Central Lancashire PhD thesis.

Palfreyman, Nick. 2016. Variation and change in the numeral system and colour terms of Indonesian sign language varieties. In Ulrike Zeshan & Keiko Sagara (eds.), *Semantic fields in sign languages*, 269–300. Berlin: Mouton de Gruyter & Nijmegen: Ishara Press.

Panda, Sibaji. 2016. Sign-switching. Presentation at the International Conference of South Asian Languages and Literatures (ICOSAL-12), Centre for Endangered Languages and Mother Tongue Studies, School of Humanities, University of Hyderabad, India, 7–9 January.

Panda, Sibaji. 2016. *Sign-switching: Indian Sign Language and Burundi Sign Language*. Ishara Signed Publications No. 4. Nijmegen: Ishara Press.

Rosenstock, Rachel. 2008. The role of iconicity in International Sign Language. *Sign Language Studies* 8(2). 131–159.

Sagara, Keiko. 2016. Aspects of number and kinship terms in Japanese Sign Language. In Ulrike Zeshan & Keiko Sagara (eds.), *Semantic fields in sign languages*, 298–328. Berlin: Mouton de Gruyter and Nijmegen: Ishara Press.

Sandler, Wendy & Diane Lillo-Martin. 2006. *Sign language and linguistic universals*. Cambridge: Cambridge University Press.

Shih, Ya-Chun. 2014. Communication strategies in a multimodal virtual communication context. *System* 42. 34–47.

Shohamy, Elana. 2015. LL research as expanding language and language policy. *Linguistic Landscape* 1(1–2). 152–171.

Stamp, Rose, Adam Schembri, Bronwen G. Evans, & Kearsy Cormier. 2016. Regional sign language varieties in contact: Investigating patterns of accommodation. *Journal of Deaf Studies and Deaf Education* 21(1). 70–82.

Supalla, Ted & Rebecca Webb. 1995. The grammar of International Sign: A new look at pidgin languages. In Karen Emmorey & Judy Reilly (eds.), *Sign, gesture and space*, 333–353. Mahwah, NJ: Lawrence Erlbaum.

Swerts, Marc, & Emiel Krahmer. 2008. Facial expression and prosodic prominence: Effects of modality and facial area. *Journal of Phonetics* 36(2). 219–238.

Tomasello, Michael. 2003. *Constructing a language: A usage-based theory of language acquisition*. Cambridge, MA: Harvard University Press.

Torres Cacoullos, Rena & Catherine Travis. 2015. Gauging convergence on the ground: Codeswitching in the community. *International Journal of Bilingualism* 19. 635–386.

Tunmer, William E. & Judith A. Bowey. 1984. Metalinguistic awareness and reading acquisition. In William E. Tunmer, Chris Pratt & M.L. Herriman (eds.), *Metalinguistic awareness in children*, 12–35. New York: Springer-Verlag.

Van Kleeck, Anne. 1982. The emergence of linguistic awareness: A cognitive framework. *Merrill-Palmer Quarterly* 28. 237–265.

Wang, Qiuying Y., Jean Andrews, Hsiu Tan Liu & Chun Jung Liu. 2016. Case studies of multilingual/multicultural Asian Deaf adults: Strategies for success. *American Annals of the Deaf* 161(1). 67–88.

Wenger, Etienne. 1998. *Communities of practice: Learning, meaning, and identity*. Cambridge: Cambridge University Press.

Whynot, Lori. 2016. *Understanding International Sign*. Washington, DC: Gallaudet University Press.

Wilbur, Ronnie B. 1979. *American Sign Language and sign systems*. Baltimore: University Park Press.

Wilbur, Ronnie B. 1990. A comparison of signs in American Sign Language and Signed English sentences. *International Journal of Sign Linguistics* 1(2). 81–105.

Wilbur, Ronnie B. 2000. Phonological and prosodic layering of non-manuals in American Sign Language. In Karen Emmorey & Harlan Lane (eds.), *The signs of language revisited: An anthology to honour Ursula Bellugi and Edward Klima*, 213–244. Mahwah, NJ: Lawrence Erlbaum.

Zeshan, Ulrike. 2004. Hand, head and face: Negative constructions in sign languages. *Linguistic Typology* 8(1). 1–58.

Zeshan, Ulrike. 2005. Sign languages. In Matthew S. Dryer & Martin Haspelmath (eds.), *The world atlas of language structures online*. Munich: Max Planck Digital Library. Available at http://wals.info/supplement/9

Zeshan, Ulrike. 2015. "Making meaning" – Communication between sign language users without a shared language. *Cognitive Linguistics* 26(2). 211–260.

Zeshan, Ulrike & Sibaji Panda. 2015. Two languages at hand: Code-switching in bilingual deaf signers. *Sign Language & Linguistics* 18(1). 90–131.

Zeshan, Ulrike & Sibaji Panda. 2017. Sign-speaking: The structure of simultaneous bimodal utterances. *Applied Linguistics Review* 9(1). 1–34.

# Repair in cross-signing: Trouble sources, repair strategies and communicative success

Kang-Suk Byun, Connie de Vos, Ulrike Zeshan and Stephen Levinson

## 1 Introduction

The scholarly recognition that signs and gestures comprise actual, genuine languages, following Stokoe's unprecedented research in 1960, made a large impact on the field of linguistics. This and other sign language linguists' research in the next decades introduced the concept of a 'visual-gestural language' for the first time and demonstrated that sign languages have their own phonology, morphology and syntax. However, there is still very little research into the use and scale of these languages.

The World Federation of the Deaf (WFD) states that out of the 7 billion people who live across the globe, about 70 million are deaf (including those who may identify as 'hard of hearing'), which is based on the tendency for 0.1 % of the population to be deaf (Hill, 2015). Thus, only a small proportion of a given population is deaf. Additionally, though sign languages are the languages of deaf communities, not all deaf people use them, making the population of deaf signers smaller still.

Because so few hearing people use sign language, deaf signers become accustomed to exploiting their own and other people's gestural skills. For example, a deaf patron in a restaurant who is unsure about what to order may point at the menu with expression of uncertainty, and the hearing, non-signing waiter may then point to a particular item in the menu and give the thumbs-up gesture. In the same way, signers bring these gestural resources to bear on their communication with signers from other countries. Though two signers may use mutually unintelligible sign languages and may come from different cultures, each is likely to have well-developed gestural abilities from years of communicating in a non-signing hearing world, and can utilise these skills to a high degree when interacting with the other in the visual-gestural modality (Bradford, Sagara and Zeshan, 2013; Crasborn and Hiddinga, 2015; Zeshan, 2015; Byun et al., 2018). Despite considerable structural and lexical differences among sign languages, it seems that deaf signers who come into contact persist through difficulties and challenges to achieve communication. This has led

https://doi.org/10.1515/9781501503528-002

researchers to remark on the surprising camaraderie that deaf people seem to enjoy at international events and when travelling to other countries, as they are already equipped with an understanding of each other due to worldwide similarities in deaf cultures (Spradley and Spradley, 1985). This gives rise to international networks of deaf signers in a similar way to what Zheng et al. (2010) describe in their paper on the concept of social networking based on locations and trajectories of users identified through a Global Positioning System (GPS). In other words, deaf signers connect based on the countries and cities they have travelled to and the sign languages they have learned along their trajectory. When connecting through overseas travel and remote communication, they use ad hoc visual-gestural improvisations to interact, which are called 'cross-signing' here (see also Bradford, Sagara and Zeshan, 2013; Zeshan, 2015; Byun et al., 2017).

Cross-cultural communication skills can play a major role in the ability to carry out repair (i.e. the process in which trouble occurs within the interaction and attempts are made to resolve it, as explained in section 1.2 below). These skills equip the cross-signers with an array of tools they can exploit, sometimes in impressive, numerous consecutive repair attempts, to get their meaning across. This study examines these tools and strategies more closely to get an insight into the nature of cross-signers' meta-linguistic abilities in the area of repair and their effect on the interaction. Being one of the very first investigations into the phenomenon of cross-signing, this study also permits the clear identification of practical conversational tools that could prove useful for deaf individuals who network with overseas peers and/or in the international deaf community or aspire to do so. This could be of benefit to the deaf world as a whole, strengthening its engagement, mutual understanding and unity. The insights offered here into cross-signing might improve the general understanding of International Sign pidgin and give clues as to its historical development and prospective future path. However, it is important to note that International Sign is largely an agreed-upon means of communication with its own lexical and structural resource base (Supalla and Webb,1995; Webb and Supalla 1994), whereas cross-signing represents an incipient, emerging system with no established rules or forms, in which repair is a key process helping interlocutors to create their shared space of meaning (Zeshan, 2015).

This chapter explains the process of conversational repair in the context of cross-signing, with a particular focus on the tools and strategies that cross-signers use to signal trouble and carry out repairs, and to what extent these are successful (cf. Dingemanse et al., 2015). This helps to illuminate what forms and structures cross-signers rely on to keep the conversation going, how they attempt to make themselves understood and sustain their own understanding, and how they build a shared toolkit for communication. After Section 1 introduces the study and some of its key concepts, Section 2 explains the method and data collection, including information about the participants and how the data were annotated. Section 3 explores the general mechanics of conversational repair as well as the specific repair tools used by the cross-signers and their relative rates of communicative success.[1]

The study of repair in cross-signing may be of value not only to people who would like to engage in cross-signing themselves, and people who use International Sign and/or travel internationally, but also to sign language teachers who need to communicate with first-time learners who do not sign at all, and teachers who want to instruct their learners on how to interact with signers who use other sign languages. It also is of value to linguists as an innovative and unusual piece of research into how signers interact when they do not share a language, and how they construct their communication almost from scratch. This is particularly relevant to scholars studying the evolution of language. In addition, the study reveals some of the abilities that humans can rely on for communicative problem-solving in the absence of language.

## 1.1 Cross-signing

'Cross-signing' is a term coined by Bradford, Sagara and Zeshan (2013) to describe the ad hoc communication of signers who do not have a shared language or established conventions to rely on. Although International Sign (IS) and cross-signing are both methods of communication between users of different sign languages, and facilitate cross-cultural social interaction, cross-signing differs from IS. For instance, IS has shared conventions and time-depth (with its use at formal conferences dating back to at least 1976, according to Rosenstock and Napier, 2016), whilst cross-signing does not. Mesch (2010) describes IS as an artificial, symbol-based, hybrid code that is improvised in certain settings, between particular interlocutors. She argues that this makes it too erratic and situation-dependent to be considered a conventional language. IS developed from intensive contact between national sign languages (Mesch 2010). A prerequisite for the successful use of IS is that both people in the interaction already know at least some IS, which usually means they have experience of travel and international communication. If neither or only one of the participants knows IS, then their interaction must necessarily be called 'cross-signing'. Conversations of three or

---

[1] It is important to point out that 'success' is used as a relative term here, because it is not possible to confirm absolutely in each and every instance whether or not a cross-signer has understood an utterance.

more signers were not investigated within this study, but interestingly, informal observation suggests that when one interlocutor in a cross-cultural group has knowledge of IS and uses IS forms, the others may tend to select those forms for their shared repertoire, and favour them over other forms; that is, the interactant with knowledge of IS, which is perceived as a prestigious lingua franca related to American Sign Language (ASL), may have more influence than the other interlocutors over the evolution of linguistic forms used in the group over time (Byun et al., 2018). Moreover, cross-signing is used only in informal two-way conversations, whereas IS may also be used for lectures or presentations, and is exploited in both formal and informal contexts (cf. Rosenstock, 2008; Whynot, 2015).

Because they lack shared conventions, cross-signers are much more reliant on shared knowledge of the immediate setting (cf. Levinson, 2006).They tend to establish grounding (in the sense of Clark and Brennan, 1991) through tools and strategies related to turn-taking, repair, and other interactive features of the conversation, such as pointing and joint attention. According to Clark and Brennan (1991:148) grounding is achieved in a situation where "we and our addressees mutually believe that they have understood what we meant well enough for current purposes" (the grounding criterion). Another related concept is intersubjectivity, in particular, the intersubjectivity of linguistic conventions, i.e. the mutual knowledge that everyone in the interaction can use and understand the conventions (Tomasello, 2003). This intersubjectivity is notably absent when two cross-signers meet for the first time.

In face-to-face communication, frequent backchannelling helps to sustain the interaction and establish common ground. Backchannels are behaviours that an addressee uses to signal continued interest and understanding, co-occurring with another interlocutor's turn (cf. Dixon and Foster, 1998; White, 1998). The multimodality of backchanneling, for example via vocalisations such as "uh-huh" in English or via nodding, has been recognized in spoken languages, and research has extended to cross-linguistic and language contact settings (e.g. Cutrone, 2005; Heinz, 2003). Interestingly, the present study supports the notion that backchannelling patterns in signed conversations differ from those found in the spoken language research (see also Manrique and Enfield, 2015, on Argentinean Sign Language). To indicate trouble in a spoken language conversation, an overtly negative backchannel (e.g. a frown) would tend to be used, whereas in sign language interactions, trouble can be indicated by the lack of a positive backchannel (i.e. a neutral face; see Section 3.2).

Where individual signs are the source of communication trouble in cross-signing, this often involves difficulty in agreeing on a shared code, i.e. shared forms that both interlocutors understand, and know that each other understand.

Zeshan (2015) discusses the intersubjective multilingual-multimodal space gradually constructed by cross-signers during their conversations. Use of a shared code is obviously problematic in cross-signing scenarios, as the interlocutors initially have no common sign language and no previous experience communicating with each other, making the non-understanding of forms quite frequent. In cross-signing conversations, sometimes the addressee is familiar with the form or sign being used, but still does not understand the intended meaning and/or context, and/or does not have enough background information to ascertain what is being communicated.

This study looks closely at how people slowly start to communicate with each other, focussing on their first interactions; motivated by the desire to interact, they surmount obstacles and cooperate to achieve their communication goals. Sometimes the goals may be achieved, but sometimes there may be trouble and both interlocutors may have to make substantial conscious efforts to resolve it, e.g. using repair strategies (Dingemanse et al., 2015).

## 1.2 Conversational repair

In this paper, the notion of repair and its associated communicative interactions and strategies constitute the main framework, as well as the coding system described in Section 2 on methodology. One of the most important areas to focus on when considering cross-signing as a phenomenon is conversational repair (Byun et al., 2018). *Repair* is a process in which trouble occurs and is pointed out, and attempts are made to resolve it; this sequence has been described within the realm of conversational analysis, or CA (Schegloff, Jefferson and Sacks, 1977). In other words, *repair* refers to the set of practices whereby a co-interactant interrupts the ongoing course of action to attend to possible trouble in speaking, hearing or understanding the talk. *Trouble* includes "misarticulations, malapropisms, use of a 'wrong' word, unavailability of a word when needed, failure to hear or to be heard, trouble on the part of the recipient in understanding, and incorrect understandings by recipients" (Schegloff, 1987). Repair is then used to ensure "that the interaction does not freeze in its place when trouble arises, that intersubjectivity is maintained or restored and that the turn and sequence and activity can progress to possible completion" (Schegloff, Jefferson and Sacks, 1977).

Interlocutors will generally make attempts to overcome the trouble instead of ignoring it or giving up. They may make repeated attempts at repair of a single trouble source before coming to a resolution. A person may for example try a number of different words or signs until one is successfully understood by their interlocutor. Very rarely is repair a one-off occurrence in a conversation; it is a phenomenon that happens continually, and is naturally expected in many contexts. Other-initiated repair (OIR) has been found to occur once every 1.4 minutes on average in any language (Dingemanse et al., 2015). Humans use repair universally, to negotiate communication in every interaction. This is shown by Dingemanse et al. (2015), who found that repair sequences across 12 languages were remarkably similar. They theorised that this was due to three factors: self-referentiality (talking about the communication itself, e.g. 'Did you mean Stephen?'); social intelligence and theory of mind (knowing that others see the world in a different way); and collaborative action (cooperating and sharing decisions about communication, e.g. how much time to spend on a repair sequence). Repair contributes to the co-creation of shared understanding. It may be a joint effort, where for example one person finishes another person's truncated sentence.

Drawing on aspects of CA, this study examines repair sequences in cross-signing situations. This is an innovative undertaking, as previously most research into repair has focused on interlocutors using the same language (Sacks, Schegloff and Jefferson, 1974; Schegloff, Jefferson and Sacks, 1977; see also Dingemanse et al., 2015).

According to Schegloff et al. (1977), there are technically two kinds of repair, one originating from the person producing the message (self-initiated repair, SIR), and one originating from the receiver of the message (other-initiated repair, OIR). These are discussed separately in the literature. In a repair sequence, there are distinct parts: T0 refers to the instance when the trouble is indicated (e.g. 'sorry, what?'). T-1 is used to mean the actual trouble source, i.e. the utterance that caused a problem (Dingemanse et al., 2015) or misunderstanding (Pietikainen, 2016). T+1 is the turn where a solution is offered. The forms of turns at T+1 and T-1 will be examined further as these are the forms that create trouble (T-1) and constitute solutions (T+1).

The main focus in this chapter is on the strategies that signers employ at T+1, as illustrated in Figure 1. In this figure, T-1 involves Signer D producing a form for 'man' from Hong Kong Sign Language (HKSL), articulated at the side of the head. At T0, Signer A signals trouble by repeating the form. At T+1, Signer D offers the Korean Sign Language (KSL) raised-thumb form for 'man' as a solution.

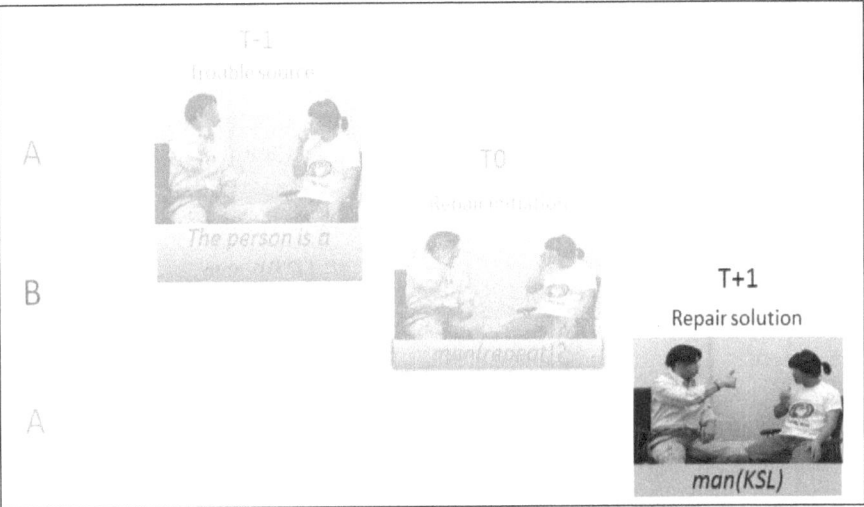

**Figure 1.** Repair solution (T+1)

Another key issue is the actual means or strategies of repair; resolving trouble through repair cannot be characterised as simply asking or urging the other person to explain more. It involves distinct and identifiable strategies. The data analysed in this chapter have been coded with a focus on these various strategies used in repair sequences.

Repair is very important in cross-signing for several reasons. Firstly, repair facilitates problem identification and joint attention, giving signers a ready framework in which to point out trouble and thus enabling them to share the same focus on a specific item. Secondly, repair sequences allow signers to build interaction with a common goal (resolving the trouble), within the structure of turn-taking. Thirdly, repair gives signers the chance to engage in problem solving, as they consider and decide on strategies to try and then retain or abandon. Lastly, cross-signers learn through repair, and acquire communicative tools for their personal toolkit or repertoire.

In cross-signing, repair appears to be more welcome and expected compared to repair in interactions between users of the same language; however, repair initiations in cross-signing occur less frequently than once every 1.4 minutes, which was the average rate for multiple languages found by Dingemanse et al. (2015). Rather, repair initiations in the cross-signing data occur about every 2.1 minutes. This is probably because cross-signing proceeds at a slower pace than same-language interactions, and because only the first repair initiation of a sequence was included in this data. A notable feature of cross-signing is the lengthy repair sequences, which often involve side-sequences and repairs-within-repairs, so if all of the initiations in a sequence were included, the rate may be closer to Dingemanse et al.'s (2015) rate of once every 1.4 minutes. As the data suggest, repair is a dialogue strategy that cross-signers seem to use readily and openly to facilitate negotiation. Their repair attempts, including other-initiated repair, seem to occur mostly without the frustration and face-threats that sometimes accompany repair in same-language conversations, which contribute to a preference for self-initiated repair amongst same-language users (Schegloff et al., 1977).

In the context of signaling specific problems or potential trouble sources, previous research (Byun et al., 2018) has demonstrated the use of try-markers by cross-signers. Drawing on Moerman (1988), Byun et al. (2018) define "try-marker" as "a device that is used to indicate a test of the addressee's recognition of a referent. The device is followed by a hesitation pause in expectation of a sign from the addressee as to whether the referent is known to the addressee". An example of how a try-marker is realized in a spoken language is a rise in intonation at on the try-marked constituent in English.

Via their interactions and repair sequences, cross-signers provide each other with opportunities to negotiate signs and meanings and develop a shared repertoire (Zeshan, 2015), and this leads to the emergence and evolution of a mutually-agreed system of communication.

## 1.3 Research question

The research question for the study reported here covers sequences in other-initiated repair (OIR) in cross-signing, and can be formulated as follows:

- In cross-signing OIR, what do the T+1 turns look like, and how does communicative success vary across the different T+1 strategies ?

This question sets the stage for the main topic of the research, that is, the deployment and success of repair strategies. Which repair strategies do signers deploy to resolve communication trouble? When there is a communication breakdown, signers theoretically have many ways of trying to resolve the trouble. For instance, they could resort to writing, fingerspelling, giving examples, or using alternative signs from other sign languages. Within the small sample of signers in this study, the aim was to track which of the possible resources signers used in real conversations. Once the repair strategies have been identified, it is interesting to consider how successful the repair attempts are when these strategies are deployed.

## 2 Methodology

This section explains what kind of data was used in this study, and the size of the two main data sets. In 2.1, the participants are introduced briefly along with relevant details about their backgrounds, in particular their languages and experience of international travel. This is important because the two data sets differ in this regard, with possible implications for the analyses. In 2.2, the annotation process is described, including how categories of repair strategies were developed, and how values were assigned to the data inductively.

### 2.1 Data and participants

The data for this study come from two sources. The first is a corpus created during the Sign Language Typology project, directed by co-author Zeshan from 2003–2006 at the Max Planck Institute for Psycholinguistics in Nijmegen, the Netherlands (see also Byun et al., 2018, for details about this corpus). The second corpus comes from one sub-group of participants in the project Multilingual Behaviours in Sign Language Users (Multisign), also led by Zeshan, which took place from 2011–2016. For both corpora, dyads of deaf signers who did not share any common language were filmed communicating. These individuals came from China, Hong Kong, India, Indonesia, Jordan, the UK, Japan, South Korea, Nepal, the Netherlands, Turkey and Uzbekistan. Figure 2 shows the interaction pairs in which signers participated in the two projects, and arrows signifying the dyads used for this chapter appear in bold. The abbreviations used to refer to the sign languages discussed in this chapter are listed in Table 1.

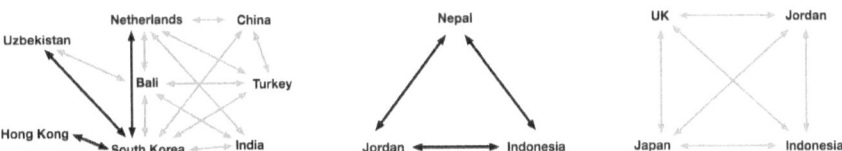

**Figure 2.** Participant configurations of cross-signing participants (Typology project dyads at left, and Multisign project dyads at right)

Table 1. Abbreviations for the sign languages used in this chapter

| Sign Language | Abbreviation |
| --- | --- |
| German Sign Language | DGS |
| Hong Kong Sign Language | HKSL |
| Indonesian Sign Language | BISINDO |
| Jordanian Sign Language | LIU |
| Korean Sign Language | KSL |
| Nepali Sign Language | NSL |
| Russian Sign Language | RSL |
| Sign Language of the Netherlands | NGT |
| International Sign | IS |

The Multisign signers, two male participants from Indonesia and Jordan, and one female participant from Nepal, had not met previously, and had minimal knowledge of English and no shared sign language. They were filmed on their first meeting in India, where the research took place, and this is the data focused on in this chapter.[2] It was important to film them on the first meeting because this was before they had a chance to see or adapt to each other's signing, providing maximal opportunities for communicative trouble. They were filmed on the same day, unlike the Typology group, whose pairs were each filmed at different times. Between the filming sessions, the Multisign group attended a deaf leadership programme, and socialised with each other and with other deaf people in their environment (see Bradford, this volume, for a detailed characterisation of the Multisign group and its setting in India). The Typology group, in contrast, were in a work setting between the filming sessions, assisting with a research project at the Max Planck Institute for Psycholinguistics, and interacted with each other in that context.

The four participants in the Typology group were all males, from the Netherlands, Uzbekistan, South Korea, and Hong Kong. The setting of data collection for this group is described in detail in Byun (this volume). Two of the

---

[2] They also were filmed after one week and after three weeks, but that data is not considered here.

participants grew up in signing environments, with deaf parents. As a group, they had more international exposure prior to data collection than the Multisign group, and some had even arguably engaged in cross-signing before, on a limited basis. However, their experience in international contexts varied. Signer A had been to an international conference which provided him with about 20 days of immersion in ASL and IS.[3] Signer D had frequently been to Taiwan and thus acquired some Taiwan Sign Language and cross-cultural communication skills. Signer B had lived in Germany for 14 years and learned German Sign Language (DGS), and was the only one of the four who was fluent in two sign languages. Signer C had attended the same conference as Signer A, in addition to a World Federation of the Deaf (WFD) conference that was held in Canada. Signers B, C and D each met with Signer A, resulting in the three dyads from this group which are analysed for this chapter.

In contrast, the Multisign participants had very little experience of international or cross-cultural communication. They had no shared language and had never been to India previously. They also advised the researcher that they had minimal knowledge of English; during the coding it became apparent that some of them knew individual fingerspelled English words, but this was sporadic. Their familiarity with English appeared to be basic, e.g. enough to fingerspell some words but not to fingerspell sentences. Therefore, the profile of these participants differs from the Typology group in terms of their international experience. This is a factor to consider, and while a focused comparison of the two groups is outside the scope of this study, it may be illuminating to bear in mind this distinction between the groups and the effects it might have. Table 2 summarises the participants' background details including language proficiencies.

---

**3** On occasion during the data collection, Signer A from the Typology group looked up definitions in an online dictionary via a hand-held device. This signer would watch a fingerspelling of an English word and then look up the equivalent word and meaning in their own written language, as discussed in Section 3.2.2 below. The context of the Typology group was rather informal and flexible, and this signer was comfortable enough to call a temporary halt to the conversation to consult a dictionary. This did not occur in the Multisign group.

**Table 2.** Socio-linguistic backgrounds of the participants

| Project | Participants | Language Background |
|---|---|---|
| Typology | **Signer A:**<br>**Family background:** Deaf parents and siblings<br>**International experience:** Attended Deaf Way II conference | **Native:** Korean Sign Language (South)<br>**Intermediate:** written Korean<br>**Minimal:** written English, International Sign |
| | **Signer B:**<br>**Family background:** Deaf parents and siblings<br>**International experience:** Moved from Uzbekistan to Germany | **Native:** Russian Sign Language<br>**Fluent:** German Sign Language, (written) German, (written) Russian<br>**Intermediate:** (written) English, International Sign |
| | **Signer C:**<br>**Family background:** Hearing parents<br>**International experience:** Attended Deaf Way II and WFD conferences | **Fluent:** Sign Language of the Netherlands, (written) Dutch<br>**Minimal:** (written) English, International Sign |
| | **Signer D**<br>**Family background:** Hearing parents<br>**International experience:** Has often travelled to Taiwan | **Fluent:** Hong Kong Sign Language<br>Intermediate: Taiwan Sign Language, (written) Chinese |
| Multisign | **Signer E**<br>**Family background:** Hearing parents<br>**International experience:** no experience | **Fluent:** Jordanian Sign Language<br>Intermediate: (written) Arabic<br>**Minimal:** (written) English |
| | **Signer F**<br>**Family background:** Hearing parents<br>**International experience:** no experience | **Fluent:** Indonesian Sign Language (BISINDO)<br>**Intermediate:** (written) Bahasa Indonesia<br>**Minimal:** (written) English |
| | **Signer G**<br>**Family background:** Deaf parents and siblings<br>**International experience:** no experience | **Fluent:** Nepali Sign Language<br>**Minimal:** (written) Nepali, (written) English |

While the groups' differing experiential and linguistic profiles offer a contrast, it is worth pointing out that these two corpora were used in part because such data are exceedingly rare, and these are the only two corpora of cross-signing known to the researchers. The chief concern in compiling the data sets was to ensure that all participants were fluent signers. The myriad factors that can influence cross-signers, such as piecemeal lexical knowledge from a variety of languages that they may have encountered at some point in their lifetime, are impossible to control for in a scientific study with such a rare data set. Therefore, while this research has made reasonable efforts to attend to language background factors and their potential impacts on the findings, it has not been feasible to control for the multiplicity of such variables.

This study examines only the initial encounters between the participants, as these most aptly display the incipient features of cross-signing, prior to lexical convergence and accommodation.[4] Therefore, the analyses were carried out on 1 hour and 20 minutes of video data from the Typology project, which when combined with the 1 hour and 48 minutes from Multisign, amount to 3 hours and 8 minutes of video data (see Table 3). These data were transcribed using ELAN video annotation software (Sloetjes, 2013). Section 2.2 explains the transcription scheme that was used in these analyses. In addition to annotating the data, three of the partants were interviewed on webcam by the first author about some aspects of their interactions, In particular, the provenance of some of the signs they had used (See Section 3.1 for details).

**Table 3.** Summary of data

| Dyad | Signers | Recording length | data |
|---|---|---|---|
| 1 | Signer A – Signer C | 37 minutes | |
| 2 | Signer A – Signer B | 10 minutes | Typology |
| 3 | Signer A – Signer D | 33 minutes | |
| 4 | Signer G – Signer F | 40 minutes | |
| 5 | Signer F – Signer E | 29 minutes | Multisign |
| 6 | Signer E – Signer G | 39 minutes | |

Several considerations were involved in choosing the pairs of signers. First of all, there is an equal number of dyads from Typology and Multisign (three pairs each). Because signers from both groups had been chosen according to different selection criteria, it was important to foresee potential comparison between the two groups. Having roughly equal amounts of data from each group is therefore beneficial. All dyads last between 30 and 40 minutes, with the exception of the conversation

---

[4] For a study that investigates how cross-signing develops over time, based on several subsequent data collection sessions, see Bradford, Michaelis and Zeshan (this volume).

between Signer A and Signer B. This video is exceptional in that the conversation lasted only 10 minutes.

For the Multisign group, the three pairs constitute the entire set of conversational data from the project sub-group that was based in India. A fourth signer was only involved in elicitation experiments but did not participate in the free conversations (see Bradford, this volume). Within the Typology group, three dyads were chosen that all involved the same signer (Signer A, who is also the first author of this chapter) as one of the participants. This distribution means that each individual's amount of data is different in terms of how many minutes they were involved in a conversation, because some people are involved in conversations more than once. For example, Signer C is present in a total of 37 minutes of conversation with one other participant; Signer F is in a total of 69 minutes with two other participants; and Signer A appears in 80 minutes of conversation with three others. However, this variation in the amount of data is not problematic because we are not analysing patterns in the use of repair strategies at the level of individuals.

## 2.2 Data coding

Data were coded using the ELAN multimedia annotation software (Sloetjes, 2013), which allows time-aligned codes to be linked to a video on parallel tiers. The tiers can be defined flexibly according to the research questions being pursued. In this case, annotations were made on separate tiers for each of the signers in the interaction. In addition, tiers were labelled according to the phase of the repair interaction (T-1, T0, or T+1). The content of the tiers includes capital letter glosses representing the manual signs, as is the usual convention in sign language linguistics, and labels for the type of repair strategy used (e.g. substitution). Figure 3 shows a screenshot of the data annotation in ELAN.

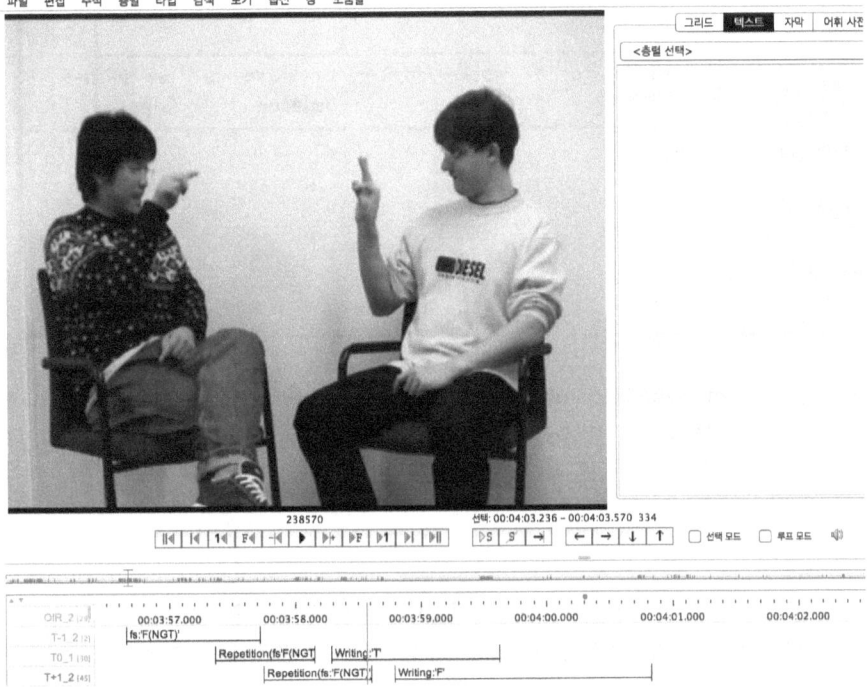

**Figure 3.** Data annotation in ELAN

Following the identification of the parts of the repair sequence, the different types of strategies and tools exploited at T+1 were categorised. This was done using an inductive data-driven approach, watching and annotating the clips and then considering how the various strategies could be meaningfully classified. The resulting types are defined in this section, and examples are given in Section 3.3. In total, 88 repair sequences were coded. The coding schema of repair strategies that emerged from the inductive process is summarised in Table 4. Repair strategies are distinguished from each other on the basis of features, with the following values:

- +    feature always applies
- (+)  feature usually applies
- -    feature does not apply
- (-)  feature usually does not apply
- 0    feature is not relevant

Each repair strategy differs from all others in at least one of the features, so that all strategies are uniquely identifiable.

**Table 4.** Repair strategies

|  | single sign | spoken language reference | trouble source included | established signs |
|---|---|---|---|---|
| Repetition | + | - | + | + |
| Substitution | + | - | - | + |
| Literacy | + | + | - | 0 |
| Explanation | - | - | - | (+) |
| Example | - | - | + | (+) |
| Productive signs | (-) | - | - | - |

If a single sign is the basis of the repair strategy, this may involve repetition of the same sign that was the trouble source at T-1, or substitution with a different sign, often but not always a close equivalent from a different sign language. Alternatively, signers may resort to a repair strategy that is based on using literacy, i.e. written representations of words from a spoken language. In most cases, this involves fingerspelling, which is the use of a manual alphabet to sign a sequence of letters spelling out the target word. Other uses of literacy include writing/tracing on a surface or in the air.

Alternatively, signers may use various multi-sign strategies. In the case of explanations, the trouble source is described using a circumlocution. For example, an explanation for 'happy' may use signs with meanings such as 'smile', 'feel good', and 'celebrate', but not a sign for 'happy' itself. If the trouble source itself is used in the repair, this is categorised as an example. Examples often work by inserting the trouble source sign into a sentence, thereby clarifying its context and allowing the addressee to infer the sign's meaning. For instance, 'age' was clarified by saying "my age is 27; what is yours?".

In addition to the above sign language based strategies that rely on established signs, another option is to use productive signs. The distinction between established and productive signs is complex and consists of a set of criteria (Johnston and Schembri, 1999: 136). In short, productive signs are characterised by their formational components (handshapes, movements, locations, etc) being meaningful. Therefore, the meaning of productive signs is componential and relatively transparent, due to non-arbitrary relationships between the sign's form and its meaning. Established signs, on the other hand, have a higher degree of conventionalisation and there may often be arbitrary relationships between the sign's form and meaning. Productive signs include those described in the literature as having a high degree of visual iconicity, namely classifiers (Schembri, 2003), size and shape specifiers, and indexical signs such as pointing. For our purposes, this category also includes gesture and mime, which is sometimes deployed by signers to resolve a trouble source. The productive strategy usually involves multiple signs, but can sometimes consist of a single sign. Since explanations and examples are also multi-sign combinations, the entire utterance may contain productive signs (hence the feature (+) instead of +). But the use of productive signs is not the main characteristic in these strategies. The established-productive distinction is irrelevant for the "literacy" strategy as it does not consist of signs as such (hence the feature 0).

In addition to these categorisations, a strategy was coded as "mixed" if a single turn at T+1 contained more than one of the above strategies. It is necessary to distinguish these cases because the coding labels the communicative turn (T+1) as a whole and not its individual components, so that each T+1 is associated with only one coding category. In the data, fingerspelling was sometimes preceded or followed immediately by another strategy, for instance fingerspelling followed by a substitute sign to convey the meaning 'difficult'. Thus the "mixed" category is a sequential combination of more than one of the above strategies within the same turn.

# 3 Repair strategies in cross-signing

This section sets out the results from our research with respect to the two research questions. Firstly, we consider the nature of the trouble source that gives rise to OIR in the sequences investigated here (Section 3.1). This is because the repair undertaken at T+1 should not be seen in isolation but with respect to the entire repair sequence. Therefore, a closer look at the trouble source at T-1 serves to situate the deployment of repair strategies in the appropriate context with respect to the specific phenomenon of cross-signing. In Section 3.2 we take a closer look at the form of the turn where one of the interlocutors signals the communication trouble (T0). Section 3.3 presents the deployment and frequency of the various repair strategies, and Section 3.4 summarises the results in terms of the differential success of the signers' repair strategies.

## 3.1 Trouble sources

There are three basic types of trouble that may occur in conversations: trouble in receiving the message, trouble in producing the message, and trouble in understanding the message (Schegloff, Jefferson and Sacks, 1977; Schegloff, 1987). A person may miss or be unable to hear (or in this case, see) a message, for example due to environmental noise (or visual obstruction); the sender might produce the message using incorrectly articulated words or signs, which can also cause trouble. Alternatively, the addressee may fail to comprehend precisely what the message means, or may come to a very different understanding than what the speaker or signer intended. In our data, the reasons for communication trouble are often complex and difficult to verify with certainty, but they appear to mostly fall into the category of trouble in understanding the message. Receiving the message was not an important factor in these data, as the setting was optimized for video filming of the conversations, so there were no visual obstructions.

In this section, we take a closer look at the sub-set of trouble sources where a communication difficulty originated in the turn preceding an OIR, i.e. the indication of a problem by the interlocutor. As noted above, our interest is in the original trouble source of repair sequences involving OIR because the current chapter is part of a larger programme of research focusing on OIR. The data include all trouble sources in OIR sequences, regardless of whether a shared understanding was ultimately achieved, and regardless of whether the indication of trouble at T0 was followed by a single repair attempt, or whether multiple attempts at repair were necessary.[5] All instances of T-1 for which the T+1 repair strategy is analysed in this chapter were coded as to the type of trouble source at T-1.

Table 5 shows the trouble source types for the 88 coded instances of T-1, which triggered repair initiations at T0. It shows that OIR was most likely to be employed for trouble related to the use of individual signs. However, it is sometimes difficult to distinguish repair initiations that are due to trouble recognising a sign or form, from those that arise from problems in understanding the content of the message. For example, if the trouble source is a fingerspelled English word, it may be unclear whether the other signer does not know that particular English word or concept, or whether they know it but just had difficulty following the spelling.

Many of the 88 occurrences of T-1 are individual signs that are unfamiliar to the other participant, most commonly due to being from a sign language that they do not know. Usually this was due to the interlocutors using signs from their own languages, but it also occurred when some signers used ASL. For example, the sign CENTER was used by a participant who knew ASL, but was not recognised by the other signers. In contrast, a repair initiation that targeted the entire utterance and left the exact nature of the trouble source unspecified occurred only once. This instance is marked by a so-called "open repair initiator" (Dingemanse et al, 2015), that is, a form that signals a general lack of comprehension. This

---

[5] In any case, each successive repair attempt builds on the entire interaction, so one cannot be sure which part of the entire interaction is responsible for an ultimate successful conclusion.

distribution suggests that either it was rare for signers to have trouble with an utterance overall, or that they preferably chose to target an individual form when initiating a repair.

Table 5. Trouble sources in all instances of OIR (T-1)

| Individual Sign | Fingerspelled word | Entire utterance |
|---|---|---|
| 79 | 8 | 1 |

For some of the individual signs causing trouble at T-1, and used to restore communication at T+1, it was possible to verify which signs were from which languages. To help with this identification of signs, the first author was able to undertake some interviews remotely via online communication with three of the participants. Signer C and Signer D from the Typology group were interviewed, as well as Signer G from the Multisign group. In addition, the first author was able to use his own judgment with respect to KSL signs, as KSL is his first language. It was not possible logistically to interview all of the participants, but it was feasible to ask these three whether a trouble source sign used by a particular signer was in fact part of this signer's lexicon in his or her own sign language. In several cases, the sign at T-1 within the first repair sequence is already a substitution, i.e. another sign language being used instead of the signer's native sign language. One example was the use of the ASL sign for 'people', based on the P-handshape, by Signer A when addressing Signer D. Signer A resolved the trouble by offering two further signs for 'people'. Thus cross-signers sometimes seem to suspect that signs from their native sign lexicon could become trouble sources even in the absence of any negative feedback, and therefore possibly avoid them; alternatively, it may be the case that they know a sign that they deem to be more suitable for the particular interaction. In Byun et al. (2018) this point is pursued in detail with respect to the try-marking of signs at T-1.

In the overwhelming number of cases, it is an individual sign, i.e. the surface form, that is pinpointed as the trouble source (89.7 %). This is in line with Byun et al. (2018), who found that individual signs are the source of trouble in over 90 % of cases in their data. For example, in the interaction between Signer C and Signer A, a NGT sign for 'why' produced by Signer C was not understood. Signer C then articulated the ASL form for 'why', which was understood. In another interaction, Signer F produced a sign meaning 'cannot', from his language, Indonesian Sign Language, when conversing with Signer G, who then indicated that she did not know this sign. In all of these cases, the signer of the trouble source was using a form that had not been agreed on, and/or that the addressee did not know. Zeshan

(2015) has documented the same phenomenon and proposed a systematic process by way of which signs are added to an agreed shared lexicon by the participants in the interaction.

Much more rarely, in 9.1% of cases, a fingerspelled word occurs as trouble source. In some instances, both signers knew the one-handed (ASL or IS) alphabet, but did not know about the variations for some letters that exist for some sign languages. For example, for the letter 'U', most versions of the one-handed alphabet have a palm-forward orientation, but Dutch signers use the opposite orientation (see Figure 4). They also position the thumb and forefinger differently for the letter 'F' compared to most other users of this alphabet, allowing them to overlap. Some of the participants were confused by these variations, especially when used in initialised signs such as 'culture' with C-handshape and 'family' with F-handshape in ASL.

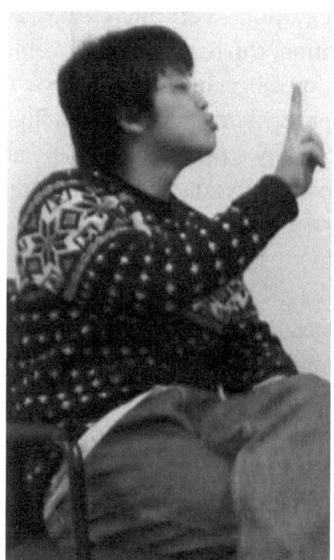 

**Figure 4.** Different orientations for the fingerspelled letter 'U' in ASL/IS and NGT

Finally, there is one case in the data where an open repair initiator is used, that is, an utterance that signals a general lack of understanding (similar to English *what?*, *huh?*) rather than focussing on a particular sign.

In addition to the lack of a shared code as such, problems with understanding the message also included a number of other types. Firstly, there were examples triggered by not understanding English, e.g. the fingerspelled word A-R-E-A; the signer knew what all the letters were, but they did not know English and thus did not understand the meaning. Next, there were examples where a signer was unfamiliar with the conventions or grammatical rules of another sign language. For example, in LIU the order of two-digit numerals is produced in a reversed fashion relative to Indonesian Sign Language, such that in a sentence meaning 'I am 24 years old', the sign for '24' appears as the sequence FOUR TWENTY.[6] This caused considerable communicative difficulty between Signer E and Signer F, and they had to resort to tracing written digits in the air (see Zeshan, 2015:222 for a similar example).

Trouble also arose with concepts that the addressee had not seen or experienced before, e.g. because they were uncommon in the addressee's culture. For example, Signer E used a sign for 'police' referring iconically to the policeman's helmet and holstered gun; this was not understood by Signer G, in whose mountainous home environment such police officers are not seen.

Finally, some signs that are relatively abstract, arbitrary or opaque were a source of problems in understanding. One illustration of this is the LIU sign for '(years of) age', which involves pointing to the teeth. This was misconstrued by Signer F as a reference to 'teeth', which prompted him to sign about the topic of dentists. It may be that in such cases, iconic parts of overall opaque or abstract signs act like 'false friends' and lead the addressee down the wrong path. Another example occurred when Signer G wanted to communicate the concept of 'exam', and signed an explanation that represented the actions of 'write on the paper and finish and turn it in'. Despite its iconic motivation, this explanation was not understood by Signer F, the addressee, who did not grasp Signer G's overall aim in this part of the conversation.

Cases of visual obstruction did not occur in the data, but there were several sources of trouble related to understanding the form of a sign. In one example, Signer C produced the ASL-derived form meaning 'family', which makes use of the F-handshape. As the F-handshape is articulated slightly differently in NGT, this caused a problem for Signer A, even though he was familiar with the ASL sign. The articulation was such that he could not grasp the sign the first time. Similarly, phonological variations in the articulation of common iconically motivated signs sometimes created trouble. For example, the sign for 'milk' that refers to milking a cow may be produced slightly differently, e.g. with more of a palm-outward versus palm-inward orientation, and with the thumb more or less extended. In such a case, both signers know the sign and its iconic motivation, but the phonological difference triggers communicative difficulty. For example, the left-hand picture in Figure 5 shows a sign for MILK at T-1 that uses a T-handshape and appears to be quite enlarged, with maximal use of the signing space. The other signer then

---

6 Following the usual conventions in sign language linguistics, a gloss using capital letters refers to a sign, while lowercase letters enclosed in single quotes refer to a sign's meaning.

repeats it at T0, using the same handshape but smaller movements, taking up less of the signing space.

**Figure 5.** MILK at T-1 and repetition at T0

As mentioned above, often examples from the data are not easily categorisable into one of the three basic types of communicative trouble, and reflect a combination of problems. For example, when conversing with Signer A, Signer B produced a form meaning 'Uzbek', referring to a person from Uzbekistan. Not only was this not part of an agreed code between the two signers, but Signer A was not aware of this country or the concept of 'an Uzbek person' at all. Therefore, this was a problem with the shared code and access to the concept.

In another instance, Signer D articulated a sign for 'man' produced at the side of the head, with which Signer A was unfamiliar, and which he took to mean 'woman'. Again, this was caused not only by the form not being within the signers' shared code, but also by a misunderstanding based on wrongly assuming what the iconic motivation was. Such misconstrual of iconic motivations of signs occurs regularly in the data. When Signer C articulated a sign for 'hearing' (in which an F-handshape moves back and forth near the ear), Signer A guessed that the sign might be iconic but was not sure what it meant, imagining that it may mean something like 'too loud'. Similarly, in the discussion between Signer G and Signer F, the former used a sign for 'woman' that refers to a pierced nose. Signer F then imagined that Signer G was talking about piercings in general. He did not realise that a pierced nose had any iconic association with the concept of 'woman', because he was not familiar with the significance of this in the cultural context of Nepal.

Not unexpectedly, the complexity of factors involved in miscommunication caused confusion and difficulty for the researchers when carrying out the analysis. One of these was related to ascertaining the specific reason behind an observed repair initiation and seeming lack of understanding by the addressee. For example, in the interaction between Signer E and Signer F, the former fingerspelled O-L-D 'old' using the one-handed alphabet, which the latter did not understand. It was unclear whether this was due to Signer F's lack of familiarity with the one-handed alphabet, or a failure to see and/or accurately identify all of the letters in the word, or a lack of English proficiency.

In terms of the three basic categories mentioned at the beginning of this section, "shared code" problems and "understanding-related" problems are especially tricky to tease apart in cross-signing. Therefore, in this section we have offered a qualitative description of examples in order to convey the complexities involved in identifying reasons of miscommunication, and the quantitative analysis of trouble sources is limited to the results in Table 5. The next section focuses on identifying the form of the TO turn.

## 3.2 Form of the TO turn

The TO turn in cross-signing can take several different forms, including repetition, offering another equivalent sign as a means of checking (so-called "restricted offer"), a blank facial expression (i.e. lack of backchannelling), or an explicit statement indicating that the signer does not understand. The range of TO forms found in cross-signing is similar to the taxonomy described by Manrique (2016) for Argentinean Sign Language (*Lengua de señas argentina*, or LSA). Manrique suggests that the TO turns produced by LSA signers can be placed into three groups: open, restricted, and 'implicit' initiators. She finds that the restricted repair initiators comprise more than half of all OIR in LSA and include requests, offers, and questions, both manual and non-manual. The most common format for open repair in LSA is non manual marking, especially by means of lowering the eyebrows (Manrique, 2016). These findings are similar to what is seen in the cross-signing data, although the sequence of repair progresses differently for cross-signers in comparison with same-language signers. The quantitative results for the occurrence of these types of TO (repetition, restricted offer, a blank facial expression, and a statement of non-understanding) in the data have been calculated, and are presented in this section along with qualitative examples.

Repetition has many functions and processes in OIR, including identifying a source of trouble, presenting what needs to be repaired, and inviting clarification, specification or confirmation (Dingemanse and Enfield, 2015). Dingemanse et al. (2015) find that in interactions between users of the same language, repetitions at T0 may be of the full trouble source, or only part of it, and that overall, repetitions comprise 48.3 % of T0 turns. In comparison, in the cross-signing data, out of 88 instances of OIR, 65 (73.9 %) took the form of repetition. Most of these occurrences (45 out of 65, i.e. 69.2 %) were repetitions of the full trouble source, whilst the rest (20 out of 65, i.e. 30.7 %) were repetitions of only part of the trouble source. One example of a partial repetition is when Signer B articulated the sign UZBEK 'Uzbekistan', which is performed at the side of the head and has a mouthing (silent lip pattern derived from the articulation of a spoken word) reflecting the articulation of 'uzbek' (see example 1). At T0, Signer A repeated the mouthing, but not the manual component of the sign.

Example 1. Partial repetition of 'Uzbekistan' at T0, using only the mouthing

Signer B:     U   Z   B   E   K
              'uzbek'
Signer A:             'uzbek'

Another example occurred when Signer A articulated two adjacent signs for 'study' at T-1 (see example 2). The first sign, with the hand located at the mouth, is from Korean Sign Language. The second, performed immediately after the first, was the American Sign Language form with the hands in front of the signer. A later interview revealed that Signer D did not know either of these signs. However, at T0, Signer D only repeated the second sign, not the first, possibly because it was easier to remember and repeat the second sign in the sequence.

Example 2. 'Study' – only the second sign was repeated at T0

Signer A:   HOW   STUDY(KSL) STUDY(ASL)   HOW   Pointing(you)
Signer D:                                                    STUDY(ASL)

There was another occasion where Signer A used this strategy of articulating two adjacent signs with the same meaning, the ASL and KSL forms for 'university' (the former based on the fingerspelled letter U, and the latter a half circle around the head; see example 3). Here, Signer D also repeats the second sign in the pair at T0, which is the KSL sign; therefore it appears that the latter sign is being selected for repetition, rather than the sign from a particular language. This is only a supposition as the nature of this phenomenon is not yet clear, but the tendency to select the second sign in an adjacent same-meaning pair for repetition at T0 may be an interesting area for further investigation.

Example 3. 'university' – only the second sign was repeated at T0

Signer A: MUST UNIVERSITY(ASL) UNIVERSITY(KSL) MUST KNOW Pointing(he)
Signer D:                                                UNIVERSITY(KSL)

Some trouble-source repetition at T0 was accompanied by other signs or strategies as well. There were 20 such cases in the data. These included repetition being used alongside non-manual features (e.g. eyebrow movements, body leans), mouthings, and restricted offers. Restricted offers are utterances at T0 with which the signer attempts to guess the meaning of the trouble-source sign; they are used to offer a candidate understanding, like saying "do you mean X?", for the other interlocutor to react to (Dingemanse and Enfield, 2015).

Restricted offers appeared after repetition in three instances. For example, Signer G articulated the concept of 'August' by presenting 8 digits and then making a sign for 'calendar' that refers to flipping the page of a wall calendar (see Figure 6). Signer F repeated the '8' and 'calendar' signs, and then made a sign for 'computer' (possibly having mistaken the 'calendar' sign for 'laptop'). This 'computer' sign (see Figure 7) therefore constituted a restricted offer, and the sign is accompanied by a questioning facial expression.

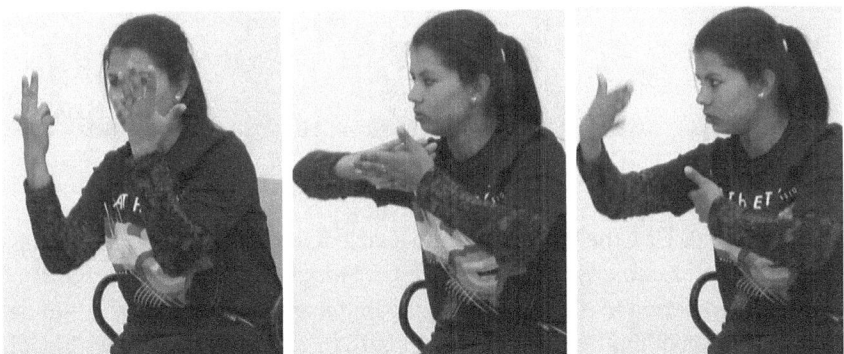

**Figure 6.** Sign for 'August' referring to a wall calendar

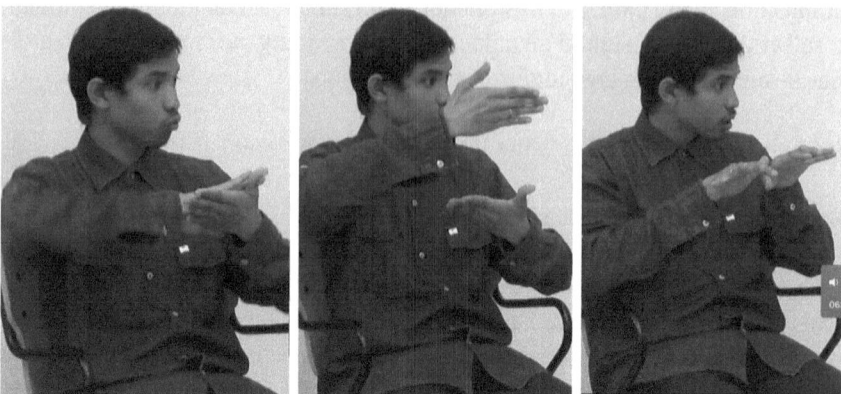

**Figure 7.** Sign for 'computer' used as a restricted offer

In another example, Signer F articulated the fingerspelled letter 'D' from ASL, and Signer G repeated this at T0 and then traced a written 'F' on her palm, because she erroneously thought the letter being signed was 'F' (see Figure 8). Similarly, Signer C fingerspelled I-F 'if' with the index finger and thumb of the F handshape overlapping, and Signer A repeated this handshape at T0 and then traced a written 'F' on his palm.

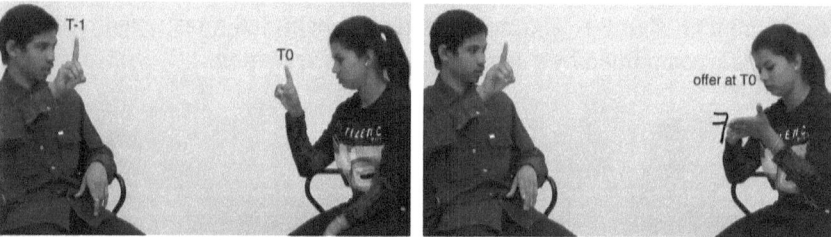

**Figure 8.** Repetition (from T-1) and then offer at T0

Another type of T0 is the blank face, with a lack of feedback or backchannelling. This can signal trouble to the interlocutor (cf. Manrique, 2016 on the occurrence of this phenomenon in Argentinean Sign Language). This kind of indication of trouble is termed 'implicit' by Manrique (2016). 'Implicit' or 'off record' repair initiators comprise a category that is rare in the research on spoken languages, which concentrates mostly on various types of explicit repair initiators (Manrique, 2016). This occurs 15 times in the cross-signing data, comprising 17.2 % of the T0 turns. Most of these are instances of the blank face appearing by itself, but occasionally it can be accompanied by other features. For example, in two cases the T-1 turn is try-marked, and the hold persists even with the blank face being apparent at T0, so the signer of the T0 turn adds another indicator of trouble, such as a head tilt or frown. In such an interaction, the person who articulates the try-marker initially has a chance to register the blank face and make the necessary adjustments or further attempts, and the signal of communication trouble is then reinforced with the additional facial expression at T0, e.g. the frown. The non-manual signals at T0 imply that the participants can minimise the addition of signs or forms to the interaction, which may potentially cause additional trouble or confusion and necessitate further repair attempts. It could also be argued that this T0 option is less face-threatening than other indications of trouble, as these non-manual indicators are more subtle and less overtly challenging.

Overt utterances signifying a lack of understanding are comparatively less frequent and are seen only 4 times in the data (4.6 %). 'I don't understand' occurs three times, and 'I don't know' appears once. The opposite scenario also occurs in the data, that is, an overt indication that the addressee understands and wants the signer to continue. The term 'continuer' refers to this function, which may be carried out by backchannelling (usually nodding). This maintains the interlocutors' shared connection. In one instance, this is done explicitly with a manual sign meaning 'I understand'.

Interestingly, there is an example in the data where the intended function of the turn at T0 itself is misunderstood. In this interaction, Signer E indicated a trouble source (involving signs about age), and Signer F then signalled a confirmation, believing that Signer E had understood when in fact he was trying to mark an instance of trouble. Therefore, the T0 was misunderstood and had to be repeated and clarified in order for the repair sequence to progress. This is the only occurrence of this sort of misunderstanding at T0 in the cross-signing data. Pietikainen (2016) postulates that this kind of misunderstanding may be due to 'common ground fallacy', wherein people assume too much common knowledge, and do not make their communication clear enough and fail to engage in sufficient monitoring. Perhaps the reason why it occurs only once is that cross-signers approach the communication with a great deal of vigilance (frequently using try-markers and delayed responses, as described in Byun et al., 2018) and little if any assumption that they share common ground. Cross-signers seem to be more ready for communication trouble, backtracking and repair sequences, whereas same-language users may tend to communicate with the default expectancy that they will be understood, so that the need for checking understanding is less salient, whereas it is heightened in cross-signing.

## 3.3 Deployment of repair strategies in cross-signing interactions

This section examines some quantitative data associated with the strategies used for other-initiated repair attempts in cross-signers' interactions. These data include signers' deployment of particular strategies and differences between attempts within the same sequence, i.e. the first, second, third and so on. However, the first attempt is the main focus here, and each of the first-attempt strategies are explored and illustrated, including repetition (3.3.1), literacy (3.3.2), substitution (3.3.3), explanation (3.3.4), examples (3.3.5) and productive signs (3.3.6). Signers' reasons for selecting these strategies are also considered. This section provides a necessary background to the subsequent section, 3.4, which presents data on which repair strategies were the most and least effective.

The data reveal, in total, 88 occurrences of other-initiated repair attempts, including repairs that were immediately successful after the first repair attempt, repairs that were successful but needed more than one repair attempt, and repair attempts that were ultimately unsuccessful. Table 6 shows the distribution of 82 ultimately successful *repair sequences* produced by participants in the Typology group and the Multisign group. Instances of repair sequences with only one attempt, i.e. one-off repair initiations, comprise 53 of these 82 occurrences, or 64.6 %. Sequences with second, third, fourth, and fifth attempts together account for 29 of the total, or 35.4 %. More than five attempts did not occur in the data.

These percentages are close to what has been reported in spoken-language research by Dingemanse et al. (2015) and Dingemanse (in press). Using much larger corpora than the one in this study, with higher numbers of repair attempts, they find that a repair initiation selected from the corpus at random has a 58 % chance of being a one-off, and a 42 % chance of being part of a longer sequence.

**Table 6.** Distribution of sequences of other-initiated repair by number of attempts

| | 1 attempt | 2 attempts | 3 attempts | 4 attempts | 5 attempts | | Total sequences |
|---|---|---|---|---|---|---|---|
| Typology group | 22 (26.8 %) | 6 (7.3 %) | 3 (3.6) | 1 (1.2 %) | 1 (1.2 %) | 1 (1.2 %) | 34 (38.6) |
| Multisign group | 31 (37.8 %) | 10 (12.1 %) | 5 (6.0 %) | 2 (2.4 %) | 1 (1.2 %) | 5 (6.0 %) | 54 (61.3 %) |
| Total | 53 (64.6 %) | 16 (16.5 %) | 8 (9.7 %) | 3 (3.6 %) | 2 (2.4 %) | 6 (7.3 %) | 88 (100 %) |

In a small minority of six instances, repair efforts were ultimately abandoned without resolution. This usually seemed to be because the person who initiated the repair failed to make clear whether the repair was successful or not. However, the specific reasons behind such abandonment and ambiguity were not investigated in this study. But in 82 of the 88 cases in Table 6, the repeated attempts resulted in successful repair. This was on the first meeting, at which point none of these individuals had communicated with each other previously.

Table 7 shows the distribution of individual *repair attempts*, since a repair sequence can include more than one individual repair attempt. Signer C, Signer E and Signer G produced trouble sources, followed by repair attempts, more often than the other participants. Moreover, three of the aforementioned instances of ultimate abandonment arose from a T-1 turn by Signer G. However, individual differences of this kind are disregarded here, and the main aim of Table 7 is to provide an overview of overall repair frequency, and the frequency of repeated repairs.

**Table 7.** Distribution of first and repeated repair attempts

|  | Signer A | Signer B | Signer C | Signer D | Signer E | Signer F | Signer G | total |
|---|---|---|---|---|---|---|---|---|
| 1st attempt | 9 | 2 | 19 | 3 | 19 | 12 | 18 | 82 |
| 2nd attempt | 1 | 1 | 8 | 1 | 10 | 2 | 6 | 29 |
| 3rd attempt | 1 | – | 4 | – | 4 | 1 | 3 | 13 |
| 4th attempt | – | – | 2 | – | 2 | 1 | – | 5 |
| 5th attempt | – | – | 1 | – | 1 | – | – | 2 |

Example 4 shows a case of repeated repair attempts. The signer first produces the sign NEPAL (1st attempt), and as this is not understood, she uses fingerspelling (2nd attempt), and then explaining (3rd attempt). The explanation clarifies that she is talking about 'the country north of India'. A visual-spatial SASS (size and shape specifier) construction happens to be embedded in the explanation but the entire sequence is categorised as an instance of 'explaining'. Unfortunately, dedicated analyses of the occurrence of specific morphosyntactic phenomena such as SASS within repair sequences is outside the scope of this paper but would be a fascinating area for future research.

Example 4. Multiple repair attempts (Success at 3rd attempt)

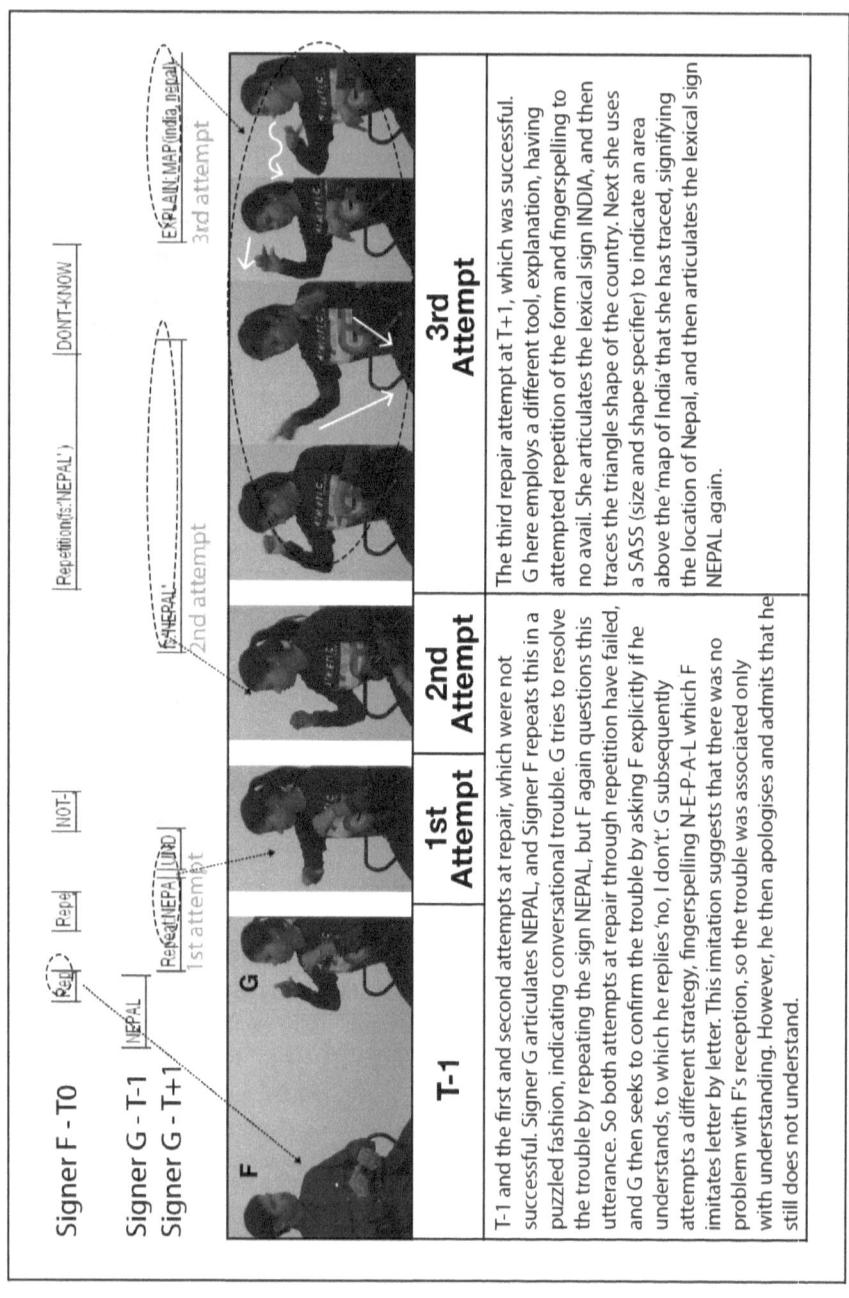

To provide a broader overview of the results, Figure 9 shows the range of communicative repair strategies that were identified in this study and the number of times they were employed in a first repair attempt. As the figure indicates, substitution and fingerspelling/writing-based (literacy-based) strategies were drawn upon most frequently overall, though the results reveal that these did not bring about successful repair at the same rate.

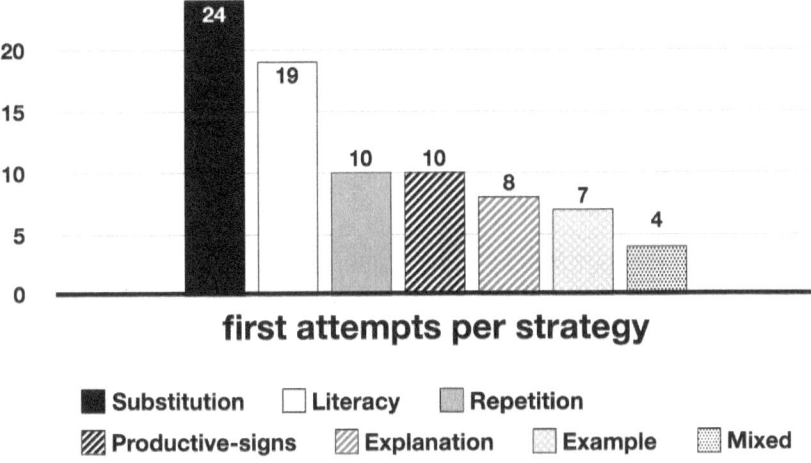

Figure 9. Number of first attempts per strategy

Not unexpectedly, we find a great deal of variation with respect to how frequently each of the strategies occurs with the individual participants. This is summarised in Figure 10. Two of the participants (Signers B and D) have a very small number of occurrences. The remaining five participants have between nine and 21 occurrences, and each individual has a somewhat different profile. For example, Signer C only uses a total of four strategies, while Signer E uses a wide variety of strategies. The largest amount of data with respect to the length of video recordings is associated with Signer A, but this participant does not have the highest number of repair occurrences. His profile also has a conspicuous absence of the Literacy (fingerspelling and writing) category.

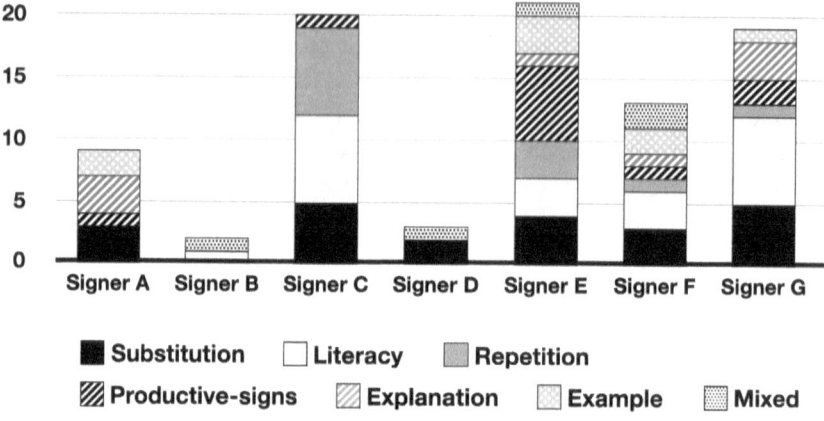

**Figure 10.** Individual variation in the use of repair strategies

Such large variation is expected because there are so many factors whose interplay determines the profile and behavior of each individual. Some participants are more active communicators, that is, they talk much more than their interlocutors. People may also be more or less inclined – for reasons of personality or culture, for example – to interrupt their interlocutor at T0. And of course the topic of the interaction also plays a role. For example, if place names are important for the conversation, fingerspelling may be a natural choice for repair. The conclusion from these considerations is that the repair strategies should primarily be characterised in terms of the range of strategies, and by demonstrating the range of options that signers can draw on for repair. Frequency counts are less revealing because individual differences are large in relation to the total number of occurrences.

In the remaining discussion, we focus on instances of first repair attempts only, because this allows us to compare like with like, and avoid any contamination from instances where a form's success was due to its use in a previous repair attempt within that sequence.[7] The plentiful first attempts in the data enable this approach to provide a useful picture of participants' strategies and assumptions at initial contact.

---

[7] This of course still leaves open the possibility of influence from previous repair sequences, but it is not possible to control for this factor within the setting of this research.

### 3.3.1 Repetition

Repetition refers to the repeating of a trouble source, as in the first repair attempt in Example 4 above. In another instance the NGT sign for 'summer' was not understood by the interlocutor, and it was repeated for the benefit of the addressee, slowly and with slightly more emphasis. There are 12 cases of repetition in the data. Example 5 shows a data segment with repetition as the repair strategy, with Signer E articulating the trouble source NAME at T-1, Signer F signaling the trouble at T0, and Signer E responding with repetition of the same sign at T+1.

One reason for deploying repetition might be that the signer wants to check which sign it was that the addressee did not understand, or give the addressee another chance to see the sign and verify if s/he still does not understand it. Further reasons could be that the signer is using repetition to stall for time as s/he has not yet selected an alternative strategy, or indeed that s/he has difficulty coming up with another strategy. Repetition may be part of the process of replication, in which one person tries to determine the results of his/her beliefs about the world by assuming that other people are also trying to determine the results of their own beliefs (Lewis, 1969). Employing repetition allows a signer to check their beliefs and those of their interlocutor.

Sometimes a form is repeated within T-1; that is, the repetition occurs before the interlocutor has signalled a problem with understanding at T0. These cases are not included in the count for repetition as a repair strategy at T+1, but are assigned to the T-1 turn. Moreover, if the repetition produced by the sender overlaps with the prompt for repair from the interlocutor at T0, the decision to assign the sender's repetition to T-1 is based on the co-occurrence of try-marking (cf. Byun et al., 2018).

Of the occurrences of repetition in the data, half are repetitions of fingerspelled words, and the other half are repetitions of signs from the signer's language or other sign languages. In very few cases did the addressee use one of the overt signals of communication trouble at T0, including a facial expression indicating uncertainty (such a facial expression was the trigger for repetition in only one case). Instead, in most cases, the T0 trigger for repetition was the absence of backchanneling.

This pattern suggests that not giving a positive backchannel counts as a T0 trigger in cross-signing, which is different from what is found in the spoken language research. In spoken languages, the lack of a positive backchannel is normally not enough to constitute a T0 trigger, and an overtly negative backchannel is needed.

Repetition is also different from the other strategies in that it is accompanied by mouthing in 83% of cases when used at T+1. All other strategies are

Example 5. Repetition

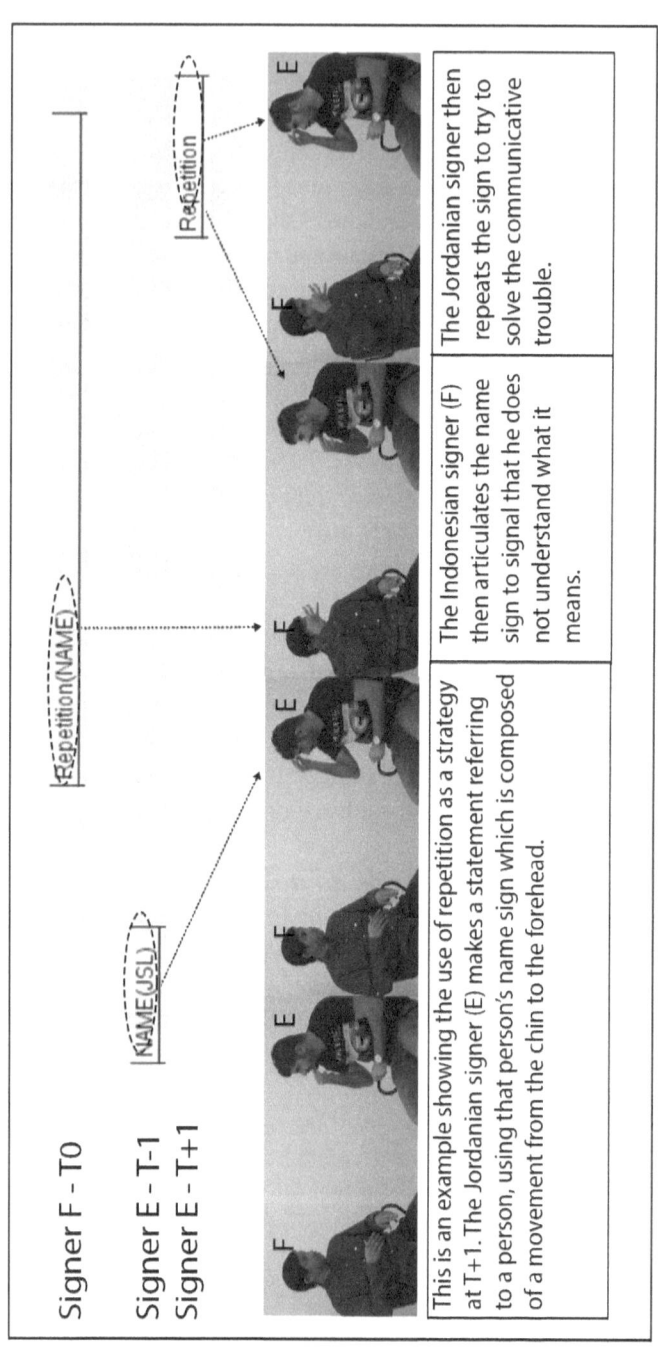

overwhelmingly produced without mouthing, and several strategies, including explanation, example, and mixed strategies are never accompanied by a mouthing at T+1. 'Mouthing' refers to a signer's partial or full, but unvoiced, production of a spoken-language word with the mouth, and it usually happens simultaneously with the manual production of a lexical sign (Boyes-Braem and Sutton-Spence, 2001). The frequency of mouthing in the two repair strategies where it does occur is as follows:

| | | |
|---|---|---|
| Repetition with mouthing | 10/12 | 83 % |
| Literacy with mouthing | 5/21 | 24 % |

In a study on regional language variation, Stamp, Schembri, Evans, and Cormier (2016) found that in addition to repetition, English mouthing, fingerspelling, and signing a different variant for the same concept were each used as a means of resolving instances of miscommunication. Similarly, cross-signers frequently seem to use mouthing, usually English mouthing, in conjunction with repetition. Repetition in first repair attempts occurs with mouthing 83 % of the time; i.e. out of 12 total instances of repetition, 10 appear with mouthing and only 2 appear without mouthing. The preference for repetition with mouthing over repetition without mouthing may lend further weight to the notion that cross-signers are replicating forms to check the results of their beliefs about the world, in the terms of Lewis (1969).

Cross-signers are less likely to use mouthing with literacy strategies. Out of 21 first-attempt instances of fingerspelling or writing-based strategies, only five were produced with mouthing, which is a rate of only 24 %, much lower than the 83 % rate at which repetition occurs with mouthing. The occurrence of mouthing with other strategies is very rare, although it is likely where other strategies are combined with repetition or utilised in a sequence alongside repetition.

### 3.3.2 Literacy

The Literacy category includes all strategies that exploit written languages, including both fingerspelling and writing. This section concentrates on the 19 cases where fingerspelling/writing was used as a first-attempt repair strategy and appeared as a 'new' tool in the sequence; that is, T+1 involved fingerspelling or writing but T-1 did not.

Fingerspelling is the most common way in which literacy is deployed in the data. For instance, if the addressee does not understand a sign for 'home', the signer may fingerspell H-O-M-E for clarification. In the data, the target language of fingerspelling is always English, so the deaf participants seem to be aware that this is the language of international communication. Successful deployment of fingerspelling thus relies on both knowledge of the manual alphabet itself and lexical knowledge of English.

The cross-signers also used writing, especially to communicate about numbers (cf. Zeshan, 2015). For example, when talking about his age, the Jordanian signer signed '27' using the cross-linguistically atypical method of articulating '7' before '20' ('seven-and-twenty'), which caused trouble for his interlocutor; he then traced the numbers on his hand to clarify his meaning.

It is noteworthy that four of the sign languages represented, KSL, NSL, LIU and HKSL, use fingerspelling systems that are different to ASL/IS, and yet the signers from these places do not use these native systems in their fingerspelling within the data. They resort instead to the one-handed English-derived alphabet seen in ASL/IS. This makes the one-handed alphabet a commonality amongst all the signers, giving them a shared resource to draw on when trouble arises.

The frequency of these strategies at T+1 suggests that literacy in the form of fingerspelling and/or writing was seen by the participants as a favourable way to attempt repair, although it was in fact less effective than some of the other strategies in actually bringing about successful repair (see Section 3.4). Unfortunately, because only the first interactions were coded and no longitudinal data were analysed, it is not possible to say whether this lack of success led participants to decrease their use of literacy-based strategies over time. Observation of the sequence of initial conversations suggests that at least some participants used this strategy less in their later pairings compared to their earlier ones.

Possibly, this favourable view toward literacy-based strategies is due to the status of English as a worldwide lingua franca, especially in technology and remote communication, and/or perhaps it reflects the great importance typically placed on writing and fingerspelling skills throughout deaf education. Fingerspelling was particularly useful when a signer was able to look up definitions in an online dictionary, as they could use the spelling to find the word and meaning in their own written language. To this end, Signer A used a hand-held device to look up the Korean translations of 'identity' and 'area' that were fingerspelled to him.

Fingerspelling is sometimes the main available way in which to introduce a concept, e.g. a country such as Nepal (see Example 6), a language such as Arabic, or a person such as Kang-Suk. Also, the first meeting usually involves many introductory items such as names, and fingerspelling is a typical way to provide these in many sign languages. Johnston (1989 and 1998, in Johnston and Schembri, 2007: 322) states that in Auslan, for example, fingerspelling is commonly employed to convey English proper nouns and concepts that have no lexicalised Auslan sign. Thus, abstract concepts like 'culture' and 'theory' may frequently need to be fingerspelled in cross-signing, as there is no immediate visually iconic means of portraying them, especially in the first meeting when the shared code might be minimal.

The fingerspelling in the data often featured noticeable holds, even at first attempt. Groeber and Pochon-Berger (2014) find that speakers maintain holds during the next speaker's turn, which shows that they are not only using holds to signal the end of their turn, but also to remain in 'speaker position' so that they can easily resume the role of speaker. They note that this behaviour appears to be common in repair situations, where the management of mutual understanding is complex and affects the interaction's progress. Holds can also help the interlocutors manage intersubjectivity as they advance the conversation, because holds are an 'embodied resource' that reveal a person's current expectations and understanding of mutual behaviour (Groeber and Pochon-Berger, 2014). The holds in the cross-signing data involved each letter being sustained long enough for the signer to seek confirmation from his or her conversational partner (although the precise length of these holds was not quantitatively analysed in this study). This could be due to signers' awareness of each other's non-fluent English, to which they made explicit reference in the data. More importantly though, it contributes to the process of grounding, giving the interlocutors time to devote their joint attention and comprehension to each individual letter. In contrast to fingerspelling, tracing (usually in the air or on the palm of the hand) tended to be used mainly in guessing the meaning at T0. In Example 7, Signer C has fingerspelled a letter, and Signer A has not fully grasped the meaning but makes a guess by tracing the letter. Interestingly, Signer C then confirms that the guess was correct by also using the tracing strategy, matching the usage of Signer A.

Example 6. Literacy strategy for clarifying a proper noun

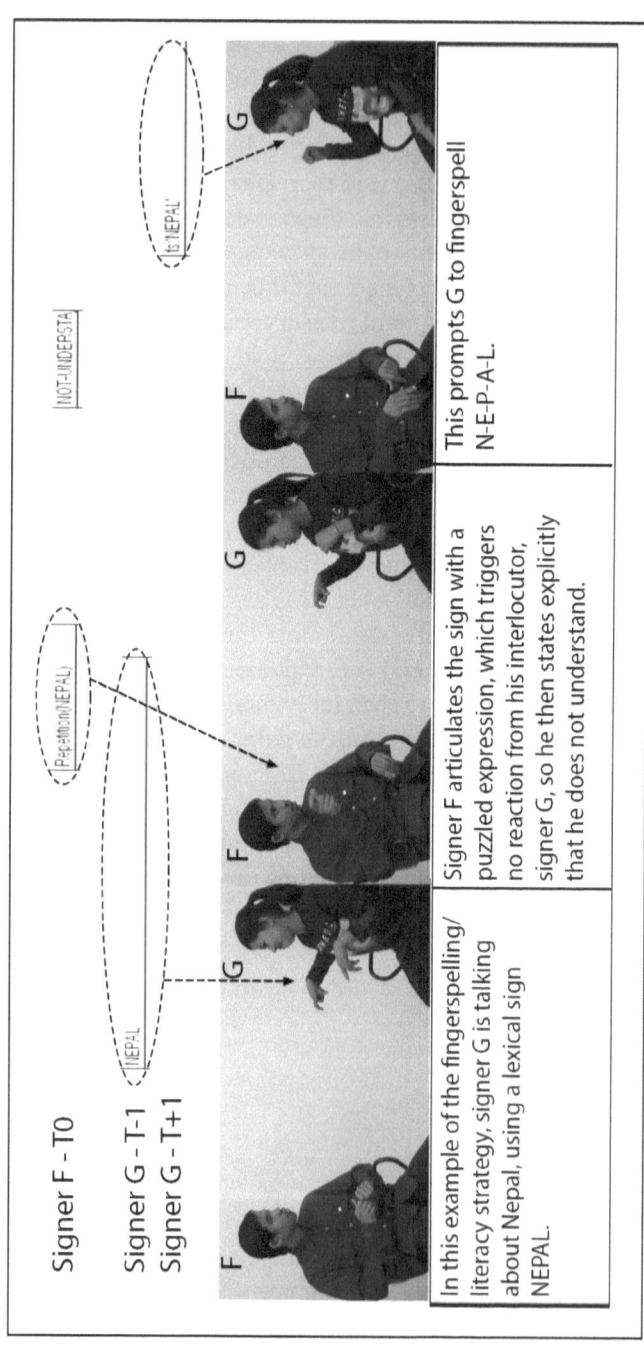

Example 7. T+1 signer accommodating strategy of T0 signer

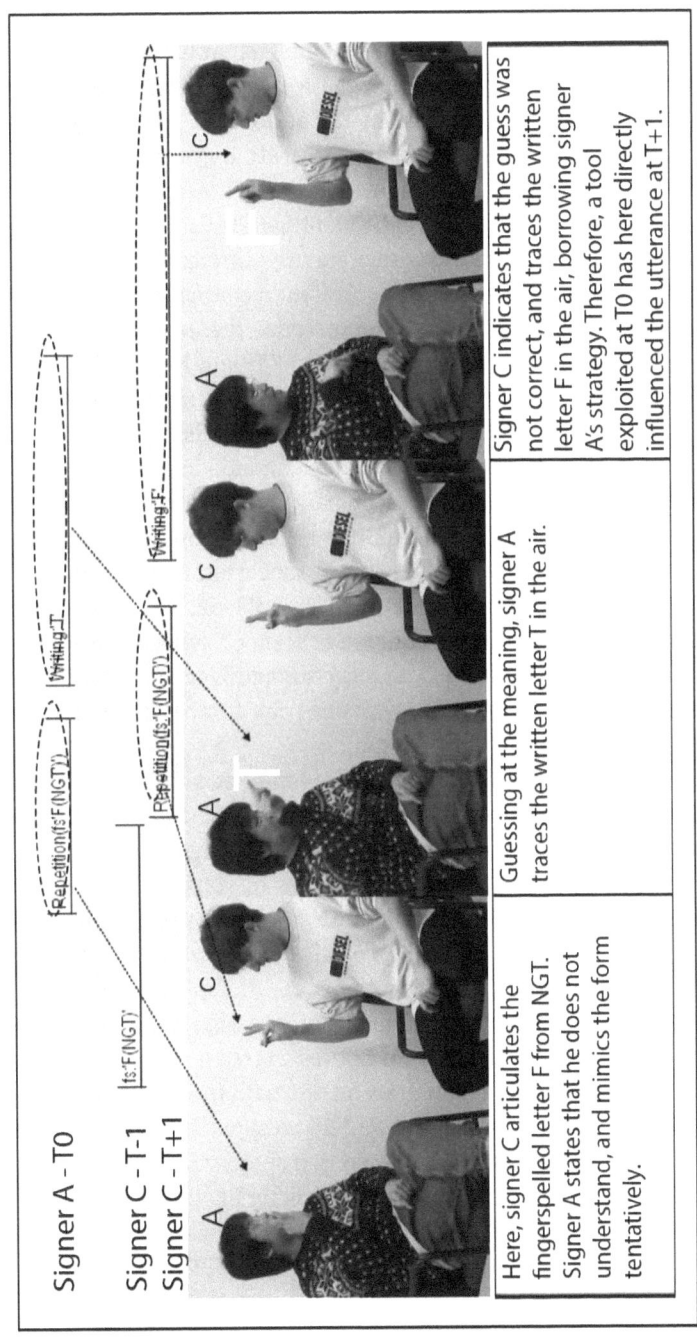

### 3.3.3 Substitution

Substitution is the use of a word from another language that has an equivalent or similar meaning to the trouble source. For example, when Signer D articulated MAN from HKSL and it was not understood by the addressee, he then tried the KSL sign for 'man'. Substitution was the most frequent strategy, with a total of 24 cases identified in the data, and substitution comprised 79 % of the successful repairs at T+1. Two types of substitution can be identified: substitution involving a sign or signs from the same language with a slightly different meaning, and substitution involving a sign with a roughly equivalent meaning from a different sign language (see Example 8). The first type includes the examples of COW at T+1 being substituted for MILK at T-1; REST for LAZY; and NO and DANGER for CANNOT. Examples of the second type include signs for 'friend' (HKSL sign substituted with KSL sign), and 'people' (ASL sign with P-handshape substituted with non-initialised IS sign). This strategy was more common in cases where the sign at T-1 was of an abstract nature and not iconically motivated.

These two types of substitution are familiar from previous research. Lee (2003) draws on the work of Tarone (1980), using Tarone's term 'approximation' to mean something similar to the strategy of 'substitution' here, i.e. the replacing of a trouble-source sign with a roughly equivalent form or synonym. Lee also uses a term from Dorneyi and Scott (1997), namely 'foreignizing', to describe the strategy of substituting a troublesome form with one from another language, e.g. the interlocutor's mother tongue or a third language.

It is notable that there are many examples of try-marked substitutions. The occurrence of try-marking fits in well with the consideration that in the context of substitution, signers think about the most promising choice of sign in terms of resolving the communication trouble. In instances of substitution, it often seemed that signers were attempting to imagine what signs their interlocutor would be most likely to understand, given their particular background and native language. A signer might be familiar with a number of different sign languages. For instance, a person from Korea might know Chinese Sign Language (CSL) and International Sign in addition to KSL. If interacting with Signer D, who is from Hong Kong, the Korean signer might draw on CSL with the assumption that this interlocutor probably knows some Chinese-derived signs. In contrast, when interacting with a European signer, the same Korean signer might guess that a substitution from International Sign would stand a higher likelihood of success.

Example 8. Substitution

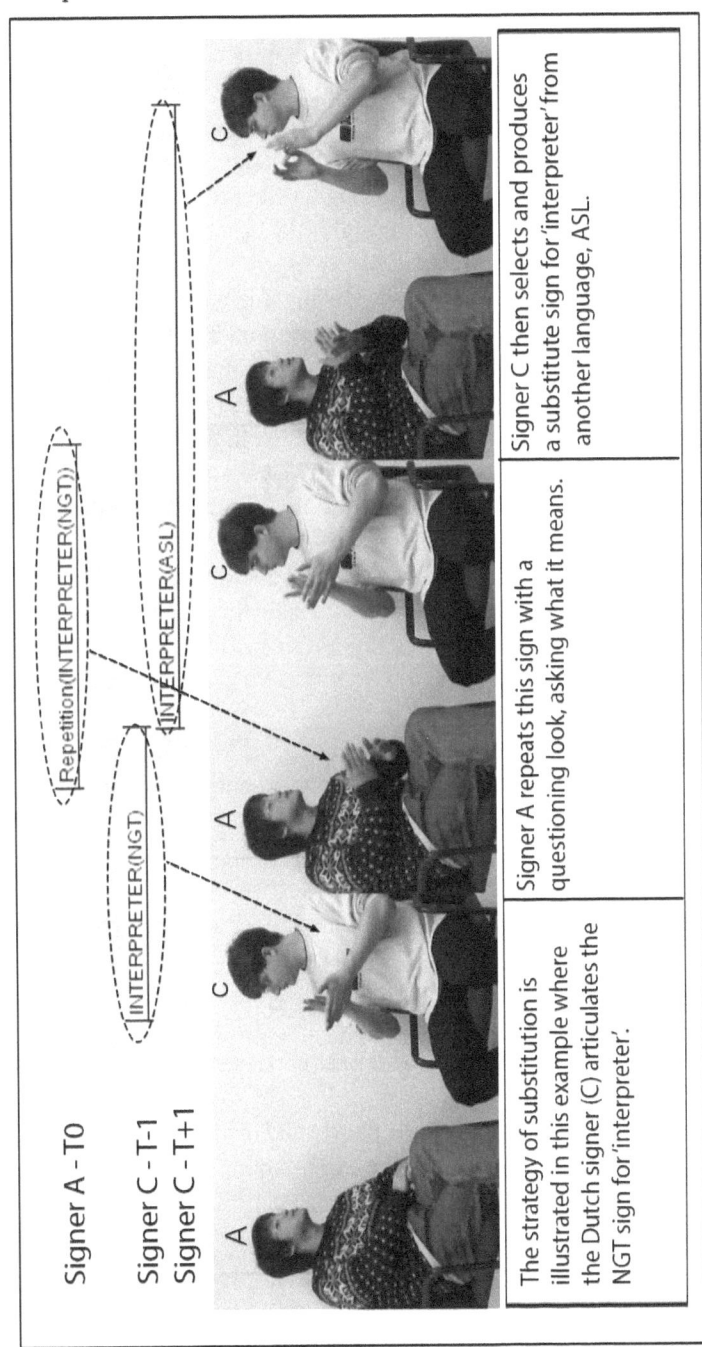

### 3.3.4 Explanation

The tool of explaining here refers to explicitly describing the meaning and/or grammatical function of the trouble source so that the addressee can make the necessary connections. This does not include the use of synonyms, as that would fall under the category of substitution. For Example 9, a signer might resolve the trouble source HAPPY by signing 'smile, glad, laugh, celebrate'; a sign for 'north' that was not understood was clarified by the signer by describing the axes of a compass and the four cardinal directions.

Lee (2003) notes that the strategies of explaining and giving examples are grouped together into one category called 'circumlocution' by Tarone (1980), as both involve 'talking around' the trouble source. The present study's separation of explaining and giving examples into two distinct categories is more similar to the taxonomy of Dornyei and Scott (1997, in Lee 2003), in which explaining is 'rephrasing' (i.e. describing or expounding on the trouble-source item further), and giving an example is 'expanding' (i.e. putting the trouble-source item into a sentence).

Explaining was useful in forging a referential understanding of the problem source sign by drawing explicitly upon the context in question. Examples include the following:

Example 10.
Trouble source:   HAPPY (performed on the chest)
Repair:           'work, achieve, feel ecstatic, grin, cheer out loud, heart is full'

Example 11.
Trouble source:   WORRY (in neutral space at head height)
Repair:           'effort, bad result, fail, wonder how (to fix), scratching my head'

Example 12.
Trouble source:   NORTH
Repair:           axis of north, south, east and west portrayed in space

Such circumlocutions give the addressee the opportunity to identify the meaning of the trouble source form via the context of the explanation.

Repair in cross-signing: Trouble sources, repair strategies and communicative success — 65

Example 9. The Explanation strategy.

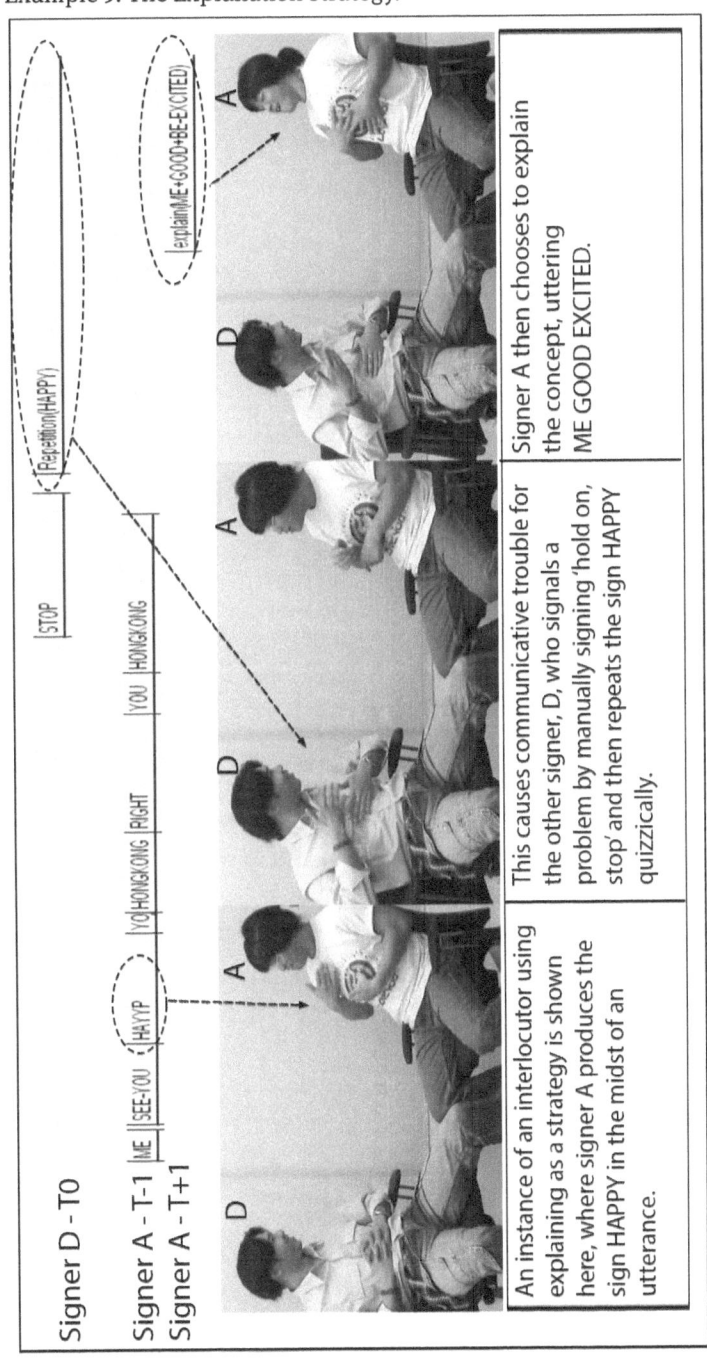

### 3.3.5 Example

Use of an example involves offering a new sentence containing an instantiation of the meaning; for example, when the sign 'age' was not understood by the interlocutor, the signer offered the example 'My age is 27' (Example 13).

Example 13. Deployment of the example strategy

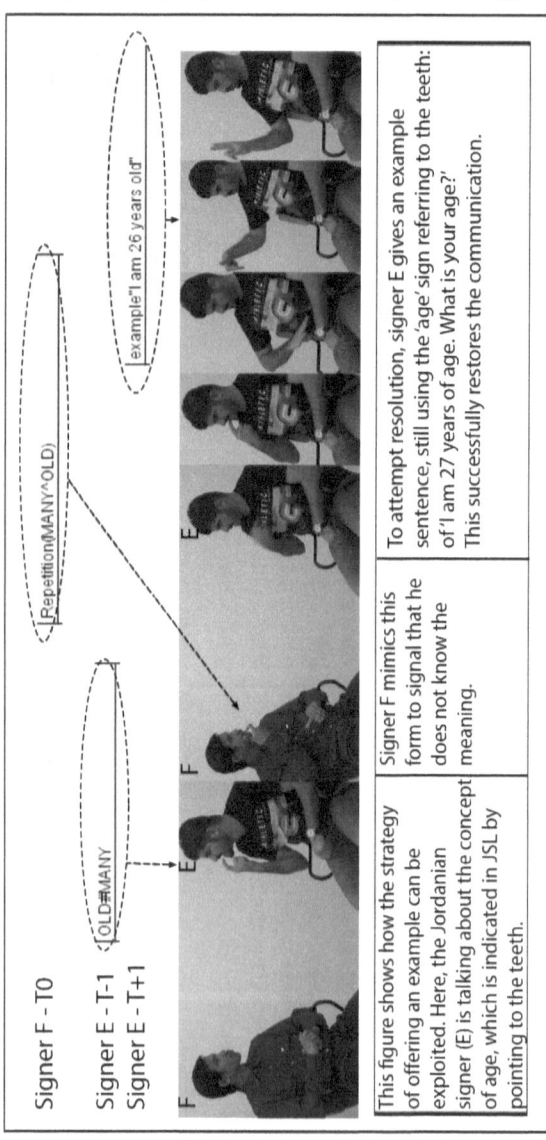

Another way of including the trouble source sign in the repair at T+1 was to mention it alongside a contrasting sign, in a "not A but yes B" kind of construction where B was the trouble source sign. In this way, the addressee could infer the meaning of B on the basis that its meaning was in contrast to, or perhaps the opposite of, the meaning of A, a sign that he could understand more easily.

Giving examples was sometimes useful in imparting the context to the addressee. When a sign was pinpointed as a trouble source, the signer sometimes gave a number of different examples of the concept. To check understanding, which would typically become apparent at the end of the clause with the example, signers tended to hold the final sign as a try-marker, seeking feedback from the addressee.

This try-marking seems to set the strategy of giving examples apart from that of explaining, as the latter is less likely to involve holds, a crucial component of try-marking. Out of seven instances of giving examples, four included try-marking,[8] whereas out of eight instances of explaining, only one involved try-marking (see Table 8). This may be because explaining usually involves longer utterances and fewer phrasal or clausal boundaries where try-markers could be added. The one occurrence of explaining that did involve try-marking was comprised of a series of visually iconic descriptions of the concept of 'party/celebration' (as the trouble-source was a Nepali Sign Language sign meaning 'party'). The explanation included signs referring to a red gown, wedding ring, headdress, noise, and drums, and the Nepali signer used holds as try-markers in between each item to check whether the Indonesian signer had understood, i.e. whether the attempted repair was successful. It was the 'drums' component that finally facilitated the repair. Like in this unusual instance of Explanation, the Example strategy also usually involves shorter utterances with more opportunities for try-marking. Nevertheless, the two strategies are similar with respect to their function of contextualising the trouble source sign.

---

**8** There was only one occurrence of giving examples that did not include try-marking (the remaining two of the seven were undetermined). This case was unusual as it was not a typical OIR. One signer was discussing 'age' using a sign that involves pointing at the teeth. The other signer misunderstood the meaning and carried on the conversation under the assumption that the sign actually meant 'teeth'. The first signer then attempted to repair the misunderstanding by giving an example (signing 'year'). This was a more complex misunderstanding, rather than a typical OIR with both signers' attention drawn to a recognised trouble-source.

**Table 8.** Use of try-markers with Example and Explanation strategies at first attempt

|                      | Example | Explanation |
|----------------------|---------|-------------|
| With try-markers     | 4       | 1           |
| Without try-markers  | 1       | 5           |
| Undetermined         | 2       | 2           |

### 3.3.6 Productive Signs

As set out in Section 2.2, this strategy includes the use of indexicality, classifiers (whole-entity, handling), SASS signs, gesture, and mime. In sign languages, such visually motivated forms tend to be selected more often than arbitrary/opaque forms by language learners, especially children (Rosenstock, 2008). Homesign, the system of communication often devised idiosyncratically by deaf children and their families, is noted for being highly iconic (Coppola and Newport, 2005).

Iconicity can be a strong means of grounding and a successful prompt for referent identification that allows a person to identify the signified item using aspects of the linguistic form itself (Perniss and Vigliocco, 2014). Thus it is perhaps not surprising that iconic constructions including productive signs were selected by participants as convenient ways to make visually-motivated, easily-understood conceptual links between signs and real-world meanings. Example 14 shows how visual iconicity was deployed in the Productive Signs strategy. In this example, the signer is representing the actions of a teacher, using a technique known as 'role shift' or 'role taking' in sign language linguistics. Quer (2013: 12) defines role shift as 'the signer [taking] on the role of the reported person [...] accompanied by an imitation of the actions by the reported agent, in a mimic-like way'.

Repair in cross-signing: Trouble sources, repair strategies and communicative success — 69

Example 14. Deployment of the Productive Signs strategy

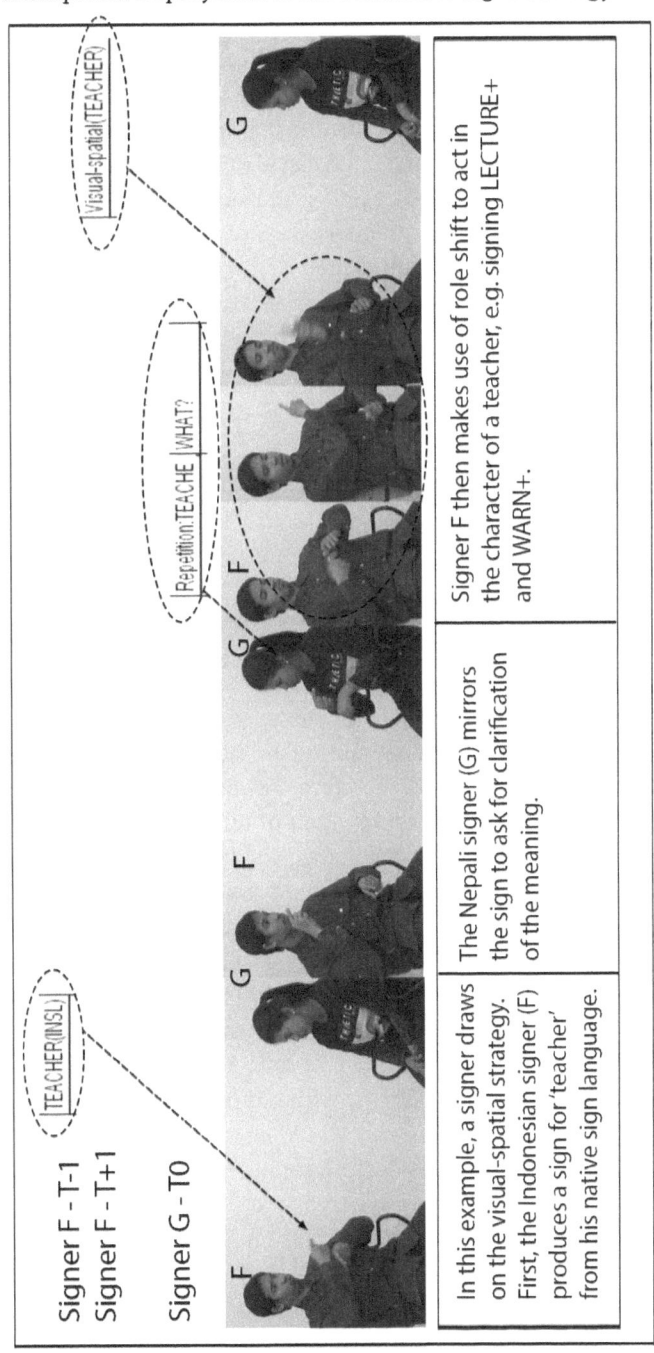

Further examples include the concept of 'careful', which was iconically presented as being nervous; 'teacher' was portrayed by writing on a board and lecturing in front of a class; and the meaning of the fingerspelled A-U-G ('August') was shown by flipping through an imaginary 'calendar' on the wall, indicating that the names of months are at the top, and then turning pages and counting up to 8. In another instance where the signers exploited visual-spatial iconicity in the Productive Signs strategy, the initialised ASL sign for 'university' was clarified as 'diploma rolled up in my hands, study (read book), higher-up'; the details and visually-motivated iconicity in these utterances made them effective as vehicles for repair. This suggests that iconicity is a strategy that signers believe will aid the understanding of their addressee, and one they are ready to rely upon when conversational trouble arises.

## 3.4 Successful and unsuccessful repair attempts

This section presents data on the success rates of the strategies described above, including how often the individual participants used each strategy, and differences between the choices made by the Multisign group versus the Typology group.

Therefore, this section looks at a different measure, the rate of success of the different repair strategies.

For this research, we investigated which of the repair strategies is successful or unsuccessful in resolving the communication trouble. Deciding what counts as "success" is not straightforward, and therefore, several safeguards were put in place to ensure reliability of the results. First of all, it is impossible to decide whether an interlocutor has really understood the intended meaning to be conveyed. To the extent that people can remember what they were thinking during the conversation, it is of course possible to ask them afterwards about their level of understanding. Consequently, the data collection reported in Zeshan (2015) for a different aspect of cross-signing included post-hoc interviews with the participants (see also Webster et al., this volume). These interviews can be very revealing and confirm that sometimes, one or both interlocutors believe that communication trouble has been resolved, while in fact they continue to misunderstand each other.

As post-hoc interviews were not considered here due to the logistics and timing of the interviews in relation to the data coding, success is defined as a signal from the addressee of T+1 as to whether or not the repair is felt to have been understood. Understanding can be signalled by an explicit meta-linguistic comment ('Oh, I understand'), a head nod, or an affirmative sign such as GOOD. Conversely, a negative facial expression such as frowning, a negative headshake, or an explicit signed comment (WHAT, NO, DON'T-UNDERSTAND, or a palm-up gesture) signal unsuccessful repair. Typically, in such cases where repair is not immediately successful, this is followed by another repair attempt.

Another measure to increase the reliability of the "successful/unsuccessful" judgment is to restrict the analysis to instances of first attempts of repair only. As each repair sequence has at least one repair attempt, the number of first attempts is equal to the total number of repair sequences, i.e. 88. However, in six cases, there was no clear positive or negative signal from the addressee after the first repair attempt to indicate whether the repair attempt had been successful or not. Hence these instances were excluded from the analysis, resulting in a final figure of 82 first repair attempts for analysis here.[9]

Restricting the analysis to first repair attempts is appropriate, because only at the first attempt it is possible to be sure that the success or otherwise of the repair is due to the particular repair strategy used at T+1. For any successive repair attempt of the same trouble source, any definite conclusion to this effect would be impossible. For example, if the first repair attempt is by way of a circumlocution ("explanation" strategy), and a second repair attempt follows using fingerspelling ("literacy" strategy), ultimate successful understanding after the second repair attempt could be due to the fingerspelling being a successful strategy. However, it could also be the case that the addressee merely needed additional time to decode the explanation given at the first repair attempt and is actually disregarding the fingerspelling altogether. Because each successive repair attempt builds on the entire interaction, one cannot be sure which part of the entire interaction is responsible for an ultimate successful resolution.

Table 9 summarises the first attempts at repair and the rate of success according to which strategy was employed, showing the absolute numbers of successful and unsuccessful instances as well as those that could not be determined (for example, because of unclear backchannelling).

---

[9] Note that this figure is different from the subset of 82 repair sequences in Table 6, in which we have deducted from the total number of 88 sequences those 6 sequences where repair was ultimately abandoned at any point in the repair sequence.

Table 9. First attempt success rate per strategy

|  | Explanation | Productive signs | Substitution | Example | Mixed | Literacy | Repetition |
|---|---|---|---|---|---|---|---|
| Immediately successful | 8 (100 %) | 9 (82 %) | 19 (79 %) | 4 (57 %) | 2 (50 %) | 9 (43 %) | 2 (17 %) |
| Not immediately successful | 0 (-) | 1 (9 %) | 5 (21 %) | 3 (43 %) | 2 (50 %) | 10 (48 %) | 8 (67 %) |
| Success unclear / undetermined | 0 (-) | 1 (9 %) | 0 (-) | 0 (-) | 0 (-) | 2 (10 %) | 2 (17 %) |

Explanation, using productive signs, and substitution have the highest rates of success at the first repair attempts, at 100 %, 82 % and 79 % respectively; they seemed to be the most effective at helping addressees to make prompt connections between signs and meanings. Giving examples and using a mix of strategies had considerably lower success rates of 57 % and 50 % respectively, though the total number of occurrences is also low for these categories.

Thus in terms of successful strategies, it would appear that there are three effective ways to achieve repair at the first attempt, namely substitution, explaining, and using productive signs. However, it is important to note that the difficulty level of the trouble-source may restrict the availability of certain strategies and influence the signers' choice of strategies, and this research has not analysed T-1 utterances in terms of difficulty or perceived difficulty. Therefore these results are suggestive only, and require further investigation to tease out how the nature of the T-1 utterance may influence the signer's selection of a particular repair strategy.

The data provide good evidence that some of the frequently-used strategies were less helpful. Repetition was associated with immediately successful repair in only 17 % of its occurrences, with the much larger proportion of 67 % being unsuccessful. It is worth considering the possible motivation behind a signer's decision to use this strategy, as it may seem counterintuitive that if the addressee failed to understand the form in question the first time, they would comprehend a second, unaltered production of it. This is explored further in Section 4.

Resorting to spoken-language-derived strategies in the Literacy category was unsuccessful 48 % of the time. Participants still continued to use such strategies, however, perhaps because they are still successful more than half the time, and because this may be a common way of attempting repair generally, particularly for signers from cultures where written literacy is widespread. In cross-signing, literacy strategies often appear to be selected for place names (e.g. 'Nepal'), languages (e.g. 'English'), and some abstract concepts (e.g. the concept of 'name' in 'what's your name'). As noted in Section 3.3.2, literacy-based strategies may be more useful for abstract concepts such as 'name' because there is much less likely to be a shared code for such items or any other way of indicating them.

Having already looked at the data as one corpus incorporating the Typology and Multisign sets together, the results from the two sets are now considered separately in order to facilitate a brief comparison. The results are summarised in Figure 11.

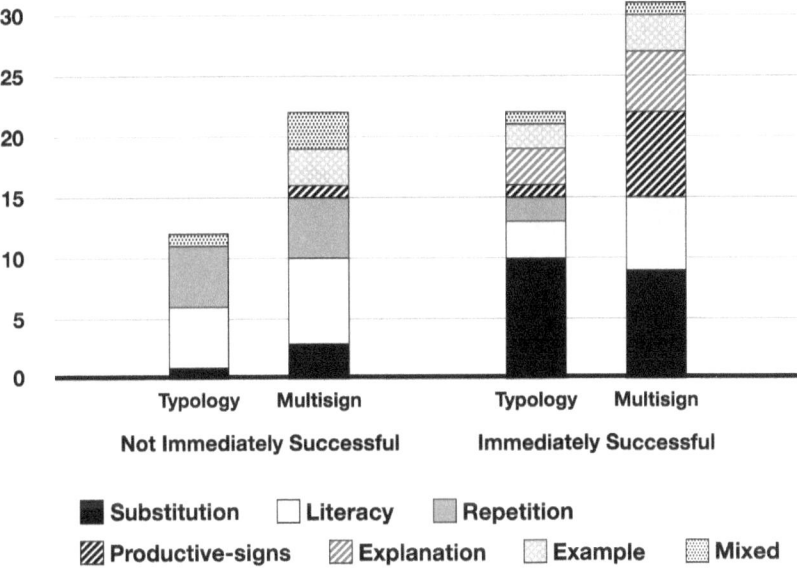

**Figure 11.** Comparison between first attempt success rates per strategy for the Typology group (left) and Multisign group (right)

In both data sets, the two strategies that most often led to successful repair at first attempt were substitution and explaining. Both sets also showed repetition to be an unsuccessful strategy. Overall, the strategy of giving examples was only successful about half of the time, possibly because putting the trouble-source sign into a sentence or exemplifying it with other signs still involves using the trouble-source sign itself. If this has been a problematic form for the addressee, their confusion may be sustained by additional articulations of the sign. It appears that explaining a form is a more successful strategy.

It is worth reflecting on why explaining was so successful as a repair strategy. Explaining was a way to clarify a form and allow the addressee to consider the context of the meaning more fully. It tended to involve imparting the meaning in a detailed manner, often with longer sequences of signs used for circumlocution, to ensure the addressee grasped the prior context and surrounding field of meaning. This strategy seems to be particularly considerate of the addressee and requires the signer to put forth considerable effort so that the addressee can gain clarity. So perhaps unsurprisingly, this tool has the highest rate of success in the data, in fact reaching 100 %.

With respect to substitution, a more detailed look at the data reveals that substitution leads to differential success rates of the repair depending on the provenance of the sign chosen. Figure 12 shows that, when a signer selects a form from the addressee's language, this is very likely to be successful. In fact, all of the four instances of this at T+1 were successful, as were the seven cases where the signer selected another sign from his or her own language (e.g. KSL CANNOT being substituted with KSL DON'T).

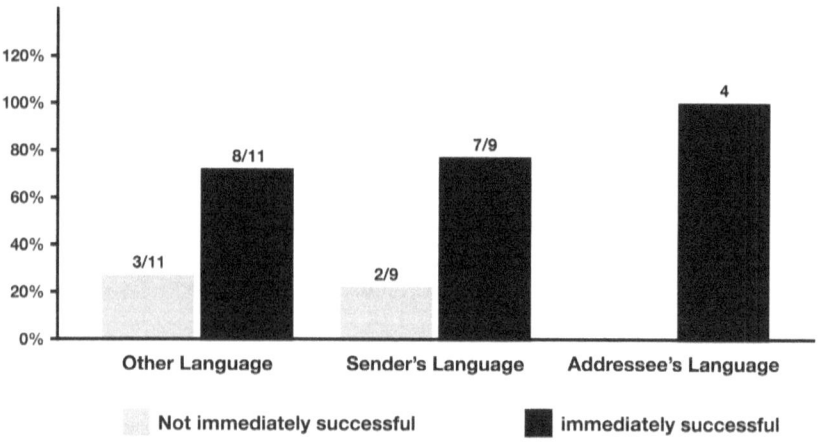

**Figure 12.** Success of substitution in 1st attempt repair strategies according to provenance of signs

The reason why substituting another sign from the signer's own language may tend to be successful is that such a form is perhaps more likely to already be in the two signers' shared repertoire, compared to a sign from a third sign language. The use of other sign languages, i.e. neither the sender's nor the addressee's language (e.g. ASL), resulted in eight instances of successful repair and three instances of unsuccessful repair, which was a much lower rate of success than substituting a form from the addressee's language or a different sign from the signer's own language.

For the Literacy strategy, there is only a slight difference between the two sets of data. There were 3 successful occurrences overall in the Typology set, compared to 5 unsuccessful ones; in the Multisign set, there were 6 successful instances and 7 unsuccessful ones.

Another difference between the two data sets is evident when looking at the use of the Productive Signs strategy. This was quite frequent in the Multisign data, with 7 successful cases. While it was also successful in the Typology set, it was infrequent, and it is as yet unclear why there were so few occurrences in this set compared to Multisign.

Overall, the similarities between these two sets are more notable than the differences, and the disparity in previous communicative experience between the two groups of signers makes the many parallels all the more remarkable. The main conclusions drawn on the basis of Table 9, with explaining, productive signs, and substitution being successful strategies, repetition being an unsuccessful strategy, and literacy-related uses presenting a more mixed picture, still hold when considering the groups separately.

# 4 Conclusions

This chapter has highlighted the considerable skills displayed by sign language users in cross-signing interactions. We have looked in detail at the range of repair strategies and their use in conversations. Despite the challenging situation, cross-signers' combined use of multilingual resources, iconicity, circumlocutions, and literacy often allows them to repair communication trouble within a single turn.

A quantitative analysis of some of the data, together with qualitative descriptions of the use of repair strategies, have revealed some of the rationale and underlying motivations when signers try to resolve miscommunication in cross-signing. While several of the strategies clearly aimed at resolving the trouble source directly, our analysis suggests that repetition merely appears to buy time to come up with better strategies, rather than being a preferred repair strategy in its own right. Overall, the results of this chapter are in line with recent research on cross-signing (Zeshan 2015, Byun et al, 2017), particularly with respect to the initial meetings between signers (see Bradford, Michaelis and Zeshan, this volume, for a comparative study tracking cross-signers' interactions over a longer time period).

The study of cross-signing is an innovation in sign language linguistics. Besides the interest in cross-signing itself as an emerging jargon, part of the potential of this research also lies in improving our general understanding of International Sign pidgin, which is itself severely under-researched. Cross-signing may provide clues as to the historical development of International Sign, and the way in which it may have emerged over time.

In addition to being of interest in the context of sign language linguistics, research on cross-signing also provides valuable new insights into and considerations with respect to established notions in the area of repair. Firstly, cross-signing leads us to consider the trouble source (at T-1) in much more detail, revealing its complexities. Because a shared code is largely absent at the beginning of cross-signing interactions, the interplay of factors leading to communication trouble cannot be adequately covered using the three categories of trouble in "receiving, producing and understanding" the message. Instead, the qualitative examples have shown, for instance, that "understanding" is itself a multifaceted notion. In cross-signing interactions, failure to understand a sign can be due to the absence of a shared code, the unfamiliarity of a concept (as in the example of 'Uzbekistan'), or misinterpretations of iconicity. The difficulty in understanding a fingerspelled word can be due to the form of the fingerspelled letter, on due to the addressee not knowing the targeted English word.

Likewise, the nature of the utterance that occurs at T+1 it is called into question by the use of the Repetition strategy. Due to this strategy being largely unsuccessful, the data have led to the conclusion that the function of Repetition may have more to do with "buying time" for the sender than with offering a repair option to the addressee. Therefore, we need to consider that either Repetition may not fully fall into the scope of repair, or that utterances at T+1 may serve multiple functions, some of which are not primarily associated with repair in a narrow sense.

Finally, this research has uncovered some preliminary evidence of how recipient design supports repair efforts. Recipient design is the concept that actors in communication tend to produce their message in a way that is tailored to their recipient (Sacks, 1974; Blokpoel, 2015). For example, when formulating their message, people will take into account their addressee's individual background, and what they assume their addressee to know. Some evidence for this is inherent in the data on the Substitution strategy, which showed that signers sometimes show sensitivity to their addressee's background by choosing a substitute sign from the addressee's sign language. The data also show that using recipient design in this way is more successful as a Substitution strategy than choosing a sign from an unrelated sign language as a substitute sign.

The present research is also of interest in terms of the communicative and cognitive skills deployed by signers in the interaction. The data analysed here have provided several clues as to the impressive metalinguistic skills that signers draw upon in this situation. On the other hand, the interplay between signers' individual and social-linguistic backgrounds, and the linguistic basis of cross-signing communication, is a difficult issue that requires further research. Part of the reason why analysing this type of communication is quite difficult is due to the issue of identifying what factors are related to the nature of the sign languages themselves, and what factors are associated with participants' general communication abilities (see Zeshan, 2019, for an analysis of factors in relation to experimental data from cross-signing).

At present, we do not have multiple dyads of signers from the same countries, with the same linguistic backgrounds, in order to determine where there are similarities due to the languages involved and where communication is idiosyncratic due to the specifics of the people involved. Having multiple pairs of signers with similar linguistic backgrounds would be very desirable for future research.

## Acknowledgements

Part of the research leading to these results has received funding from the European Research Council under the European Union's Seventh Framework Programme; we are grateful for funding of this research under the project "Multilingual behaviours in sign language users" (MULTISIGN), Grant Agreement number 263647.

We are very grateful to the participants in the study: Waldemar Schwager, Rutger-Jan Savelkoul and Kenny Chu from the Typology group; and Anita Sharma, Baha Freihat, and Adam Mailk from the Multisign group. Other members of the wider research team are also gratefully acknowledged, in particular Muhammad Isnaini, Mohammed Salha, and Anju Jain, whose dedication as facilitators for the Multisign group has been invaluable, and Sibaji Panda who coordinated the Multisign field site setting.

We are also grateful to the Max Planck Institute for Psycholinguistics and to the Dr Shakuntala Misra National Rehabilitation University, Lucknow, for hosting the Typology and Multisign groups of signers.

## References

Blokpoel, Mark. 2015. *Understanding understanding: A computational-level perspective*. Nijmegen: Radboud University PhD thesis.

Boyes Braem, Penny & Rachel Sutton-Spence. 2001. *The hands are the head of the mouth: The mouth as articulator in sign languages*. Hamburg: Signum Press.

Bradford, Anastasia, Keiko Sagara & Ulrike Zeshan. 2013. Multilingual and multimodal aspects of "cross-signing" – A study of emerging communication in the domain of numerals. Poster presented at the 11th conference on Theoretical Issues in Sign Language Research (TISLR11), University College London, 10–13 July.

Byun, Kang-suk, Connie De Vos, Anastasia Bradford, Ulrike Zeshan & Stephen C. Levinson. 2018. First encounters: Repair sequences in cross-signing. *Topics in Cognitive Science* 10(2). 314–334. doi:10.1111/tops.12303

Byun, Kang-Suk, Seán Roberts, Connie De Vos, Ulrike Zeshan & Stephen C. Levinson. 2018. Interactive sequences modulate the selection of expressive forms in cross-signing. *Proceedings of the 12th International Conference on the Evolution of Language (Evolang12), Torun, Poland*. Torun: Nicolaus Copernicus University.

Clark, Herbert. H & Susan E. Brennan. 1991. Grounding in communication. In Lauren B. Resnick, John M. Levine & Stephanie D. Teasley (eds.), *Perspectives on socially shared cognition*, 127–149. Washington, DC: American Psychological Association.

Coppola, Marie & Elissa L. Newport. 2005. Grammatical subjects in home sign: Abstract linguistic structure in adult primary gesture systems without linguistic input. *PNAS* 102(52). 19249–19253.

Crasborn, Onno & Anja Hiddinga. 2015. The paradox of International Sign: The importance of deaf-hearing encounters for deaf-deaf communication across sign language borders. In Michelle Friedner & Annelies Kusters (eds.), *It's a small world. International deaf spaces and encounters*, 59–69. Washington DC: Gallaudet University Press.

Cutrone, Pino. 2005. A case study examining backchannels in conversations between Japanese-British dyads. *Multilingua* 24(3). 237–274.

Dingemanse, Mark. & Nick J. Enfield. 2015. Other-initiated repair across languages: Towards a typology of conversational structures. *Open Linguistics* 1. 98–118.

Dingemanse, Mark, Seán G. Roberts, Julija Baranova, Joe Blythe, Paul Drew, Simeon Floyd, Rosa S. Gisladottir, Kobin H. Kendrick, Stephen C. Levinson, Elizabeth Manrique, Giovanni Rossi & Nick J. Enfield. 2015. Universal principles in the repair of communication problems. *PLoS One* 10(9): e0136100. doi:10.1371/journal.pone.0136100.

Dingemanse, Mark. In press. Recruiting assistance in interaction: a West-African corpus study. In Simeon Floyd, Giovanni Rossi & Nick J. Enfield (eds.), *Getting others to do things: A pragmatic typology of recruitments*. Berlin: Language Science Press.

Dixon, John. A & Foster, D.H. 1998. Gender, social context and backchannel responses. *Journal of Social Psychology* 138(1). 134–136.

Dörnyei, Zoltán & Mary Lee Scott. 1997. Communication strategies in a second language: Definitions and taxonomies. *Language Learning* 47. 173–210.

Groeber, Simone & Evelyne Pochon-Berger. 2014. Turns and turn-taking in sign language interaction: A study of turn-final holds. *Journal of Pragmatics* 65. 121–136.

Heinz, Bettina. 2003. Backchannel responses as strategic responses in bilingual speakers' conversations. *Journal of Pragmatics* 35. 1113–1142.

Hiddinga, Anja & Onno Crasborn. 2011. Signed languages and globalization. *Language in Society* 40(4). 483–505. doi:10.1017/S0047404511000480
Hill, Joseph C. 2015. Data collection in sociolinguistics. In Eleni Orfanidou, Bencie Woll & Gary Morgan *Research methods in sign language studies: A practical guide*, 193–205. Chichester, UK: John Wiley & Sons.
Johnston, Trevor & Adam Schembri. 1999. On defining lexeme in a signed language. *Sign Language & Linguistics* 2(2). 115–185.
Johnston, Trevor & Adam Schembri. 2007. *Australian Sign Language: An introduction to sign language linguistics*. Cambridge: Cambridge University Press.
Levinson, Stephen C. 2006. On the human "interaction engine". In Nick J. Enfield & Stephen C. Levinson (eds.), *Roots of human sociality: Culture, cognition and interaction*, 39–69. Oxford: Berg.
Lewis, David. 1969. *Convention: A philosophical study*. Oxford: Blackwell.
Manrique, Elizabeth. 2016. Other-initiated repair in Argentine Sign Language. *Open Linguistics* 148(4). 308–314.
Manrique, Elizabeth & Nick J. Enfield. 2015. Suspending the next turn as a form of repair initiation: Evidence from Argentine Sign Language. *Frontiers in Psychology* 6(1326). doi: 10.3389/fpsyg.2015.01326
Moerman, Michael. 1988. *Talking culture: Ethnography and conversation analysis*. Philadelphia: University of Pennsylvania Press.
Perniss, Pamela & Gabriella Vigliocco. 2014. The bridge of iconicity: From a world of experience to the experience of language. *Philosophical Transactions of the Royal Society B* 369(1651). doi:10.1098/rstb.2013.0300
Pietikäinen, Kaisa S. 2016. Misunderstandings and Ensuring Understanding in Private ELF Talk. *Applied Linguistics* 39(2). 188–212.
Quer, Josep. 2013. Attitude ascriptions in sign languages and role shift. In Leah C. Geer (ed.), *Proceedings from the 13th meeting of the Texas Linguistics Society*, 12–28. Austin: Texas Linguistics Forum.
Rosenstock, Rachel. 2008. The role of iconicity in International Sign. *Sign Language Studies* 8(2). 131–158.
Sacks, Harvey, Emanuel Schegloff & Gail Jefferson. 1974. A simplest systematics for the organization of turn-taking in conversation. *Language* 50. 696–735.
Schegloff, Emanuel A. 1987. Some sources of misunderstanding in talk-in-interaction. *Linguistics* 25(1). 201–218.
Schegloff, Emanuel A., Gail Jefferson & Harvey Sacks. 1977. The preference for self-correction in the organization of repair in conversation. *Language* 53. 361–382.
Schembri, Adam. 2003. Rethinking "classifiers" in signed languages. In Karen Emmorey (ed.), *Perspectives on classifier constructions in sign languages*. 3–34. Mahwah, New Jersey: Lawrence Erlbaum Associates.
Sloetjes, Han. 2013. The ELAN annotation tool. In Hedda Lausberg (ed.), *Understanding body movement: A guide to empirical research on nonverbal behaviour with an introduction to the NEUROGES coding system*, 193–198. Frankfurt a/M: Lang.
Spradley, Thomas S, & James P. Spradley. 1985. *Deaf like me*. Washington, DC: Gallaudet University Press.
Stamp, Rose, Adam Schembri, Bronwen G. Evans & Kearsy Cormier. 2016. Regional sign language varieties in contact: Investigating patterns of accommodation. *Journal of Deaf Studies and Deaf Education* 21(1). 70–82.

Stokoe, William C. 1960. *Sign language structure: An outline of the visual communication systems of the American deaf (Studies in linguistics: Occasional papers no. 8)*. Buffalo: Dept. of Anthropology and Linguistics, University of Buffalo.

Supalla, Ted & Rebecca Webb. 1995. The grammar of International Sign: A new look at pidgin languages. In Karen Emmorey & Judy Reilly (eds.), *Language, gesture, and space*, 333–352. Mahwah, NJ: Lawrence Erlbaum.

Tarone, Elaine. 1980. Communication strategies, foreigner talks, and repair in interlanguage. *Language Learning* 30. 417–431.

Tomasello, Michael. 2003. *Constructing a language: A usage-based theory of language acquisition*. Cambridge, MA: Harvard University Press.

Webb, Rebecca & Ted Supalla. 1994. Negation in International Sign. In Inger Ahlgren, Brita Bergman & Mary Brennan (eds.), *Perspectives on sign language structure (Papers from the Fifth International Symposium on Sign Language Research, Salamanca, Spain, May 25–30, 1992)*, 173–185. Durham: International Sign Linguistics Association and Deaf Studies Research Unit, University of Durham.

White, Sheida. 1989. Backchannels across cultures: A study of Americans and Japanese. *Language in Society* 18. 59–76.

Whynot, Lori A. 2015. *Assessing comprehension of International Sign lectures: Linguistic and sociolinguistic factors* (Unpublished doctoral dissertation). Sydney: Macquarie University.

Zeshan, Ulrike. 2015. "Making meaning" – Communication between sign language users without a shared language. *Cognitive Linguistics* 26(2). 211–260.

Zeshan, Ulrike. 2019. Task-response times, facilitating and inhibiting factors in cross-signing. *Applied Linguistics Review* 10(1). 9–30.

Zheng, Yu, Xing Xie & Wei-Ying Ma. 2010. GeoLife: A collaborative social networking service among user, location and trajectory. *IEEE Data Engineering Bulletin* 33(2). 32–39.

# Two languages at hand – Code-switching in bilingual deaf signers[1]

Ulrike Zeshan and Sibaji Panda

## 1 Introduction

Research on bilingual sign language users has previously centred on two subfields: "Sign bilingualism" and "bimodal bilingualism". Sign bilingualism is situated in the context of deaf education, where a sign language is acquired alongside a spoken language, usually in its written form, such as British Sign Language and written English (e.g. Swanwick 2010, Knight and Swanwick 2013). Because of its link with deaf education, the study of sign bilingualism often involves linguistic data from children and is often allied with issues from applied linguistics, such as the acquisition of literacy and language policies in education (Wilbur 2000, Plaza-Pust and Morales-López 2008).

Bimodal bilingualism involves hearing people, often hearing children of deaf adults (CODAs), co-using a sign language and a spoken language. This includes the study of data from both children and adults (e.g. Emmorey et al. 2008 on American Sign Language and English, Donati and Branchini 2013 on Italian Sign Language and Italian). Bimodal bilingualism has been approached as a particular language contact phenomenon that is not found in spoken language linguistics, and has been of interest in psycholinguistics because of the effects on language processing (e.g. Emmorey 2009). By contrast, research on unimodal bilingual signers, that is, signers using two or more different sign languages in conversation, is a recently emerging research area.

There are very few studies dealing with data on the co-use of two sign languages. Previous studies have concentrated on the phonological and lexical levels, as in Quinto-Pozos (2000) on Mexican Sign Language (LSM) and American Sign Language (ASL), and Yoel (2007) on Russian Sign Language and Israeli Sign Language, specifically dealing with attrition of the former. More recently, work has also emerged on psycholinguistic aspects of bilingual language

---

[1] This chapter was originally published in 2015 as an article with the same title. It appeared in the journal *Sign Language & Linguistics* 18(1): 90–131 and is republished here with permission from the original publisher. In keeping with the format of this volume, the abstract that appeared with the journal article has been omitted here.

processing in unimodal sign bilinguals (Adam 2013). Very little is known about the contribution that two sign languages make to utterances at clause and discourse level (see Adam 2012 on British Sign Language / Auslan and (Australian) Irish Sign Language).

In this article, we first summarise the fieldwork setting and the linguistic backgrounds of the participants (Section 2), followed by information about the data and methodology (Section 3). We then discuss the research domain, which focuses on negative clauses and wh-questions, and our approach to the data (Section 4). The following sections detail the results emerging from an analysis of the data, including both lexical choice (Section 5) and clause structures (Section 6). In the conclusion (Section 7), it is argued that the data support a view of this group of participants as a "community of practice" in sociolinguistic terms.

# 2 The language contact situation and the participants

## 2.1 The fieldwork site and its linguistic situation

This research was conducted in New Delhi with participants from Burundi who were enrolled in a BA programme for deaf students. This programme had attracted students from India and other countries, as it was taught entirely in a sign language environment and included a preparatory university access programme. At the time of fieldwork, which was conducted outside the campus, six Burundian students were enrolled in the programme, four of whom participated in video recordings of signed interactions with each other (see Section 3.1 on data collection).[2]

The context of this research is unusual in that the setting involves a group of signers from a range of different nationalities. This produces a particularly rich multilingual situation, also considering that the Indian students joined the programme from locations all over India. Our research has developed over a substantial time period, but at the time of collecting these data, the student cohort consisted of the following:

Indian students: 50

Non-Indian students: Mexican (1), Nepalese (8), Burundian (6), Chinese (2), Ugandan (2), Afghanistan (1), Burma (1)

---

[2] Chapter 8 describes the Burundi Sign Language-Indian Sign Language bilingual subcommunity in more detail, though the chapter refers to a later point in time.

In addition, individual students in the cohort have varying degrees of fluency in American Sign Language (ASL) and International Sign, while the written language of communication is English only. Despite the multilingual nature of this setting, it is clear that the main language of interaction for both academic and social purposes is Indian Sign Language (ISL),[3] as may be expected given the predominant number of Indians in the cohort. All teaching staff, both hearing and deaf, use ISL to deliver the course. Moreover, all interactions with Indian signers outside the campus are in ISL, and as students live off-campus, they are not segregated from the wider Deaf community. In fact, all students have multiple, continuous links with local deaf communities in India, and all newcomers to the programme acquire communicative competence in ISL during their first few months.

The complexity of this multilingual situation is fully recognised here, and we do not wish to downplay its importance. However, as argued in Section 4, the research domain is such that this complex context does not impinge on the conclusions drawn from our data. Firstly, previous research has shown that ISL dialects have remarkably uniform grammatical structures and vary principally with respect to the lexicon. In particular, Zeshan (2006) investigated dialectal variation with respect to negation and wh-questions in ISL regional dialects, and found no major grammatical differences. Secondly, in the preparatory planning phase, the research team made informal observations regarding sub-groups of students from different nationalities. These observations confirmed that the Burundian group continued to use BuSL signs in interactions with each other, rather than switching completely to ISL, or using any of the other available sign languages within this setting.[4] Our informal observations of interactions between students from Burundi further suggest that they tended to mix BuSL and ISL for most purposes when communicating with each other. BuSL on its own seemed to be the predominant language mode only in situations of emotional intensity, for example during a conflict.

---

[3] The term *Indian Sign Language* is used here in the sense of representing the urban sign language varieties within India, although sign language varieties across the border in Pakistan constitute dialects of one and the same language otherwise labelled *Indo-Pakistani Sign Language* (cf. Zeshan 2000).
[4] This was in marked contrast with the two signers from China, for example, who were never seen using Chinese signs with one another.

## 2.2 The participants and their linguistic background

In addition to the setting as a whole, the linguistic backgrounds of the participants are complex. The majority of the data are from three of the BuSL-ISL bilinguals (identified as CN, AB and SN), who were selected with the aim of capturing the bilingual productions of signers who had been acquiring ISL for varying periods of time. The three have similar linguistic backgrounds and educational biographies. None of them have other deaf family members, but all of them have some family members who can sign, particularly younger siblings. SN (female, aged 24) was born deaf, while AB (female, aged 28) and CN (male, aged 32) became deaf in early childhood, aged four and seven respectively. The fourth participant (WK, male, aged 27) also became deaf in early childhood. Thus all participants have BuSL as their functional first language (L1).

Educational options for deaf children are very limited in Burundi, as there are only a few special schools for the deaf. Thus, all participants attended the same primary school for deaf children (CN attended a hearing school for one year, before the onset of deafness). Primary school in Burundi goes up to year six, after which SN and AB continued in a hearing secondary school (year 7–10), while CN continued in a deaf secondary school. At school in Burundi, the language of literacy was French, and all participants acquired English later in life, after secondary school.

It is common for deaf Burundians to seek further educational opportunities, or to seek work, in neighbouring countries; all participants spent between 1–3 years outside Burundi: SN and WK in Kenya, and AB and CN in both Kenya and Uganda. They have therefore become familiar with the sign language varieties in these countries too.

At the time of data collection, CN had been in India for three years, AB for two years, and SN for one year. This factor has motivated the choice of this set of participants for data analysis, i.e. one person from each year group of students, as we were interested in potential correlations between length of stay in India and bilingual language patterns. Data from the fourth signer, WK, have been included in a more limited way (see Section 5 for details), as the three other signers produced a larger number of the target structures within the video segments analysed here.

Before coming to India, the four participants had been in regular contact with each other, typically several times a week. They belonged to the same church in the capital city of Bujumbura, and as church is a central part of social life in Burundi, their contact with each other before arriving in India can be described as intensive. There is no doubt that all participants were using BuSL together very regularly in Burundi for the several years that they had been living in Bujumbura. Within the group, CN has a leadership role because he is a church minister and was the first student to arrive in India, after which he was instrumental in assisting the other Burundian students in the transition to India.

While this article distinguishes between monolingual BuSL and the bilingual BuSL-ISL variety, we also recognise that referring to monolingual BuSL is a simplification, due to the presence of other linguistic influences from sign languages outside Burundi in general, and the participants' individual travel biographies in particular. Typically, the complexities of linguistic settings in much of sub-Saharan Africa, both for signed and spoken languages, make it difficult to identify any situation as truly "monolingual" (see, for instance, Lüpke and Chambers 2010 and Nyst 2010 on the complexities of linguistic settings in West Africa for spoken and signed languages, respectively).

In the remainder of this article, we therefore refer to "monolingual BuSL" as shorthand for the variety that our participants would have used before they arrived in India and learned ISL. While it is recognised here that this variety of BuSL may itself be a composite system whose history and development from contributor languages has not been described, we also argue in Section 4.2 that for the purpose of the present research, it is not necessary to decide on this issue.

It is clear from the data that the Indian Sign Language used by the participants is a learner variety, that is, none of them has native competence in ISL. On the other hand, all of them have been using ISL in their everyday lives for a period between one and three years, and use their communicative competence daily in interactions with deaf Indians. Of course, there is no requirement in bilingualism research to study only people with equal competence in both languages (so-called "balanced bilinguals"), if indeed such an idealised situation exists in real life. In fact, Grosjean (2010: 20) points out that it is a misapprehension to consider only balanced bilingualism as "real" bilingualism: "If one were to count as bilingual only those who can pass as monolinguals in each language, one would have no label for the vast majority of people who use two or more languages regularly but do not have native-like fluency in each." Our bilingual participants do not have balanced bilingualism, but clearly do have a usage-based functional bilingualism, or rather multilingualism. Their total multilingual repertoire includes written English, written French, BuSL, sign language varieties in Kenya and/or Uganda, and ISL.

Of the four participants, AB has the highest degree of fluency in ISL, due to more intensive contact with ISL users (see the comments in Section 5.1), and it is interesting to note that the degree of fluency in ISL does not correlate neatly with the time spent in India. However, none of the participants, including WK and SN who are among the latest arrivals in India, reported any communication difficulties with ISL signers at the time when data collection took place for this research.

## 3 Methodology and data

The data presented here form part of a larger data corpus of bilingual BuSL-ISL productions. Data collection from BuSL-ISL bilinguals involved three stages:
1.  Collecting information about each participant's background, including the kind of information presented in Section 2.2, which was gathered using a written questionnaire about the person's linguistic biography and bi-/multilingual language use; and qualitative questions (for which the answers were videotaped) to get a sense of the participants' language attitudes, for example how they felt about the mixing of several sign languages.
2.  Free conversations involving the whole group of four participants, which were videotaped. The researcher asked some guiding questions in order to encourage and steer the conversation, but did not otherwise interfere. These conversational data, comprising over 3 hours of video, are the basis of the present article.
3.  At a later stage of the research, pairs of participants were involved in a linguistic elicitation game based on maps of places familiar to them, resulting in nearly 2 hours of data which are more recent and have not been analysed yet. These data include two further BuSL-ISL bilinguals who were only involved at this stage.

Interestingly, the four participants expressed different language attitudes with respect to their bilingual use of BuSL and ISL during the qualitative interviews. While all of them found it valuable to know more than one sign language, they did not agree on the mixing of different sign languages in communication. CN and SN felt that keeping their different sign languages quite separate was preferable, while AB and WK supported the idea of mixing sign languages in the same discourse. However, these expressed attitudes do not correlate with the actual linguistic behaviour of the participants. In the actual discourses analysed here, all four participants mix BuSL and ISL and freely code-switch between the two.

### 3.1 Data from bilingual interactions

The conversational bilingual interactions were recorded in a relaxed private home setting, with participants sitting in a half-circle (see Figure 1 for a screen shot of this). All four individuals were active in the conversation, some more than others. Before the start of data collection, participants were briefed about the aims and implications of the research and intended use of the data, following the project's standard informed consent procedures.

**Figure 1.** The data collection setting

The recording session was led by one of the co-authors, who is a deaf Indian and native ISL user. He used guiding questions to start the conversation, but then left the room and was not present for the rest of the interaction, except to add a few further guiding questions when the participants ran out of topics to talk about, after which he again left the room. The intention of these questions was to prompt the signers to talk about situations and experiences that were hypothesised to elicit code-switching between the two sign languages. For example, participants were asked how they had first learned ISL upon arrival in India, and what this experience felt like to them. They were asked about their experiences of travelling to New Delhi and their future plans upon their return to Burundi at the end of their studies. These kinds of guiding questions were successful in eliciting conversations with a large amount of code-switching. In addition, some of the conversational segments include a lot of negative and interrogative constructions, which are the main grammatical target of the analysis here.

The participants were not asked explicitly to use both BuSL and ISL, and the aims of the research with its focus on bilingualism were explained only in very general terms. It is therefore unlikely that the initial briefing or the researcher's brief presence have influenced the data, especially as the participants' code-switching between BuSL and ISL had already been observed informally. There is no reason to suppose that the data represent anything other than the natural discourse style of the participants when discussing the topics that they were asked to address.

In response to the topic of their initial journey to India, CN, AB and SN each produced a longer, coherent text. A segment of ca. 3 minutes was selected from each of these narratives on the basis of a substantial number of negatives and wh-questions occurring therein. As in each case the journey from Burundi to India was fraught with difficulty, it is natural for these texts to contain a lot of negation. Wh-questions were somewhat less frequent, as would be expected in a monologue narrative segment, and most questions are rhetorical or in the form of reported speech rather than being directed at another participant in the conversation, although the latter also occurs a few times. These short segments are the basis of overall word counts across all signs, irrespective of the occurrence of negative clauses and wh-questions. The segments also provided an opportunity to consider the discourse level with respect to the lexical choice of BuSL and ISL signs. Although the total transcribed data is only a small proportion of the entire videotaped data, the process did result in the substantial number of nearly 1,000 transcribed and labelled signs, which allows an initial insight into bilingual sign language use, without claiming that the data are strictly representative of the entire corpus collected for this research.

In order to gain a more comprehensive impression of the bilingual use of negatives and wh-questions, we also analysed individual clauses that occurred outside these three texts. These are taken from longer segments totalling over half an hour of video, which contain the three narratives. Additional negative and WH-clauses from all four signers appear in these data, and all additional clauses are fully transcribed in the same way as the three short text segments. These additional clauses are relevant for the specific analysis of negatives and wh-questions only. Table 1 provides a summary of the video data.

**Table 1.** Video data summary

| Clip number | Clip time | Transcribed text length within clip | Signer of transcribed text |
|---|---|---|---|
| 2 | 11 min 48 sec | 2 min 50 sec | AB |
| 3 | 11 min 25 sec | 3 min | SN |
| 5 | 10 min 59 sec | 2 min 56 sec | CN |
| Total | 34 min 12 sec | 8 min 46 sec | |
| Relevance of data | For clauses containing negatives and wh-questions only | Word counts across all signs and analysis of lexical choice in discourse | |

## Data annotation and analysis

Much work on code-switching in spoken languages relies on the analysis of conversational texts (see, for instance, the contributions in Auer 1998). For sign languages, with few exceptions, such work is not yet widely available, and thus there are no established standards for analytical procedures in working with bilingual signed texts. A number of methodological issues were encountered during the research process (see Section 4.2). For instance, there were obstacles related to annotation and glossing. The analysis mainly relies on annotations produced with the multimedia annotator programme ELAN. Both the narrative texts and the individual clauses were first glossed sign-by-sign. As we were interested in the relative contributions of BuSL and ISL signs, each sign gloss is prefixed with the language that it comes from (e.g. I:PROBLEM vs. B:PROBLEM). Interestingly, there is a high percentage of signs that cannot unambiguously be assigned to either language, and these were annotated as S:GLOSS (for "same").

The implications of this lexical overlap for the analysis are discussed in more detail in later sections. The initial glossing was done by some of the BuSL-ISL bilinguals themselves, and then reviewed by the research team. In addition, a separate ELAN tier coded the occurrence of negative signs and WH-signs, which made it easier at the analysis stage to search for and compile all relevant clauses. The codes on this tier are NEG-BUSL, NEG-ISL, NEG-SAME, WH-BUSL, WH-ISL, and WH-SAME, reflecting the same three-way distinction as in the sign glosses on the main tier. An additional tier was used for open comments of any kind.

Subsequently, all negative and wh-utterances were compiled into an Excel spreadsheet. This enabled us to categorise the utterances according to lexical choice and grammatical properties. In addition, it was of interest to get an overall word count as to proportions of BuSL signs, ISL signs, and signs that could be from either language. This was done for the narrative texts only, as an overall word count is most informative with respect to longer connected discourse. Deciding which signs to include in this count has not been straightforward, and a number of sign categories had to be excluded in order for the analysis to be meaningful. Overall, 991 signs from the three narratives were used for this analysis, and the methodological details and results are discussed in Section 5.1.

## 3.2 Monolingual data from Burundi Sign Language

This research on code-switching has been unusual in that one of the sign languages involved, BuSL, is undocumented. Code-switching research on spoken languages usually relies on information about the lexicons and the grammars of both languages being available, as is seen in work on French and English by Grosjean (see Grosjean 2008: 286–289), or work on Swahili and English by Myers-Scotton (1993, 1997), for example. However, there are a number of arguments supporting the viability of our research, even in the absence of BuSL documentation. First of all, this situation is not unheard of in other areas of contact linguistics. Thus Creole researchers are not always familiar with the substratum languages[5] of the respective Creole languages being studied. Although some work in creole linguistics such as by Lefebvre (1998) emphasises the importance of grammatical substrate in Creoles, in this case with respect to the role of West African languages in Creoles in the Caribbean, this is not always the case, and work that does not rely on detailed knowledge of the grammars of contributing substratum languages is not automatically considered unsound or invalid.

Secondly, we were able to rely on the fact that BuSL is one of the numerous sign languages in sub-Saharan Africa that have arisen under strong influence from American Sign Language (ASL). Thus a large amount of lexical material as well as grammatical aspects of BuSL have been carried over from ASL into BuSL. This applies, for instance, to all of the WH-signs used in the sub-corpus (coded WH-BUSL), and all negator signs that were coded NEG-BUSL. The details of how ASL arrived and spread in Burundi are not documented, but Nyst (2010) provides possibly comparable scenarios of ASL spread in West Africa, emphasising the role of deaf education in the process. This includes regions of West Africa where, as in Burundi, French rather than English has been the dominant language of education. The discussion in this article is limited to negation and wh-questions as well as constituent order in these clauses, and for this limited purpose, it is not necessary to have a comprehensive description of BuSL grammar.

Moreover, for the purpose of this research, we do not aim to decide where the various non-ISL signs and structures used by our participants ultimately come from, and as mentioned above, the way in which BuSL has been shaped by influences from ASL and other sign languages is beyond the scope of this research. Rather than trying to analyse each sign's ultimate source, the rationale for categorising BuSL in our data, discussed further in Section 4.2, has been by

---

5 These are the native languages of the original contributor populations to the development of a Creole, such as the slave populations from various West African countries that were involved in the formation of Creoles in the Caribbean (see Lefebvre 1998).

way of exclusion, concentrating on signs that are clearly not part of ISL (labelled B:GLOSS, WH-BUSL and NEG-BUSL).

Monolingual BuSL data were included in order to have at least some direct evidence of negatives and wh-questions in BuSL. We recorded two female signers from Burundi (SN and AB) in conversation for 45 minutes, asking them to communicate using BuSL only. While not fully comprehensive or free of ISL interference, this has provided at least an approximate model of BuSL on its own. Moreover, another member of the research team, who is an American fluent in ASL, reviewed this video recording and confirmed the very substantial degree of overlap with ASL. While there are also some interesting differences between ASL and BuSL, these are beyond the scope of this article, and the important point to note is the considerable overlap with ASL in the negative and WH-structures of BuSL. The BuSL video recording was not glossed in ELAN as its role was limited to providing a sample of BuSL for comparison with the bilingual conversations.

Finally, one of the co-authors conducted a specific elicitation session with four BuSL signers (AB, SN, CN, WK), where they were asked explicitly about negative and interrogative constructions as well as constituent order options in BuSL. These responses, which were videotaped, confirmed our expectations derived from the bilingual and the monolingual conversational recordings. The monolingual BuSL data, the similarities with ASL, and the elicitation session together provide a relatively clear picture of BuSL with respect to the target grammatical domains. Taking all the available evidence into account, we can draw valid conclusions from the data. The scope of this research is narrowed in Section 4.1, while further challenges in the analysis process are discussed in Section 4.2, and a summary of ISL and BuSL negatives and wh-questions is given in Section 4.3.

# 4 The research domain

## 4.1 Aims of the research

This research has several interrelated aims. First of all, we aim to document the ways in which two sign languages may be used in bilingual interactions, thereby adding to the thin data base currently available in the area of code-switching involving sign languages. As pointed out in Section 1, there are very few studies of bilingual sign language use, and there is a particular gap with respect to findings above and beyond the level of individual signs.

More specifically, we are interested in the lexical and grammatical choices that bilingual signers make in conversations that involve code-switching. In order to identify patterns and draw conclusions about the differential contributions that both languages make in terms of lexical choice and grammatical structures, the domains of negation and wh-questions have been chosen as the primary focus of analysis because they are relatively well-documented across sign languages (cf. Zeshan 2004a, 2004b, 2006) and thus the discussion here can be informed by a typological perspective against which to evaluate the data.

This research also reveals some individual differences between the signers who participated in the study. Not all signers exhibit the same code-switching patterns to the same degree. The findings in Sections 5 and 6 are differentiated where appropriate according to whether they are equally compatible with all data, or are found more rarely or not at all in some of the participants.

## 4.2 Challenges encountered during analysis

In other studies on code-switching, the analysis generally relies on more or less detailed prior knowledge of the two or more languages involved in the bilingual situation. This is the case particularly where the research question centres on the grammar of utterances at the clause level, as in work by Muysken (2001, 2011, 2013). The present research can similarly rely on previous documentation of the grammar of ISL, which is by now a relatively well-documented language. Both grammatical overviews (e.g. Zeshan 2000, 2003) and documentation of individual grammatical domains (e.g. Panda and Zeshan 2011 on reciprocal constructions, Zeshan 2006 on negation and wh-questions, Sinha 2009 including clause types) are available. Moreover, both co-authors are fluent in ISL, and one is a native signer.

On the other hand, the lack of BuSL documentation presents challenges for the analysis, particularly in view of the fact that no monolingual BuSL users were available. Under these circumstances, an important line of argumentation proceeds by way of exclusion: those lexical and grammatical elements that are not found in ISL are likely to be from BuSL, especially if they are also found in ASL, which has heavily influenced the BuSL variety used by our participants. Importantly, it has been straightforward for the research team to identify structures that are ungrammatical in ISL, and this has often provided crucial arguments for the analysis. ISL syntax in negative clauses and content questions follows very strict constituent orders, making it straightforward to identify clauses that would be ungrammatical in ISL. Conversely though, where a particular structure is compatible with ISL grammar, it was usually not possible to identify whether the same structure also occurs in BuSL or is ungrammatical in BuSL, and this limitation must be borne in mind. In other words, negative evidence on the ungrammaticality of constructions is only available for ISL, but not for BuSL.

A different challenge arises from an unexpected angle, given that BuSL and ISL are genetically unrelated and have not had any prior historical contact. Despite this situation and somewhat surprisingly, the bilingual conversations contain a substantial number of lexemes that exist in both languages. In a few cases, this is due to shared contact with a third sign language, ASL, but unlike in BuSL, the number of ASL borrowings in ISL is very small. Although there are some groups of ASL-ISL bilinguals in India,[6] their number is vanishingly small compared to the total number of ISL users, which is estimated to be at least 2–3 million, if not more (cf. Bhattacharya, Grover and Randhawa 2014). The greater number of lexemes that are identical in BuSL and ISL are more likely to have arisen from shared iconicity. The iconic nature of many signs results in the likelihood of a baseline level of shared vocabulary across sign languages, even if these sign languages are completely unrelated. For instance, Guerra Currie et al. (2002) identified a baseline level of lexical similarity between Mexican Sign Language and Japanese Sign Language, two unrelated languages, at 23% of the lexical entries that they investigated. Interestingly, several negator signs are among those that exist in both BuSL and ISL, while WH-signs are quite distinct in the two languages (see Section 4.3).

The frequent occurrence of signs that could be either BuSL or ISL creates a particular complication with respect to coding and analysis. In much of the lit-

---

**6** One important enclave using an ASL lexicon (though not always an ASL grammar) is in Bangalore, due to the presence of a large deaf school. Other ASL users are individuals who have spent time in the US and returned to India, but these individuals do not tend to form any coherent linguistic sub-groups in India.

erature on code-switching in spoken languages, the point of switch between two languages is of particular interest, and it has been important to discuss at which point in the clause code-switching should be possible or impossible, in order to find general constraints on code-switching. Constraints proposed have not always been successfully validated by subsequent research, as pointed out in Muysken (2013), but nevertheless, this aspect has been important in the spoken language literature. It has also been pointed out that lexemes potentially belonging to either of the languages involved in the bilingual interaction can facilitate code-switching by acting as ideal switch points, as in this English-Dutch bilingual example cited in Muysken 2013:194, which relies on the similarity between English what and Dutch wat:

(1)  Weet  je   what she is doing?
     Do you know…?
     'Do you know what she is doing?'

With respect to our data, it is clear that the existence of signs that cannot be assigned clearly to either BuSL or ISL creates complications for the analysis in terms of the point at which code-switching occurs. These signs are very frequent in the data and thus warrant the aforementioned separate coding category S:GLOSS. In many cases, the S signs are interspersed with unambiguous BuSL and ISL signs. In particular, in any sequence where signs of the type S:XXXX occur in between BuSL and ISL signs (examples 2 and 3), it is impossible to determine where exactly the switch point is because the signs in the middle could belong to either sign language. Non-manuals are not glossed in the examples except where particularly relevant, but can be seen in the video clips provided with this article.

(2) B:WHY S:IX1 S:MEET S:IX1 B:HONEST S:DON'T-KNOW I:OWN$_3$ I:BACKGROUND S:DON'T-KNOW
'Because when I'd meet her, honestly, I don't know her background.'
clip 5, 02:17, WK

(3) I:MONEY B:UTENSILS S:FOOD S:COOK S:IX1 I:PAY B:HOW
'How would I pay for utensils (kitchenware) to cook food?'   clip 2, 04:12, AB

This issue is also recognised in Quinto-Pozos (2007:11), who recommends that due to these difficulties in labelling a particular utterance as from one sign language or another, we need to work towards "an in-depth syntactic analysis of code switching between two sign languages". Some initial steps towards such an analysis are attempted in Section 6. However, it should be noted that the problem is not limited to open-class lexical signs, but also affects closed-class grammatical items. The frequent occurrence of S type signs is particularly pertinent with respect to the negative signs that are shared between BuSL and ISL (see Section 4.3.1), and these are important grammatical morphemes. Thus if we were to consider the potential role of one of the sign languages as the grammatically dominant language, following the model proposed in Myers-Scotton (1993, 1997) and subsequently elaborated, it would be essential to identify the language of the negative morphemes in a negative clause. The Matrix Language Frame model is intended to account for intra-sentential code-switching such as in examples (2) and (3), and posits that in a bilingual utterance one language usually is the dominant language (Matrix Language, ML) that provides the grammatical frames for the sentence, and the other one is the Embedded Language, EL, that mainly provides lexical material (see Myers-Scotton 2002:10ff). Similar complications arise when trying to apply the typology proposed in Muysken (2001) in terms of insertion (of individual lexemes from language A into Language B) and alternation (between chunks of language A and Language B), particularly in the latter instance. The third term in this typology, congruent lexicalisation, is useful and explored below.

There is no obvious solution to these problems, and therefore, the analysis here does not focus on determining the switch point in mixed utterances, and neither do we explore the "fit" of our data against the Myers-Scottons ML-EL model or Muysken's three-way typology. Instead, it can be argued that the existence of these shared signs plays an important role in shaping the particular bilingual variety used by these signers in conversation. This argument is pursued in Sections 6 and 7.

## 4.3 Negation and wh-questions

### 4.3.1 Negation

BuSL and ISL have a number of similarities with respect to negative clauses, while wh-questions are quite different in both sign languages. Both BuSL and ISL principally rely on negative particles for clause negation, and this is also the option most commonly found across sign languages in general (Zeshan 2004a). The basic clause negators, that is, those signs that merely reverse the polarity of a sentence without any additional semantic content, are represented in Figure 2. For ISL, the sign is derived from a common communicative gesture used by hearing people in the Indian subcontinent (Zeshan 2006). The BuSL basic clause negator sign is identical to the ASL sign.

**Figure 2.** Basic clause negators in ISL (left) and BuSL (right)

Interestingly, BuSL and ISL share a number of other negative particles. These are from among the same types of signs that have also been shown to occur with some frequency across sign languages in general. Zeshan (2004a) identified the wagging index finger, the side-to-side open hand wave, and the closed round handshape (F- or O-handshape) as three forms that occur frequently in a typological sample of 37 sign languages. It is therefore not surprising that such signs would occur in BuSL and ISL as well. However, the number of these overlapping signs is striking, as there are a total of five negators that occur in both sign languages (see Figure 3). The first three signs have the formal characteristics just mentioned, while the fourth sign is a borrowing from ASL (based on the one-handed fingerspelling N-O). As ISL does not use one-handed fingerspelling, this sign is clearly not indigenous to India, but is one of the relatively few ASL borrowings used by some deaf Indians. In addition, both sign languages also share the use of a negative predicate DON'T-KNOW. Again, this form is found in a number of unrelated sign languages and is sometimes part of a larger paradigm of related forms (e.g. in Ugandan Sign Language, see Lutalo-Kiingi 2014), but this is not the case in ISL and BuSL.

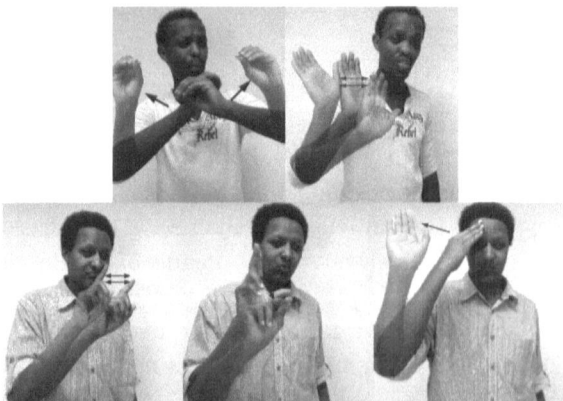

**Figure 3.** Negative signs common to ISL and BuSL

Negative signs that do not overlap in the two sign languages include the signs CANNOT in ISL and BuSL, as well as NEVER in BuSL, and the basic clause negators mentioned above. It should be noted that for the purpose of this research, it was not possible to ascertain whether all negative particles that are shared between BuSL and ISL have the same function and meaning.[7] We have only been able to note their identical form and their global function as negatives, while details on the use of these negatives in BuSL have not been available. However, it is striking that in the paradigm of negative particles of both sign languages, more signs are shared than are different.

### 4.3.2 Wh-questions

Wh-questions are quite different in BuSL and ISL, especially with respect to the paradigm of question words. Cross-linguistically, this is in line with the radical differences found in question word paradigms across sign languages (Zeshan 2004b). The only similarity is the use of an ASL variant for 'who' in both BuSL and ISL, glossed S:WHO. Other than this, the interrogative signs of BuSL and ISL have no known overlap.

In ISL, all specific question signs except two monomorphemic signs (WHEN in the sense of 'what date' and S:WHO) are compounds with a general WH-sign. The general WH-sign can be used, in principle, for any interrogative meaning, but often the meaning is specified by creating a compound with another sign, with WH always being the second member of the compound. These are FACE+WH for 'who', PLACE+WH for 'where', NUMBER+WH for 'how many', TIME+WH for 'what time, when', and a distributive form of INDEX+WH for 'which' (see Figure 4). The functions 'why', 'how', and 'what' are subsumed under WH. With the possible exception of S:WHO, all WH interrogatives are obligatorily clause-final, as they behave in the same way syntactically as other functional particles in ISL including negatives, and thus there is no doubling of wh-signs either (Zeshan 2000, 2003).

---

[7] Thus the variants combined under the gloss S:NONE with different handshapes and movements, and those combined under the gloss S:NO with different handedness and movement patterns, could well be considered separate signs if warranted by a detailed analysis of BuSL and/or ISL separately. However, they have been combined here under the same glosses, and separating out variant forms would make no difference for the conclusions arising from their analysis.

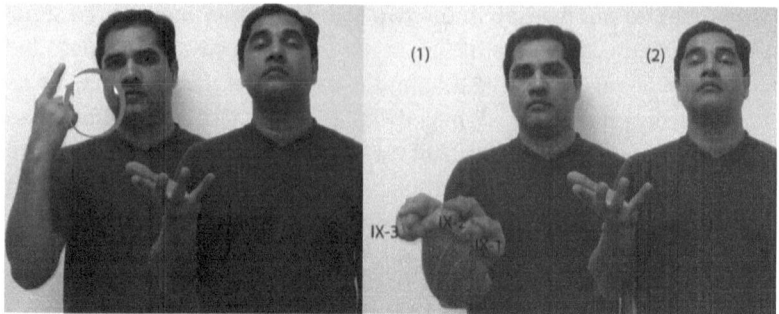

**Figure 4.** FACE+WH 'who' and IX$_{dist}$+WH 'which' in ISL

In BuSL, wh-questions behave very differently. First of all, WH-signs regularly appear clause-initially, though they can appear clause-finally too. In addition, WH-signs can be doubled, as is also the case in ASL, and there can be multiple wh-questions in one clause (cf. Fischer 2006). All WH interrogatives found in the bilingual and monolingual data as well as those reported by BuSL signers during elicitation are identical to ASL signs. This includes WHO, WHERE, WHEN, WHY, and HOW (see Figure 5).

**Figure 5.** WH-interrogatives in ASL and BuSL

The main difference between ASL and BuSL in terms of question signs is the use of a PALM-UP sign, of gestural origin, which is used in ASL as a question word meaning 'what'. The use of PALM-UP in various functions, such as clause linker, negative, or discourse particle, is common across sign languages, as reported, for instance, in Zeshan (2006) for Turkish Sign Language and in Lutalo-Kiingi (2014) for Ugandan Sign Language. In ASL, a PALM-UP indefiniteness marker has been identified by Conlin, Hagstrom and Neidle (2003), in addition to a PALM-UP sign for 'what'.[8]

In BuSL, PALM-UP is not used as a question word, but is a question particle that can occur to mark both yes/no-questions and wh-questions, and in the latter case can co-occur with other question signs. For the interrogative 'what', BuSL uses the sign in Figure 6, which is also a possible variant in ASL. In the elicitation session, our participants unanimously reported that PALM-UP is not used as a WH-sign in BuSL. Therefore, all occurrences of PALM-UP signs used as WH-interrogatives are glossed I:WH and considered ISL signs here. In citation form, the general WH-sign in ISL has a handshape with the finger tips pointing in different directions as shown in Figure 4, but in discourse, the handshape can often be more relaxed with all fingers in parallel, as is typical of PALM-UP signs in other sign languages.

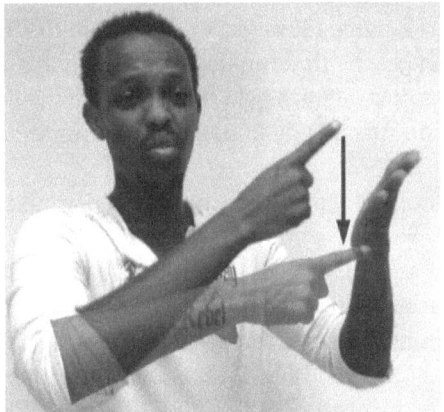

**Figure 6.** The ASL variant WHAT used in BuSL

---

**8** These authors use various glosses other than PALM-UP to describe the respective signs. We refer to all these signs as PALM-UP here merely for the sake of comparison.

# 5 Lexical choice in unimodal bilingual signed texts

The specific aim of this article is to investigate the way in which code-switching operates in negative clauses and wh-questions in BuSL-ISL bilinguals. However, it is also of interest to look at lexical choice in general, that is, to consider the contributions to signed texts by signs that are from BuSL, from ISL, or that could be from either sign language. This is considered in Section 5.1. Lexical choice with respect to clause negators and question words is discussed in section 5.2. Finally, section 5.3 considers the ways in which signs from the two sign languages are combined in discourse.

## 5.1 Lexical choice in example texts

For the data discussed in this section, we have used the three-minute texts produced by the three signers AB, SN and CN. The motivation was to establish which percentage of signs in these texts are BuSL signs, ISL signs, or signs from the S category that could belong to both languages. As there are few if any such text-based studies on unimodal sign bilinguals, it is interesting to compare the overall use of signs with the lexical choices made specifically in negative clauses and wh-questions.

From the three signed texts, a total of 991 signs were initially coded and assigned to one of the three categories – BuSL, ISL and S. The number of signs coded for SN and CN is very similar (308 and 293), while AB's text has a higher number of signs (390), mainly due to a faster signing tempo.

During the analysis, it became apparent that some categories of signs in the S category should be excluded from consideration. In fact, the number of signs that could not unambiguously be assigned to either BuSL or ISL is very high, which was surprising at first. Overall, only about a third of all signs in the texts are unambiguously from BuSL or from ISL. The results are summarised in Table 2.

The reasons for this high incidence of shared signs become clear once we consider various subcategories within the S categories. First of all, there is a large amount of index finger pointing, which is unsurprising given that research on other sign languages has shown a similar prevalence of pointing signs (cf. de Vos 2012). In the three texts considered here, AB and CN are in line with the findings from other sign languages, and only the text by SN includes relatively few instances of index finger pointing (4.9 %).

Another category that has been excluded from the analysis consists of classifier constructions (CL) including size and shape specifiers (SASS).[9] These highly visual constructions often show a great degree of overlap across unrelated sign languages due to their iconic nature (cf. Emmorey 2003). As might be expected, the use of these signs depends to some extent on the topic of the text. Therefore, there are large differences in the number of signs in these categories across the three texts. The text by CN, in particular, includes a large number of handling constructions, as the text is about interactions at the border crossing into India. CN describes in much detail the handling of his passport and other documents, which results in a high number of handling classifiers. This category also includes general directionals, that is, an open hand shape moving towards or away from the signer, glossed COME and GO.

These signs have been excluded from the analysis here because our aim has been to quantify lexical choices with respect to conventional lexical signs. If signers express 'giving', 'taking', and 'putting', the use of appropriate handling classifiers with high visual iconicity does not constitute a lexical choice between BuSL or ISL lexemes. Similarly, pronominal index finger points do not constitute a locus of lexical choice between BuSL and ISL. Finally, a few other types of signs were excluded for the same reason (listed under the *Other* category in Table 2); these include proper names for both persons and places, pointing signs with other hand shapes, manual actions categorised as communicative gestures, and signing without a manual component. The *Other* category has a particularly high word count for SN because there are many proper names in this text. The remaining signs in the S category which are included in the analysis (fifth column from the left in Table 2) include both iconic signs that happen to be identical due to shared iconicity (e.g. DEAF, BEFORE, CHOOSE, PHONE) and non-iconic signs that may have come about due to shared borrowing from other sign languages, primarily ASL (e.g. N-O, INTERPRETER, OK).

It should be noted that the S category is possibly an overestimation. Both the BuSL and the ISL variety used within this fieldwork setting have been subject to influences from several other sign languages e.g. from Kenya, Uganda, and the US, as mentioned in Section 2, and there is often more than one sign in use for a particular concept. Therefore, only those signs that were certain to be exclusively from ISL on the one hand, or were clearly assigned to BuSL through the rationale explained in Section 4.2 on the other hand, were coded as such. Any doubtful

---

**9** This also includes signs of visual perception that are made with extended index and middle finger, glossed SEE, WATCH, etc. Although these signs are not always included in the CL category in linguistic analyses of sign languages, it makes sense to subsume them under CL in this case as the aim has been to exclude signs that are highly visually motivated.

cases that could be instances of lexical overlap between the two languages were assigned to the S category. This also applies to cases where it is unclear whether there may be a small phonological difference between similarly articulated signs in BuSL and ISL, parallel to English what and Dutch wat in example (1). As any such cases are difficult to ascertain given the wide dialectal range of ISL and the lack of BuSL documentation, no distinction is made between strictly identical and very similar signs, and all are assigned to the S category.

This was done in order to have more conservative estimates of BuSL and ISL signs, which are the main target of comparison here. On the other hand, while the high number of S signs may seem surprising at first, these figures are similar to what has been found in a previous study on Mexican Sign Language (LSM) and ASL. Quinto-Pozos (2000: 101) summarises that "slightly more than 50 % of all elements in the group and interview sessions could be understood by monolingual users of either LSM or ASL. The average percentage of SA signs throughout all sessions was 20 %.[10] Gestural and pantomimic elements totalled more than 13 % of the group discussion elements. Further, points averaged slightly more than 20 % for all the sessions."

**Table 2.** Frequency of sign categories: All signs

| Participant | All signs | BuSL | ISL | S | IX | SASS/CL | Other |
|---|---|---|---|---|---|---|---|
| AB | 390 | 63 | 89 | 128 | 71 | 21 | 18 |
|  |  | 16.2 % | 22.8 % | 32.8 % | 18.2 % | 5.4 % | 4.6 % |
| SN | 308 | 92 | 50 | 93 | 15 | 12 | 46 |
|  |  | 29.9 % | 16.2 % | 30.2 % | 4.9 % | 3.9 % | 14.9 % |
| CN | 293 | 51 | 31 | 56 | 41 | 85 | 29 |
|  |  | 17.4 % | 10.6 % | 19.1 % | 14 % | 29 % | 9.9 % |
| Total | 991 | 206 | 170 | 277 | 127 | 118 | 93 |

Table 2 shows the frequency counts for the 991 coded signs in terms of the sign categories described above. The columns headed *IX*, *SASS/CL* and *Other* contain the excluded signs. The proportion of excluded signs is around a fourth of signs for AB and SN, although distribution across the three excluded categories is very different. For CN, the proportion of excluded signs is substantially higher due to the large number of SASS/CL signs. However, there are still a total of 652 tokens of signs in the first three categories (BuSL, ISL and S), and these are the signs that are of specific interest here.

---

[10] SA signs are "similarly articulated" signs.

The data in Table 2 at first sight suggest that there are considerable differences in the percentages of BuSL, ISL and S signs across the three texts, ranging, for instance, from 19.1 % of S signs for CN to 32.8 % of S signs for AB. However, these figures are expressed as a percentage in relation to all signs, and thus are affected by the percentage of excluded signs. As these vary significantly across the three texts, a better measure of lexical choice is to look only at the subset of 652 signs consisting of the first three categories (BuSL, ISL and S). This has been calculated in Table 3.

**Table 3.** Frequency of sign categories: BuSL, ISL and S tokens

| Participant | All tokens | BuSL tokens | ISL tokens | S tokens |
|---|---|---|---|---|
| AB | 280 | 63 | 89 | 128 |
|  |  | 22.5 % | 31.8 % | 45.7 % |
| SN | 235 | 92 | 50 | 93 |
|  |  | 39.1 % | 21.3 % | 39.6 % |
| CN | 137 | 50 | 31 | 56 |
|  |  | 36.5 % | 22.6 % | 40.9 % |
| Total | 652 | 205 | 170 | 277 |

Table 3 shows the distribution of our three target categories. This confirms that all three signers are indeed using a bilingual signing variety that includes substantial lexical contributions from both BuSL and ISL; none of the signers has a negligible, marginal number or percentage of signs in any of the categories. Results for CN must be considered with more caution as the number of tokens is much lower than for the other two texts; AB has over twice as many tokens in the text. The figures for AB are interesting in that there is a comparatively high number of ISL tokens (89, i.e. 31.8 %) and a low number of BuSL signs (63, i.e. 22.5 %). AB is the only signer who produces more ISL signs than BuSL signs. This finding is corroborated by several other observations that were made informally during fieldwork. We had already noticed before data collection that AB was conspicuous in using a larger number of ISL signs. She had spent four weeks in a residential deaf school in central India where Hindi was the predominant spoken language, and also spent a lot of time socialising with Indians outside the campus. AB is the only signer from Burundi who was ever observed using mouthings from Hindi. Many of the Indian students in the BA course tend to use English mouthings, but some also use Hindi mouthings. Thus the figures triangulate well with other observations. Interestingly, the result of focusing only on the three target categories is that now CN and SN look very similar, with differences of 2.6 %, 0.3 % and 1.3 % over the three categories; only AB has a different pattern due to the stronger preference for ISL signs.

It is possible to think of the amount of BuSL, ISL and S signs in these texts in two different ways: on the one hand, we could consider the total number of signs (i.e. the tokens) in each category, as has been done in Table 3. On the other hand, we could consider how many different signs (i.e. how many types) are used in each category. This can be significant because it could be argued that producing a larger number of different ISL signs, though they may be fewer in total number of tokens, is a more significant ISL contribution to the text than using a few ISL signs repeatedly. We have not aimed to pursue this argument in detail, although it is clear that type-token relationships are different across the signers. For instance, AB uses the ISL sign BETTER six times in the text, and the ISL signs MONEY, DIFFICULT and SOME four times each, while CN does not use any ISL sign more than twice, with the exception of I:WH (used five times).

With such reasoning in mind, Table 4 shows the number of types (i.e. different signs) in each category. The results confirm the figures from Table 3 in that CN and SN have very similar patterns, with differences no larger than 5.2%. Again, AB has a more divergent pattern, especially with respect to the larger number of ISL signs. We return to the possible significance of these figures, in combination with other data, in Section 7.

**Table 4.** Frequency of sign categories: BuSL, ISL and S types

| Participant | All types | BuSL types | ISL types | S types |
|---|---|---|---|---|
| AB | 140 | 39 | 48 | 53 |
| | | 27.8% | 34.3% | 37.9% |
| SN | 104 | 35 | 27 | 42 |
| | | 33.7% | 25.9% | 40.4% |
| CN | 81 | 25 | 19 | 37 |
| | | 30.9% | 23.5% | 45.6% |
| Total | 325 | 94 | 87 | 144 |

Another interesting conclusion from Tables 3 and 4 is that the number of ISL signs (either tokens or types) does not correlate with the length of each participant's stay in India. The signer with the longest exposure to ISL is CN, but his BuSL and ISL percentages are very similar to SN, who has had the shortest exposure to ISL. Contrary to what could be expected in this situation, it is not the signer with the longest exposure to ISL who uses the most ISL signs. Instead, it is AB whose signing shows a greater contribution by ISL than is the case for the two other signers.

## 5.2 Lexical choice in negative clauses and wh-questions

Returning to the main purpose of discussing negative clauses and wh-questions, we now turn to the respective contributions that BuSL and ISL make to the lexical expression of clause negators and question words. Strikingly, the data show that the patterns are quite different from what has been shown in Tables 2, 3 and 4, where there are no radical disparities between the three categories of signs.

For the clause negators and question words, an extended data set was used, consisting of all occurrences within the three 3-minute texts as well as all additional occurrences in the three corresponding video clips, i.e. within a total of 34 min 12 sec of video data. This was done in order to generate a sufficiently large number of example utterances on which to base more meaningful conclusions. The wider dataset also includes all negative clauses and wh-questions from the fourth signer, WK. For the purpose of the analysis here, cases where the same clause was repeated (either immediately or shortly after each other) were excluded, on the grounds that these do not constitute separate instances of negative clauses and wh-questions; 8 negators and 1 WH sign were excluded on these grounds. Moreover, there were 4 instances of a sign glossed CANNOT (see Figure 7), which is sometimes seen in Burundi but is considered by our participants to be a loan from neighbouring African countries. As this is also used as a foreign loan by many of the Indian students, this sign could not be assigned clearly to either BuSL or ISL, and these instances were also excluded from the analysis, although use of this sign is important for some of the arguments made in Section 6. The BuSL sign for 'cannot' did not occur in the data. This leaves a total of 97 clause negators and 47 question words for the analysis. Most clauses have just a single negator or question word, but there are instances with two negatives or two question words within the same clause (see Section 6 for a discussion of these).

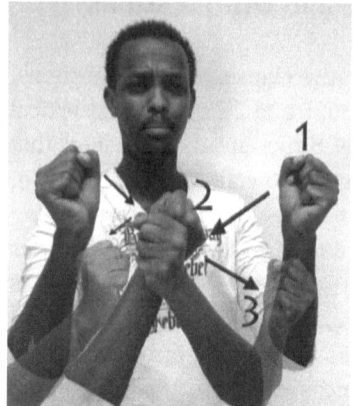

**Figure 7.** CANNOT

As discussed in section 4.3.1, BuSL and ISL have a shared pool of clause negators, as well as a shared negative predicate. A total of nine different negatives were identified in the data: 2 belonging to BuSL, 2 belonging to ISL, and 5 with a shared form between BuSL and ISL, i.e. in the S category. Table 5 lists the occurrences of all negatives in the data.

**Table 5.** Frequency of clause negators

| | | |
|---|---|---|
| B:NEVER | 2 | 2.10% |
| B:NOT | 8 | 8.20% |
| I:CANNOT | 2 | 2.10% |
| I:NOT | 9 | 9.30% |
| S:DON'T-KNOW | 11 | 11.30% |
| S:DON'T | 3 | 3.10% |
| S:NO/NOT-AT-ALL | 15 | 15.50% |
| S:N-O | 11 | 11.30% |
| S:NONE/NOTHING | 36 | 37.10% |
| Total | 97 | 100% |

Several interesting observations emerge from these data. First of all, the basic clause negators B:NOT and I:NOT, which are distinct in the two sign languages, do not occur with any frequency, constituting only 8.2% and 9.3% of occurrences respectively. This is quite surprising, given that basic clause negators are widely applicable in negative clauses and represent the most neutral way of expressing negation. In particular, the use of B:NOT is very prevalent in the monolingual BuSL data. This sign is the same as in ASL, but is used in BuSL in a wider range of contexts. For instance, the bilingual data include utterances such as TAP B:NOT 'The tap is not working.' and BAG B:NOT 'The bag is not there.' However, despite this prevalence, B:NOT is rare in the data and is not used at all by SN and AB.[11]

Instead of a prevalence of basic clause negation, we find that the negators in the S category clearly predominate, as they constitute 78.3% of all clause negators. Except for S:DON'T, all signs in the S category are more frequent than any of the B and I negators. S:NONE is particularly frequent and is the most frequent clause negator for all signers except SN.[12] CANNOT as in Figure 7, while of different origin and not included in this count, is also a shared sign. Other clause negators particular to BuSL or ISL do not occur in these data. Thus it seems clear that items in the "overlap" S category are privileged both in terms of their frequency and whether they occur at all in the data. The frequency of the three categories of signs is given in Table 6.

**Table 6.** Categories of clause negators

| | | | |
|---|---|---|---|
| B negators | | 10 | 10.30% |
| I negators | | 11 | 11.40% |
| S negators | | 76 | 78.30% |
| Total | | 97 | 100% |

The distribution of wh-question signs in the data is quite different from the distribution of clause negators and the distribution of all B, I and S signs. First of all, the question word paradigms in BuSL and ISL are very different as described in Section 4.3.2. Apart from S:WHO, all question signs are distinct between BuSL and ISL. Thus we can only expect a very minor overlap at the lexical level. Instead, it is interesting to observe the choice between BuSL and ISL question signs. As can be seen in Table 7, this choice is far from balanced.

---

[11] Of course this does not mean that these signers never use B:NOT in their bilingual interactions; these observations apply to the snapshot of data analysed for this particular research.
[12] However, total frequency counts for all negators are low for SN (between 1–4 instances each), so this observation is not really meaningful.

**Table 7.** Frequency of WH-interrogatives

| | | | |
|---|---|---|---|
| B:HOW | ▬ | 6 | 12.80% |
| B:WHAT | ▎ | 2 | 4.30% |
| B:WHERE | ▍ | 3 | 6.40% |
| B:WHY | ▬▬ | 13 | 27.70% |
| I:WH | ▬▬▬ | 18 | 38.20% |
| S:WHO | ▬ | 5 | 10.60% |
| Total | ▬▬▬▬▬▬ | 47 | 100% |

From the data in Table 7, the first imbalance we observe is in terms of the number of different question signs: While BuSL is represented with four different question signs, only a single ISL question sign, the general interrogative I:WH, is used. Not unexpectedly, this sign occurs with the greatest frequency, as it can stand for a wide range of interrogative meanings, and it is the only WH-sign that is used by all four signers in the data. However, what is striking is that there is not a single instance of a question word compound from ISL, and thus the ISL input into the bilingual conversational data is reduced to the most basic, general question word in the paradigm. All specific question words, including those meaning 'where' and 'who' with their available WH-compound signs in ISL, are monomorphemic and do not use the ISL question word compound strategy.

**Table 8.** Categories of WH-interrogatives

| | | | |
|---|---|---|---|
| B interrogatives | ▬▬▬ | 24 | 51.10% |
| I interrogatives | ▬▬ | 18 | 38.30% |
| S interrogatives | ▬ | 5 | 10.60% |
| Total | ▬▬▬▬▬ | 47 | 100% |

Table 8 shows the overall predominance of BuSL question words in the data. Just as with the S type negators, the BuSL WH-signs are prevalent both in terms of the range of signs used and overall frequency (51.1% of WH-signs are particular to BuSL). However, it should be pointed out that the data on WH interrogatives are limited in that for most question signs, there are only a few tokens, due to the narrative, non-dialogic nature of the 3-minute texts that constitute the main source of data. Therefore, it would seem that the very restricted range of ISL interrogatives is a more important finding than the frequency counts.

The function of I:WH signs in clauses is of particular interest to the discussion of the data at clause level in Section 6. We argue that the selection of negators and WH interrogatives by the signers does not constitute merely lexical choice.

These choices also have consequences for the construction of the negative and interrogative clauses in which they occur, and this topic is explored in Section 6. It is in this qualitative analysis that WH-signs are important despite not being highly frequent in the data.

## 5.3 Lexical choice in discourse

In much of the data, there is a continuous to-and-fro between signs from BuSL, signs from ISL, and signs that are shared between the two. Typically, any given clause includes at least two of the three sign categories, and often there is more than one switch within a single clause. There are very few instances in the data of clauses that are entirely in BuSL or in ISL. The existence of many signs that cannot unambiguously be assigned to either of the two languages makes it very difficult to determine switch points between BuSL and ISL. Examples from spoken languages such as (1) above with English *what* and Dutch *wat*, with the shared lexical item argued to facilitate a switch to the other language, seem to imply that there are few such items available. In a situation where such shared items are numerous, the effect is that the distinction between parts of clauses in different sign languages becomes blurred, and it is very difficult to determine switch points in the way that has been done for spoken languages. This issue is very evident in our data and is partly a result of the visual-gestural modality including a higher level of iconicity.

The text below, taken from SN's discourse, exemplifies these patterns. To illustrate the interplay between the different sign categories, the text examples in this section are represented on three lines, with one line for each sign category and the shared S signs in the middle. Where parts of the text have been left out, this is indicated by (...) in the transcription.

Clip 3, 02:50 – 03:11, SN

(4a)           B:LIKE                                      B:DIFFCULT
     S:IX3           S:NONE / S:IX3-dist S:SOLVE
        I:INDIA                           I:DIFFICULT+
    'She did not like India. To resolve this with all of them was very difficult.'

(4b)  B:MOTHER B:MY B:MOTHER B:ACCEPT B:BUT
                                             S:FAMILY
     B:ACCEPT
          I:NOT / I:DIFFCULT (...)
    'My mother accepted, but my family did not accept; it was difficult.'

(4c)           B:COUSIN B:THIRD        B:COUSIN
    S:INTERPRETER S:PHONE              S:PHONE           S:FIRST

         B:SISTER
    S:PHONE                   S:PHONE S:DISCUSS
                    I:DIFFICULT
    'An interpreter phoned my third cousin, phoned my first cousin, phoned my sister, and it was     difficult, discussing on the phone.'

(4d)   S:HEY        (false start) S:FLY S:WHO S:PICK-UP S:WHO(...)
           I:INDIA
    'Listen, when she flies to India, who will be picking her up?'

(4e)        B:C-H-A-R-L-E-S                                       B:FINE
       S:KNOW              S:BEFORE                    S:IX3
                              I:START I:INDIA I:EXISTENTIAL
    'You know, Charles, he has started (studies) and is already in India, so that is fine.'

It remains to be seen whether such patterns are also characteristic of other sign language combinations in bilingual interactions between signers. Within the three example texts examined here, parts of AB's text stand out as qualitatively somewhat different. AB's text contains sections with no or minimal BuSL signs, and this is not the case with the other two signers, who use BuSL signs more continuously. The following text segment exemplifies AB's style with a higher proportion of ISL signs; the only BuSL sign is B:WHY. AB's text also includes other sections that are more in line with CN's and SN's co-use of ISL and BuSL, but the existence of ISL-dominant text segments supports earlier observations about AB's greater preference for ISL signs compared to the other signers.

Clip 2, 04:39 – 04:49, AB
(5a)   S:CYNTHIA S:BOTH S:SHARE S:PROGRESS
                                        I:GOOD
    'Cynthia and I were both progressing well together.'

(5b)              B:WHY
        S:FEEL           S:IX1 S:FLY
   I:STUDY    I:DIFFICULT I:BUT    I:ENGLISH I:BASIC I:SOME
   'I felt it was difficult to study, but because when I came here, I only had some basic English.'

(5c)       S:IX1  S:FEEL       S:LITTLE S:PROGRESS S:FEEL
   I:BUT          I:PRACTICE                    I:BETTER
   'But I felt with practice I could progress a little and felt better.'

(5d)        S:IX1          S:NONE
   I:YEAR    I:WH I:FEAR
   'In one year, what (would happen), I was not scared.'

Usually, the choice of lexical items in the texts seems to be unconnected to the content of the discourse. One exception is part of the story by CN, where he reports on interactions with a female staff member at the Indian border crossing. While the preceding text has both BuSL and ISL elements, some of the reported interactions with the Indian woman are predominantly in ISL, with no BuSL signs, as is the segment starting from (6b) below:

Clip 5, 04:07 – 04:25, CN
(6a)                    B:WHERE / _____hs
   S:IX1 S:THINK S:IX1 S:THROUGH      S:PALM-UP (...) /

             B:BUSY /
   S:IX1 S:IX3
         I:GIRL
   'I thought where am I going to go through? No idea. I (saw) a girl there, busy.'

(6b)  S:HEY S:IX1 S:DEAF S:PALM-UP /
   'Excuse me, I am deaf.'

(6c)  I:GIRL                  I:WH      I:PASSPORT
         (staring action) / S:WRITE S:IX2 S:GO   (...) S:HEY     S:GIVE-IT-HERE
   'The girl stared at me. She wrote "Where are you going?" (...) "Give me your passport."'

This segment is clearly intended to reconstruct the scene linguistically, although of course the border agent was a non-signer. Thus the text contains not only ISL signs but also gestural elements (non-manual staring action, PALM-UP with headshake, and the sign glossed GIVE-IT-HERE). However, this ISL-dominant pattern is not sustained throughout the text, and further reported conversations with the Indian woman do use BuSL lexical items.

In addition to lexemes shifting between categories, the data also contain a good number of instances of what has been called "reiterative code-switching" (Quinto-Pozos and Adam 2013:389) and involves the repetition of the same concept expressed with lexemes from two different languages. This can occur either in immediate adjacency (examples 7–9) or with a few signs or a short clause intervening (see examples 17 and 18 in Section 6).

(7)  S:IX3-dist S:SOLVE I:DIFFICULT+ B:DIFFCULT         – clip 3, 02:52, SN
    'To resolve this with all of them was very difficult.'

(8)  B:FATHER B:MONEY I:MONEY B:MONEY S:THERE I:PLUS I:ADD-UP-TOTAL S:OK S:AGREE
    'My father agreed to gather the funds.'                – clip 3, 02:13, SN

(9)  B:HOLIDAY I:HOLIDAY S:IX1 S:$_r$FLY$_l$ S:$_l$FLY$_r$ S:IX1 S:NO   – clip 2, 02:07, AB
    'During holidays, I do not fly over (to Burundi).'

Reiterative code-switching is perhaps the most overt indication that throughout a conversation between bilinguals, there is a constant opportunity for choice as to which language contributes which lexemes. It can occur either without any obvious function, or for emphasis. For instance, 'difficult' is emphasised in example (7), by first repeating the ISL sign and then adding the BuSL sign, thus resulting in multiple expressions of the concept. Moreover, that signers are conscious of their choices is further evidenced by the occurrence of false starts in the data, which sometimes overlap with reiterative code-switching. Thus in a false start, production of a sign from one language may be initiated first, sometimes only partially, and then the signer interrupts him-/herself to choose the equivalent lexeme from the other sign language instead. Two examples are shown in (10), with the first sign fully formed followed by a short hesitation, and in (11), with the first sign partially formed and then replaced.

(10)  I:INDIA I:LIKE (hesitation) B:LIKE S:IX1 I:NOT     clip 3, 01:08, SN

(11)  I:ENGL.. B:ENGLISH     clip 11, 05:36, CN

As we have seen in this section, the choice of lexemes in a bilingual signed discourse is clearly a complex matter that cannot be reduced to a single factor. For further discussion of the functions of code-switching in our data, see Section 7.

# 6 Grammatical patterns in negation and wh-questions of BuSL-ISL bilinguals

In this section, we investigate the grammatical patterns found in negative clauses and wh-questions. In particular, the aim is to gain some insight into the ways in which the two grammars of BuSL and ISL combine with the lexicons in the construction of clauses. Therefore, this section focuses on the level of the clause.

Table 9 shows the summary of data from both the three-minute narratives and the other clauses appearing throughout the half-hour conversation. As the Table shows, these data amount to a total of 90 negative clauses and 43 wh-clauses. Occasionally, the arguments also draw on other types of clauses in the data.

As far as negation is concerned, the grammars of BuSL and ISL are largely compatible, as seen in Section 4.3.2. In addition to a substantial number of shared signs that are clause-final negators, this overlap is further supported by the fact that most other clause negators in BuSL and ISL are also clause-final. In fact, only the sign CANNOT, which is neither from BuSL nor from ISL, occurs in pre-verbal position in the data, while in all other instances of negation the negators occur in clause-final position. The role of non-manual negation in these languages has not been investigated in this research.

Thus it would seem that negation in the bilingual mode is close to what Muysken (2001) terms "congruent lexicalisation". Congruent lexicalisation applies when "the two languages happen to display the same word order in the two languages according to their specific grammars "(Donati and Branchini 2013:107), and this is the case for most of the BuSL-ISL bilingual examples with negatives. Thus there is a single, overlapping grammatical structure that can be filled in with lexical material from either language ad libitum. This structure consists of Argument(s)-Predicate-Negator word orders and their variants, e.g. clauses with adjuncts or with repeated subject pronouns as arguments, such as examples (12) and (13). Exceptionally, example (14) shows a clause with CANNOT preceding the main verb; other clauses with CANNOT in clause-final position are also attested.

**Table 9.** Data summary of negative and WH-clauses

**Texts**

| Clip number | Negative | WH |
|---|---|---|
| 2 | 14 | 9 |
| 3 | 12 | 2 |
| 5 | 13 | 9 |
| Total | 39 | 20 |

**Other clauses**

| Clip number | Negative | WH |
|---|---|---|
| 2 | 15 | 3 |
| 3 | 14 | 10 |
| 5 | 22 | 10 |
| Total | 51 | 23 |
| Total all | 90 | 43 |

(12)   B:MOTHER S:TELL₃ S:NONE                                clip 3, 02:29, SN
       'Mother said nothing.'

(13)   S:DEAF B:GOVERMENT B:SUPPORT I:CLEAR S:NONE     clip 2, 00:23, AB
       'It is not clear (how) the government supports deaf people.'

(14)   S:₃TELL₁ CANNOT S:₃HELP₁                               clip 2, 04:28, AB
       'He told me he could not help me.'

One major difference between BuSL and ISL grammars arises from the fact that BuSL also allows SVO word orders,[13] while these are ungrammatical in ISL, which is a strongly head-final language and does not allow objects to follow main verbs (Zeshan 2003). SVO word order does occur with some regularity in the data (there

---

**13** Sometimes SVO order seems to be required in BuSL. In one of the elicitation sessions, the participants rejected some of the SOV clauses we discussed as ungrammatical and insisted that the word order must be SVO. This line of inquiry has not been pursued further.

are 11 SVO clauses), but none of them is a negative clause. Wh-questions with SVO word order are discussed below.

Looking at those clause negators that are particular to BuSL and ISL, the question arises as to the language of other lexemes in the same clause. For instance, is it just as likely to have a combination of an ISL verb with a BuSL negator as it is for a BuSL verb to combine with a BuSL negator? Indeed, we find examples of all combinations in the data. In (15) and (16), the ISL basic clause negator I:NOT is combined with verbs from both sign languages.

(15) B:MY B:MOTHER B:ACCEPT B:BUT S:FAMILY B:ACCEPT I:NOT   clip2, 02:56, SN
'My mother accepted, but my family did not accept.'

(16) B:MOTHER S:IX1 S:BEFORE S:IX1 S:CHOOSE+ B:COUNTRY / S:SIDONIE I:LIKE I:NOT / I:LIKE I:NOT / I:LIKE I:NOT
'My mother (said), I had chosen countries before, but Sidonie doesn't like any of them.'

Examples such as (17) and (18), which are instances of reiterative code-switching akin to those discussed in Section 5.3, are particularly interesting in that the verb or predicate is repeated in both sign languages. Although in (17), it is not entirely clear whether the negator actually negates the verb, and (18) has an S negator, such utterances do suggest that the choice of verb in bilingual utterances is probably not influenced by the choice of negator, and vice versa. It seems that verb and negator can combine freely as long as they are in the word order that is grammatical in both languages.

(17) B:GIRL   thoughtful-expression B:SEARCH B:OFFICE S:IX-circular I:SEARCH B:NOT / S:IX-circular B:SEARCH B:NOT
'The girl thought about it and searched (my bag) everywhere around the offices. Searching everywhere had no result.'           Clip 5, 05:54, CN

(18) I:PROBLEM S:NONE / S:IX2 S:KNOW / B:PROBLEM S:NONE – clip 3, 09:31, WK
'There is no problem, you know, no problem.'

In wh-questions, there is less grammatical overlap between BuSL and ISL, just as there is little lexical overlap as discussed in Section 5.2. Again, it is ISL that has the more constrained constituent order: the only acceptable order is argument(s)-verb/predicate-interrogative, with the exception of the foreign borrowing S:WHO, which can be clause-initial. In BuSL, argument(s)-verb/predicate-interrogative is also a possible word order, though it may not be applicable equally to all BuSL question words; this has not been investigated in detail. Examples such as (19) and (20) are compatible with both grammars and therefore, bilingual utterances can function under congruent lexicalisation. Again, these two utterances are similar except that the question word is from BuSL in (19) and from ISL in (20).

(19)  B:PLAN S:FLY S:IX2 S:THINK S:THERE I:INDIA S:THINK B:WHAT (...)
 clip 3, 06:32, CN
 'As you were planning to fly, what were you thinking about India?'

(20)  S:IX2 S:THINK I:INDIA S:THERE S:THINK I:WH     clip 3, 06:41, CN
 'What were you thinking about India?'

However, several other grammatical options occur in the data that are ungrammatical in ISL, and it is reasonable to assume that they are carried over from BuSL, especially as all of them are available in ASL. These wh-questions include the following structures:

a) Clause-initial question signs

There are several examples of clause-initial WH-signs in the data where the utterance is an interrogative clause type. The most common clause-initial WH-sign is B:WHY, but in the majority of cases, this is used as a conjunction 'because'. B:WHY as an initial interrogative is shown in example (21), and example (22) uses initial B:WHERE (note that this is a multiple wh-question in the English translation, but in the signed utterance, the second wh-question has no overt question sign). I:WH does not occur clause-initially except as a conjunction (see example (26d) below). Example (23) shows a subordinate conditional clause followed by S:WHO at the beginning of the main clause; it is unclear whether this is a possible construction in ISL, but the equivalent construction with the ISL compound interrogative I:FACE+WH is certainly ungrammatical in this case.

(21)  B:WHY I:LIE S:IX1 / S:UNDERSTAND I:FAIL     clip 2, 06:26, AB
 'Why did they lie to me? I don't understand.'

(22)  B:GIRL B:WHERE S:IX2 B:FROM S:FLY S:IX-fly I:NAME    clip 5, 06:08, CN
 'The girl (asked): Where did you fly in from with which airline?'

(23) _____cond
I:BUT B:HAPPEN I:INDIA B:HAPPEN S:SICK S:WHO B:CARE B:HERE
– clip 3; 03:44, SN
'But if (you) should get ill in India, who will take care here?' (i.e. now that I am here)

b) Multiple wh-questions

In multiple wh-questions, there is more than one question word in the clause, and more than one piece of information is being sought using one and the same clause. In ISL, a multiple wh-question needs to be split up into several clauses because two clause-final question signs cannot compete for the single available syntactic slot. As S:WHO may be clause-initial, this may open an option for a multiple wh-question in monolingual ISL, but the grammaticality of such a construction has not been investigated for ISL. In the bilingual data, we find an example of clause-initial S:WHO in combination with a second clause-final question word both from BuSL (example 24).

(24)   S:WHO S:KAKOOZA B:WHERE                           clip 5, 07:27, CN
       'Who and where is Kakooza?'

c) Doubling of WH interrogatives

In some sign languages, WH-signs constitute one of the sign categories that may be doubled within a single clause, usually clause-initially and clause-finally. This construction is exemplified in (25), with a subordinate clause followed by the main WH-interrogative clause. Doubling of WH-interrogatives does not occur in monolingual ISL.

(25)   S:HEY I:INDIA (false start) S:FLY S:WHO S:PICK-UP S:WHO   clip 3, 03:13, SN
       'Hey, when you fly to India, who will be picking you up?'

These examples indicate that the WH-signs from BuSL and ISL are used in accordance with the grammatical patterns and constraints of their respective source languages.[14] Similarly, CANNOT in example (14) is pre-verbal because this is a structural possibility in its source languages, while I:CANNOT is always

---

**14** There is just one possible example of WH-doubling with I:WH in the data (I:WH S:BAG I:WH 'Where is the bag?'), but this is where CN reports on his communication with the hearing woman at the border, and the communication style here is peculiar in that it uses ISL signs in a way that

clause-final in the data, as it is in ISL. Further confirmation for the view that WH interrogatives carry over the grammatical patterns of their source language into the bilingual discourse comes from the use of I:WH, which is used with exactly the same range of functions and syntactic positions as in monolingual ISL. I:WH is commonly used in ISL to mean 'what', 'how' and 'why', as there are no separate lexical interrogatives for these meanings (Zeshan 2000). In addition, I:WH is also used as a complementiser following certain predicates such as verbs of communication ('say that...'), and it is used clause-initially as a conjunction 'because' (Panda and Zeshan 2006). These same functions occur in the bilingual data as illustrated in examples (26a-d):

I:WH meaning 'what'
(26a)  S:BIBLE  B:NAME  B:ENTER  B:STORY  I:WH – clip5, 02:38, SN
'What is the name of the story in the Bible?'

I:WH meaning 'how'
(26b)  I:I-F  S:IX1  S:ARRIVE  S:IX1  I:RENT  I:WH – clip 2, 04:10, AB
'If I arrive, how will I pay the rent?'

I:WH as complementiser 'that'
(26c)  I:LAST  S:IX3  S:SAY  S:WH – clip2, 00:40, AB
'At last, he said that...'

I:WH as conjunction 'because'
(26d)  I:BUT  S:FEEL  S:IX1  I:DEVELOP  S:NONE  I:WH  I:STUDY  S:NOTHING
– clip 2, 00:19, AB
'But I felt I had not developed because I had not studied.'

It is worth pointing out that while negators and question words are used in accordance with the grammatical patterns of their respective source languages, preliminary evidence suggests that this may not be the case for other sign classes. Again, in order to demonstrate this, we look at constructions that are known to be ungrammatical in ISL, as we do not have sufficient information about constructions which would be ungrammatical in BuSL. Examples (27) – (29) show ISL verbs used in constructions which are ungrammatical in ISL, namely SVO constituent order in (27), main verb followed by complement in (28), and modal

---

more closely matches the conversational gestures used by hearing Indians. Thus this does not represent strong counter-evidence.

followed by main verb in (29).¹⁵ In ISL, modals are clause-final like other functional signs, but pre-verbal modals occur in BuSL, as in the phrases B:NEED S:SEE and B:NEED S:GIVE-PAPERS, in the data from CN. Similarly, ISL predicates co-occur with BuSL negators and vice versa, as discussed above.

(27)  S:IX1 I:SEARCH B:V-I-S-A  S:IX3           clip 2, 03:42, AB
      'I looked for the visa.'

(28)  I:START  S:IX1 I:SEARCH                   clip 2, 03:42, AB
      'I started searching.'

(29)  S:3TELL1 S:IX1 S:ALONE B:CAN I:D-O        clip 2, 05:54, AB
      'He told me I could do it alone.'

Another way of looking at these examples is to emphasise that the predicates in the above examples do not contribute to the grammar of the clause. This makes the use of I:SEARCH and I:D-O appear akin to insertion as defined by Muysken (2001), which is defined as material from one language appearing in a structure from the other language, with the latter providing the grammar of the clause. An inserted word or constituent does not contribute to the grammar of the clause.¹⁶ Signs from open lexical classes can be inserted in this way and are used within the grammar of the 'host' sign language, making it possible for the above ISL verbs to be used in non-ISL constructions, such as ISL SEARCH being used in an SVO construction in (27). This agrees with the observation in Muysken (2001:63) on Bolivian Quechua and Spanish that inserted elements "tend to be content words rather than function words". Although we have identified only a few such clauses in our data, they demonstrate at least the possibility of insertion with signs from open lexical classes.

On the other hand, this section has demonstrated that signs from closed grammatical classes such as negators and WH-interrogatives cannot be subject to insertion into a clause with a conflicting structure. An apt explanation is that when choosing a sign with a grammatical function for the construction of a bilingual utterance, the sign cannot be dissociated from its grammatical rules

---

**15** As all examples are from the same signer, this needs further investigation to check if other signers also produce similar utterances elsewhere in the data corpus.
**16** Considering these examples as proper instances of insertion may require disregarding the occurrence of S-type signs, and the absence of B-type signs in example (28). However, this has no bearing on the motivation for discussing insertion here, which is to show that the ISL verbs are used in non-ISL structures.

and constraints. Instead, signs from closed grammatical classes seem to carry over their grammatical properties into the bilingual utterance, which is why they cannot be used in constructions from the other sign language when the grammatical structures would conflict. By contrast, so far there is no evidence in our data of signs from open lexical classes bringing any grammatical constraints along with them when integrated into a bilingual utterance.

# 7 Discussion and conclusions

It is well known from literature on code-switching in spoken languages that bilingual language use including code-switching can serve as a marker of social identity and be indicative of various factors within social actions and interactions (e.g. Romaine 1989, Heller2007), including in Deaf communities (cf. contributions in Metzger 2000). Auer (1995:116) takes the perspective of the bilingual language user seriously and states that "it is the task of the linguist [...] to reconstruct the social processes of displaying and ascribing bilingualism." Thus the choice of language in groups of bilingual people may depend on multiple factors including the participants in the conversation, the topic(s) of the conversation, and the relative status of both languages (e.g. Heller 2007 on code-switching and power relationships). In the BuSL-ISL bilingual data, the approach used in this research has been successful in eliciting conversations where all participants use significant amounts of code-switching. From the data analysed so far, it seems that the mixing of the two sign languages as such is the main factor motivating these data. With few exceptions, it was not obvious in the data that either BuSL or ISL is preferred for particular topics or situations.

One exception was observed in the text by CN, as discussed in Section 5.3, when CN reports on his interaction with a female hearing staff member at the Indian border crossing. However, as mentioned before, this is not a consistent pattern throughout the signed text. Both SN and AB report lengthy discussions with their families in Burundi, but there is no conspicuous use of increased BuSL signs or absence of ISL signs. ISL signs occur freely even when the participants report conversations with family members in Burundi.

From the evidence discussed in this article, it seems that the Burundian students living in New Delhi have developed into a small 'community of practice', along the lines of what Eckert and McConnell-Ginet (1992) discuss in a different context, for language and gender: "A community of practice is an aggregate of people who come together around mutual engagement in an endeavour. Ways of doing things, ways of talking, beliefs, values, power relations – in short, practices – emerge in the course of this mutual endeavor" (Eckert and McConnell-Ginet

1992: 464, see also Lave and Wenger 1991). In this case, this small community of practice is characterised by their shared life experiences and intensive contact with each other during their stay in India, and bilingual sign language communication is obviously an important aspect of the community's "ways of talking".

Linguistically, this is reflected in a range of shared characteristics of their bilingual outputs analysed here, and we argue that this small group of students has developed a relatively stable bilingual linguistic variety. Although it has been noted that there are some individual particularities, such as the use of Hindi mouthings by AB, it is also possible to pinpoint the characteristics of the linguistic variety used by all three signers (and also evident, though based on less data, in the fourth signer WK). The linguistic variety used by this bilingual community of practice is thus characterised by the following features:

- Consistently substantial contributions of both BuSL and ISL signs, with similar proportions, especially in terms of types
- Considerable use of the available pool of shared signs that exist in both sign languages
- Strong preference for S negators
- No ISL compound WH-signs
- Signs from closed grammatical classes follow patterns of the source language
- Signs from open lexical classes may not follow patterns of the source language

These preferences and patterns are not in any way more natural or obvious than any others. For example, it would be perfectly feasible for each person to have very different proportions of BuSL and ISL signs, or for one signer to use only ISL-type WH compounds and another signer to use only BuSL interrogatives. However, this is not what we see.

Additional strong evidence for the fact that the bilingual linguistic variety develops with some consistency within the group comes from errors in the use of ISL signs. As all participants have been learning ISL as an additional language for varying length of time, it is natural that they do not always successfully acquire native-like ISL. What is interesting, however, is that we can pinpoint errors made by several participants in the same way. One of these is the sign I:DIFFICULT (see Figure 8). In ISL, this is articulated with a closed fist hand shape and a small repeated up-and-down movement. However, all four of our participants sometimes produced this sign differently, with repetition at two different points of articulation to the right and left of the signer. This is never seen in ISL and is an acquisition error that has apparently spread throughout the group of Burundian students.

**Figure 8.** DIFFICULT in ISL

The research conducted here has had very few, if any, precedents, and therefore, there had been no specific expectations as to what the bilingual signed communication might look like in this group. Thus the observations made here have been genuine novel discoveries; we have seen that lexical choices and grammatical patterns of code-switching are not random but follow certain regularities as discussed above. It has also become apparent that some of the research questions addressed in spoken language linguistics in the domain of code-switching are not easily applicable to the bilingual signed discourses investigated here, such as the Matrix Language-Embedded Language distinction, and the discussion of possible switch points between two languages. Most importantly, this research has contributed to the very scarce data on unimodal sign language bilingualism, and we have demonstrated how research questions and methodologies for tackling them can develop in the case of bilingual sign language data. It is hoped that further work on other combinations of sign languages in bilinguals may either support or qualify the findings reported in this article in the near future.

## Acknowledgements

The research leading to these results has received funding from the European Research Council under the European Union's Seventh Framework Programme; we are grateful for funding of this research under the project "Multilingual behaviours in sign language users" (MULTISIGN), Grant Agreement number 263647.

Thanks to Tashi Bradford for advice on the similarities/differences between Burundi Sign Language and American Sign Language, and to Dr. Susanne Michaelis at the Max Planck Institute for Evolutionary Anthropology in Leipzig for helpful comments on an earlier version of this article.

Most importantly, we would like to thank our participants from Burundi who have played such an active role at all stages of this research: Charles Njejimana, Aline Berahino, Sidonie Nduwimana, and Willy Kamugisha.

## References

Adam, Robert. 2012. *Unimodal bilingualism in the Deaf community: Contact between dialects of BSL and ISL in Australia and the United Kingdom*. PhD dissertation, University College London.

Adam, Robert. 2013. *Cognate facilitation and switching costs in unimodal bilingualism: British Sign Language and Irish Sign Language*. Paper presented at the 9th International Symposium on Bilingualism (ISB9), 10–13 June 2013, Singapore.

Auer, Peter. 1995. The pragmatics of code-switching: A sequential approach. In Lesley Milroy & Peter Muysken (eds.), *One speaker, two languages. Cross-disciplinary perspectives on code-switching*, 115–135. Cambridge: CUP.

Auer, Peter. 1998. *Code-switching in conversation: Language, interaction and identity*. London: Routledge.

Bhattacharya, Tanmoy, Nisha Grover & Surinder P.K. Randhawa (eds.). 2014. *Indian Sign Language(s). People's Linguistic Survey of India, Vol. 38*. New Delhi: Orient Blackswan Private Limited.

Conlin, Frances, Paul Hagstrom & Carol Neidle. 2003. A particle of indefiniteness in American Sign Language. *Linguistic Discovery* 2(1).1–21.

De Vos, Connie. 2012. *Sign-spatiality in Kata Kolok: how a village sign language of Bali inscribes its signing space*. Nijmegen: Radboud University PhD dissertation.

Donati, Caterina & Chiara Branchini. 2013. Challenging linearization: simultaneous mixing in the production of bimodal bilinguals. In Theresa Biberauer & Ian Roberts (eds.), *Challenges to linearization*, 93–128. Berlin a.o.: Walter de Gruyter.

Eckert, Penelope & Sally McConnell-Ginet. 1992. Think practically and look locally: Language and gender as community-based practice. *Annual Review of Anthropology* 21. 461–490.

Emmorey, Karen. 2009. The bimodal bilingual brain: Effects of sign language experience. *Brain and Language* 109(2–3). 124–132.

Emmorey, Karen. 2003. *Perspectives on classifier constructions in sign languages*. Mahwah, NJ: Lawrence Erlbaum.

Emmorey, Karen, Helsa Borinstein, Robin Thompson & Tamar Gollan. 2008. Bimodal bilingualism. *Bilingualism: Language and Cognition* 11(1). 43–61.
Fischer, Susan. 2006. Questions and negation in American Sign Language. In Ulrike Zeshan (ed.), *Interrogative and negative constructions in sign languages. Sign Language Typology Series No. 1,* 165–197. Nijmegen: Ishara Press.
Grosjean, François. 2008. *Studying bilinguals.* Oxford: OUP.
Grosjean, François. 2010. *Bilingual. Life and Reality.* Cambridge, Mass. and London: Harvard University Press.
Guerra Currie, Anne-Marie, Richard P. Meier & Keith Walters. 2002. A cross-linguistic examination of the lexicons of four sign languages. In Richard P. Meier & Kearsy Cormier (eds.), *Modality and structure in signed and spoken languages*, 224–236. New York: Cambridge University Press.
Heller, Monica. 2007. Code-switching and the politics of language. In Li Wei (ed.), *The bilingualism reader*, 163–176. New York a.o.: Routledge.
Knight, Palema & Ruth Swanwick. 2013. *Working with deaf children: Sign bilingual policy into practice*. Routledge.
Lave, Jean & Etienne Wenger. 1991. *Situated learning: Legitimate peripheral participation*. Cambridge: CUP.
Lefebvre, Claire. 1998. *Creole genesis and the acquisition of grammar.* The case of Haitian creole. Cambridge: CUP.
Lüpke, Friedeike & Mary Chambers. 2010. Multilingualism and language contact in West Africa: towards a holistic perspective. *Journal of Language Contact THEMA Series No. 3*.
Lutalo-Kiingi, Sam. 2014. *A descriptive grammar of morphosyntactic constructions in Ugandan Sign Language.* Preston: University of Central Lancashire PhD dissertation.
Metzger, Melanie (ed.). 2000. *Bilingualism and identity in deaf communities.* Washington, DC: Gallaudet University Press.
Muysken, Pieter. 2001. *Bilingual speech. A typology of code-mixing*. Cambridge: CUP.
Muysken, Pieter. 2011. Bridges over troubled waters: Theoretical linguistics and multilingualism research. *Stellenbosch Papers in Linguistics* 40. 20–38.
Muysken, Pieter. 2013. Two linguistic systems in contact: grammar, phonology and lexicon. In Tej K. Bhatia & William C. Ritchie (eds.), *The handbook of bilingualism and multilingualism,* 193–216. 2nd ed. London: Blackwell.
Myers-Scotton, Carol. 1993. *Social motivation for codeswitching: Evidence from Africa*. Oxford: Clarendon Press.
Myers-Scotton, Carol. 1997. *Duelling languages: Grammatical structure in codeswitching.* Oxford: Clarendon Press.
Myers-Scotton, Carol. 2002. *Contact linguistics: Bilingual encounters and grammatical outcomes.* Oxford: Oxford University Press.
Nyst, Victoria. 2010. Sign languages in West Africa. In Diane Brentari (ed.), *Sign languages*, 405–432. Cambridge a.o.: Cambridge University Press.
Panda, Sibaji & Ulrike Zeshan. 2006. *Professional course in Indian Sign Language.* Mumbai: Ali Yavar Jung National Institute for the Hearing Handicapped.
Panda, Sibaji & Ulrike Zeshan. 2011. Reciprocal constructions in Indo-Pakistani Sign Language. In Nicholas Evans, Alice Gaby, Stephen C. Levinson & Asifa Majid (eds.), *Reciprocals and semantic typology. Typological Studies in Language Series,* 91–114. Amsterdam: John Benjamins.

Plaza-Pust, Carolina & Esperanza Morales-Lopez. 2008. *Sign bilingualism: Language development, interaction and maintenance in sign language contact situations.* Amsterdam: John Benjamins.

Quinto-Pozos, David. 2000. *Contact between Mexican Sign Language and American Sign Language in two Texas border areas.* Austin: University of Texas PhD dissertation.

Quinto-Pozos, David. 2007. Editor's introduction: outlining considerations for the study of signed language contact. In David Quinto-Pozos (ed.), *Sign languages in contact*, 1–28. Washington, DC: Gallaudet University Press.

Quinto-Pozos, David & Robert Adam. 2013. Sign language contact. In Robert Bailey, Richard Cameron & Ceil Lucas (eds.), *The Oxford handbook of sociolinguistics*, 379–403. USA: Oxford University Press.

Romaine, Suzanne. *Bilingualism.* 2nd edition. Oxford: Blackwell.

Sinha, Samar. 2009. *A grammar of Indian Sign Language.* PhD dissertation, Jawaharlal Nehru University, New Delhi, India.

Swanwick, Ruth. 2010. Policy and practice in sign bilingual education: development challenges and directions. *International Journal of Bilingual Education and Bilingualism* 13(2). 147–158.

Wilbur, Ronnie B. 2000. The use of ASL to support the development of English and literacy. *Journal of Deaf Studies and Deaf Education* 5(1). 81–104.

Yoel, Judith. 2007. First-language attrition of Russian Sign Language. In David Quinto-Pozos (ed.), *Sign languages in contact*, 153–191. Washington, DC: Gallaudet University Press.

Zeshan, Ulrike. 2000. *Sign language in Indo-Pakistan: A description of a signed language.* Amsterdam: John Benjamins.

Zeshan, Ulrike. 2003. Indo-Pakistani Sign Language grammar: A typological outline. *Sign Language Studies* 3(2). 157–212.

Zeshan, Ulrike. 2004a. Hand, head and face – negative constructions in sign languages. *Linguistic Typology* 8(1). 1–58.

Zeshan, Ulrike. 2004b. Interrogative constructions in sign languages – cross-linguistic perspectives. *Language* 80(1). 7–39.

Zeshan, Ulrike. 2006. Regional variation in Indo-Pakistani Sign Language – evidence from content questions and negatives. In Ulrike Zeshan (ed.), *Interrogative and negative constructions in sign languages. Sign Language Typology Series No. 1*, 303–323. Nijmegen: Ishara Press.

# Stabilisation of the lexicon in an emerging jargon: The development of signs to express animate referents in a sign language contact situation

Tashi Bradford, Susanne Michaelis and Ulrike Zeshan

## 1 Background: Lexicon development in pidgins and jargons

While there has been extensive research on language contact between spoken languages, much less work has been conducted on contact between signed languages. In this chapter, we study the emerging nature of the stabilising lexicon in a situation of language contact that has been called "cross-signing" (Zeshan 2015). In situations of cross-signing, sign language users who have no language in common engage in ad hoc improvised communication. When this communication and its emergent regularities are studied from the very beginning of the contact, as is the case in the present research, the closest equivalent in spoken languages is research on jargons. Jargons represent the earliest point of departure on a developmental path from jargons to pidgins and further to creoles (Thomason and Kaufman 1988, Bakker 2008). Before we address the data and results from this study, it is useful to review the topic of lexical development in contact languages from spoken language research, including both pidgins and jargons, and relate it to what we know about sign language contact situations.

When members of different language communities come in contact with each other and share no common language, verbal communication develops over time by evolution of reduced languages known as pidgins (Holm 2000, Winford 2003). Historically this has most often occurred in the context of trade, slavery, and territorial occupation (Baptista 2005). Pidgins are not spoken by anyone as a first language, but are used between speakers who have different languages as their first languages (Winford 2003). Pidgins have stable grammars and are passed on to other speakers, with norms to be followed if one wants to be a "good speaker" of a pidgin (Bakker 2003). When pidgins are passed on to the next generation of speakers and thus become the native first languages (L1) of these speakers, the resulting language varieties are usually referred to as creoles.

https://doi.org/10.1515/9781501503528-004

Spoken pidgins share several common features. Dependent upon pragmatic context, they are simplified in both lexicon and grammatical structure compared to their contributing languages (Botha 2006). Tones, for instance, only transfer to pidgins if the contributing languages themselves also have tone (Mühlhäusler 1997:138), but in the process of pidginisation the tone paradigm always seems to get reduced.[1] Some pidgins lack copulas (Romaine 1993), and pidgins rarely exhibit inflectional morphology, such as inflectional marking for gender, number, tense, case, and possession. However, as Bakker (2003) showed, some pidgins may show a significant amount of inflectional morphology. This seems to be due to a historical accident insofar as a number of documented pidgins, such as Eskimo Pidgin, happened to develop from highly inflectional contributing languages in the first place. As a result of pidginisation, the simplified inflectional morphology is still more complex than you would expect from pidgins and even creoles evolving from less strongly inflecting or even isolating languages (like Chinese Pidgin English).

But how do spoken pidgins come about? They must evolve from unstable jargon varieties when people without any language in common try to rudimentarily communicate in a specific interethnic context. These linguistically and socially unstable jargon varieties show a high degree of variation since they are based on speakers' individual ad-hoc strategies to bridge the communication gap.[2] Different speakers apply different strategies dependent on their education, their personality, but also dependent on their experience with other non-native speakers (Mühlhäusler 1997). This is exactly the situation that cross-signers also find themselves in.

Jargons thus lack linguistic norms and speakers heavily rely on discourse and pragmatic context to reconstruct the intended meaning, often with a fair amount of misunderstandings. Linguistically, jargons reflect very basic grammar, e.g. holophrastic utterances, pragmatic structuring, iconic ordering of time events.

The division between jargon and pidgin is rather fuzzy and allows for many intermediate steps between the two types. We conceive of jargons as unstable individual ad-hoc solutions to communicate between speakers of different languages who occasionally interact for various purposes, whereas pidgins are

---

[1] See also data on pidgins and creoles in APiCS, Michaelis et al. 2013, http://apics-online.info/parameters/120#4/3.06/-21.64)
[2] The following passage is largely based on Mühlhäusler (1997) and Parkvall and Bakker (2013).

stabilised languages with clear grammatical and social norms. Both types of languages are non-native languages.[3]

Contact between speakers of different signed languages has been less studied, as have been sign languages in general. At the international level, early mention of contact among deaf people from different language backgrounds exists regarding banquets in Paris which began in 1834, bringing together deaf people from all over Europe. In 1850, Ferdinand Berthier reported how successful communication occurred amongst the revellers of different countries (Moody 1987). In the twentieth century, as international travel and communication became more prevalent, this contact signing progressed as a vehicle of communication with the organisation of such entities as the Comité International des Sports Silencieux (CISS) in 1934, the World Federation of the Deaf (WFD) in 1951, and the International Workshop for Deaf Researchers in 1985. This linguistic phenomenon was called International Sign, later referred to as IS. In an attempt to extend and formalise the communication taking place in such contexts, in the 1950s committees were established to expand the International Sign lexicon under the name of *Gestuno*. The WFD published dictionaries of this lexicon in 1959 and in 1965 (Supalla and Webb 1995). However, the impact of these compilation efforts did not last, in contrast to the more fluid and naturally occurring International Sign which lived on and continued to mature.

Research on International Sign in the past several decades has categorised it as a pidgin. In parallel with spoken pidgins such as Eskimo Pidgin mentioned above, IS has quite a complex grammatical structure, particularly with respect to processes that rely on the grammatical use of the three-dimensional space (Rosenstock 2008, Supalla and Webb 1995). As in spoken pidgins, this complexity is likely due to the fact that the sign languages among which the contact occurs share some of the same complex grammatical features, and thus they are not reduced or eliminated (Webb and Supalla 1994). For instance, there are regular grammatical patterns in marking relations among arguments of the verb (Supalla and Webb 1995), and as in national sign languages, in IS there is use of locating referents in space, adverbial inflection, nonmanual grammatical

---

**3** In spoken languages, some pidgins and even creoles (which have become the L1 of a speech community) have "jargon" in their language denomination, e.g. Mobilian Jargon or Chinook Jargon (which is referred to as Chinuk Wawa in APiCS http://apics-online.info/contributions/74, Grant 2013). But here "jargon" does not refer to unconventionalised language/speech varieties, but to stable pidgins with quite strict grammatical norms. However, there are also cases where linguists have called unstable jargons pidgins, for instance Bickerton named the variety which he recorded in Hawai'i a pidgin even though it becomes quite clear that this variety is far from being a stable pidgin with fixed linguistic rules (see Bakker 2003: 4).

markers, rhetorical questions as a linking device, classifiers, and referential role-shifting (Locker-McKee and Napier 2002).

Sign language contact situations that would be equivalent to spoken jargons are only just beginning to be studied systematically, and studies on cross-signing (Zeshan 2015, Byun, De Vos, Zeshan, Bradford, and Levinson 2017) are among the first such investigations.

As for the lexicon, jargons and pidgins overwhelmingly draw their words from one so-called "lexifier" language, e.g. Chinese Pidgin English from English or Fanakalo from Zulu. But there are some exceptions where pidgins have two main lexifier sources, e.g. Russenorsk, Yimas-Arafundi Pidgin (see APiCS, http://apics-online.info/contributions/69), or Ndjuka-Trio Pidgin (see Parkvall and Bakker 2013: 47).

Linguists have tried to correlate these data with social factors in the sense that two-lexifier-pidgins, i.e. pidgins that are substantially based on the lexicons of two languages, are more likely to develop in a symmetric power relationship (e.g. in trade situations) and therefore both languages contribute equally to the nascent jargon/pidgin lexicon, whereas one-lexifier-pidgins more naturally evolve in an asymmetric hierarchical social situation where one group clearly dominates the other (e.g. in slave, military, or working contexts) (see e.g. Fill and Mühlhäusler 2001). However, besides social power relations, Baker and Huber (2001) invoke mobility as the key factor that decides on which lexifier basis the pidgin lexicon is built. Traders and sailors who interact with many different local peoples are more likely to impose their lexicon on the jargon/pidgin variety and in this way the lexicon of the most mobile group in the language contact situations becomes the linking element between the different substrate communities (Parkvall and Bakker 2013: 47).

It seems that in the very first stages of the lexicon development in jargons we find a lot of mixture. The jargon only shows a small stable core lexicon (often from one lexifier), with many variable non-core items as speakers with different substrate languages borrow words from their L1s (Mühlhäusler 1997: 153). It is only at later stages that one lexifier source prevails. As the number of lexical items in a jargon is small and at the same time the meaning of each item is very general, interlocutors have to draw on context and pragmatics to infer the intended meanings. The aim of the present chapter is to investigate how such lexicon selection may play out in the sign language modality.

Jargons can undergo stabilisation processes so that a stable pidgin may arise. For this to happen, the speakers have to develop socially accepted language norms. Mühlhäusler (1997:135) observes that "(...) it is in the lexicon that stable conventions begin to develop first". Speakers of stabilising pidgins converge in preferred lexical variants out of the feature pool of highly unstable jargon varieties. The emergence of language norms in the stable pidgin implies certain restrictions on the developing lexicon: First of all, only a small part out of the lexifier lexicon is taken over into the pidgin. Siegel (1982: 12) shows that out of 80 cutting verbs in Fijian, only two verbs are found in the corresponding pidgin. Second, the meaning of lexemes in pidgins can differ with respect to the corresponding lexeme in the lexifier(s) and/or the substrate(s). The meaning can be overgeneralised as Mühlhäusler (1997: 153) shows for Pidgin German in Papua New Guinea where *kaput* 'broken' corresponds to Standard German *zerrissen* 'torn to pieces', *zerbrochen* 'broken', *zerplatzt* 'burst', *zerfetzt* 'slashed', *durchlöchert* 'perforated' etc. The meaning of a lexifier or substrate item can also be attenuated in the pidgin, as is the case of *too much* meaning 'much' in many English-based pidgins or Tok Pisin *sit* ( < English *shit*) meaning 'leftovers, faeces' (Mühlhäusler 1997: 155f.).

There are other typical lexical strategies to systematically enlarge pidgin lexicons (cf. Mühlhäusler 1997: 157f.). Antonyms can be created by adding a word to a given item which corresponds to 'no', e.g. *no hatwok* 'easy' in Tok Pisin, or *hayi saba* 'not fear' meaning 'brave' in Fanakalo. Female and male animates are composed by preposing 'man' and 'woman' to a lexeme, as in Cameroon Pidgin English *man got* 'billy goat' and *wuman got* 'nanny goat' (for more examples see also the *APiCS* feature "Female and male animals" http://apics-online.info/parameters/117#2/13.8/5.0). Finally, nomen agentis are encoded by adding 'man' or 'person' to the relevant verb or predicate, as in Hiri Motu *hadibaia tauna* 'teach person' meaning 'teacher'.

The conventionalised lexicon of International Sign, in contrast with its complex grammatical structure in some domains, is limited (Rosenstock 2004, Allsop et al. 1995). To compensate for its "impoverished" lexicon, strategies in production of IS include substitutions (lexical and metaphorical), repetitions in more than one form (Quinto-Pozos and Adam 2013 and Zeshan and Panda 2015 use the term reiterative code-switching for this), reductions of phrases, and expansion of lexical items (Rosenstock 2008). Reiterative code-switching is also a salient feature of cross-signing, as well as occurring in bilingual interactions where all the signers are familiar with both languages (Zeshan and Panda 2015). Woll (1990) comments on this IS use saying that "[t]he use of multiple representation for the same referent, whether of alternative lexical signs, of a paraphrase series, or of a mix of signs and gestures appears designed to give the widest opportunity of comprehension to the addressees." Allsop et al. (1995) found that while the rate of signing in IS is the same between experienced and novice signers (signs per second), the length of stories told in IS by experienced signers is substantially longer due to the circumlocutions and duplications used to compensate for the limited lexicon.

In Rosenstock's (2004) study of IS interpreting at the Deaf Way II international conference in Washington DC in 2002, various sources of lexical items were identified. Over 60% of the IS vocabulary was the same or similar as signs from more than eight national sign languages (not borrowed from a specific sign language). In comparison, 38% of vocabulary was borrowed from one sign language or group of related sign languages. Only 2% of IS signs were found to be unique to IS. Signs from Gestuno had all but disappeared, having been replaced in IS by signs with higher iconicity and loan vocabulary (Rosenstock 2004). Although this research is not framed with respect to the issue of "lexifier languages", it does raise interesting issues given that spoken language pidgins are so often dominated by a single lexifier language or, more rarely, two lexifier languages.

In this chapter, we investigate first-time contact between two groups of sign language users who come together from different countries and have no language in common. The aim is to track processes within the earliest stages of lexicon development in the emergent cross-signing jargon. The abovementioned notions of jargonisation, lexifier language, feature pool, etc, are relevant to the discussions in the remainder of the chapter. In Section 2, we discuss the data and methodology used for this study. Section 3 presents the result of the study structured in terms of several processes that have occurred in the signed output over the several weeks' duration of the study, and section 4 presents the conclusions.

## 2 Data and methodology

The logistics of undertaking this study of signers with no common language necessitated bringing together participants from different countries to a single location for up to six weeks. As the first filming of the study is of their very first encounter with each other, it had to be arranged for them to have no contact with each other or with local Deaf people upon arrival until the filming of the first meeting was finished. For the remainder of their stay, they must have had not only time as a group but with the local Deaf community as well. Besides participating in the study, they also took part in capacity-building training and activities. Coordinating all of the above was not an easy task.

## 2.1 Participant selection and language backgrounds

Identifying participants was the first step. Criteria for participation included a strong command of their native sign language; lack of knowledge of other signed languages or of International Sign; little or no knowledge of English (with the exception of the British participant CP); and leadership potential in order to disseminate in their home community the skills and information learnt through capacity building. The principal investigator (hearing) and staff members (Deaf) of the International Institute for Sign Languages and Deaf Studies (iSLanDS) are affiliated with various countries and chose participants from familiar communities. The staff members also served as intermediaries and interpreters for the participants. Outside of the research environment this ensured that the participants had the support they needed to reduce the stress of being in a foreign country, and having research team members who were fluent in the native sign languages of the participants was an essential aspect of the study.

For the 2012 study located in Preston, UK, one male participant each was chosen from Indonesia, Japan, and Jordan, as well as a female participant locally in the UK. All were personally known by iSLanDS staff members and fit the above criteria. In addition to the role of iSLanDS staff members as hosts, they served as interpreters for the participants at key times during the study. This was the same with the second group of participants, who got together in Lucknow, India, in 2014, though in a slightly different arrangement.

For the Lucknow 2014 group, the Preston 2012 participants from Indonesia and Jordan returned in the capacity of intermediaries and interpreters for two new male study participants who were identified by the guides and the same iSLanDS staff members working in those countries. New participants from India and Nepal were also chosen by an Indian iSLanDS staff member. One Indian male participant was recruited to participate in the elicitation games. This participant was not included in the conversational data in the interest of time management, as he was a full-time student at the time. The female participant from Nepal was accompanied by another young Deaf Nepalese woman who was familiar with Indian Sign Language, International Sign, and English. All participants as well as the research team were housed in university lodging on site.

Chapters 10 and 11 in this volume provide details of the Preston and the Lucknow cross-signing groups, describing their constellations and relationships with each other during their stay. The research period lasted six weeks in Preston and five weeks in Lucknow, enough time for the groups to constitute themselves as small communities with joint routines and objectives.

During the research activities, interpreting between the participants and the research team was provided by the intermediaries in both groups. For consent to the study, intermediaries delivered the project description and consent form in the participants' native sign languages. This was videotaped for record of consent along with the signed forms. Instructions for the filming sessions were also delivered to participants in their own sign languages. Finally, the post-hoc interviews (see below) between researchers and participants were interpreted by the same intermediaries.

Participant profiles are listed in Table 1. All participants are highly fluent in their native sign language, and also have advanced or intermediate competence in the written languages of their home countries. In addition, most participants have some very limited skills in written English, restricted to familiarity with a few isolated words, and most are somewhat familiar with the fingerspelling system used in International Sign. Only participants CP and NG have had extensive exposure to users of other sign languages due to respectively working and studying among international groups of signers.

**Table 1.** Participant profiles

| Group | Alias name | Country | Gender | Native sign language | In-country written language |
|---|---|---|---|---|---|
| Preston | CP | UK | F | British SL (BSL) | English |
| Preston | HM | Japan | M | Japanese SL (JSL) | Japanese |
| Preston | MI | Indonesia | M | Indonesian SL (BIS) | Bahasa Indonesia |
| Preston | MS | Jordan | M | Jordanian SL (LIU) | Arabic |
| Lucknow | NG | India | M | Indian SL (ISL) | Hindi & English |
| Lucknow | AS | Nepal | F | Nepali SL (NSL) | Nepali |
| Lucknow | AM | Indonesia | M | Indonesian SL (BIS) | Bahasa Indonesia |
| Lucknow | BF | Jordan | M | Jordanian SL (LIU) | Arabic |

## 2.2 Data collection

For both groups, once all was explained and consent given, data was obtained from sessions of free conversation in pairs, lasting about 40 minutes, as well as an elicitation game of about 30 minutes. The Lucknow participants also took plart in an additional elicitation game of equal length. For the conversational sessions, participants were free to talk about anything they wished. If they ran out of topics, the researcher filming at the time would suggest a new topic such as family, sport, or work.

The elicitation game was a director-matcher task (e.g. Clark and Wilkes-Gibbs 1986), consisting of paired pictures and drawings. Participant A would have just one picture to describe. Participant B had the same picture on a paper along with one or two related but different pictures. Participant A, the "director" of the game, would describe the picture and participant B, the "matcher", would have to indicate which picture A described by pointing to it on camera. A and B could not see each other's pictures, so there was often some questioning and to-and-fro to determine which was the correct choice.

Pictures were chosen for the cards to include a balance of inanimate objects and animate beings such as people and animals. Figure 1 shows a typical example.

| Participant B | Participant A |
|---|---|

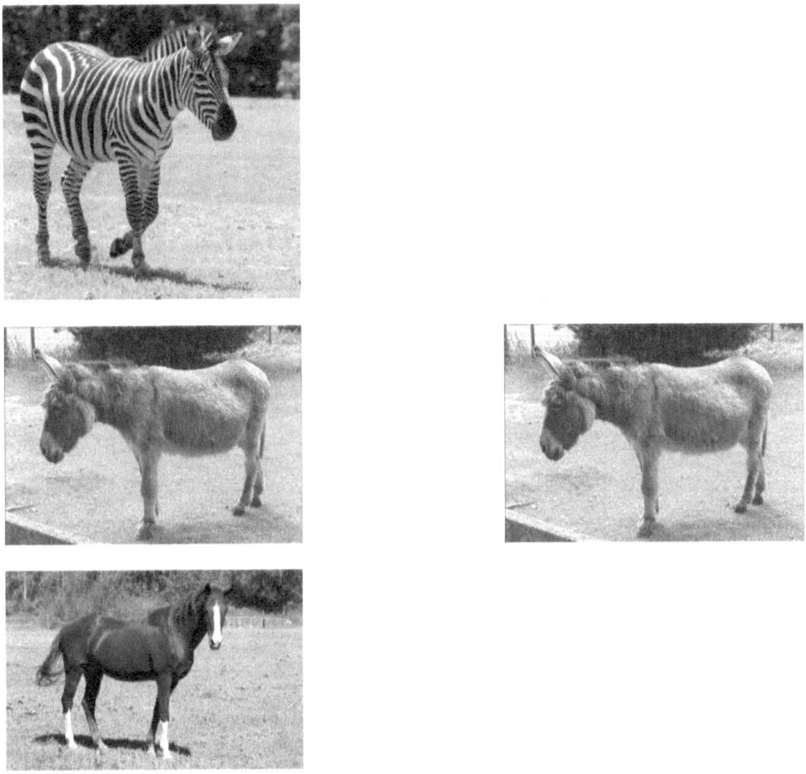

**Figure 1.** Stimulus materials

On the first day of meeting, after the project description and consent form, each dyad had one session of free conversation and one session of the elicitation game(s). It was essential to complete the first sessions before participants had opportunity for socialising with each other and with the local Deaf community. If time ran out or participants became too tired, the remainder of filming of first meetings was postponed to the next day.

Once the first round of data collection was finished, post-hoc interviews took place between a research team member and each participant in turn (see Chapter 7 of this volume for details on this methodology). The interviewers conducted the session in International Sign, and an intermediary functioning as interpreter was present at each interview (except for the interview with CP which did not need an interpreter). Video of the free conversations was shown and any instance of communication difficulty was discussed. Participants were invited to comment openly on the footage and were also asked specific questions by the researchers. In the interview a participant could explain what they had understood their interlocutor to say, and what they themselves were trying to express in each segment of the conversation. These interviews yielded valuable insights into the data, including the mental processes by which a sign was chosen. Often signers were unaware that a miscommunication had happened at all until each person was asked to explain what they had understood and wanted to say. Although these data provided a useful qualitative framing for the research, the post-hoc interviews are not used explicitly for the purpose of analysis in this chapter.

One week after the initial meetings, filming of free conversations was repeated. Around three weeks later, i.e. ca. one month after arrival and shortly before participants' departure for their home countries, filming was repeated of both free conversation and the director-matcher elicitation game. This is illustrated in Table 2.[4] Interspersed and in parallel with the data collection sessions, the participants in both groups (expect NG) pursued various capacity building activities. These are described in detail in Chapter 10 and Chapter 11.

---

[4] The exact dates of research sessions varied because the arrival of participants was staggered over a week, rather than having them all arrive on the same day. This was done to keep the logistics for the research sessions manageable.

**Table 2.** Summary of data

|  | 1st day | 2nd day | After 1 week | After 1 month |
|---|---|---|---|---|
| Conversation | X |  | X | X |
| Elicitation game | X |  |  | X |
| Post-hoc interview |  | X |  |  |

## 2.3 Coding and analysis

For this chapter, analysis focuses on the experimental data from both the Preston group and the Lucknow group, covering both instances of the conversational game, with a period of about a month in between. The present analysis focuses on the expression of animate referents, including both people and animals, as occurring in the data gathered via the elicitation games. The coding schema that identifies the various strategies used in referring to animate beings in this study includes the following coding categories.
- SASS: Size And Shape Specifier
- CL:handle: Handle classifier
- CL:limb: Limb classifier
- CL:whole: Whole entity classifier
- LEX: Lexical item
- CA: Constructed Action
- SPACE: Use of real space around the signer, e.g. pointing
- GEST: Communicative gestures

SASS – The most frequent strategy in the data is use of a size and shape specifier. A SASS describes the referent in terms of its geometrical features, hence its name referring to size and shape (Klima and Bellugi 1979). The example in Figure 2 refers to a tree, outlining first the tree trunk (the first two pictures) and then the crown of the tree (pictures 3–5).

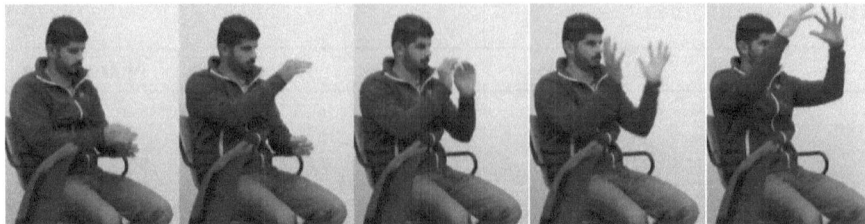

**Figure 2.** SASS construction for the referent "tree".

Different sub-types of SASS signs are recognised in the literature. For instance, size and shape can be shown by a static hand configuration, or, as in the present example, by tracing the outline, which involves a path movement of the hands. Various handshapes are used depending on the shape to be indicated; for example, the handshape in picture 1-2, with the thumb and index finger making contact, is compatible with a long and narrow shape. The signer then changes to an open hand shape in picture 3-5 to indicate a round and bulky shape. For the purpose of the coding in our research, we do not differentiate between the different sub-types of SASS signs, and they are all included within one in the same category.

Three types of signs that are collectively referred to as "classifiers" in sign language linguistics are distinguished in the coding system. It is important to note that these signs do not correspond to "classifiers" in the spoken language literature (cf. Schembri 2003; Aikhenvald 2014), but the difference in terminology is not discussed here. The three types are coded CL:handle, CL:whole and CL:limb.

CL:handle – In a handling classifier, the hand moves as if it were holding and handling the object in question (Sutton-Spence and Woll 1999: 49). This results in a very iconic representation of actions, in particular actions carried out by human referents. The meaning of the sign is often ambiguous between and object and the action carried out with this object (e.g. hammer/to hammer). Figure 3 shows an example of CL:handle where the location of the sign in space is also meaningful. In this case, it refers to a mechanic repairing something located above the head.

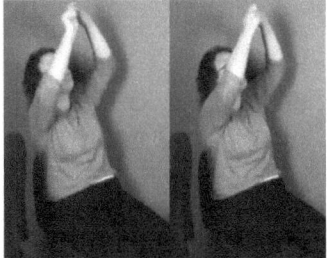

**Figure 3.** Handling classifier construction showing "work with a tool"

CL:whole – A whole-entity classifier represents the entire being, projected onto the hand, which takes on a handshape representative of a class of referents (Johnston and Schembri 2007). Typically, the movement and location of the hand or hands is also meaningful and mapped onto the movement and location of the referent. These complex "classifier predicates" are very common across sign languages, though not universal (Nyst 2007), and the choice of handshape is language-specific. An upright index finger, as shown in Figure 4, is used in many sign languages to represent a person, but other handshapes are also found across sign languages.

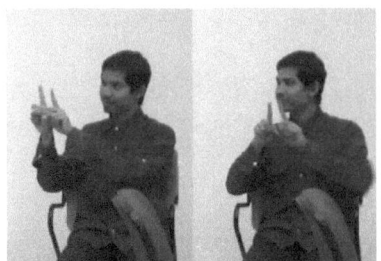

**Figure 4.** Whole-entity classifier construction showing "a couple dancing".

CL:limb – In producing a limb classifier, a part of the body is represented and mapped onto the hand, sometimes including the forearm, of the signer (Supalla 1986). Body parts are not limited to the extremities, such as arms and legs, but can also include parts such as the tongue, the ears, or a beak. Figure 5 shows an example of CL:limb being used to represent ears. In this case, the whole hand "stands in" for the ears. If, on the other hand, the signer chose to trace the outline of the ears, such a sign would be coded as SASS. In many cases in the data, signers can choose between a number of options to represent one and the same referent, and the choices made are important for the analysis.

**Figure 5.** Limb classifier showing the ears of a donkey

CA – Constructed Action is "a re-construction" of the action by the signer (Johnston and Schembri 2007), such that the signer performs the action as if taking the place of the referent. In other words, signers "act out" with their entire body the situation they aim to convey, adopting the perspective of the character in question. This distinguishes CA from whole-entity classifiers, which adopt a bird's-eye view or observer perspective (see Perniss 2007 on observer perspective and character perspective). In Figure 6, the action of dancing is described in response to the same picture that Figure 5 refers to, but using Constructed Action.

**Figure 6.** Constructed Action referring to the action of dancing.

LEX – This code refers to a conventional lexical item, whether from the signer's own language, another language, or a sign constructed and agreed upon within the group. Unlike all the other categories of signs, LEX signs include signs that are purely the result of linguistic convention and may have no motivated link between form and meaning, such as the Indian Sign Language sign GREEN mentioned in Section 3.1. It is a typical development in sign languages that more iconic signs, including SASS, constructed action, and classifier constructions, become conventionalised over time, and acquire increasingly arbitrary properties (Zeshan 2003). It is therefore natural that signs may have partially iconic and partially arbitrary components, and during coding, the differences between a LEX sign and a related sign from another category are sometimes subtle.

SPACE – Use of this category is not frequent in the data. A sign is coded as SPACE when the signer uses real physical space to convey information, usually via pointing. For example, this can be used to indicate colour, as shown in Figure 7.

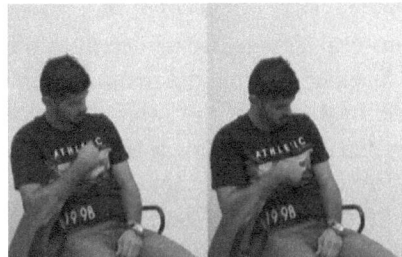

**Figure 7.** SPACE used to indicate "colours" by pointing to the colourful T-shirt.

In a few cases in the data, signs do not fit any of the above categories, but are drawn from communicative gestures (coded GEST). Such gestures often stem from the surrounding culture, where the communicative gestures are also used by hearing people. One example was a gesture of crossing oneself. These instances are rare and are excluded from the data counts in Section 3.

# 3 Results and discussion

The main aim of this research has been to track changes in the emerging communication of cross-signers over time. As mentioned above, the data analysed here for this purpose are from the two sets of communication games (i.e. the "Game" row of Table 2 above).

As the groups of signers become familiar with one another and one another's communicative resources, several aspects of routinisation and reduction can be expected to take place. In the following subsections, we look at different aspects of these changes over time. Section 3.1 provides an example of the signed interactions, to illustrate the kinds of differences we find between the first and second round of the elicitation games. Section 3.2 considers the participants' overall performance in the task, particularly with respect to response times, over the entire data from both rounds of the elicitation game. In section 3.3, quantitative results relating to the use of the various sign types discussed above are presented. Section 3.4 then investigates and exemplifies several sub-processes of jargonisation, using the notion of "feature pool". Sections 3.3 and 3.4 are based on a subset of the data, including only those instances where the stimulus pictures show animate referents.

## 3.1 Signed interactions in elicitation games

In order to illustrate the kinds of productions that signers use to describe and identify the target pictures, we now turn to an example from the first and from the second rounds of the elicitation games. In this case, the same signer is describing the same target picture, namely the donkey shown in Figure 1. As one of the aims of target picture selection was to avoid repetition of the same picture, the example is exceptional in this respect. However, a direct comparison is good for illustrative purposes, and the points made here are also typical of other productions where target pictures are not constant across both games for the same participant.

Figure 8 shows a series of screenshots that are part of the description of the donkey in the first round of the game, with AM as director and BF as matcher. To recall, this was the first time that the two signers have met, and the elicitation game was filmed immediately after their initial 45-minute free conversation.

At the beginning of the description, AM uses a series of visual-spatial constructions. The SASS sign, with the hand moving downward, is articulated very slowly. Moreover, the torso bends down too and there is a diminutive facial expression. Thus the concept of small size is marked multiply in three different ways, involving a considerable articulatory effort.

The addressee then wants to confirm the colours on the picture, using the Jordanian sign COLOUR. AM immediately repeats the sign in order to indicate that it has not been understood. This is a common strategy to initiate a conversational repair in cross-signing, as reported in Byun et al (2017). The roundabout strategy of asking for the colour naturally presents itself because the signers do not have established lexical signs for the three different animals.[5]

---

[5] It is quite possible that the matcher at this point actually intends to ask about the colour of the animal, but the response mentions the grassy surface because this is a vibrant colour in the picture and the director does not know that the other two pictures show similar but differently-coloured animals.

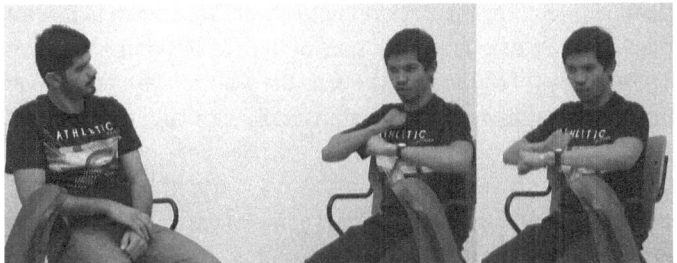

CL:handle 'riding'

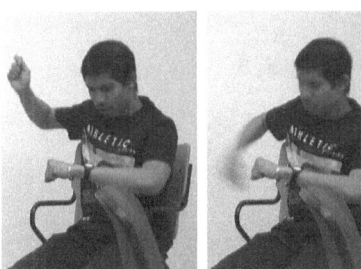

CL:handle 'whipping'

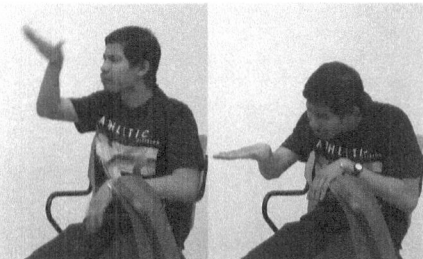

SASS 'small size'

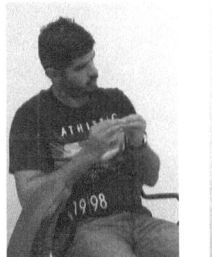 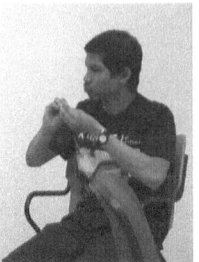

COLOUR (LIU)   COLOUR (LIU)

**Figure 8.** Description of the donkey in first round, with AM (director) and BF (matcher)

After some further negotiation involving other strategies (not shown in Figure 8), AM has understood the question and responds with the next sequence (Figure 9). Describing the green surface of grass on the picture, AM uses an Indonesian (BIS) sign GREEN (see Palfreyman 2016 on colour signs in Indonesian sign language varieties). This is followed by several more sequences with further visual-spatial descriptions, and both signers are engaged in back-and-forth checking for successful communication (including regular eye contact), such as shown in the last two pictures of Figure 9. Here BF asks about the ears of the donkey, and AM makes full use of the visual possibilities of signing, by showing the exact shape and position of the ears with a limb classifier. As with the previous SASS sign, and the COLOUR sign, this limb classifier is again produced slowly and deliberately. Increased holding duration of the sign and eye contact has been identified by Byun et al. (2017) as characteristic of try-marking in cross-signing interactions. Try-marking is a mechanism to flag up a sign to the addressee for checking comprehension, and invites the other participant to ask for clarification and repair if needed.

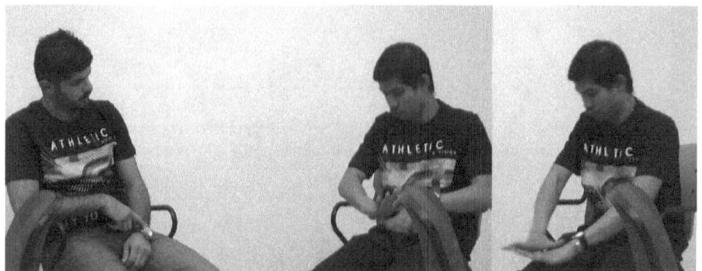

SASS 'low horizontal surface'

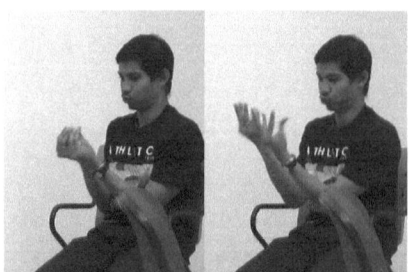

GREEN (BIS)

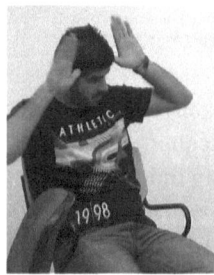 

CL:limb 'large ears'  CL:limb 'large ears facing forward'

**Figure 9.** Description of the donkey in first round, with AM (director) and BF (matcher)

Figure 10 shows the same reference picture being described by AM after three weeks of the group of participants having spent time together. The first two pictures are the same constituents also used in the initial description. However, the SASS is produced much faster and in quick succession with the preceding sign, almost like a compound, although formationally there are two separate signs. Such reduction and tighter combination of sign sequences is typical as communication between signers has become more established, and this is further explored in Section 3.4.

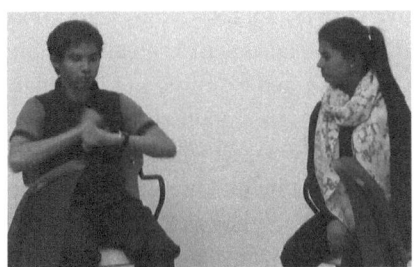
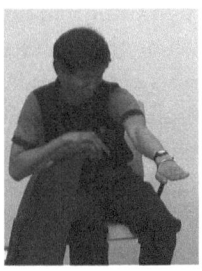

CL:handle 'riding'          SASS 'small size' CA 'forelegs'

CL:handle 'whipping'        CL:handle 'riding' + CA 'rearing up'

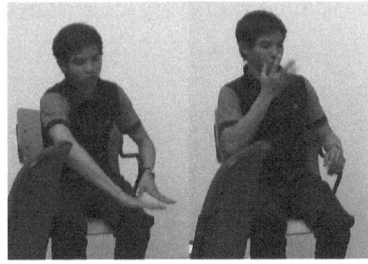

COLOUR (ISL)    SASS 'low surface' GREEN (BIS)    GREEN (ISL)

**Figure 10.** Description of the donkey in second round, with AM (director) and AS (matcher)

The next sequence is also similar to the initial rendition, with visual-spatial constructions, namely classifier, and constructed action. The main difference is that the description overall is much shorter, as the target picture is identified much more quickly by the addressee. Again, this is typical of the data overall, as argued in Section 3.2.

In the final sequence, the colour of the picture is again questioned. Interestingly, both the question and the answer use Indian Sign Language signs. This shows the increasing influence of the surrounding language, which is typical in the development of the jargon (see Section 3.4 on this point). In the response, AM actually starts to sign GREEN in his native variety, but it is a false start, and is immediately replaced by the ISL sign GREEN. The false start is clearly visible as only an initial opening of the handshape is performed resulting in a lax open hand, and then the articulation of the BIS sign GREEN is abandoned mid-way. The fully formed BIS sign shown in Figure 9 has a repeated opening and closing motion with clearly defined handshapes. Thus it appears that by this time, signers have enriched their repertoires and are able to make conscious choices from among the available signs, including those that are entirely in non-iconic, as is the case with the ISL sign GREEN. In a separate study, Byun et al. (forthcoming) have traced the choice of colours signs over time within the same (Lucknow) group of participants.

## 3.2 Reduction of response times

As an initial first-pass estimate of the extent to which communication becomes more efficient in the second round of the elicitation games, it is informative to consider the overall time taken for completing the elicitation games. Table 3 shows the total time taken by each pair of signers in Set 1 (that is, the initial game when the signers met for the first time) and Set 2 (that is, the second round of the elicitation game after the signers had spent 3-4 weeks together). Within each set of four signers, every signer is paired with every other signer, resulting in six pairs.

**Table 3.** Total response times

| Participant pair Preston group | SET1 times in sec | SET1 turns | SET2 times in sec | SET2 turns | Time difference in sec |
|---|---|---|---|---|---|
| CP-HM | 428 | 16 | 188 | 16 | 240 |
| HM-MI | 600 | 20 | 459 | 20 | 141 |
| HM-MS | 480 | 21 | 161 | 21 | 319 |
| MI-MS | 278 | 21 | 329 | 21 | -51 |
| CP-MI | 327 | 21 | 217 | 21 | 110 |
| MS-CP | 270 | 20 | 203 | 20 | 67 |
| TOTAL | 2383 | 119 | 1557 | 119 | 826 |
| Participant pair Lucknow group | SET1 times in sec | SET1 turns | SET2 times in sec | SET2 turns | Time difference in sec |
| AS-BF | 394 | 20 | 165 | 20 | 229 |
| NG-AS | 541 | 20 | 172 | 20 | 369 |
| AM-NG | 460 | 20 | 266 | 20 | 194 |
| AM-BF | 314 | 20 | 169 | 20 | 145 |
| BF-NG | 388 | 20 | 246 | 20 | 142 |
| AS-AM | 333 | 20 | 185 | 20 | 148 |
| TOTAL | 2430 | 120 | 1203 | 120 | 1227 |

For both the Preston and the Lucknow data, the total time taken by all signers to complete the entire task decreases over time. For the Preston group of participants, the second round of the game is 34.66% faster, and for the Lucknow group the second round is 51.49% faster. In the Lucknow data, each pair resolved the task for a total of 20 pictures ("turns" in Table 3). However, in the Preston data, the total number of pictures resolved per pair was not constant, varying between 16 and 21 pictures. In several cases, Set 2 had more pictures than Set 1, in which case the number of pictures in Set 2 was capped so that Set 1 and Set 2 had an equal number of pictures. Table 3 shows the capped figures. Despite this difference in rigour of the data, the reduction itself is not in question.

The total times taken are very similar between the two groups for SET1, with 2383s and 2430s respectively, while the Lucknow group has faster overall response times in SET 2 with 1203s compared to 1557s for the Preston group. Another similarity was the fact that the error rate, that is, the number of times that the matcher identified the wrong target picture, was well below 10% in both groups and in both sets. Therefore, differences in error rate are not useful in determining change over time in the task, and it is more appropriate to consider the response times, which do vary considerably.

While an overall reduction in the time taken is of course expected, a specific interest lies in differentiating between the individual cross-signers and considering how much each person's response time differs between SET1 and SET2. This is shown in Table 4 as the "time saved" by each individual, in the role of director (the person giving the signed description), in the role of matcher (the person choosing the target picture), and for both roles combined.

Table 4. Time saved per participant.

| Time saved | as director | as matcher | in both roles |
|---|---|---|---|
| Preston group | | | |
| CP | 270 | 147 | 417 |
| HM | 332 | 368 | 700 |
| MS | 195 | 140 | 335 |
| MI | 29 | 171 | 200 |
| Lucknow group | | | |
| AS | 252 | 494 | 746 |
| BF | 234 | 282 | 516 |
| NG | 478 | 227 | 705 |
| AM | 263 | 224 | 487 |

A detailed investigation of the individual response time figures is pursued in Zeshan (2019), so this issue will not be discussed exhaustively here. The participant standing out from amongst the Preston group is HM, the signer from Japan. Both as sender and as receiver, the time saved is greatest where HM has been involved in the task, and the total time saved at 700s is the largest by far among the four signers. Moreover, Table 3 shows that the pairwise response times in Set 1 are larger where HM is involved as a participant. Subsequently, this difference disappears in Set 2, where HM is intermediate between the other signers. These figures point to HM having taken a larger step towards establishing effective communication compared with the other signers in this group. Zeshan (2019) argues that several factors come into play to explain this effect, including the greater typological divergence of Japanese Sign Language relative to the other sign languages, and its lower level of internal dialectal diversity. These results are in line with some characteristics of HM's signing discussed in section 3.4.

For the Lucknow group, a reasonable prediction would have been for the Indian signer (NG) and the Nepali signer (AS) to be in a position of advantage, due to the geographic proximity of their sign languages and some similarities (cf. Section 3.4), and the fact that Indian Sign Language was the surrounding language for the group. However, the actual pattern does not support this hypothesis, as the "time saved" for these two individuals is in fact greater than for the other participants. Moreover, among all pairs of signers the total pairwise response times are in fact highest for the NG-AS pair in Set 1 at 541s (see Table 3). These few examples illustrate that there is a complex interplay of factors that may account for differences in response times. This conclusion is supported by the findings reported in Zeshan (2019), where the analysis highlights a number of factors and discusses their positive (facilitating), negative (inhibiting) or neutral effect on the likely communicative success of a given pair of signers among the same groups of participants as those discussed here. From this research, it seems that "exposure to the other group members, typological distance, the family constellation in terms of growing up with deaf family members, and the dialectal diversity [in the home area] all may have influenced the level of communicative ease among participants" (Zeshan 2019). By contrast, shared semiotic resources based on literacy, including writing and fingerspelling, seemed to have no effect. Zeshan (2019) also does not find a facilitating effect for signers who are from the country where the research is taking place, i.e. CP in SET1 and NG in SET2 (forthcoming discussion of this point in Section 3.4.3).

## 3.3 Sign types

We now turn to a more detailed investigation of the signed output produced by the participants in round 1 and 2 of the elicitation task. In order to understand how the output changes over time, the first aspect considered has been the occurrence of various types of signs, according to the categorisation and coding set out in section 2.2. Table 5 shows the overall occurrence of signs in all types that were used to express animate referents in the task. Descriptions produced in response to pictures showing inanimate referents are not included in the analysis.

Table 5. All signs used in round 1 and round 2 of the elicitation game

|  | SASS | CL:handle | CL:limb | CL:whole | LEX | CA | SPACE | TOTAL |
|---|---|---|---|---|---|---|---|---|
| first game | 359 | 62 | 126 | 43 | 204 | 134 | 36 | 964 |
| second game | 198 | 29 | 92 | 32 | 197 | 164 | 32 | 744 |

At first sight, it is not easy to draw firm conclusions from these data. Unsurprisingly, in total fewer signs are used in the second round of the experiment. Beyond this, other generalisations are not straightforward because some sign types have nearly the same frequencies in round 1 and 2 (LEX, SPACE) and one type (CA) even occurs more frequently in round 2.

Upon reflection, it becomes clear that in the many cases the preferential occurrence of sign types is cued by what is depicted on the target pictures. For example, handling classifiers will only occur if they logically fit the target picture. If only faces are shown, a handling classifier or a CA construction would be unexpected. This consideration is supported by the fact that there are large degrees of variation between signers and sign pairs with respect to the frequency of sign types CA, CL:limb, CL:handle and CL:whole in the data.

Therefore, frequency data on the occurrence of the CA and the classifier sign types is not a useful parameter of comparison. There is, however, one sign type that is equally applicable irrespective of what is displayed on the target picture. This is the SASS category. Size and shape specifiers (SASS) are compatible with virtually any target picture because all pictures have visual content for which size and shape can be described. We therefore look more closely now at the occurrence of the SASS category across the different signers and experiment rounds.

Table 6 shows all signs categorised as belonging to the SASS sign type, comparing their frequency in the first and the second round of the elicitation game, for the participants from both the Lucknow and the Preston group. As a measure of overall tighter compression of the signed message over time between first and second round, we would expect the absolute number of SASS signs to reduce. In addition, we would also expect the proportion of SASS signs relative to all signs to decrease. This is because SASS signs are highly iconic and thus can be expected to have a high level of intelligibility across different sign languages. In the absence of a conventional shared vocabulary at the beginning of contact between participants, we may therefore expect a higher number of SASS signs, particularly in the form of longer sequences of SASS signs, as the referents on the pictures are described in terms of their visual-spatial properties rather than being labelled with conventional lexical items. The initial rendition of the description of the target picture 'donkey' in section 3.1 is a typical example.

The data confirm this hypothesis. Table 6 shows a reduction of all SASS signs from 163 to 99 in the Preston group, and from 196 to 99 in the Lucknow group. Moreover, the overall proportion of SASS signs also decreases in both groups so that the average percentage of SASS signs in the second round of games drops to a fourth of all signs for both groups (26.51 and 25.02% respectively) Moreover, within the Preston group, these reductions in SASS signs apply individually to all six dyads. Within the Lucknow data, the percentage of SASS signs is lower in round 1 than in round 2 for two of the participant pairs. In both cases, this involves the Indian signer NG, whose pattern diverges somewhat from the other signers in that there are many instances of repetition, which is why the total number of round 1 signs is higher in the dyads involving NG. As Byun et al (this volume) point out, repeating the same signs is a way of "buying time" in order to come up with alternative expressions, and this strategy is used by NG more than by the other signers. Many of these repetitions involve LEX signs, resulting in a lower percentage of SASS signs. If these repetitions are eliminated, the proportion of SASS signs is in line with the other dyads, including the decrease of SASS signs between round 1 and round 2.

**Table 6.** First and second round frequencies for SASS type signs

**PRESTON GROUP**

|  | 1st game | | | 2nd game | | |
|---|---|---|---|---|---|---|
|  | SASS | all signs | SASS % | SASS | all signs | SASS % |
| CP-HM | 21 | 55 | 38.18 | 8 | 54 | 14.81 |
| CP-MI | 20 | 42 | 47.62 | 10 | 51 | 19.61 |
| CP-MS | 22 | 49 | 44.90 | 15 | 51 | 29.41 |
| MI-HM | 28 | 74 | 37.84 | 39 | 108 | 36.11 |
| MS-HM | 42 | 65 | 64.62 | 14 | 43 | 32.56 |
| MS-MI | 30 | 57 | 52.63 | 13 | 49 | 26.53 |
|  | 163 | 342 |  | 99 | 356 |  |
| SASS average |  |  | 47.63 |  |  | 26.51 |

**LUCKNOW GROUP**

|  | 1st game | | | 2nd game | | |
|---|---|---|---|---|---|---|
|  | SASS | all signs | SASS % | SASS | all signs | SASS % |
| NG-AM | 25 | 124 | 20.16 | 27 | 94 | 28.72 |
| NG-BF | 47 | 142 | 33.10 | 22 | 89 | 24.72 |
| NG-AS | 30 | 118 | 25.42 | 16 | 56 | 28.57 |
| BF-AM | 21 | 87 | 24.14 | 7 | 33 | 21.21 |
| BF-AS | 24 | 51 | 47.06 | 13 | 52 | 25.00 |
| AS-AM | 49 | 100 | 49.00 | 14 | 64 | 21.88 |
|  | 196 | 622 |  | 99 | 388 |  |
| SASS average |  |  | 33.15 |  |  | 25.02 |

Another category to look at in more detail in our research has been the LEX sign type. Here the question is not simply a matter of frequency because there are different, competing motivations for using LEX signs. On the one hand, we may expect participants to use a substantial number of LEX signs from their own sign language because initially, these would be the only conventional signs available to them, and at times they may struggle to come up with more iconic options (e.g. SASS or CA) as an alternative to their conventional vocabulary. Use of LEX signs stemming from this motivation may be expected to decrease over time. However, newly acquired LEX signs that have been adopted as the group's "standard" may increase. The dynamics of this "feature pool", that is, the pool of signifiers that becomes the shared standard over time, is discussed in detail in section 3.4. The feature pool tends to start out as a larger, less constrained pool of options and become more constrained and smaller over time.

## 3.4 Feature pool of variants

In this subsection, we look at the various strategies and linguistic outcomes that the signers in the elicitation games devise to get their intended concept across to the other signers, who do not share the same sign language. Here, we restrict our analyses to the expression of a sub-set of animate referents, namely the various options to sign FEMALE, MALE, and PERSON(S).[6] It is interesting to see which signs are used in the first and second rounds of the game and to examine the selection and propagation of signs in the second round, which would hint at an incipient process of conventionalisation and stabilisation of the shared cross-signing lexicon.

Following linguists like Mufwene (2001, 2002) and Aboh and Anselmo (2007), we refer to the concept of the "feature pool" for describing the linguistic situation created in the various communication situations (conversations, games, post-hoc interviews) over the 3-4 weeks in both groups. "Feature pool" is a notion which alludes to "gene pool" in the sense that in a given multilingual speaker/signer community, linguistic variants are in competition with each other and subjected to a process of selection until they finally become part of the grammars

---

6 In many sign languages, the signs for 'woman' and 'female', and for 'man' and 'male' are the same, so FEMALE and MALE also encompass the meanings of 'woman' and 'man'. Moreover, there is no difference between singular and plural forms in these signs, whereas some of the signs used for PERSON have separate plural forms glossed PERSONS.

of individuals and whole speaker/signer communities.[7] Relevant factors which may influence the selection of a given feature (be it a phoneme, lexeme or construction) are numerous, such as frequency of usage, salience of the relevant forms, their transparency and iconicity, the typological disparity between the languages in contact, and the social status of speakers/signers in the group and differences in the demography.

In what follows, we lay out and evaluate the various processes of competition and selection traceable in the data from the elicitation games of the two groups in Preston and Lucknow. One of the most fascinating aspects of the data here lies in the possibility to observe the different communication strategies in *statu nascendi*, which is much less possible, if at all, in spoken languages. In the one-to-one settings of the language games, multiple levels of cross-signing communication are targeted. In the first games, we mainly deal with processes at the individual level. On the other hand, the second games took place after several weeks of intense contact between the four participants in each group, and with surrounding sign language users in Preston and Lucknow, so these data reflect the more interpersonal processes of mutual negotiation and initial conventionalisation of lexemes.

### 3.4.1 Occurrence of LEX signs

The present analysis focuses on several signs from the category of lexical signs (LEX as defined in Section 2.2) that refer to humans, namely those glossed MALE, FEMALE and PERSON(S). Unlike many of the visual-spatial highly iconic signs, these LEX signs can be assigned to a specific sign language, which is important for the argumentation here. The expressions of FEMALE, MALE and PERSON(S) were coded in the following way: For every token of a target LEX sign that was used in the games, we indicated the corresponding sign language, abbreviated ISL (India), NSL (Nepal), BIS (Indonesia), LIU (Jordan), BSL (UK), JSL (Japan) and IS (International Sign). We also distinguished the agent from the recipient of the signing, for instance "HM with CP" refers to the data in which HM was acting as the director while signing with CP as the matcher. Tables 7 and 8 show the occurrence of LEX signs for FEMALE and MALE, organised by the provenance of the signs from the various contributing sign languages, from the Lucknow games (both first

---

7 "An important caveat about this analogy is that the transmission of linguistic features is typically with modification, unlike in biology, where the default condition of the transmission of individual genes is perfect replication and innovations arise from how they are recombined into genotypes." (Mufwene 2002: 46)

and second round), and the Preston games (second round only). Additionally, we differentiated whether a given LEX was a native or non-native sign for the user in question, and these figures are discussed in Section 3.4.3.

In the first game round of the Preston group we find only one token of MALE and four tokens of FEMALE expressed using a LEX sign, so only the data from the second round of games are included in Table 7. In the Lucknow data, the LEX signs for both MALE and FEMALE are much more evenly distributed over the first and second games. Over the entire data, PERSON(S) did not occur often enough to warrant a numerical analysis, though examples are mentioned in the qualitative discussion further below.

There may be several reasons for this uneven usage. In principle, signers in the first round might be expected to use fewer LEX signs and more CA, CL and SASS signs, as the latter are highly iconic and therefore useful for conveying meaning across different sign languages. Therefore, the Preston group's strategy is not unexpected,[8] while the Lucknow signers seem to have followed a different strategy that included LEX signs from the beginning. Also, the few references to PERSON(S) are even scarcer in the second round of games for both groups. This may be due to specifying individuals as male or female, which leads to a decrease of the more generic PERSON(S) signs.

---

[8] The lack of LEX signs in these data is not due to a lack of pictures with people as referents, as there were a total of 36 target pictures showing people in the first round of the game.

Table 7. Results from the Lucknow games[9]

| LUCKNOW | First round MALE | | | | Second round MALE | | | |
|---|---|---|---|---|---|---|---|---|
| | IS | ISL/NSL | LIU | BIS | IS | ISL/NSL | LIU | BIS |
| NG with AS | | 3 | | | | | | |
| NG with AM | | | | | | 5 | | |
| NG with BF | | 12 | 1 | | | 2 | | |
| AS with NG | | 3 | | | | 2 | | |
| AS with AM | | 2 | | 1 | | 3 | | |
| AS with BF | | | | | | | | |
| AM with NG | | 2 | | | | 2 | | |
| AM with AS | | | 1 | | | 2 | | |
| AM with BF | | | | | | | | |
| BF with NG | | | | | | | | |
| BF with AS | | | 2 | | | | | |
| BF with AM | | 1 | 3 | | | | | |
| ALL | | 23 | 6 | 2 | | 16 | | |
| | FEMALE | | | | FEMALE | | | |
| NG with AS | | 9 | | | | 3 | | |
| NG with AM | | 5 | | | | 3 | | |
| NG with BF | | 11 | 1 | | | 2 | | |
| AS with NG | | 4 | | | | 3 | | |
| AS with AM | 2 | 4 | | | | 5 | | |
| AS with BF | | 1 | | | | 3 | | |
| AM with NG | 1 | 7 | | 2 | | 2 | | |
| AM with AS | | 1 | | | | 5 | | |
| AM with BF | | | 2 | 4 | | 1 | | |
| BF with NG | | 2 | 11 | | | 5 | | |
| BF with AS | | | 1 | | | 3 | | |
| BF with AM | | | 4 | 1 | | 1 | | |
| ALL | 3 | 48 | 19 | 3 | | 36 | | |

9 A slash is used where the same sign occurs in two different sign languages, e.g. ISL/NSL for signs occurring both in India and in Nepal.

Table 8. Results from the Preston games (second round only)

| PRESTON | Second round FEMALE | | | | | Second round MALE | | | | |
|---|---|---|---|---|---|---|---|---|---|---|
| | IS | BSL | LIU | BIS/IS | JSL | IS | BSL | LIU | BIS | JSL |
| MH with CP | | 4 | | 1 | | | | | | |
| MH with MI | | | | 1 | | | | | | |
| MH with MS | | 2 | | 2 | | | | | | |
| CP with MH | | 6 | | | | | 4 | | | |
| CP with MI | | 3 | | | | 1 | 3 | | | |
| CP with MS | | 1 | | | | 1 | | | | |
| MI with MH | | | | 2 | | 2 | | | 1 | |
| MI with CP | | | | | | 1 | | | | |
| MI with MS | | | | 2 | | | | | 1 | |
| MS with MH | | | | | | | | | | |
| MS with CP | | | | 2 | | | 1 | | | |
| MS with MI | 2 | | | 2 | | | 1 | | | |
| ALL | 2 | 16 | | 12 | | 5 | 9 | | 2 | |

### 3.4.2 Strategies and innovations

Let us now look at the different strategies that the signers used in the first elicitation game to communicate across sign languages. A major strategy is to first **try one's own native sign**. HM, for instance, uses the JSL sign FEMALE three times in the first game, whereas in the second he does not produce this form, but instead shifts to BSL (six times) and IS/BIS (four times). The issue of using native vs non-native signs is discussed in more detail below. One strategy to circumnavigate the problem of directly signing MALE or FEMALE is to refer **metonymically** to properties which are iconically linked to a referent, e.g. a moustache for 'man'. One example is when CP signs MOUSTACHE as a SASS when conversing with HM (1st, 0:47). Another way to solve the communication task is to refer to the more **generic sign PERSON** while targeting the gender-specific referent. When signing with MI in the first game (1st, 2:47) CP uses PERSON to refer to 'man', a strategy which is also well-attested in spoken jargons (Mühlhäusler 1997: 137).

Furthermore, we can detect processes that affect the phonological shape of the targeted non-native signs. Attempts to articulate non-native signs sometimes lead to **mispronunciations**: AM, for instance, produces the wrong movement for ISL FEMALE (1st, 6:16). Often the signer shows **hesitation phenomena** while targeting non-native forms. This is seen in an example from BF, who hesitates before signing non-native ISL FEMALE (India-Jordan, 2nd, 0:21). Hesitation phenomena and slower rates of delivery in general are again known to be evident in spoken jargons (Mühlhäusler 1997: 142). A slower rate of signing is not only a signer-driven strategy to better monitor the production of non-native signs, but at the same time it also enables the receiver to decode the message more effectively. This can also be seen in the example text in Section 3.1, for example the delivery of the sign for 'small size' in the initial round 1 rendition.

This brings us to another major strategy which unfolds in multilingual contact situations, which is the reinforcement of information in order to reach **extra-clarity** with respect to the targeted meaning (see Haspelmath and Michaelis 2017 on extra-clarity in contact languages). Extra-clarity can be expressed by various means, e.g. signing segments with reduced speed, or reinforcing the information via the **increase of articulation effort**, as shown in the first dyad between AM and BF (1st, 1:16), where AM uses two hands instead of one to sign MALE in his L1 (example 1).

(1) AM:  MALE (2 handed)    point-to-own-shirt    NO
         LEX(BIS)            SPACE                 LEX
         'The man is not wearing any shirt.'

Another means of extra-clarity consists of **reiterative code-switching**, where signers combine lexical signs from more than one language to refer to a human referent. Most often signers start with their native sign and then code-switch to either IS, the L1 of the signing partner, or the surrounding sign language (BSL in Preston, ISL in Lucknow). One example is when AS (Nepal-Indonesia, 1st, 5:01) combines her native NSL sign FEMALE and the IS sign FEMALE (example 2). She even code-switches repeatedly using four signs: NSL to IS to NSL to IS.

(2) AS:  SAME FEMALE FEMALE FEMALE FEMALE LONG-STRAIGHT-HAIR
         LEX   LEX(NSL) LEX(IS) LEX(NSL) LEX(IS) SASS
         COLLAR LONG-HAIR
         SASS     SASS
         'The woman has long straight hair up to her collar.'

Interestingly, it is HM in the Preston group who most often shows reiterative code-switching. This may be because, as the signer whose sign language is the most typologically distinct, HM may have felt a need for extra-clarity. This he attempted to achieve by combining at least two signs referring to the same referent (MALE, FEMALE) to get his intended meaning across. Overall, instances of reiterative code-switching are not very widespread in our data. We coded nine occurrences from Preston (HM four times, MS three times, CP once, and MI once), all stemming from the first game, whereas there are five from Lucknow (AM twice, AS twice, and NG once), all produced in the second game.

A further strategy to express extra-clarity is the reinforcement of MALE/FEMALE through the **additional use of the sign PERSON** in order to emphasise the gender, with both orders (MALE/FEMALE + PERSON, and PERSON + MALE/FEMALE) being possible. At the very beginning of the first game between HM and CP, HM produces the sequence PERSON(IS) FEMALE(JSL) (1st, 0:01) to clearly indicate the female referent (example 3).

(3) HM:  PERSON   FEMALE   PERSON FEMALE
         LEX(IS)  LEX(JSL) LEX(IS) LEX(JSL)
         'There is a woman.'

Some of these reinforcements via PERSON or the reiterative code-switching sequences discussed above are fused into **compounds** which are produced under one single integrated signing contour. Example (4) comes from the first game between NG and AS (1st, 1:55), where NG combines two native signs, MALE and PERSON, into one compound.

(4) NG: MALE      TALL  AMERICAN  MALE+PERSON          AMERICAN  FACE  SHOUT
        LEX(ISL)  GEST  LEX       LEX(ISL)+LEX(ISL)    LEX       SASS  CA
        'A tall American man is shouting.'

### 3.4.3 Selection of variants

The strategies described so far reflect innovations of signs by the individual signers to make themselves better understood in the demanding multilingual settings of the elicitation games. These are ad-hoc solutions typical of jargonisation situations (cf. Mühlhäusler 1997 for similar strategies in spoken jargons). All these innovations contribute to the feature pool of variants shared in each dyad and eventually among all the participants of a group. As many of the innovations (e.g. reiterative code-switching, new compounds, other reinforced signs) are very unstable, it is interesting to trace the processes of selection and propagation of certain signs from the feature pool (see Croft 2000 for the notions of innovation and propagation in language change processes). Here, we look at the social dimension of the transmission of variants between each pair of signers and within the whole group. In order to do this, we first evaluated the figures in Tables 7 and 8 to see whether there has been any process of crystallisation of preferred variants between the first and the second games in each group. Our expectation was such that the surrounding sign language would have a strong influence on the selection of the variants from the feature pool. Indeed, this is the picture that we observe in the Lucknow group, that is, in the second round, only the ISL/NSL signs are used. The situation for the Preston group is more mixed, as there are two preferred variants for FEMALE and MALE, one being the BSL sign and the other an IS sign (which in the case of FEMALE is identical to the BIS sign). This pattern is still consistent with the claim that in both groups, the surrounding sign language exerts a pressure on the choice of the preferred variants. As already mentioned, a first indicator of this selection and stabilisation process is that the signers who travelled to the host country shift to using non-native signs in the second game, whereas those from the host country maintain their L1 signs. This pattern of native and non-native signs (relative to each signer) is shown in Table 9, with the top half of the table showing the signers whose L1 signs become the preferred variants (NG and AS for the India-based group and CP for the UK-based group), and the other signers shown in the bottom half of the table. The non-native signs used by HM, MI and MS include both BSL and IS signs. The two non-native signs used by CP in round 2 are due to using the IS sign for MALE, and four of the native signs used by MI in round 2 are due to the IS/BIS sign FEMALE that is one of the preferred variants in the Preston group.

Table 9. Use of native and non-native signs in the Lucknow and Preston games

| LUCKNOW/PRESTON | | | | | MALE/FEMALE |
|---|---|---|---|---|---|
| | Signers with host country variants as L1 | | | | |
| | First round | | Second round | | |
| | n-nat | nat | n-nat | nat | |
| NG | 2 | 40 | | 15 | |
| AS | 1 | 14 | | 16 | |
| CP | | 1 | 2 | 17 | |
| Total | 3 | 55 | 2 | 48 | |
| | Signers with other variants as L1 | | | | |
| | First round | | Second round | | |
| | n-nat | nat | n-nat | nat | |
| AM | 12 | 7 | 12 | | |
| BF | 4 | 21 | 9 | | |
| HM | | 3 | 10 | | |
| MI | | | 3 | 6 | |
| MS | | | 8 | | |
| ALL | 16 | 31 | 42 | 6 | |

The clearest example for selection of the sign from the surrounding sign language can be seen in the expression of FEMALE by the Lucknow group. The sign for FEMALE in ISL and NSL has the same form, meaning that in the feature pool of the Lucknow group, this sign already had a high frequency right from the beginning of the first contact. In the first game, the two non-ISL/NSL participants, AM and BF, produce native and non-native signs for FEMALE. However, in the second game, they shift to the majority variant of the ISL/NSL sign. In the Preston group, the Japanese signer HM only produces native JSL signs for FEMALE in the first game but shifts to producing only non-native signs in the second game.

Interestingly, the choice of preferred variant does not seem to be driven primarily by the extent of the sign's iconicity or transparency (in the sense of a non-arbitrary relationship between the sign's form and its meaning). For instance, the two preferred variants for FEMALE in the Preston group include the sign from BIS/IS, which makes reference to an earring and could be argued to be an instance of metonymy, but the BSL sign (an index finger brushing the cheek twice) does not have any apparent form-meaning correspondence and appears arbitrary. Yet both signs become preferred variants. Moreover, although the ISL/NSL sign FEMALE also involves metonymy (referring to the nose ring worn by women), it is transparent only in the region and would not have been transparent to signers from the other countries.

Another noteworthy consideration is that the preference for variants from the surrounding sign language does not seem to correlate with communicative ease for the participants from these countries in any straightforward way. Zeshan (2019) argues that there is no "home advantage" for the British signer in SET1 and the Indian signer in SET2 with respect to their response times in the director-matcher task. This is despite the fact that their native variants come to be preferred by the group as a whole. Therefore, the choice of variants from the feature pool is a separate issue from the degree of communicative success, which, as mentioned above, is subject to a number of factors.

### 3.4.4 Propagation of variants

It is informative to trace some particular instances of selection and propagation processes of variants from the overall feature pool. One typical process is what Zeshan (2015) calls "IAP sequence". This sequence consists of three sub-processes: **I**ntroduce, **A**ccommodate, and **P**ersist. In the prototypical sequence, a sign for a new concept is introduced by one of the signers, and copied by the other signer, thereby accommodating the choice of lexical item. Once the sign has been established as part of the "shared space" between the interlocutors, it then persists in the further discourse. The prototypical sequence is subject to some variation, e.g. repeated introduction of defferent options where a concept is difficult to convey, or partial accommodation where the interlocutor only accommodates some aspects of an introduced sign. Zeshan (2015) does not specify the source of the signs occurring in an IAP sequence, in terms of where a sign that is introduced comes from – the signer's own sign language, another sign language, or an invented form are some possibilities. However, in our data there is a tendency for a particular type of sequence, whereby one signer introduces their native sign and the interlocutor, with a different native sign language, accommodates to this signer's sign by immediately picking it up and using it as their non-native sign. Once this non-native sign has been picked up, it is likely to persist in the subsequent discourse. Example (5) is from the first game between NG and AM. NG uses his native sign for FEMALE and immediately after this AM reproduces this sign, i.e. he code-switches to a non-native sign (1st, 1:54, see also 1st, 3:43).

(5) NG: FEMALE USE-WALKING-CANE FEMALE USE-WALKING-CANE
         LEX(ISL) CL:handle          LEX(ISL) CL:handle
         'An old woman...'
    AM:  FEMALE USE-WALKING-CANE
         LEX(ISL) CL:handle
         'An old woman...'

However, the process of maintaining a non-native LEX sign is not straightforward. For instance, throughout the succession of picture-matching tasks in the first round of the game, BF initially produces his native LIU sign for FEMALE (1st, 0:10 ff.). Then NG introduces the ISL sign for FEMALE (1st, 2:02). In the direct reply to NG, BF continues to produce his own native LIU sign, but then accommodates to the ISL sign (1st, 2:25). In the remainder of the game, BF switches back to his native LIU sign, but after a second introduction of the ISL sign for FEMALE by NG (1st, 4:28), BF reproduces the non-native ISL sign. Conversely, NG also code-switches to LIU after producing his native sign, mispronouncing the LIU sign for FEMALE (1st, 4:28). The sequence is illustrated in (6).

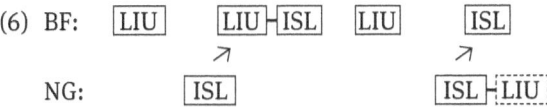

(6) BF: [LIU]  [LIU]-[ISL]  [LIU]     [ISL]
              ↗                    ↗
    NG:       [ISL]                [ISL]-[LIU]

Comparing AM and BF's references to 'woman' in the first and second Lucknow games, we see differences, but also similarities. In the first game, AM stands out in using nearly twice as many non-native signs as native ones (11 vs 6). Most non-native occurrences are articulations of the ISL/NSL sign for FEMALE (8 out of 11 non-native signs), indicating a shift away from the L1 even at this early stage. BF, on the other hand, produces over three times more native signs for FEMALE than non-native ones in the first game (11 vs 3), which corresponds to the more widespread pattern of initial sign production for both groups. However, in the second game, both signers behave identically in that they exclusively produce the non-native ISL/NSL sign for FEMALE. Instances of IAP processes must have been turning points toward the production of more non-native (ISL/NSL) signs and fewer native signs.

Given the greater impact of iconicity in sign languages compared to spoken languages, one may expect that in multilingual cross-signing settings it is the more iconic signs that are selected from the feature pool. However, our data discussed here seem to contradict such a simplistic hypothesis. In fact, it is the overall high usage frequency and dominating social role of the surrounding sign language that appear to emerge as the two overarching factors in the selective processes in cross-signing situations, not the degree of iconicity of the competing signs. These findings seem to fit with Croft's position (2000: 178) that social factors determine the successful propagation of competing variants in language change processes, not functional factors like iconicity or transparency, which operate only at the level of innovation by each individual signer/speaker.

# 4 Conclusions

As there are few precedents for the kind of research reported on in this chapter, it is worth summarising which of the research team's initial hypotheses have been borne out by the data and which predictions could not be supported by data analysis.

Firstly, the team hypothesised that the data would show a general improvement in communication between the first and the second rounds of the elicitation game, in an overall quantitative sense, with participants taking less time to complete the task in the second round. This was borne out by the data in Section 3.2. However, another reasonable expectation, namely that the matchers would make fewer mistakes in the second round in identifying the target picture, was not borne out by the data.

We further expected that there would be a decrease in iconicity over time in the sense of an "iconicity cline", with the SASS, CA, CL:handle and CL:limb signs being more iconic (in the sense of a non-arbitrary correspondence between form and meaning) than whole entity classifiers, followed by the LEX signs which include entirely non-iconic signs, as in the Indian sign GREEN. According to the "iconicity cline" hypothesis, use of sign types higher on the iconicity cline would decrease and use of more arbitrary signs would increase over time. However, the results in Section 3.3 showed that this was not the case when considering all sign types together. This may be partly due to some of the types such as CA and handling classifiers, being largely dependent on what is actually shown on the target picture. However, we argued that SASS signs are universally applicable to almost any picture, and there is a decline in these signs between the first and second meetings in Lucknow, both in absolute numbers and with respect to percentages.

With respect to LEX signs, we discussed potentially divergent tendencies for their frequency or occurrence, in terms of preferring native LEX signs because of a lack of adaptability, or avoiding LEX signs initially in favour of visual-spatial sign categories. Section 3.4 demonstrated that this is related to another consideration, namely that the choice of signs from the initial feature pool becomes constrained over time, with a marked influence of the surrounding sign language as a lexifier language. Signers show considerable readiness to adopt signs other than their own, and there is an overall reduction of variation to refer to the same referent after 3-4 weeks of contact. Examples of signs that are used in the first round of games and then discarded include FEMALE in JSL, two different variants for PERSON in LIU, and another variant for PERSON in ISL.

As explained in Section 1, in spoken language jargons, the closest equivalent to cross-signing, we also find a pattern of initial lexical variability with items from several L1s followed later by a prevailing lexifier language (Mühlhäusler 1997). The present research suggests that in cross-signing this later stage may be reached after 3-4 weeks of exposure of signers to each other. This is a significant result, given that for spoken language jargons, there is no information about the time it takes for the lexifier language to prevail over other variants. The cross-signing research has made it possible to track this development and specify a time-line because the unique research set-up has enabled us to observe the jargonisation process right from the beginning. Such research is not available for speakers of jargons.

At the level of morphology, we have observed various two-sign combinations. This includes both cases where the two-sign combination would qualify fully as a compound under the criteria posited by Johnson and Liddell (1986), and two-sign combinations that do not yet fully meet all these criteria. Therefore, such data are interesting in terms of observing the gradual creation of compounds in real-time. An example of a fully qualifying compound is FEMALE+FEMALE used by CP, which is a combination of a BSL and an international sign. An example of incipient compounding is RIDING+SMALL-SIZE for referring to the donkey in the second round of the games (detailed in section 3.1)

The gradual morphological change from separate signs to compounds is akin to the gradual grammaticalisation of classifier constructions posited in Zeshan (2003), where it is argued that ambiguous intermediate stages are to be expected. Moreover, reiterative code-switching, i.e. occurrence of two signs with the same meaning from different sign languages immediately after one another (see Quinto-Pozos and Adam 2013), is observed in the data. For example BF first using a Jordanian sign PERSON immediately followed by the international sign PERSON. Interestingly, reiterative code-switching can be a source of compounding, as in FEMALE+FEMALE used by CP.

Reiterative code-switching is also characteristic of conversations among bilingual groups, for both signed and spoken languages. However, for sign-speaking, this seems to be a strategy for increasing the chance that the message will be understood, whilst among bilingual groups, the function would be more as a marker of bilingual identity, as everyone in the group already knows both sign languages. Zeshan and Panda (this volume) describe reiterative code-switching among bilingual signers in a group of deaf students from Burundi who have acquired Indian Sign Language.

Interestingly, there is little evidence that iconic signs are generally preferred in the process of selecting variants from the feature pool, as argued in detail in section 3.4. Rather, we see considerable influence from the surrounding sign languages. This is in line with the findings of Byun et al. (forthcoming), who track the development of colour terms in a different experiment with the same signers in the Lucknow group. Here the data show that the non-arbitrary relationship between a sign and its meaning is not one of the main factors determining which signs are retained and which are discarded for communication over time.

Finally, one of the most interesting considerations from this study is in terms of comparisons between signed and spoken jargons. Our study has allowed an in-vitro observation of the formation of an incipient jargon right from the beginning. An equivalent study has not been done for spoken languages, and in fact, it is unlikely to be viable because by the time a spoken language jargon is identified, it necessarily has already undergone some development. The fact that we can study the development of cross-signing ab initio also has to do with the deaf signers' ability to communicate across language boundaries with remarkable success (cf. the arguments on meta-linguistic processes in cross-signing in Zeshan 2015). Moreover, in cross-signing we can observe a very fast process of conventionalisation, which we think proceeds much more rapidly than what would typically be found in spoken jargons. For instance, the data from India show that by the second round of the elicitation games, the ISL/NSL signs for MALE and FEMALE are used by the entire group, to the exclusion of other variants. Similarly, the research on colour terms in Byun et al. (forthcoming) shows a radical reduction in the size of the pool of variants over a three-week period.

Another intriguing difference between cross-signing and spoken language jargons is related to linguistic innovation. In spoken jargons, speakers re-combine already existing language material from the different contributing languages, and we see the same processes in our data, for example in the formation of compounds, and in reiterative code-switching. However, cross-signers also produce genuine innovations in the sense of inventing entirely new signs that are not part of any of the contributing sign languages. This does not actually occur in the data analysed here, perhaps because the target domain was not conducive to such innovations. But Zeshan (2015) provides examples of such newly invented signs from the domain of numerals. In cross-signing, the evidence so far suggests that these innovations are always iconically motivated. If this is the case, it also explains why sign languages are at an advantage compared to spoken languages in the creation of such new lexical material independently of the available contributing languages.

## Acknowledgements

The research leading to these results has received funding from the European Research Council under the European Union's Seventh Framework Programme; we are grateful for funding of this research under the project "Multilingual behaviours in sign language users" (MULTISIGN), Grant Agreement number 263647. In addition, Susanne Maria Michaelis gratefully acknowledges the support of the European Research Council (ERC Advanced Grant 670985, Grammatical Universals). We are very grateful to the participants in the study: Claire Perdomo, Hayashi Masaomi, Muhammad Isnaini, Mohammed Salha, Anita Sharma, Navneet Gupta, Baha Freihat, and Adam Mailk. Other members of the iSLanDS Institute who were members of the wider research team are also gratefully acknowledged: Paul Scott, Nicholas Palfreyman, Keiko Sagara, and Anju Jain, whose dedication as facilitators for the international participants throughout the project duration supported the research process in many crucial ways; Sibaji Panda who trained and coordinated a substantial team of student annotators in India; and Sam Lutalo-Kiingi who was responsible for important parts of data collection and participant briefings.

## References

Aboh, Enoch O. & Umberto Ansaldo. 2007. The role of typology in language creation: A descriptive take. In Umberto Ansaldo, Stephen Matthews & Lisa Lim (eds.), *Deconstructing creole*, 39–66. Amsterdam: Benjamins.

Aikhenwald, Alexandra Y. 2014. Number and noun categorisation: A view from north-west Amazonia. In Anne Storch & Gerrit J. Dimmendaal (eds.), *Number – Constructions and semantics. Case studies from Africa, Amazonia, India and Oceania*, 33–56. Amsterdam: John Benjamins Publishing Company.

Allsop, Lorna, Bencie Woll & Jon Martin Brauti. 1995. International sign: The creation of an international deaf community and sign language. In Heleen Bos & Gertrude Schermer (eds.), *Sign Language Research 1994: Proceedings of the Fourth European Congress on Sign Language Research, Munich, September 1-3, 1994* (International Studies on Sign Language and Communication of the Deaf, 29), 171–188. Hamburg: Signum.

Baker, Philip & Magnus Huber. 2001. Atlantic, Pacific, and world-wide features in English-lexicon contact languages. *English World-Wide* 22(2). 157–208.

Bakker, Peter. 2003. Pidgin inflectional morphology and its implications for creole morphology. In Geert Booij & Jaap van Marle (eds*.), Yearbook of morphology 2002*, 3–33. Dordrecht: Kluwer.

Bakker, Peter. 2008. Pidgins versus creoles and pidgincreoles. In Silvia Kouwenberg & John V. Singler (eds.), *Handbook of pidgin and creole studies*, 130–157. Oxford: Wiley-Blackwell.

Baptista, Marlyse. 2005. New directions in pidgin and creole studies. *Annual Review of Anthropology* 34. 33–42.

Bickerton, Derek. 1981. *Roots of language*. Ann Arbor: Karoma Publishers
Bickerton, Derek. 1984. The language bioprogram hypothesis. *The Behavioral and Brain Sciences* 7. 173–188.
Bloomfield, L. 1933. *Language*. New York: Henry Holt.
Bolton, Kingsley. 2002. Chinese Englishes: From Canton jargon to global English. *World Englishes* 21(2). 181–199.
Botha, Rudolf. 2006. Pidgin languages as a putative window on language evolution. *Language & Communication* 26. 1–14.
Byun, Kang-Suk, Connie De Vos, Ulrike Zeshan, Anastasia Bradford & Stephen Levinson. 2017. First encounters: Repair sequences in cross-signing. *Topics in Cognitive Science (Special Issue on Miscommunication)* 10. 314–334.
Byun, Kang-Suk, Sean Roberts, Connie De Vos, Ulrike Zeshan & Stephen Levinson. Forthcoming. Content-, conformity- and frequency-biased selection in the evolution of expressive forms in cross-signing. *Journal of Language Evolution*.
Clark, Herbert & Deanna Wilkes-Gibbs. 1986. Referring as a collaborative process. *Cognition* 22(1). 1–39.
Croft, William. 2000. *Explaining language change: An evolutionary approach*. London: Longman.
Fill, Alwin & Peter Mühlhäusler. 2001. *The ecolinguistics reader*. London: Continuum.
Grant, Anthony P. 2013. Chinuk Wawa. In Susanne M. Michaelis, Philippe Maurer, Martin Haspelmath & Magnus Huber (eds.), *The survey of pidgin and creole languages. Vol. III: Contact languages based on languages from Africa, Asia, Australia, and the Americas*, 149–157. Oxford: Oxford University Press.
Haspelmath, Martin & Susanne Maria Michaelis. 2017. Analytic and synthetic: Typological change in varieties of European languages in Language Variation. In Isabelle Buchstaller & Beat Siebenhaar (eds.), *European Perspectives VI: Selected Papers from the 8th International Conference on Language Variation in Europe (ICLaVE 8), Leipzig 2015*, 3–22. Amsterdam: Benjamins.
Holm, John. 2000. *An introduction to pidgins and creoles*. Cambridge: Cambridge University Press.
Liddell, Scott K. & Robert E. Johnson. 1986. American Sign Language compound formation processes, lexicalization, and phonological remnants. *Natural Language & Linguistic Theory* 4(4). 445–513.
Johnston, Trevor & Adam Schembri. 2007. *Australian Sign Language: An introduction to sign language linguistics*. Cambridge: Cambridge University Press.
Klima, Edward S., & Ursula Bellugi. 1979. *The signs of language*. Cambridge, Massachusetts: Harvard University Press.
Knorr, Jacqueline. 2010. Contemporary creoleness, or: the world in pidginization? *Current Anthropology* 51(6). 731–759.
Liddell, Scott K. & Robert E. Johnson. 1986. ASL compound formation processes, lexicalization, and phonological remnants. *Natural Language and Linguistic Theory* 4(4). 445–513.
Locker-McKee, Rachel & Jemina Napier. 2002. Interpreting into International Sign Pidgin: An analysis. *Sign Language & Linguistics* 5(1). 27–54.
Moody, William. 1987. Berthier, Jean-Ferdinand (1803-1886). In John V. Van Cleve (ed.), *Gallaudet Encyclopedia of Deaf People and Deafness, vol. 1*, 141–143. New York: McGraw-Hill.
Mufwene, Salikoko S. 2001. *The ecology of language evolution*. Cambridge: Cambridge University Press.

Mufwene, Salikoko S. 2002. Competition and Selection in Language Evolution. *Selection* 3 (2002) 1, 45–56.
Mühlhäusler, Peter. 1997. *Pidgin and creole linguistics*. London: Battlebridge.
Nyst, Victoria. 2007. A descriptive analysis of Adamorobe Sign Language (Ghana). Utrecht: LOT.
Palfreyman, Nick. 2016. Colour terms in Indonesian sign language varieties: A preliminary study. In Ulrike Zeshan & Keiko Sagara (eds.), *Semantic fields in sign languages: Colour, kinship and quantification*, 269–300. Berlin: De Gruyter.
Parkvall, Mikael & Bakker, Peter. 2013. Pidgins. In Peter Bakker & Yaron Matras (eds.), *Contact Languages: A Comprehensive Guide*, 15-64. Berlin: De Gryuter Mouton.
Perniss, Pamela. 2007. Achieving spatial coherence in German Sign Language narratives: The use of classifiers and perspective. *Lingua* 117(7). 1315–1338.
Perniss, Pamela, Robin Thompson & Gabriella Vigliocco. 2010. Iconicity as a general property of language: evidence from spoken and signed languages. *Frontiers in Psychology* 1. 227.
Quinto-Pozos, David & Robert Adam. 2013. Sign language contact. In Robert Bayley, Richard Cameron & Ceil Lucas. (eds.), *The Oxford handbook of sociolinguistics*, 379–400. Oxford: Oxford University Press.
Reinecke, John E. 1937. *Marginal languages: A sociological study of creole languages and trade jargons*. Yale University PhD thesis.
Rosenstock, Rachel. 2004. *An investigation of International Sign: Analyzing structure and comprehension*. Washington, DC: Gallaudet University PhD thesis.
Rosenstock, Rachel. 2008. The role of iconicity in International Sign. *Sign Language Studies* 8(2). 131–158.
Schembri, Adam. 2003. Rethinking "classifiers" in signed languages. In Karen Emmorey (ed.), *Perspectives on classifier constructions in sign languages*, 3–34. Mahwah, New Jersey: Lawrence Erlbaum Associates.
Siegel, Jeff. 1982. Plantation Pidgin Fijian. *Oceanic Linguistics* 21. 1–72.
Supalla, Ted. 1986. The classifier system in American Sign Language. In Colette Craig (ed.), *Noun classes and categorization: Typological studies in language, Vol. 7*, 181–214. Amsterdam: Benjamins.
Supalla, Ted & Rebecca Webb. 1995. The grammar of International Sign: A new look at pidgin languages. In Karen Emmorey & Judy S. Reilly (eds.), *Language, gesture, and space*, 333–352. Hillsdale, New Jersey: Erlbaum.
Sutton-Spence, Rachel & Bencie Woll. 1999. *The linguistics of British Sign Language: An introduction*. Cambridge: Cambridge University Press.
Thomason, Sarah G. & Terrence Kaufman. 1988. *Language contact, creolization, and genetic linguistics*. Berkeley: University of California Press.
Webb, Rebecca & Ted Supalla. 1994. Negation in international sign. In Inger Ahlgren, Brita Bergmann & Mary Brennan (eds.), *Perspectives on sign language structure: Papers from the 5th International Symposium on Sign Language Research, Vol. 1, Salamanca, Spain, 25-30 May 1992*, 173–186. Durham: ISLA.
Winford, Donald. 2003. *An introduction to contact linguistics*. Oxford: Blackwell.
Woll, Bencie. 1990. International perspectives on sign language communication. *International Journal of Sign Linguistics* 1(2). 107–120.
Zeshan, Ulrike. 2003. "Classificatory" constructions in Indo-Pakistani Sign Language: Grammaticalization and lexicalization processes. In Karen Emmorey (ed.), *Perspectives on classifier constructions in sign languages*, 41–113. New Jersey/London: Lawrence Erlbaum Associates.

Zeshan, Ulrike. 2015. "Making meaning" - Communication between sign language users without a shared language. *Cognitive Linguistics* 26(2): 211–260.
Zeshan, Ulrike & Sibaji Panda. 2015. Two languages at hand: Code-switching in bilingual signers. *Sign Language & Linguistics* 18(1). 90–131.
Zeshan, Ulrike & Sibaji Panda. 2017. Sign-speaking: The structure of simultaneous bimodal utterances. *Applied Linguistics Review* 9(1). 1–34.
Zeshan, Ulrike. 2019. Task-response times, facilitating and inhibiting factors in cross-signing. *Applied Linguistics Review* Special Issue 10(1). 9–30.

# A minimalist perspective on code blending in TİD – Turkish bimodal bilingualism[1]

Selçuk İşsever, Bahtiyar Makaroğlu, İclâl Ergenç and Hasan Dikyuva

**Abstract:** This study investigates how code blending is produced in the context of TİD – Turkish bimodal bilingualism. We follow Donati and Branchini (2013) for the classification of code blending but propose a slight revision for the types of code blends attested in our database. As for the question of how bimodals can generate blended utterances, we scrutinise two types of models for their accuracy to account for this type of data: the 'interactive' model (Emmorey et al., 2008) and the 'minimalist' model (MacSwan, 1997, 2000, 2005; Lillo-Martin et al., 2010, 2012, 2014; Quadros et al., 2013). It is shown that, having the fewest assumptions possible, the minimalist model is conceptually more accurate as well as theoretically simpler than the interactive model. We further investigate the applicability of the minimalist model to actual examples found in our database and conclude that it is not only conceptually accurate but also technically capable of accounting for different types of code blending.

## 1 Introduction

Language users with simultaneous access to the resources of two languages have the ability to mix them when producing an utterance. This ability to engage in language mixing appears to be the main factor that draws a line between bilingual

---

[1] This research is a part of the project entitled "Multilingual Behaviours in Sign Language Users (Multisign)", which was supported by European Research Council (ERC), Seventh Framework Programme under grant agreement no 263647 awarded to Ulrike Zeshan and the University of Central Lancashire.
We would like to thank the reviewers and editors for their insightful comments and efforts in helping us improve the article. Of course, all shortcomings are our own.

https://doi.org/10.1515/9781501503528-005

and monolingual speakers. This difference between the two types of language user has led researchers to think about what is going on in a bilingual mind in terms of language production. For some researchers, the grammatical system of a bilingual speaker includes specific constraints with respect to code switching such as the Equivalence Constraint, Free Morpheme Constraint (Poplack, 1980, 1981), and Closed-Class Constraint (Joshi, 1985), all of which have been proposed to account for linguistic boundaries where code switching is possible. Works by Azuma (1991, 1993) and Myers-Scotton (1993), proponents of the Matrix Language Frame (MLF), can also be added to this list. Under MLF, one of the languages in the code switching context functions as the matrix language, whose role is to define the surface structure positions for content words and functional elements. The central idea shared by these proposals, then, is that the grammatical system of a bilingual is essentially different from that of a monolingual such that the former's language production process is controlled by specific grammatical constraints that pertain to bilingual grammar only.[2]

However, this line of research has been subject to criticism by scholars who defend the view that bilingual and monolingual grammars should include the same set of rules, and thus there should be no code-switching-specific constraints or the like operating exclusively in bilingual language production (Woolford, 1983; Mahootian, 1993; Belazi et al., 1994; MacSwan, 1997, 2000, 2005; Chan, 2003, 2008). In line with Chomsky's (1995) Minimalist Program, MacSwan (1997, 2000, 2005) developed a system where bilingual sentence production is accounted for on a par with monolingual production so that both are subject to the same rules and constraints of universal grammar. He points out that "[m]aking the simplest assumptions, we would posit that all grammatical relations and operations which are relevant to monolingual language are relevant to bilingual language, and only these" (MacSwan 2000:43), an idea which is also called the Null Theory (Mahootian, 1993; MacSwan, 1997, 2000, 2005; Chan, 2003, 2008).

Although a great deal of research has been done on bilingualism in the context of spoken languages, studies in sign language linguistics have shown that spoken and signed languages can be produced simultaneously as well, bringing about a different aspect of the phenomenon, which is generally termed *bimodal bilingualism*. However, due to the differences in modality in each type of language production, we also find divergences between the aspects of bilingualism in unimodal and bimodal contexts. In the case of spoken languages, i.e. the unimodal context, the user has to switch between languages because s/he

---

[2] We refer the interested reader to MacSwan (2000, 2005) for more detailed information about these constraints on bilingual grammar.

can use only one modality, the vocal tract. Therefore, in this type of bilingualism we only find code switching. However, bimodals may use both the vocal tract and the hands and other body parts, which allow them to use two languages with different modalities simultaneously. Thus, in contrast to the former type of bilingualism, bimodal bilingualism also includes *code blending* (Emmorey, Borinstein, and Thompson, 2005), i.e. the simultaneous articulation of sign and speech. In fact, bimodals tend to use code blending far more often than code switching. Emmorey et al. (2005), for example, reports that 95% of all code mixing in their American Sign Language (ASL) – English data are code blends while code switching occurs as little as 5% of the time. This rate is 94% (code blends) vs. 6% (code switches) in Petitto et al. (2001), and 65% vs. 35% in Emmorey et al. (2008). These findings suggest that we need to pay special attention to the phenomenon of code blending in order to gain a better understanding of the language production mechanism in bimodal bilingualism.

One of the biggest questions in this field has been how a bimodal bilingual, who is generally a CODA (Child of Deaf Adults), can simultaneously produce language in two different modalities.[3] One answer is that in the language production system of a CODA, the spoken and signed languages are produced individually but amidst continuous interaction with each other throughout (Emmorey et al., 2005, 2008). This we will call the interactive model of language production. Another view relies on MacSwan's (1997, 2000, 2005) proposal, although it was originally developed to account for the bilingual production of spoken languages, i.e. unimodal bilingualism. In line with MacSwan's minimalist analysis, recent studies have shown that it is indeed possible for a single grammatical system to permit concurrent linguistic items in both signed and spoken modalities to form an utterance. The idea behind the Null Theory and MacSwan's model of 'making the simplest assumptions' has, therefore, been corroborated by these studies.

In this context, our aim here is to investigate some aspects of bimodal language production, focusing on code blending generated by TİD – Turkish bimodal bilinguals. After introducing our method and database in section 2, we explore the types of code blending attested in our data in section 3, building on but slightly revising the classification given in Donati and Branchini (henceforth, D&B) (2013). In section 4, we introduce the interactive model of Emmorey et al. (2008) as well as MacSwan's (1997, 2000, 2005) minimalist model together with

---

[3] Although CODAs constitute the main group of bimodal bilinguals, recent studies have shown that deaf bilinguals may also produce sign and speech simultaneously (van den Bogaerde, 2000; Fung, 2010, among others). However, within the limits of our study we will be dealing with data from CODAs only.

the Language Synthesis model (Lillo-Martin et al., 2010, 2012, 2014; Quadros et al., 2013), which builds on MacSwan's minimalist approach and the framework of Distributed Morphology (henceforth, DM; Halle and Marantz, 1993). In this section we also analyse samples from our data in line with the minimalist approach to see how it can cope with actual cases of code blending. Section 5 concludes the study.

## 2 Method and data

The data of this study consist of TİD – Turkish bimodal bilingual utterances taken from conversations of CODAs with mixed groups of deaf signers and hearing non-signers. These CODAs were exposed to skilled usage of both languages at early ages and acquired them in a similar way to how unimodal bilingual children acquire two spoken languages (Newport and Meier, 1985). There were 12 of these participants, all TİD – Turkish bilinguals with normal hearing (6 males, 6 females) who were born into Deaf signing families and acquired TİD as a first language; they communicated with 12 hearing native Turkish speakers who had no knowledge of TİD, and 12 deaf native TİD signers with knowledge of written Turkish.

To collect the code blending data, it was necessary to construct a token audience consisting of non-signing hearing people and deaf signers, in order to create a semi-natural context for the bimodals. The participants could then address this mixed audience and become therefore motivated to produce both signed and spoken language structures. The bimodals were instructed to try to be as clear as possible so that both the deaf and hearing members of this audience could follow the conservations equally well.

During the conversations, each CODA addressed different signers and speakers and to encourage natural conversational data they were prompted to talk about various topics such as family, hobbies, work, travel, and education, that were felt to be likely to cue them into code blending. The deaf – hearing group interacted without the availability of sign language interpreting, so that the bimodal had to address both the deaf signers and hearing non-signers. There was also a social situation of equality between the deaf and hearing interlocutors, so that the bimodal could be equally concerned about the message getting across intact in both of the languages. Controlling these specific socio-linguistic parameters helped the code blending event emerge as naturally as possible in the context of our study.

We recorded about 460 minutes of data, which is substantial compared to the length of data generally used in similar studies, thanks to the fact that code blending was generally carried out for long stretches of conversation. Finally, as for the technical details of data processing, conversations between the participants were videotaped and then transcribed with the multimedia annotator program ELAN, which is ideal for showing both signed and spoken output on a multi-tier transcription interface, including the precise temporal relationships between signing and speaking.

## 3 Types of code blending in TİD – Turkish bimodal bilingualism

As expected from the fact that code mixing in bimodal bilingual language production includes large amounts of code blending (instead of code switching), it is possible to find different types of code blending in the data from CODAs in bimodal contexts. As pointed out in previous studies, 'congruence' appears to be one of the main phenomena to look for when attempting to classify code blends. In a blended pair of linguistic items, the nature of congruence may be semantic or structural. As for the former, the literature reveals that the linguistic items of two languages blended in bimodal speech are in general semantically congruent (Petitto et al., 2001; Emmorey, Borinstein, and Thompson, 2005, among others), which is to say that although linguistic forms are generated in two different modalities, it is basically the same meaning that is conveyed in each one. From this, Emmorey, Borinstein, and Thompson (2005: 671) conclude that "... code-blending is not produced in an effort to distribute distinct information across modalities".

As for the latter, on the other hand, what we see is that the linguistic items of two languages in a blended production may or may not be structurally congruent. In many cases, one of the languages plays a pivotal role and influences the structural shaping of the other one, as in what Emmorey, Borinstein, and Thompson (2005) call "ASL-influenced English". This is a case where in CODAs' bimodal utterances, the structure of English phrases is affected by that of ASL.

However, the size of the influence between the languages may vary, or there might be no influence at all. That is to say, although semantic congruence, in a sense, is full, structural congruence is a graded phenomenon. For example, in a study of code blending in Sign Language of the Netherlands (NGT) – Dutch bimodal bilinguals, Baker and van den Bogaerde (henceforth, B&B) (2014) classify it using a four-way distinction, which is based on the influence and/or contribution of each language in the linguistic coding of a proposition: 'Dutch-based', 'full blend', 'mixed blend', and 'NGT-based'.[4] In the 'Dutch-/NGT-based' types, the proposition is expressed entirely in one language, either Dutch or NGT, while only some words/signs are produced in the other one. In the 'full blend' type, each of the languages individually articulates the proposition in full. Finally, the 'mixed blend' is a type of code blend where the proposition can only be understood by the individual contributions of the two languages, i.e. each word is provided by only one of the languages to the effect that the sentence would be incomplete if any of the words were missing. It should be noted that this classification seems to be based on the three-way classification given in van den Bogaerde (2000), where the blending categories 'full', 'supplementary', and 'complementary' are the counterparts of the above categories 'full blend', 'mixed blend', and 'Dutch-/NGT-based blend', respectively.

Another classification was given in D&B (2013), where code blending of Italian Sign Language (LIS) – Italian bimodals is investigated in terms of linearisation issues. Noting that their categorisation is substantially different from previous 'purely descriptive' ones because of their focus on linearisation, the authors make a more elaborate classification, although there are certain overlaps with other classifications in the literature. Their 'dominant blending', for example, corresponds to 'complementary blending' in van den Bogaerde (2000) and 'Dutch-/NGT-based blending' in B&B (2014). The cases of 'full blending' in van den Bogaerde (2000) and B&B (2014) are categorised as 'independent blending' in D&B's work but they further categorise this blending type into sub-types: 'congruent lexicalisation', 'syntactic calque', and 'two word orders'. Finally, the 'supplementary blending' and 'mixed blend' types of van den Bogaerde (2000) and B&B (2014), respectively, are termed 'blended blending' in D&B's classification. Table 1 summarises the blending types in these classifications:

---

[4] Here we use a shortened version of their category labels. The actual labels in their study are as follows: (a) Code-blended Dutch Base Language, (b) Code-blended NGT Base Language, (c) Code-blended Mixed, (d) Code-blended Full.

Table 1. Previous classifications of blending types

| van den Bogaerde (2000) | B&B (2014) | D&B (2013) |
|---|---|---|
| Complementary blending | Dutch-/NGT-based blend | Dominant blending |
| Full blending | Full blend | Independent blending<br>– congruent lexicalisation<br>– syntactic calque<br>– two word orders |
| Supplementary blending | Mixed blend | Blended blending |

For the classification of blending types in our TİD – Turkish bimodal data, we basically follow D&B's categorisation but slightly revise it in light of our data. Now let us introduce the blending types that emerged from our database.

## 3.1 Dominant blending

In bimodal language production, one of the languages, either the spoken or the signed one, frequently plays a pivotal role in the linguistic realisation of the utterance, hence the label 'dominant' blending. Our findings as well as the ones previously reported in the literature show that this kind of situation could happen in either of the following ways:
1. In one modality the structure is fully articulated while it is 'supported' by a few words/signs in the other. We call this type *supportive blending*.
2. The linguistic structure of the utterance to be produced in each modality is determined by the structure of the language having the pivotal role. We call this type of dominant blending *syntactic calque*, following D&B (2013).

Note that although we borrow the label 'dominant blending' from D&B (2013), it is only the first case above that is included in their respective category. Therefore, what they call 'dominant blending' is supportive blending in our classification. As for the second case, syntactic calque, they sub-categorise it under the label 'independent blending' since the proposition is fully articulated in each modality. However, because the structure of the utterance in one of the modalities is dependent on the other, this is, from our point of view, also a case of dominant blending.

Having noted the differences between our classification and that of D&B concerning dominant blending, let us now take a closer look at each case with examples from our database.

### 3.1.1 Supportive blending

As explained above, in this type of blending the utterance is fully formed in one of the modalities, with the other modality supporting the utterance with duplicates of a few linguistic items. Consider the example given in (1):[5]

(1) O-nun         için       mimik-ler-i       kullan-ıyor-UZ       [TURKISH]
    that-GEN   because   mimic-PL-ACC   use-PROG-1PL
                              MIME                 WE                        [TİD]
    'That's why we use mime'

In (1), although the utterance is complete in spoken Turkish, the few TİD lexical items are uttered as duplicates, which are deemed 'supportive' in the literature. It is also notable that the duplication of a lexical item does not need to be one-to-one on the morphological side, as both the lexical verb and aspectual information are missing in TİD while the subject agreement marked by the suffix –*uz* '1pl' on the verb in the Turkish structure is duplicated by the pronoun WE.[6]

Another example of supportive blending is given in (2), but in this case it is TİD that has the pivotal role.

(2)                              İste-r-sen                                  [TURKISH]
                                  want-AOR-2SG
    SELF      TELL     DO     WANT     YOU                  [TİD]
    'Tell (them) for yourself, if you like'

Here, the proposition is fully articulated in TİD while only the verb is uttered in the spoken channel. Interestingly, although TİD is pivotal, the Turkish verb is still

---

[5] Throughout the paper, examples are presented in the following structure: the first line represents the spoken modality, which is followed by interlinear translation (using Leipzig Glossing Rules) in the second line, and the signed modality in the third line. The fourth line shows the English translation.

[6] As pointed out by an anonymous reviewer, the fact that Turkish is an agglutinative language while TİD is not makes an interesting blending pattern in that morphological information marked by affixes in the spoken modality may be individually coded in the signed modality by respective signs. On the other hand, although the agreement information in the Turkish structure is seemingly duplicated by a pronoun in the TİD string, the linguistic status of the sign WE in (1) is not clear. It seems like a subject pronoun but it may also be an agreement marker, especially when we consider the fact that TİD, like Turkish, is typologically both a SOV and a pro-drop language. In the absence of literature, we leave this issue open here.

grammatical. This indicates that, although partially articulated, the role of the supporting language is not just to duplicate some lexical items uttered in the other channel; instead, its grammar is active. This is also seen where the production of the pronoun WE in the TİD channel in (1) duplicates the grammatically encoded information given by the subject agreement suffix in the Turkish structure.

### 3.1.2 Syntactic calque

As opposed to supportive blending, in syntactic calque the utterance is linguistically realised in full form in both modalities. However, one of the languages in the blended pair is again dominant in the sense that it takes control over the structure of the other. In D&B (2013: 107), from whom we borrow the label, syntactic calque is when the two utterances, one for each modality, "… follow the word order prescribed by only one of the two languages". In (3), the post-verbal position of the locative *allo zoo/ZOO* is unmarked in Italian but in LIS no locative would appear in this position. Therefore, it is the Italian word order that compels it to follow the verb in the LIS utterance. In (4), on the other hand, LIS grammar takes control over the structure of the Italian utterance: both the position and the actual presence of the aspectual marker *finito* in the Italian utterance is dictated by LIS grammar (D&B, 2013: 108).

(3) Una     bambina    va         allo       zoo                              [ITALIAN]
    A       girl       go.3SG     to.the     zoo
    GIRL               GO                    ZOO                              [LIS]
    'The girl goes to the zoo'

(4) Il      Papà la    mamma la   sorella    mangiato   finito                [ITALIAN]
    The     father the mother the sister     eat.PTCP   finish.PTCP
    FATHER  MOTHER     SISTER     EAT        DONE       [LIS]
    'The father, mother and sister are done eating'

Although syntactic calque is discussed within the scope of word order in D&B's study, our data clearly show that it is not limited to word order. For example, in (5), through the influence of the Turkish light verb construction *cevap ver-* 'to answer' (lit. 'answer give'), the verb GIVE happens to occur in the TİD utterance as well, although it is not required grammatically. To wit, although redundant, Turkish grammar prompts the occurrence of the TİD counterpart of the verb *ver-* 'to give':

(5) Adam         cevap        ver-iyor                                [TURKISH]
    Man          answer       give-PROG.3SG
    MAN          ANSWER       GIVE                                    [TİD]
    'The man answers'

By contrast, in (6) it is seen that this time it is TİD grammar that has the pivotal role. In this example, because the TİD lexical verb HELP does not require a light verb, the one necessitated by the Turkish verbal construction is missing. In the Turkish structure, the noun *yardım* 'help' should have been followed by the light verb *et-* 'to do' as in *yardım et-* 'to help' (lit. 'help do'), contrary to what we have in (6):

(6) Onlar        yardım       lütfen                                  [TURKISH]
    They         help         please
    THEY         HELP         PLEASE                                  [TİD]
    'Could they help, please?'

Example (7) displays a similar case to (5), although this time it is the adverb *yanlış* 'wrong' that is duplicated in TİD. As before, this duplication is redundant because the TİD lexical verb MISREMEMBER inherently carries the meaning contributed by the adverb:

(7) Seksen dört     puan      al-dı         yanlış    hatırla-m-ıyor-sa-m    [TURKISH]
    Eighty four     point     get-PAST.3G   wrong     remember-NEG-PROG-COND-1SG
    EIGHTYFOUR POINT GET                    WRONG     MISREMEMBER+NOT        [TİD]
    'If I'm not mistaken, (s)he got eighty-four points'

Another interesting example is (8), which shows that syntactic calque may happen in nominal structures as well. Here, the Turkish NP consists of two words and its meaning is reflected by a single sign in TİD, i.e. SECOND^CLASS. Still, the TİD structure includes a second sign, SECTION, mimicking the Turkish NP structure in question, although the sign SECTION is semantically different from what it appears to duplicate, which is the Turkish word *sınıf* 'class' heading the NP.

(8) İkinci              sınıf                                         [TURKISH]
    second              class
    SECOND^CLASS        SECTION                                       [TİD]
    'Second grade'

The last case we would like to offer involving the application of syntactic calque is concerned with reduplication. In the following examples, it is seen that reduplication may create three copies of the relevant category in TİD, which is a verb in (9) and an adverb in (10), to express habitual aspect. Due to the influence of TİD's reduplication strategy, we have three instances of the word in the spoken modality as well, although in these contexts Turkish reduplication would usually permit only two copies (e.g. *öğrendim, öğrendim* instead of *öğrendim, öğrendim, öğrendim*):

(9)  Öğren-di-m        öğren-di-m        öğren-di-m        geliş-tir-di-m              [TURKISH]
     learn-PAST-1SG    learn-PAST-1SG    learn-PAST-1SG    improve-CAUS-PAST-1SG
     LEARN             LEARN             LEARN             IMPROVE                     [TİD]
     'I've learned and improved'

(10) Anlık             anlık             anlık             yaşamak    ol-ma-z           [TURKISH]
     instant           instant           instant           live       be-NEG-PRES.3SG
     INSTANT           INSTANT           INSTANT           LIVE       NO                [TİD]
     'You can't live just for the moment'

Having seen some instances of dominant blending, let us now look at examples of independent blending from our data.

## 3.2 Independent blending

In contrast to dominant blending, utterances produced in each modality might be independent from each other in terms of their grammatical structures. In such a case, there are, of course, two possibilities: they might incidentally have similar structures or there might be differences between their structural constitutions. In the first case we have a blending of *congruent structures*, while the latter is a case of blending with *discrete structures*. In D&B (2013), these blending types are sub-categorised as 'congruent lexicalisation' and 'two word orders', respectively, under the main category of independent blending, which also includes 'syntactic calque' that we sub-categorise under dominant blending for the reasons explained above. Recall that their work focuses on linearisation issues, so these blending types are exclusively investigated in terms of word order. However, as is the case with syntactic calque, our data reveal that the cases of blending with either congruent or discrete structures are not limited to word order. These blending types are discussed in the following two sub-sections.

### 3.2.1 Congruent structures

As shown in (11) and (12), if two languages in a bimodal context happen to share similar features for a grammatical structure, we may have utterances that look similar or exactly the same, without any grammatical influence between them. In these examples, the sentences in both modalities are grammatical in their respective grammars.

(11) Çok     kötü    bir    yer    değil                [TURKISH]
     very    bad     a      place  not
     VERY    BAD     A      PLACE  NOT                  [TİD]
     'It's not a very bad place'

(12) Bu      yüzden   Bursa-yı    çok    sev-iyor-um    [TURKISH]
     this    reason   Bursa-ACC   very   like-PROG-1SG
     THIS    REASON   BURSA       VERY   LIKE           [TİD]
     'For this reason, I like Bursa very much'

Here it is seen that the sentences in both modalities have the same word order. We consider these blending examples congruent structures because typologically TİD and Turkish are both head-final languages; so, we assume no grammatical influence between them. Recall, on the other hand, that the LIS – Italian blendings seen in (3) and (4) above are categorised by D&B as syntactic calques, although in these examples as well, the blended sentences have the same word order. This is because LIS is a SOV language while the unmarked word order in Italian is SVO; thus, in each example the word order is prescribed by one of the languages. Therefore, as pointed out by an anonymous reviewer, from the contrast in blending types between these TİD – Turkish and LIS – Italian examples, we can conclude that the typological features of languages seem to have an impact on the blending patterns.

### 3.2.2 Discrete structures

As mentioned above, in addition to blending congruent structures, it is also possible for a bimodal language user to independently produce and blend the linguistic structures of two languages even if they are not similar. Consider the example below:

(13)  Kız-ınız-dan         ayrıl-ıyor-um           de-di-m           [TURKISH]
      girl-POSS.2PL-ABL    leave-PROG-1SG          SAY-PAST-1SG
      GIRL                 ENGAGEMENT THROW        I SAY             [TİD]
      'I said that I'm breaking off the engagement with your daughter'

In (13), the sentences in both channels are grammatically encoded and there is again no structural influence between them. Note, first, that typologically different properties of Turkish and TİD in terms of agglutination are kept intact in each modality. Second, although the Turkish NP *kızınız* 'your daughter' has a possessive structure, the TİD sign GIRL 'daughter' is a simple NP, as in these contexts TİD usually relies on contextual information for the interpretation of possessive relations. Finally, the TİD counterpart of the Turkish one-word lexical verb *ayrıl-* 'to leave' includes two signs (ENGAGEMENT THROW). Recall that in a similar structure shown in (8) above, the structure of the Turkish NP *ikinci sınıf* 'second grade' (lit. 'second class') prescribed the use of a redundant word in the TİD NP structure, i.e. SECTION, for the Turkish word *sınıf*, although the meaning of the Turkish NP is normally reflected by a single sign in TİD (SECOND^CLASS). This indicates that different structures in the two modalities may be blended by either 'syntactic calque', as in (8), or 'discrete structures' as in (13).

Now let us take a look at a quite different instance of independent blending with discrete structures:

(14)  Soru-n-u                anla-ma-dı-m                [TURKISH]
      question-POSS.2SG-ACC   understand-NEG-PAST-1SG
      $_{2sg}$ASK$_{1sg}$     UNDERSTAND        NOT       [TİD]
      'I didn't understand your question'

As is the case in (13), both sentences in (14) are grammatical. What is striking here, though, is the blending of an NP with a verb: the Turkish object NP *soru-n* 'your question' is blended with $_{2sg}$ASK$_{1sg}$, which is an agreement verb in TİD that roughly means 'you ask me'. Thus, this example reveals quite an interesting aspect of blending, namely, the possibility of blending with words that belong to different word classes. As is discussed in section 4.2, we think that the blending in question is possible because the blended words have similar underlying structures.

These examples clearly suggest that code blending can include quite different structures independently uttered in the two modalities. In the context of Italian – LIS code blending, D&B (2013) have shown that the sentences produced in each modality may include different word orders, as Italian and LIS are typologically different in terms of their canonical word orders, i.e. SVO and SOV respectively, as mentioned above. They categorise this type of blending under the label 'two word orders', which is a sub-category of independent blending in their classification (see Table 1). As Turkish and TİD are both SOV languages, 'two word orders' is not a frequent type of blending in our data. However, as we have seen in this section, code blending between these two languages involves not only word order, but also other structures associated with differences in the grammars of the two languages. The label 'discrete structures' would, therefore, be a more generic term for the blending types in question, including the cases with 'two word orders'.

## 3.3 Blended blending

As a final type of blending, we have a mixed utterance consisting of some linguistic items from one modality and some from another, such that each modality only provides part of the meaning. As D&B (2013: 110) observe, "… the utterance is complete and meaningful only if the fragments distributed in the two channels are put together in a unique, blended utterance". Sentence (15) is a clear example of this type of blending attested in their LIS – Italian corpus and (16) shows that some of the elements may be reduplicated in the other channel:

(15)  Io                                          [ITALIAN]
      I
      WIN                                         [LIS]
      'I won'

(16)  Parla           con         Biancaneve      [ITALIAN]
      talk-PRES-3SG   with        Snow White
      TALK            HUNTER                      [LIS]
      'The hunter talks to Snow White'
                      (D&B, 2013: 110)

Our TİD – Turkish bimodal data include this type of blending as well. In (17), apart from the duplicated elements, we see that the direct object *film* 'movie' and the verb *izle-* 'to watch' are generated in the signed and spoken modalities, respectively. Therefore, the VP structure is fragmented into two channels, and to form a complete VP, these parts should be put together.

(17)  Ben       de      gid-ip      izle-me-di-m          [TURKISH]
      I         too     go-CONJ     watch-NEG-PAST-1SG
      I                 GO          MOVIE  NOT            [TİD]
      'I didn't go to watch the movie, either'

For another example, consider the blended pair of sentences given in (18):

(18) Baba-m            çalış-ıyor              [TURKISH]
     father-POSS.1SG   work-PROG.3SG
     NO,   FATHER      WORK                    [TİD]
     'No, my father is working'

Here, the sentential adverb *no* is contained in the signed modality, while the rest of the utterance includes duplicated elements. Thus, although the meaning contributed by the sentential adverb could be inferred from the context, it is linguistically encoded only in the signed channel, and to get the complete meaning, the linguistic items encoded in both modalities should be interpreted together.

## 4 A minimalist analysis of code blending in TİD – Turkish bimodal bilingualism

As stated in the Introduction, the main division between the studies on bilingual language production has concerned the question of how to account for a grammatical system that is capable of mixing two languages to produce an utterance. Some studies propose that it is a system with certain grammatical constraints specific to bilingual grammar, e.g. the Equivalence Constraint, Free Morpheme Constraint (Poplack, 1980, 1981); Closed-Class Constraint (Joshi, 1985); and Matrix Language Frame (Azuma, 1991, 1993; Myers-Scotton, 1993). Others claim that no such grammar exists, maintaining the Null Hypothesis, which basically says that all we have is a single grammatical system that is responsible for both monolingual and bilingual language production (Woolford, 1983; Mahootian, 1993; Belazi et al., 1994; MacSwan, 1997, 2000, 2005; Chan, 2003, 2008). From the viewpoint of bimodal bilingualism, this issue becomes even more interesting because of the extensive use of code blending instead of code switching, especially when we think that the grammatical constraints and operations suggested to be at work in 'bilingual grammar' are all designed to account for code switching only. It is, thus, unclear how these constraints can account for code blending data such as those shown in the previous section. On the other hand, the Null Hypothesis, especially the version proposed by MacSwan (1997, 2000, 2005) in line with the assumptions of minimalist grammar, is supported by some recent studies focusing on bimodal data, revealing that it can be applicable to this type of bilingualism as well (e.g. Toribio, 2001; van Gass, 2002; Lillo-Martin et al., 2010, 2012, 2014; Quadros et al., 2013; D&B, 2013, among others).

As we mentioned above, there is, however, another view on the production of language in bimodal bilingualism, which is defended by Emmorey et al. (2005, 2008). They suggest that in bimodal production, systems of both spoken and signed languages are individually active and responsible for generating the respective linguistic structures, although they have an interactive relationship throughout the production process, which accounts for the existence of code blendings. Therefore, in terms of bimodal bilingualism, we have two opposing views, 'minimalist' and 'interactive', to explain what is going on in bimodal production. Our task in this section is, then, to try to figure out which one would offer a more reliable explanation for the issue at hand, using our bimodal data. It is worth remembering, however, that Emmorey et al.'s interactive model is a psycholinguistic production model, whose main aim is to account for the interactions between the two articulatory channels, while the minimalist model first proposed by MacSwan is a model of grammar. Although the scopes of the two models are not exactly the same in the general sense, keep in mind that in the following sections we compare just the grammatical system of Emmorey et al.'s interactive model, i.e. Formulator, with the minimalist model.[7]

## 4.1 Interactive and minimalist models

Emmorey et al. (2008) propose a highly complex model of language production for bimodal bilingualism, especially designed for ASL – English code blend production (see Figure 1). It adapts Levelt's (1989) Speech Production model and partly incorporates the model of speech and gesture production put forth by Kita and Özyürek (2003). The authors hypothesise that the ASL and English Formulators contain the lexicons and grammatical, morphological, and phonological encoding processes for each language. In other words, Formulators represent the grammar proper for each language in the production model.

---

[7] We would like to thank the reviewer who suggested that we make clear this important difference between the two models.

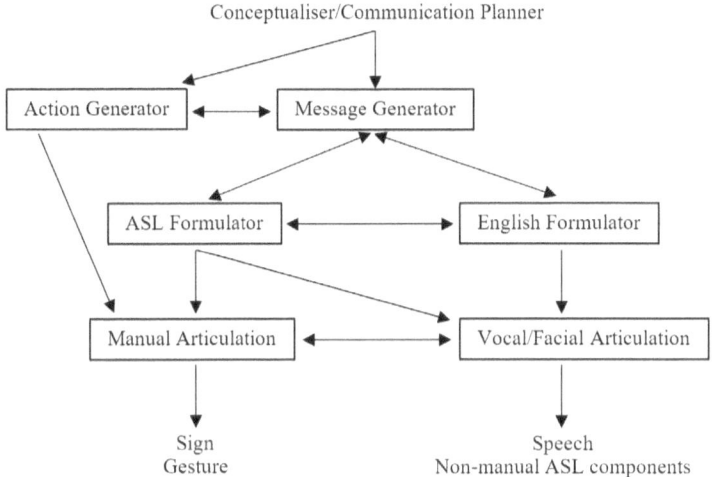

**Figure 1.** Emmorey et al.'s (2008) 'interactive' model of ASL – English code blend production.

Focusing only on the most important part for our purposes (for details, we refer the interested reader to Emmorey et al.'s paper), here we see that the Formulators of signed and spoken languages are both active, which means that all grammatical processes needed to generate the linguistic structures of ASL and English are individually taken care of by the relevant grammatical system/Formulator. However, as the two-way arrow in the figure indicates, these grammatical systems are in an interactive relationship and, along with the interactions between other modules, this accounts for the possibility of code blends.

On the other hand, in line with the Null Hypothesis, MacSwan's (1997, 2000, 2005) model involves almost no extra assumptions regarding bilingual data, except two lexicons and two PFs (one for each language) as input and output channels of the syntactic (overt) component of the computational system (CHL) (see Figure 2). Thus, the mechanism of the model is quite simple and can allow for bilingual utterances in a similar way as it does for monolingual ones.

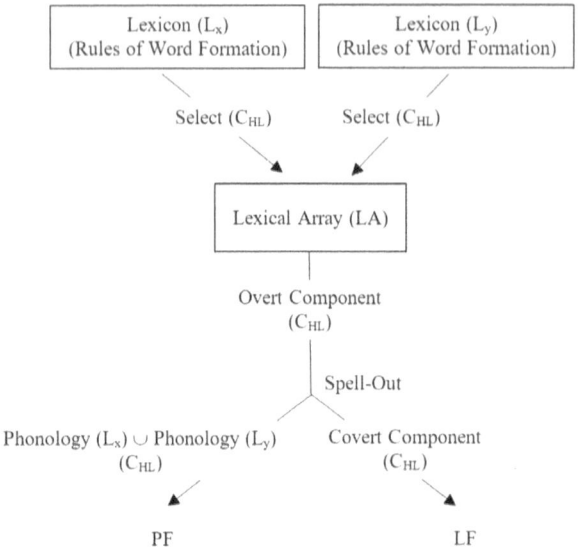

**Figure 2.** MacSwan's (1997, 2000, 2005) minimalist model of bilingual production.

In a nutshell, the production process in this model works as follows. The operation SELECT mediates between the Lexicons ($L_x$ and $L_y$) and the Lexical Array (LA, i.e. numeration) so that the lexical items in the utterance can be added to the LA. Then, by successive applications of MERGE, the lexical items in the LA are taken into the syntactic (overt) component to build the linguistic structure needed. After the syntactic component completes the structure, it is Spelled-Out to interfaces, PF (phonetic form) and LF (logical form), as would normally be done in a monolingual production. There is only one semantic (covert) component, LF, because there is only one proposition to be conveyed in the sentence. However, there are two PFs, Phonology ($L_x$) and Phonology ($L_y$), one for each language, to ensure that each lexical item in the structure can have an appropriate phonological realisation.

Recall that MacSwan's model is intended to account for code switching in unimodal bilingualism. His model has basically the same architecture of grammar as proposed in the generative framework (Chomsky, 1995), except double lexicons and PFs. From this, we can infer that code switching occurs in these components only. In other words, there are no code switching phenomena in overt and covert components, i.e. syntax and LF. MacSwan (2000) points out that "a bilingual may be assumed to have a unitary system of syntactic operations" since "all cross-linguistic variation is lexically encoded", and because of that, "syntactic operations of the computational system may be assumed to be invariant" (pp. 51-52). LF is assumed to be unitary as well, because there is only one proposition to be conveyed, as we mentioned above. However, in this model lexical items are morphologically formed in the lexicon, so there must be one lexicon for each language in the system. This is the same for PF. MacSwan points out that "... since operations associated with the computation which maps the numeration to PF (...) are ordered with respect to one another, no merging of the phonological systems is allowed. A bilingual speaker must therefore have separate and discrete phonological systems for each language" (p. 52).

Building on MacSwan's minimalist model, Lillo-Martin et al. (2010, 2012, 2014), and Quadros et al. (2013) have developed the Language Synthesis model, which adapts the approach proposed by den Dikken (2011) following the framework of DM (Halle and Marantz, 1993). Under this model, linguistic elements traditionally assumed to be in the Lexicon, a pre-syntactic component, are of two types that are inserted at different derivational points as can be seen in Figure 3: (i) Roots and morphemes (Lexical Items –LIs), which are abstract entities that are the input to the syntactic derivation; and (ii) Vocabulary Items (VIs), which include phonological expressions of syntactic terminals subject to Late Insertion, i.e. inclusion of elements at the point of Vocabulary Insertion. For a bilingual, there are two sets of LIs as well as VIs to choose from, $L_x$ and $L_y$, and insertion of linguistic elements at different points accounts for different outcomes of bilingualism as follows:

> During syntax, featural requirements [of LIs] must be satisfied; and in some cases, elements from language A may satisfy the requirements of elements from language α, leading to structures with cross-linguistic influence or transfer. At the point of Vocabulary Insertion, elements from either language may be inserted, as long as all featural requirements are satisfied, leading to code-switching. Finally, when two independent sets of articulators [i.e. Phonology $L_x$ and Phonology $L_y$] are available, lexical items from both languages are possible, making code-blending possible. (Lillo-Martin et al., 2014: 2).

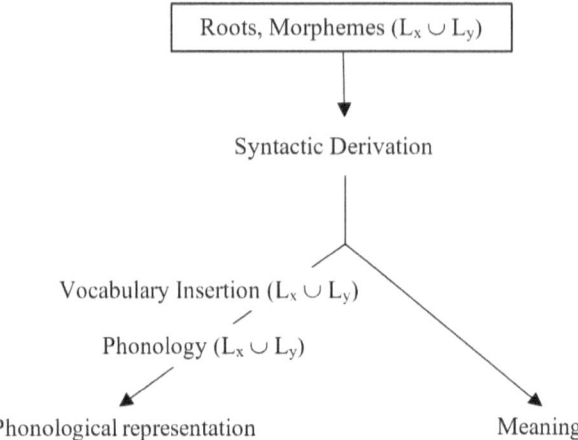

**Figure 3.** Language Synthesis model (Lillo-Martin et al., 2012; Quadros et al., 2013)

If we compare the grammatical systems of the interactive and minimalist models in terms of the difficulty of computation that they require on the user side, it appears that the minimalist models (i.e. MacSwan's model and the Language Synthesis model) have an advantage. To produce a blended utterance, the interactive model assumes that each structural unit is generated individually by the grammars of both of the languages. On the other hand, in line with the generative view, the minimalist models start with the assumption that as the grammar of both languages have the same set of syntactic rules, they are generated in a single syntactic derivation, which saves the computational system having to produce a linguistic structure twice. Obviously, in terms of producing syntactic objects, the minimalist models definitely have a less costly procedure than the interactive one. We can therefore safely state that in this regard the former are conceptually stronger than the latter.

It should also be noted that the internal mechanism of the grammar in the interactive model, i.e. the Formulator, appears to be very vague, although the minimalist models introduced above involve a precise mechanism in this respect thanks to generative architecture. Because of the obscureness of its grammatical mechanism, it is actually not clear how the interactive model would exactly account for a particular case of code blending in our data, except for a possible explanation that the grammars of the two languages in that case are in 'mutual interaction', a concept which is by no means lucid to us. With the minimalist models, on the other hand, we have a complete set of principles and rules for a full-fledged formal grammar, which allows us to decide whether it works in a particular instance.

The minimalist approach therefore represents our main perspective for the remainder of this section where we put it into action to analyse actual examples of code blends taken from our TİD – Turkish bimodal data.

## 4.2 Sample cases of TİD – Turkish code blends in a minimalist framework

### 4.2.1 Dominant blending

To begin with a relatively simple type of blending, let us consider an instance of *supportive blending*, a sub-type of dominant blending in our classification, given in (1) and repeated below:

(19)  O-nun      için       mimik-ler-i        kullan-ıyor-uz         [TURKISH]
      that-GEN   because    mimic-PL-ACC       use-PROG-1PL
                            MIME               WE                     [TİD]
      'That's why we use mime'

In (19), Turkish is the pivotal language while TİD has a supportive role with two lexical items that surface. Under the minimalist approach, the standard procedure to generate a blended utterance starts with selecting the lexical items needed for the derivation from one of the languages, $L_x$ or $L_y$. As Turkish is the leading language in (19), we can assert, following the Language Synthesis model, that in this example all LIs, i.e. roots and morphemes, are selected from the respective list of Turkish. Recall that LIs are the input to the syntactic derivation, so in this example it is the featural requirements of Turkish items (such as the subject agreement on the verb) that must be satisfied via syntactic operations, which accounts for the pivotal role of Turkish grammar. For instance, the syntactic derivation of the Turkish word *mimik-ler-i* 'mimics' includes three LIs: the lexical root *mimik* 'mimic' (a l(exical)-morpheme) and two f(unctional)-morphemes, the plural and accusative suffixes *-ler* and *-i*. At Syntax all morphemes are abstract and they are paired with phonological expressions only at the point of Vocabulary Insertion, as seen in our example *mimikleri* ('↔' and √ indicate the pairing relation and lexical roots, respectively): /mimik/ ↔ √MIMIK; /-ler/ ↔ [+plural]; /-i/ ↔ [+accusative].

As mentioned above, the Language Synthesis model asserts that code switching occurs at the point of Vocabulary Insertion if the phonological expressions of VIs to be inserted are selected from different languages, while code blending arises at Phonology thorough articulation of the elements, through Vocabulary Insertion, in both modalities. According to this system, then, at Vocabulary Insertion all elements in (19) should have been selected from the Vocabulary of Turkish, since this is not an instance of code switching; blending of the elements, realised as MIME and WE in TİD, on the other hand, is obtained by articulating them in both modalities at Phonology. Thus, in the input to Phonology there are only Turkish elements that were inserted and sent by Vocabulary Insertion but no elements from TİD. This raises the question of how Phonology determines exactly which lexical item from the Vocabulary of TİD will be articulated to blend with a Turkish word. Note that under the standard assumptions of DM, it is the responsibility of Vocabulary Insertion to assign phonological expressions to lexical items and the role of Phonology is limited to articulating them, i.e. no phonological expression that is not sent by Vocabulary Insertion can be articulated by Phonology. In keeping with this assumption, we accept that blended elements such as MIME and WE in (19) should also be inserted at the point of Vocabulary Insertion, which allows Phonology$_{TID}$ to blend them with the Turkish words.

*Syntactic calque* is another dominant blending type where the architecture of the minimalist models allows a possible explanation for the facts. Recall that also in this type of blending, one of the languages has a pivotal role in leading the structure and the other one follows it. Again, consider some of the examples given before:

(20)  Adam      [$_{VP}$  cevap      ver-iyor]       (= ex. 5)    [TURKISH]
      man              answer     give-prog.3sg
      MAN       [$_{VP}$  ANSWER     GIVE]                        [TİD]
      'The man answers'

(21)  Onlar     [$_{VP}$ yardım]     lütfen          (= ex. 6)    [TURKISH]
      They              help        please
      THEY      [$_{VP}$ HELP]       PLEASE                       [TİD]
      'Could they help, please?'

As mentioned in 3.1.2, Turkish and TİD have pivotal roles in building the structure of the VPs in (20) and (21), respectively. In (20), the structure of the Turkish VP compels the TİD VP to include the counterpart of the light verb *ver-* 'to give', although it should contain only the verb ANSWER. Following the minimalist assumptions, this can be accounted for if the VP is built by the LIs taken from Turkish, hence the structure of a Turkish VP. In (21), on the other hand, the effect of the TİD VP is that the Turkish VP does not have a light verb, even though it would normally have one, as in *yardım etmek* 'help + do: to help'. That in this case the structure of the VP follows TİD grammar suggests that the syntactic derivation in

(21) is fed by the LIs taken from TİD. Therefore, the pivotal roles of the languages in forming the VP structures in these examples could get a natural explanation by simply assuming that (i) as in monolingual production, (unimodal/bimodal) bilingual production includes a single syntactic derivation, and (ii) it can be fed by LIs taken from either of the languages. As before, at the point of Vocabulary Insertion, elements from either language are inserted and sent to the respective phonological component, Phonology$_{Turkish}$ or Phonology$_{TİD}$, for articulation.

### 4.2.2 Independent blending

In each case above, we saw that either of the languages can have a pivotal role in prescribing a structure for the blended utterance. To these cases, we can add the instances of *congruent structures* as well, which is a sub-type of independent blending as discussed in 3.2.1, although in this type of blending the structures of the utterances in each channel overlap incidentally, i.e. without any kind of prescription. Take, for example, the blending we saw in (12), repeated in (22):

(22) Bu        yüzden    Bursa-yı      çok      sev-iyor-um         [TURKISH]
     this      reason    Bursa-ACC     very     like-PROG-1SG
     THIS      REASON    BURSA         VERY     LIKE                [TİD]
     'For this reason, I like Bursa very much'

Here we see that each element in one language is blended with its counterpart in the other one and the sentences in each channel are grammatical. The strings in the two modalities look the same because TİD and Turkish are both head-final languages, not because the word order is prescribed by either of them. This suggests that the syntactic derivation of the phrases in (22) may be fed by LIs from either of the languages without any effect of prescription. Consider, for example, the derivation of the object *Bursa-yı* 'Bursa-acc' / BURSA. As discussed above, we accept, following the standard assumptions of DM, that in the case of code blending, the VI of a LI should include two phonological expressions, each taken from one language. Consequently, phonological expressions for the lexical root as well as the accusative f-morpheme should be inserted for both languages. Thus, at the time of lexical selection/Vocabulary Insertion, the VIs for these LIs should appear as follows: /bursa/, /BURSA/ ↔ [$_{NP}$ √BURSA]; and /-ı/, /Ø/ ↔ [$_{Case}^0$ +accusative]. In these representations, it is seen that the lexical root √BURSA is placed in a NP and should be phonologically realised as /bursa/ and /BURSA/ by Phonology$_{Turkish}$ and Phonology$_{TİD}$, respectively. As for the f-morpheme, we see that it is the head of the CaseP, i.e. Case$^0$, and should be pronounced as

/-ı/ in Turkish while it must be null in TİD.[8] Therefore, in accordance with the minimalist assumptions, there is a single syntactic derivation for the direct object although its linguistic realisation differs in each modality.

For all three blending types discussed above, it seems quite reasonable to assume a single grammatical structure, which is fed by lexical items selected from either of the lexicons. For these cases, then, the grammatical architecture provided by the minimalist models proves to be a useful working ground. However, in some instances of blending it is not so obvious that there is only one grammatical structure for the utterances in each modality to follow. One of the most interesting cases of this kind of blending we have found in our data involves *discrete structures*, also a sub-type of independent blending, repeated in (23):

(23)  Soru-n-u                anla-ma-dı-m                        [TURKISH]
      question-POSS.2SG-ACC   understand-NEG-PAST-1SG
      $_{2sg}$ASK$_{1sg}$                UNDERSTAND      NOT      [TİD]
      'I didn't understand your question (to me)'

In (23) we see that a noun in one modality is blended with a verb in another. More specifically, the Turkish noun *soru* 'question' is blended with $_{2sg}$ASK$_{1sg}$, which is an agreement verb in TİD, meaning something like 'you ask me'. Given the fact that these items belong to two different lexical categories and that under the minimalist models there is only one syntactic component for them to be encoded, it is important to ask how they could be derived from a single syntactic structure. We suggest that the answer lies in the fact that the Turkish noun has the same underlying argument structure as the TİD agreement verb. Note that the Turkish word *soru* 'question' is a deverbal noun derived by a nominal suffix *-I* (realised here as *-u*) from the verbal root *sor-* 'to ask', i.e. *sor-u*. Thus, in (23) the agreement verb and the deverbal noun have the same argument structure, which includes a second person singular subject and a first person singular indirect object, as shown in (24):

---

[8] As mentioned above, here we assume that at Vocabulary Insertion, for every morpheme sent by the syntactic derivation there should be a phonological expression inserted for each modality. Under this assumption, /-ı/ and /Ø/, for example, are inserted as phonological expressions of the accusative morpheme in Turkish and TİD, respectively. Alternatively, one would assume that f-morphemes such as the accusative morpheme here, i.e. /Ø/, are simply missing in TİD since they are not phonologically realised in this modality. Although either analysis would explain the blending facts in question, we choose the former option for the sake of consistency with the original assumptions of DM. We would like to note, however, that further investigation is needed for a better understanding of this issue.

(24) [$_{vP}$ DP$_{subject}$ [$_{v'}$ [$_{VP}$ DP$_{Ind\text{-}Object}$ [$_{v'}$] sor-/ASK] $v^0$ ]]

Note also that the Turkish deverbal noun with the structure *soru-n-u* 'question-poss.2sg-acc' means, in this context, 'your question to me' and we believe this is why it can be blended with the TİD agreement verb. Importantly, to get that meaning it has to be derived from a *v*P structure like (24), which is shared by the TİD agreement verb as well.

Obviously, the Turkish nominalisation suffix *–u* has to be added to the verbal root to derive the deverbal noun at some point in the derivation after the structure in (24) has been created. We assume that the suffix is a nominal head, $n^0$, which takes the *v*P structure as its complement, hence the deverbal noun with the structure *sor-u*. This nP, in turn, occupies the complement position of a DP/PossP, headed by the possessive suffix *–n*, which itself is the complement of CaseP, whose head position is filled by the accusative suffix *–u*. Thus, in line with DM, the syntactic derivation of the Turkish word *sorunu* 'your question' includes a *v*P structure as well as a nP, a DP/PossP, and a CaseP, as seen in (25):

(25) [$_{CaseP}$ [$_{DP/PossP}$ [$_{nP}$ [$_{vP}$ ... [$_{VP}$ sor-] $v^0$ ] –u] –n] –u]

On the other hand, we do not see any of the suffixes in (25) on the TİD agreement verb ASK, due to the fact that it is not an agglutinative language. Under the Language Synthesis model, this can be accounted for by positing the suffixed morphemes /–u/, /–n/, and /–u/ in the Turkish string are all realised as null morphemes in TİD. For example, at the point of Vocabulary Insertion there should be two phonological expressions of the nominalisation morpheme inserted for each language: /–u/ for Turkish and /Ø/ for TİD. This is the same for other f-morphemes in the structure; namely, for the heads of the DP/PossP and CaseP, the suffixes /–n/ and /–u/, respectively, are inserted for Turkish, and the TİD counterparts of them are null morphemes (/Ø/) that are also inserted at this point along with the Turkish morphemes (but see ftn. 5). As these are silent morphemes in TİD, the outcome of the structure looks seemingly different from its Turkish counterpart as if it is an agreement verb, although the two share the same nominal syntax, seen in (25).

Note that our analysis is supported by the general finding in the literature we mentioned before, that is, code blending is always semantically congruent. That is to say, the fact that the Turkish nominal expression *sorunu* 'your question' has underlyingly the same argument structure with the TİD agreement verb $_{2sg}$ASK$_{1sg}$ makes it possible for the language user to produce them together in a blending structure.

## 4.2.3 Blended blending

As a last case, we need to look also at the derivation of blendings where the linguistic structure is fragmented into two channels, i.e. blended blendings. In fact, this may be one of the best of all blending types to support the assumptions of the minimalist approach, for in this type it is easy to see that there is a common syntactic structure in the derivation. Consider the example repeated in (26):

(26)   Ben     de      gid-ip      izle-me-di-m                    [TURKISH]
       I       too     go-CONJ     watch-NEG-PAST-1SG
       I               GO          MOVIE        NOT                [TİD]
       'I didn't go to watch the movie, either'

Focusing on the structure of the matrix VP, here it is seen that the spoken modality includes only the transitive verb *izle-* 'to watch', while the signed modality contains just the direct object MOVIE. Instead of assuming two different VPs with omitted items for each language, as an interactive analysis would do, we believe that the most reasonable assumption also for this particular blending would be to accept that there is a common VP structure formed with LIs that are selected from one of the participating languages and phonologically realised in different phonological components, Phonology$_{Turkish}$ and Phonology$_{TİD}$, as shown in (27):

(27)   ... [$_{VP}$ [$_{V'}$ MOVIE] izle-] ...

That the lexical items in (27) are each phonologically realised in different modalities suggests that at Vocabulary Insertion each lexical item is assigned just one phonological expression, i.e. one from each language, not from both. Thus, in our analysis, independent blending differs from other types of blending in the process of lexical insertion: for each VI, insertion from the Vocabulary of just one language leads to independent blending, while insertion from the Vocabulary of each language results in other blending types. Note that code switching (in both unimodal and bimodal situations) as well as monolingual utterances can also be derived from the former type of lexical insertion, as suggested also by the Language Synthesis model. Therefore, thanks to the minimalist architecture, we are able to account for different types of language production, i.e. monolingual, unimodal bilingual and bimodal bilingual, with one simple model, an obvious advantage of the minimalist approach over other approaches, including the interactive model as well as the earlier ones.

# 5 Conclusion

In this study we have investigated how code blending is produced in the context of TİD – Turkish bimodal bilingualism. Our aim was twofold: first, to explore the types of blending used by TİD – Turkish bimodals, and second, to discuss how to account for their production. To explore the blending types, we used the classification proposed by Donati and Branchini (2013), suggesting a slight revision for the types of blending attested in our database. As for the question of how bimodals can generate blended utterances, we scrutinised two language production models in terms of their grammatical processes to see how straightforwardly they can account for this type of data, namely Emmorey et al.'s (2008) 'interactive' model, as we call it, proposed for ASL – English code blend production; and the 'minimalist' model, which was originally developed for unimodal bilingualism by MacSwan (1997, 2000, 2005) and adapted by the Language Synthesis model by Lillo-Martin et al. (2010, 2012, 2014) and Quadros et al. (2013) to include bimodal production as well. A comparison between the grammatical production processes of the two models has shown that due to having the fewest assumptions possible, the minimalist model is conceptually more accurate as well as theoretically simpler than the interactive model. We further investigated the applicability of the minimalist model to real life examples of each blended type taken from our data. Although a more detailed investigation is needed, our technical analysis has revealed that the minimalist model is not only conceptually accurate but is also technically capable of accounting for different types of code blending.

## References

Azuma, Shoji. 1991. *Processing and intrasentential code-switching*. Austin: University of Texas dissertation.

Azuma, Shoji. 1993. The frame-content hypothesis in speech production: Evidence from intrasentential code switching. *Linguistics* 31(6). 1071–1093.

Baker, Anne E. & Beppie van den Bogaerde. 2014. KODAs: a special form of bilingualism. In David Quinto-Pozos (ed.), *Multilingual aspects of signed language communication and disorder (Communication disorders across languages)*, 211–234. Bristol, UK: Multilingual Matters.

Belazi, Hedi M., Edward J. Rubin & Almeida Jacqueline Toribio. 1994. Code switching and X-Bar Theory: The Functional Head Constraint. *Linguistic Inquiry* 25(2). 221–237.

Bogaerde, Beppie van den. 2000. *Input and Interaction in Deaf Families*. University of Amsterdam dissertation, LOT Series No. 35. Utrecht: LOT.

Chan, Brian Hok-Shing. 2003. *Aspects of the syntax, the pragmatics, and the production of code-switching: Cantonese and English*. New York: Peter Lang.
Chan, Brian Hok-Shing. 2008. Code-switching, word order and the lexical/functional category distinction. *Lingua* 118(6), 777–809.
Chomsky, Noam. 1995. *The minimalist program*. Cambridge, MA: MIT Press.
Dikken, Marcel den. 2011. The distributed morphology of code-switching. Paper presented at 2010 UIC Bilingualism Forum. University of Illinois at Chicago.
Donati, Caterina & Chiara Branchini. 2013. Challenging linearization: Simultaneous mixing in the production of bimodal bilinguals. In Theresa Biberauer & Ian Roberts (eds.), *Challenges to linearization*, 93–128. Berlin/Boston: Mouton de Gruyter.
Emmorey, Karen, Helsa B. Borinstein & Robin Thompson. 2005. Bimodal bilingualism: Code-blending between spoken English and American Sign Language. In James Cohen, Kara T. McAlister, Kellie Rolstad & Jeff MacSwan (eds.), *ISB4: Proceedings of the 4th International Symposium on Bilingualism*, 663–673. Somerville, MA: Cascadilla Press.
Emmorey, Karen, Helsa B. Borinstein, Robin Thompson & Tamar H. Gollan. 2008. Bimodal bilingualism. *Bilingualism: Language and Cognition* 11(1), 43–61.
Fung, Cat H.-M. 2010. Code-blending in Hong Kong Sign Language. Paper presented at the Theoretical Issues in Sign Language Research Conference (TISLR 10). Purdue University. (http://www.purdue.edu/tislr10/pdfs/FUNG,CatH-M.pdf)
Gass, Kate van. 2002. Grammatical constraints on intrasentential code switching: Evidence from English-Afrikaans code switching. *Stellenbosch Papers in Linguistics Plus* 31, 91–113.
Halle, Morris & Alec Marantz. 1993. Distributed morphology and the pieces of inflection. In Ken Halle & Samuel Jay Keyser (eds.), *View from building 20*, 111–176. Cambridge: MIT Press.
Joshi, Aravind K. 1985. Processing of sentences with intrasentential code switching. In David R. Dowty, Lauri Karttunen & Arnold M. Zwicky (eds.), *Natural language parsing: Psychological, computational and theoretical perspectives*, 190–205. Cambridge: Cambridge University Press.
Kita, Sotaro & Aslı Özyürek. 2003. What does cross-linguistic variation in semantic coordination of speech and gesture reveal? Evidence for an interface representation of spatial thinking and speaking. *Journal of Memory and Language* 48(1), 16–32.
Levelt, Willem J. M. 1989. *Speaking: From intention to articulation*. Cambridge, MA: MIT Press.
Lillo-Martin, Diane, Ronice Müller de Quadros, Helen Koulidobrova & Deborah Chen Pichler. 2010. Bimodal bilingual cross-language influence in unexpected domains. In João Costa, Ana Castro, Maria Lobo & Fernanda Pratas (eds.), *Language acquisition and development: Proceedings of GALA 2009*, 264–275. Newcastle upon Tyne: Cambridge Scholars Press.
Lillo-Martin, Diane, Helen Koulidobrova, Ronice Müller de Quadros & Deborah Chen Pichler. 2012. Bilingual language synthesis: Evidence from wh-questions in bimodal bilinguals. In Alia K. Biller, Esther Y. Chung & Amelia E. Kimball (eds.), *BUCLD 36: Proceedings of the annual Boston University Conference on Language Development*, 302–314. Somerville, MA: Cascadilla Press.
Lillo-Martin, Diane, Ronice Müller de Quadros, Deborah Chen Pichler & Zoe Fieldsteel. 2014. Language choice in bimodal bilingual development. *Frontiers in Psychology* 5(1163). doi: 10.3389/fpsyg.2014.01163.
MacSwan, Jeff. 1997. *A minimalist approach to intrasentential code switching: Spanish-Nahuatl bilingualism in Central Mexico*. Los Angeles: University of California dissertation.
MacSwan, Jeff. 2000. The architecture of the bilingual language faculty: Evidence from intrasentential code switching. *Bilingualism: Language and Cognition* 3(1), 37–54.

MacSwan, Jeff. 2005. Codeswitching and generative grammar: A critique of the MLF model and some remarks on modified minimalism. *Bilingualism: Language and Cognition* 8(1), 1–22.

Mahootian, Shahrzad. 1993. *A Null Theory of Codeswitching*. Illinois: Northwestern University dissertation.

Myers-Scotton, Carol. 1993. *Dueling Languages: Grammatical Structure in Code Switching*. Oxford: Clarendon Press.

Newport, Elissa L. & Richard P. Meier. 1985. The acquisition of American Sign Language. In Dan Isaac Slobin (ed.), *The crosslinguistic study of language acquisition. Volume 1: The data*, 881–938. Hillsdale, NJ: Lawrence Erlbaum Associates.

Petitto, Laura Ann, Marina Katerelos, Bronna G. Levy, Kristine Gauna, Karine Tetreault & Vittoria Ferraro. 2001. Bilingual signed and spoken language acquisition from birth: Implications for the mechanisms underlying early bilingual language acquisition. *Journal of Child Language* 28(2), 453–496.

Poplack, Shana. 1980. Sometimes I'll start a sentence in Spanish y termino en Espanol: Toward a typology of code-switching. *Linguistics* 18, 581–618.

Poplack, Shana. 1981. The syntactic structure and social function of code-switching. In Richard P. Durán (ed.), *Latino language and communicative behaviour*, 169–184. Norwood, NJ: Ablex.

Quadros, Ronice Müller de, Diane Lillo-Martin & Deborah Chen Pichler. 2013. Early effects of bilingualism on WH-question structures: Insight from sign-speech bilingualism. In Stavroula Stavrakaki, Marina Lalioti & Polyxeni Konstantinopoulou (eds.), *Advances in language acquisition*, 300–308. Newcastle upon Tyne, UK: Cambridge Scholars Press.

Toribio, Almeida Jacqueline. 2001. On the emergence of bilingual code-switching competence. *Bilingualism: Langage and Cognition* 4(3). 203–231.

Woolford, Ellen. 1983. Bilingual code-switching and syntactic theory. *Linguistic Inquiry* 14(3), 520–536.

# Blending languages: Bimodal bilinguals and language synthesis

Ronice Müller de Quadros, Diane Lillo-Martin and Deborah Chen Pichler

## 1 Introduction

As the chapters of this book illustrate, multilingual signers, as multilinguals everywhere, have specific rule-governed ways of allowing their languages to interact. In this chapter,[1] we focus on multilinguals who use a sign language alongside a spoken language in its oral form (as opposed to the written form of a spoken language); these are bimodal bilinguals since their languages occupy two different modalities. The primary members of the group of bimodal bilinguals so defined are often known as Codas – a name derived from the name of an organization called CODA, for Child of Deaf Adults (see Bishop 2006), which serves as a social organization for adults who share the experience of having grown up in a household with Deaf, signing parents. Codas are bilingual by virtue of their exposure to a sign language at home together with a spoken language in the majority (hearing) community.

Multilinguals sometimes produce structures that combine aspects of more than one language. We will use the term 'code-mixing' as a cover term for different types of language combinations (without intending to impute confusion or unorderliness to such 'mixing'). One type of mixing presents as words in one language produced in the order appropriate to the other. Children's production of such structures is sometimes referred to as 'cross-linguistic influence', while for adult learners such mixing is considered 'transfer'. As will become clear, we see such cases not necessarily as intermediate stages limited to learners, but as natural products of multiple linguistic components.

---

[1] We are grateful to the participants in our research and their families, without whom such research would be impossible. We also thank the research assistants and collaborators who work with us in the larger project of which this is a part. This project was supported in part by Award Number R01DC009263 from the National Institutes of Health (National Institute on Deafness and Other Communication Disorders). The content is solely the responsibility of the authors and does not necessarily represent the official views of the NIDCD or the NIH. Support was also provided by The Gallaudet Research Institute, and CNPq (Brazilian National Council of Technological and Scientific Development) Grant #200031/2009-0 and #470111/2007-0.

https://doi.org/10.1515/9781501503528-006

Utterances by Codas involving use of spoken words in the order or form appropriate to a sign language are sometimes called Coda-Talk. This label is also applied to a particular style of talking which may involve spoken glosses of signs that are not actual translation equivalents (e.g., 'orange eyes' for ASL 'SURPRISED', because the form of that sign is similar to that of ORANGE, but located near the eyes; Bishop and Hicks 2005), or vocal patterns that imitate the voices sometimes produced by the Deaf parents of Codas. Codas also often engage in 'sign-speaking' simultaneously, or what we call 'code-blending', following Emmorey, Borinstein, Thompson, and Gollan (2008). Code-blending refers to the simultaneous use of both speech and sign within a single utterance; for example, while primarily speaking, a bimodal bilingual may produce a signed word that is a translation equivalent to a spoken word (see below for other examples). In some ways, code-blending is similar to code-switching, the (possibly intra-sentential) change from one language to the next produced by unimodal bilinguals, in that it is prevalent among highly proficient bilingual users, and may be an identifier of members of a particular sociolinguistic community, namely (adult) children with typical hearing whose Deaf parents use a sign language. Code-blending may also follow grammatical restrictions similar to those observed for code-switching. This possibility leads to one of the major questions of our research: what are the grammatical characteristics of code-blending produced by bimodal bilinguals?

Our chapter focuses on Kodas ('kids of Deaf adults,' a term used for young Codas) and as such, is the only chapter in this book to address multilingual signers as very young children. In particular, we ask how the languages of a young bimodal bilingual child develop, how they influence each other and interact, and how they are kept distinct in appropriate contexts. The children in our study and their interlocutors use American Sign Language (ASL) and English (Eng), or Brazilian Sign Language (Libras) and Brazilian Portuguese (BP). In the remainder of this first section, we summarize previous studies on unimodal and bimodal bilinguals that help to set the stage for our research by defining the characteristics of language 'mixing' in developing bilinguals.

## 1.1 Adult Codas

Adult bimodal bilinguals (Codas) have been raised with a sign language as their home language. Given that the dominant language of the majority surrounding (hearing) community is a spoken language, Codas resemble 'heritage speakers' in that their home language is different from that of the community (see Chen Pichler et al. 2017; Quadros et al. 2016). One common pattern for heritage speakers is highly variable proficiency in the home language, ranging from passive receptive knowledge of the home language to, in rare cases, dominance in the home language. Typically, heritage speakers become dominant in the community language after being immersed in it at school. Similarly, Codas report a wide range of ability in their sign language proficiency, but the majority become dominant in the community spoken language once they enter school.

For Codas who keep in contact with other Codas (such as through the CODA organization), the intermixing of sign and speech may be a special phenomenon used in language play and in close social groupings (Bishop and Hicks 2005), parallel to the use of a combination of German and Spanish known as Esplugish, used by students of a particular German-Spanish bilingual school (González-Vilbazo and López, 2011). Bishop (2010) studied the interactions of 19 ASL/Eng Codas, divided into six different groups, conversing about various Coda-related topics. She found that when instructed to "communicate in any way that is comfortable for you," almost all of the participants code-blended. She also noted a relationship between participants' attitudes towards Coda-talk and CODA events and their use of code-blending, with those showing no interest in such events choosing to use almost exclusively either English or ASL, without blending. Nevertheless, she suggested that code-blending generally emerged across groups as a "strategy of neutrality" or an unmarked choice for communication between Codas.

Emmorey et al. (2008) also studied adult ASL/Eng Codas interacting in conversation, and additionally recorded them retelling a story from an animated cartoon clip. They found that the Codas used code-blending in almost 36% of the utterances analyzed (as opposed to code-switching, which only occurred in 6% of the utterances). They reported that the code-blends typically expressed semantically congruent information in both speech and sign. They also found a high degree of temporal synchronization of the blended speech and sign: the onset of the ASL sign was almost always simultaneous with that of the English word, or only slightly offset.

We should clarify at this point why we consider code-blending to be distinct from Simultaneous Communication or "Sim-Com." First, code-blending results from interaction between sign and spoken language grammars, while Sim-Com is driven by spoken language grammar only. Sim-Com nearly always follows the structure of the spoken language, artificially imposing linear organization onto signs and stripping away prosodic information important for parsing signed utterances (e.g. rhythm, brow movement and other nonmanual cues that mark phrase boundaries). As a result, Sim-Com is easily understood by hearing listeners, but largely inaccessible to Deaf viewers, especially when it is used for extended stretches in high-stake contexts such as classroom lectures, meetings, etc. (Johnson, Liddell and Erting 1989, Tevenal and Villanueva 2009). In contrast, code-blending is a natural outcome of bimodal contexts comparable to code-switching in unimodal bilingual contexts, occurring spontaneously in mixed Deaf-hearing households or among bimodal bilinguals. Unlike SimCom, code-blending reflects both the spoken language and the sign language grammars, a balance that is easier to manage for the relatively short utterances typical of spontaneous code-blends used by young children. Finally, code-blending is better suited than SimCom to the visual modality in its maintenance of nonmanual prosodic cues typical of sign languages, facilitating accessibility for Deaf addressees. Because successful code-blending requires knowledge of the grammatical and prosodic rules of the sign language, researchers have proposed that its use indicates skill in both languages (van den Bogaerde and Baker 2002), whereas SimCom is typical of individuals who speak well, but do not sign well.

## 1.2 Kodas

Petitto et al. (2001) studied three Kodas ages 1 to 4 acquiring French and la Langue des Signes Québécoise (LSQ; the sign language used in parts of Quebec); they compared these children to three unimodal bilinguals acquiring French and English. Their study focused on establishing parallels between the bilingual acquisition of a sign language and a spoken language versus two spoken languages. By comparing the two groups of children, they established that both the unimodal and bimodal bilinguals achieved linguistic milestones such as first words, first two-word combinations, and a 50-word vocabulary at equivalent ages, within the typical age range observed for monolingual children developing each language. Furthermore, they reported that the bilingual children demonstrated sensitivity to the language of their interlocutors by modifying their language choices accordingly, even if they were unable to achieve a complete match to the interlocutor's use in their non-dominant language.

Petitto et al. (2001) also reported that the older participants produced more of what they called 'mixed' language use, particularly, 'simultaneous language mixing', which we are now calling code-blending. They noted that this mixing generally consisted of semantically 'congruent' mixes, in which a sign and a word express congruent meanings (which we would characterize as rough translation equivalents) expressed simultaneously. They also observed much less frequent 'non-congruent' mixes, in which signs and words each contributed some part of the utterance meaning.

Extensive studies of Kodas acquiring Dutch and Nederlandse Gebarentaal (NGT; Sign Language of the Netherlands) have been conducted by van den Bogaerde and Baker (2005, 2008). They categorized children's code-blending into four categories according to which language provided what they considered the semantic base for a given utterance. In Dutch BL (base language) code blends, the full content is expressed in Dutch, with no additional content expressed by the accompanying signs; NGT BL code blends have the opposite profile: full NGT content with redundant Dutch words; mixed utterances contain some content from each language; full blends express the same content in both languages.

Van den Bogaerde and Baker (2008) reported that the three Kodas they studied produced code-blending with increasing frequency when interacting with their Deaf mothers at ages 1;06, 3;00, and 6;00, moving from a relatively higher proportion of spoken utterances to a higher proportion of signed and code-blended utterances. At 3;00, the majority of code-blends were Dutch BL, moving to more Mixed and Full blends by 6;00.

Finally, a recent longitudinal study of language choice and code-blending by eight Finnish Kodas (Kanto, Laasko, and Huttunen, 2015, 2016) reported patterns very similar to those of the Canadian and Dutch Koda studies above. Already at the age of 12 months, the youngest age at which the Finnish Koda children were observed, they used more FinnSL with their Deaf parents and more spoken Finnish with hearing interlocutors, exhibiting early sensitivity to language choice that became more pronounced with time (the final observation point occurring at 24 months). The authors propose that this early language differentiation also manifested in the children's use of a wider range of gesture, sign and speech combinations when interacting with Deaf adults than with hearing adults. Specifically, the Finnish Kodas used more code-blended utterances with their Deaf parents than with hearing interlocutors, although this tendency did not clearly reflect parental use of code-blending, as was the case in van den Bogaerde and Baker's study (2005, 2008). With respect to the structure of the code-blends produced by the Finnish Kodas, most were redundant congruent blends ("Equally strong," in the terminology of Kanto et al. 2016) in which FinnSL and Finnish words contributed equivalent content to the utterance and avoided violations of either grammar. Like van den Bogaerde and Baker (2002), Kanto et al. (2016) reasoned that code-blending of this type requires considerable language competence in both FinnSL and Finnish, and so should not be regarded as an indication of weak language skills or lexical gaps. Notably, the MLU of Equally strong code-blends was shorter than for code-blends categorized as either Finnish base language or FinnSL base language, and mostly reserved for labeling, a common occurrence in spontaneous child language.

The general pattern that emerges from the three Koda studies summarized here is that young Koda children differentiate between their signed and spoken languages from a very young age, adjusting their use of one or the other according to interlocutor. They use code-blending from an early age, particularly with their Deaf parents, and display a preference for congruent structures, in which there is redundancy and synchronization across spoken and signed content. We will return to discuss these characteristics of code-blending with respect to our own Koda data later in this chapter.

## 1.3 Unimodal bilingual development

Numerous studies of unimodal bilingual spoken language acquisition have explored the ways that languages interact in development (for recent reviews, see Serratrice 2013, Unsworth 2013). In many cases, researchers have noted that children combine aspects of their two languages. For example, children acquiring a Germanic (e.g. Dutch or German) language and a Romance (e.g. French or Italian) language seem to follow the Germanic pattern permitting object drop in their Romance language, for a longer period than monolingual children do (Hulk and Müller 2000). Such effects have been attributed to temporary cross-linguistic influence in the developing grammars. Note that such influence may be facilitative, as in the case of faster acquisition of German determiners by German-Italian bilingual children (Kupisch 2007). In either case, researchers have treated this phenomenon as a stage of language development that is abandoned once children receive sufficient input.

On the other hand, researchers have also observed that young bilingual children engage in code-switching, which is considered a bilingual phenomenon related to high levels of proficiency (Cantone 2007). In code-switching, speakers combine their languages sequentially, whether inter- or intra-sententially. While researchers agree that this phenomenon is not haphazard, characterizing the constraints that regulate where switches can and cannot (grammatically) occur remains a topic of energetic debate.

On our view, cross-linguistic influence and code-switching are two natural outcomes of a bilingual language system, given that vocabulary items from two languages are available to contribute towards any given derivation. Likewise, code-blending, the simultaneous production of speech and sign, is also a natural result of combining languages in two modalities. However, we expect that it is constrained, as code-switching and cross-linguistic influence are, according to the principles of the language computational system. We will discuss this view of bilingual language architecture in more detail in section 7. In order to investigate the constraints on code-blending, however, we need to see just how it is used in young bimodal bilingual children. For this reason, the rest of this chapter will focus on describing the types of code-blending produced by bimodal bilingual children in our study.

## 2 Binational bimodal bilingual language acquisition project

For several years our research team has been engaged in investigation of bimodal bilingual language development for two language pairs: ASL and English, and Brazilian Sign Language (Libras) and Brazilian Portuguese (BP). Our original grant project, The Development of Bimodal Bilingualism, is unique in that it involves two groups of bimodal bilinguals: hearing children from Deaf families (Kodas) and young Deaf children from Deaf families with a cochlear implant (DDCI). We have collected both longitudinal spontaneous data and experimental data from these children between the ages of roughly 1;0 to 7;0.

Our research project addresses multiple research questions and includes several design features that are unique among existing studies of bimodal bilingualism. Most fundamentally, we are interested in how the developmental patterns for simultaneous acquisition of a signed and spoken language compare to those previously reported for each language individually, and those reported for young unimodal bilinguals and bimodal bilinguals learning other language pairs. By including two sets of languages with different grammatical properties, we can study the effects of particular languages on the development process, resulting in a greater degree of generalizability for our findings. Generalizability is a critical aspect of our research project as we articulate a theoretical model of language interaction that applies over the course of childhood development and into adulthood. We call our model the *Language Synthesis Model* and will introduce it in more detail below.

We are also interested in the effects of cochlear implants on bimodal bilingual acquisition, specifically for children who receive sustained exposure to a natural sign language from birth. Most of the existing literature on cochlear implanted children focuses on those with severely restricted exposure to signing, usually in the form of Total Communication rather than a full and natural sign language. Not surprisingly, such studies typically report poor development of the spoken language, compared with that of cochlear implanted children who adhere to an "oral-only" philosophy (e.g., Niparko et al. 2010). However, none of these studies has examined the development of sign language and spoken language as two systems of a child bilingual, comparing them with the natural bilingual situation of Kodas. Our project has observed extensive similarities between bimodal development of our Koda and DDCI participants (Davidson, Lillo-Martin and Chen Pichler 2014, Goodwin 2016). With respect to their sign language developmental patterns, some resemble those reported for (non-implanted) Deaf signing children, while others are noticeably divergent (Palmer 2015). We are investigating the degree to which the latter can be considered characteristics of *heritage signers,* parallel to developmental patterns reported for heritage speakers of minority spoken languages (for more on our heritage signer analyses, see Chen Pichler et al. 2017).

## 3 Method

### 3.1 Participants

The participants for the data reported in the present chapter are two hearing Koda bimodal bilingual children, one (Ben) from the U.S. and one (Igor) from Brazil. The children are participants in our long-term project, 'Development of Bimodal Bilingualism' (see www.bibibi.uconn.edu for more information on this research project). Ben has two Deaf, signing parents, and both Deaf and hearing siblings. Igor has a Deaf father and a hearing mother who is a fluent L2 signer. Like all of the children in our project, Ben and Igor receive input in a signed home language (ASL or Libras, respectively) from their parents, and a spoken majority language (English or BP, respectively) from other relatives, neighbors, and the community.

For this chapter, we have analyzed four videos collected from each child (ranging from 30 to 60 minutes in length each), in the age range from 2;00 (years;months) to 2;07, as detailed in Table 1 (see section 3.3 for information on how the utterances were coded). The linguistic productions of the adults interacting with Ben in all four sessions, and those of the adults in one speech-target session with Igor, were also analyzed. For Ben, the adults in the Sign target sessions were his mother (2;00) or a Deaf experimenter (2;06); the adult in the two Speech target sessions was the same hearing, fluent signer. For Igor, the adult in the Sign target sessions was his father, and in the Speech target sessions it was his mother.

**Table 1.** Participants and number of analyzable utterances produced in each modality as a function of the session target language (NB: participants generally used the target language, but most did not adopt that language exclusively)

| Participant | Total | # Signed | | # Spoken | | # Bimodal | |
|---|---|---|---|---|---|---|---|
| Target lang. | | Sign | Spch | Sign | Spch | Sign | Spch |
| Ben (2;00, 2:06) | 1349 | 211 | 31 | 17 | 783 | 66 | 241 |
| Adults to Ben | 1197 | 436 | 2 | 25 | 610 | 6 | 118 |
| Igor (2;02, 2;07) | 1239 | 137 | 21 | 261 | 523 | 134 | 163 |
| Adults to Igor (2;02 sp only) | 817 | | 7 | | 615 | | 195 |

## 3.2 Data collection

Participants were video-taped to collect a sample of their ordinary language use that was as natural as possible. Generally, a target language was established for each session (either Sign or Speech) and alternated every week. Our goal was to elicit natural language use and observe any mixing that occurred; we did not try to enforce language separation. See Chen Pichler et al. (2016), Quadros et al. (2014) for more detail about our filming methods and the best practices we developed for building our corpora.

## 3.3 Coding

Our first step was to annotate all speech and sign produced by the child subject and his interlocutor(s). Our procedures and conventions are described in detail in Chen Pichler et al. (2010) and summarized here. We used the ELAN program (http://tla.mpi.nl/tools/tla-tools/elan/; Crasborn and Sloetjes 2008) for all video annotation. Ordinary orthography supplemented with special symbols was used for all spoken language utterances. Glosses were used to annotate signs, following the principles of ID glossing, using a written word in Eng/BP to stand for a particular sign generally having overlapping meaning (Johnston 1991).

Utterance breaks were determined by considering both prosodic and syntactic information. An utterance is a group of signs/words usually delimited by prosodic patterns, which in the case of signing includes lowering or relaxation of the hands, a longer pause than normal, or lengthening of the final sign in the group; or in the case of speech, falling tone or a stretch of silence following the last syllable. Although prosodic information is used to help determine utterance boundaries, at the analysis stage we also used syntactic and meaning information in constructing an utterance for analysis that essentially follows the AS-unit (analysis of speech unit) described by Foster et al. (2000: 365): "consisting of an independent clause, or sub-clausal unit, together with any subordinate clauses associated with either". Each utterance is classified as sign-only or speech-only or bimodal, where utterances are bimodal if any part contains both speech and sign simultaneously.

We further coded all bimodal utterances for several features. First, we coded the Content of a bimodal utterance as falling into one of five possible categories, according to how much content was expressed in each language (independent of structural differences between the information expressed in each language). These categories, which were developed from the categories used by van den Bogaerde and Baker (2008), are listed below.

- Fully bimodal: Utterances that have the same information expressed in sign and speech. There may be some differences, such as an overt article in speech without a corresponding element in sign, but the information content is considered the same in both modalities.
- Sign-base: Utterances that have more information expressed in sign than in speech.
- Speech-base: Utterances that have more information expressed in speech than in sign.
- IX+Speech: Utterances in which speech is accompanied by a point (IX) but no other signed element. These are a special type of Speech-base utterances, since the point usually corresponds to content that is also expressed in speech. Although non-signers often point while speaking, we consider IX+Speech a potential type of blending for bimodal bilinguals (see Gökgöz et al. under revision).
- Complementary: Utterances in which neither language expresses a subset of information expressed in the other language. For these utterances, both languages are needed to grasp the total content (labeled 'Mixed' by van den Bogaerde and Baker 2008).

A second type of coding related to the Timing of sign and speech in bimodal utterances. For each utterance we determined the relative extent of signed and spoken material as shown in Table 2. Note that this coding concerns the timing of the full utterance rather than individual signs and words, diverging in this regard from the timing coding employed by Emmorey et al. (2008).

**Table 2.** Three types of timing between sign and speech in bimodal utterances

| Coextensive | sign<br>speech | ----------------<br>---------------- | Sign and speech start and end<br>at the same time |
|---|---|---|---|
| Included | sign/speech<br>speech/sign | ----------------<br>---------- | The extent of one modality is<br>completely within the other |
| Mismatch | sign/speech<br>speech/sign | ----------<br>---------- | One modality starts before the<br>other; the second ends later |

Finally, we examined the Syntax of bimodal utterances produced by Ben and his adult interlocutors in more detail. In particular, we examined those bimodal utterances containing more than one sign and more than one spoken word, so we could compare the word order used in either modality. We coded these utterances in two steps. First, we determined whether the corresponding signed and spoken words were in the same order ('congruent') or not. Next, we considered whether the signed and the spoken utterances would be considered grammatical (target-like) on its own. Utterances missing obligatory elements (e.g. articles in English), in the wrong word order for the target language, or with additional inappropriate elements (e.g. signs for English prepositions used where ASL does not normally use prepositions) were coded as ungrammatical (even though in some cases, such as missing verbal inflections in English, these are common productions for 2-year-old children).

# 4 Results – Content and timing

The results of the coding of Content and Timing for Ben and his interlocutors, and Igor and his interlocutor, are given in Figures 1-2 and 3-4, respectively. The charts show the proportion of each utterance type out of all the bimodal utterances produced for a particular session.

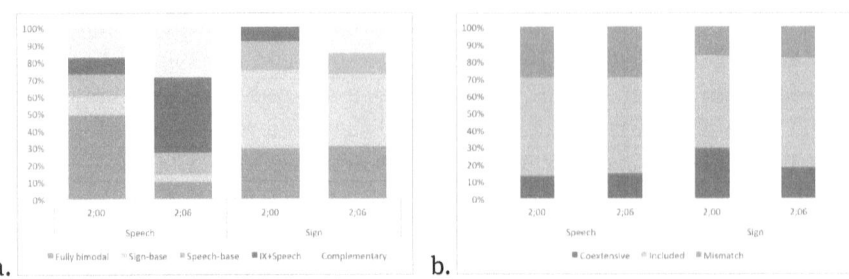

**Figure 1.** Ben's utterances: Proportion of utterances produced at each age for each target language (a) Bimodal content; (b) Bimodal timing

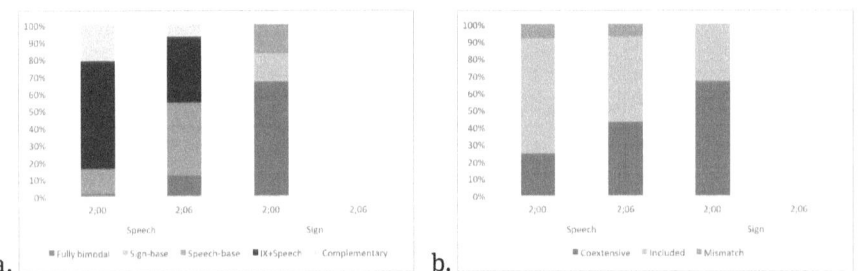

**Figure 2.** Adults' utterances to Ben: Proportion of utterances produced at each of Ben's ages for each target language (a) Bimodal content; (b) Bimodal timing (no bimodal utterances were produced in the 2;06 Sign session)

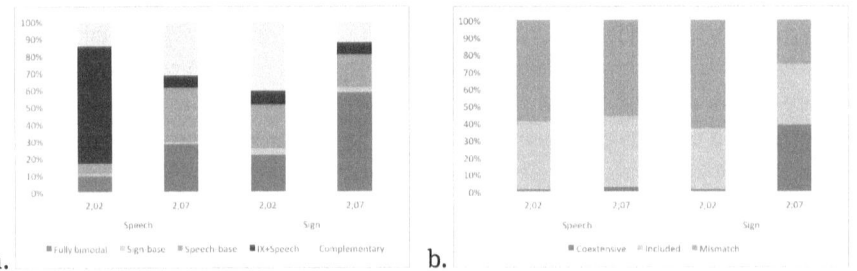

**Figure 3.** Igor's utterances: Proportion of utterances produced at each age for each target language (a) Bimodal content; (b) Bimodal timing

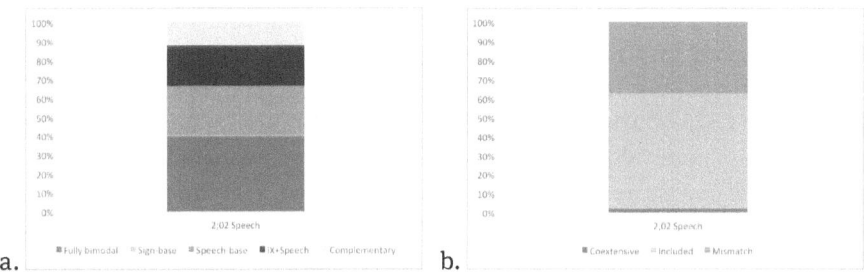

**Figure 4.** Adult's utterances to Igor in Speech-target session at 2;02: Proportion of utterances (a) Bimodal content; (b) Bimodal timing

## 5 Discussion – Content and timing

In this section we consider the bimodal utterance types produced by the children and their interlocutors by content and timing. For Ben, there is a clear difference in his blending content during sign-target sessions compared to speech-target sessions. In the sign-target sessions his blends are mostly Sign-base. An example of such a Sign-base blend produced by Ben during a sign-target session is given in (1a).[2] Sign-base plus Fully-bimodal blends (as in (1b)) constitute 70% or more of his blended utterances during sign-target sessions. This does not change over time for Ben.

(1) a.     ASL:    HAVE    COOKIE     (Ben, 2;00, sign-target)
            Eng:                cookie
            '(he) has a cookie'

    b.     ASL:    GREEN    TRIANGLE   (Ben, 2;00, sign-target)
            Eng:      green      triangle
            '(it's a) green triangle'

In speech-target sessions, half of Ben's blends are Fully bimodal at the youngest age, as illustrated in (2). It should be borne in mind, however, that at this age

---

[2] We follow the sign linguistics convention of using glosses in all caps to represent signs, with additional annotations as needed. IX represents a pointing sign, with the referent of the point indicated in parentheses. For code-blending examples, the signed production is indicated on the top tier, and the spoken production on the bottom tier. Vertical alignment indicates co-temporal production, with dashes following a sign gloss to indicate the temporal extent when needed.

his utterances generally consist of only one or two words/signs. By 2;06, Ben's blends in speech-target sessions are either Speech-base, as in (3a), or IX+speech, as in (3b). In fact, overall Ben's output is highly speech-dominant by 2;06; as reported in Lillo-Martin et al. (2014), nearly all of his output in speech-target sessions was speech alone by that age. His blending shows parallel development to his overall output: speech-target sessions move from a mixture of speech-only and speech-based blending to almost all speech; sign-target sessions include sign-only utterances and a fair amount of blending, but blending is primarily Full or Sign-base, and hence comprehensible to a Deaf interlocutor even without access to his speech.

(2)     ASL:    BIRD                    (Ben, 2;00, speech-target)
        Eng:    bird
                '(it's a) bird'

(3) a.  ASL:            POUR            (Ben, 2;06, speech-target)
        Eng:    I wanna dump this
                'I wanna dump this'

    b.  ASL:            IX(off-camera)
        Eng:    I wanna train
                'I want a train'

The timing of Ben's bimodal utterances is generally Included, meaning that in most cases, the utterance in one modality had a longer duration than in the other, as in example (3a) above. Even for Full bimodal utterances, it is possible for production in one modality to extend longer than in the other, such as when extra words are present in one modality but not the other (e.g. articles 'the/a' that are produced in English output but not in the accompanying ASL output). In some Included cases as well as many Mismatch cases, there is a clear asymmetry in timing, as in example (4a), where we reproduce the ELAN segment showing that the spoken word begins much earlier than the signed word (approximately 18 video frames). Occasionally such mismatch examples are corrected with repetition, as in (4b), which comes from a session in our database that was not analyzed for this chapter. In (4b), after a couple of tries, Ben moves his hand to the location for the second signed instance of SNAKE and produces the sign movement exactly together with the third spoken instance of 'snake'. According to the study by Emmorey et al. (2008) on adult Codas, individual signs and words usually start simultaneously or within a few video frames of one another, but this tight temporal coordination appears to still be under development for the two-year olds observed in the current study.

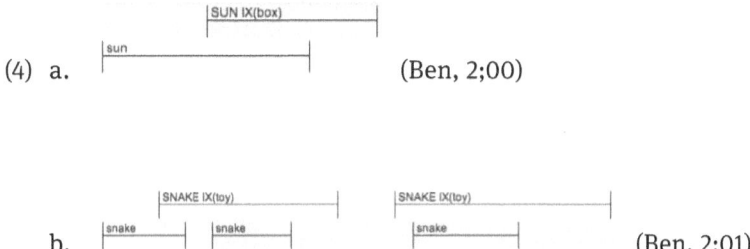

(4) a. (Ben, 2;00)

b. (Ben, 2;01)

Ben's adult interlocutors in speech-target sessions also differ dramatically from interlocutors in sign-target sessions in their use of blending content types. In the speech-target sessions, the adult produces mostly Speech-base utterances, especially IX+speech, as illustrated in (5), with some Complementary cases as well. As reported by Lillo-Martin et al. (2014), speech-target interlocutors for Ben had a higher proportion of blending at earlier sessions than later, with the majority of utterances being speech-only. On the other hand, interlocutors in sign-target sessions used very little blending at all after age 1;11. The categories represented in Figure 2 for the sign-target session at 2;00 are based on only 6 blended utterances, mostly Full bimodal, as illustrated in (6).

(5) ASL:   IX(plane)------                (Hearing adult to Ben, 2;00)
    Eng:   he  flies in the plane
           'He flies in the plane there'

(6)                                         (Deaf adult to Ben, 2;06)
    ASL:   IX(DCP)    ALLERGIC    CLEAN  IX(DCP)
    Eng:   she's      allergic to cleaning
           'She's allergic to cleaning, she is!'

As for timing, in sign-target sessions the Full type adult blends are always coextensive in length, while the others are Included. In speech-target sessions, this pattern generally holds, except that there are also some Full types that are Included, a combination that Ben himself also uses. Additionally, there are Mismatch cases, which are either Complementary or IX+speech types.

Turning to Igor, the largest contrast in blending types comes between his youngest speech-target session and the other three. In the former, his blends are primarily IX+speech, as illustrated in (7a). In the other three sessions, his blends are generally either Full bimodal or Speech-base, illustrated in (7b, c). This pattern is not surprising in view of the observation by Lillo-Martin et al. (2014) that even in sign-target sessions, Igor produced more blending and speech-only than sign-only (although his distribution of these modes is different in speech-target sessions, where speech-only is dominant).

(7) a. Libras: IX(brinquedo) (Igor, 2;02 Speech target)
　　　　　　　IX(toy)
　　　BP:　　olha, olha aqui vermelho
　　　　　　　look look here red
　　　　　　　'Look, it's red here!'

　　b. Libras: PÁSSARO (Igor, 2;02 Sign target)
　　　　　　　BIRD
　　　BP:　　pássarinho
　　　　　　　birdie
　　　　　　　'(it's a) birdie

　　c. Libras:　　　　　　　IX(brinquedo)　NÃO　(Igor, 2;07, Speech target)
　　　　　　　　　　　　　　IX(toy)　　　　NO
　　　BP:　　mãe quer　　esse　　　　　　não
　　　　　　　Mom wants　this　　　　　　no
　　　　　　　'Mom doesn't want this'

In terms of timing, Igor's blends are often Mismatches; this category includes blends of each content type produced. In his last sign-target session he produced a number of Coextensive blends, all of which are Full content type.

The adult interlocutor in Igor's speech-target sessions was his mother, and her code-blending was analyzed for one session (2;02). His interlocutor in sign-target sessions, his father, blended very infrequently, so no adult code-blending data from sign sessions was analyzed. Unlike Ben's interlocutors, blending by Igor's mother was more likely to be Fully bimodal, as illustrated in (8a). Speech-base and IX+speech made up most of the rest of the blending she produced, illustrated in (8b). Like Igor, his mother used code-blends that included Mismatch examples from every content type produced.

(8) a. Libras: E(caiu)  (Hearing adult to Igor, 2;02)
            E(fell)
       BP:  acabou
            fell-3sg
            '(s/he) fell down!'

   b. Libras: UM------------------
             ONE
       BP:   uma florzinha    só
             one  little-flower only
             'only one little flower'

Our finding that Sign-base blending is the least frequent type overall is consistent with reports by van den Bogaerde and Baker (2005, 2008) for Kodas acquiring NGT and Dutch. This is also the pattern observed in Bishop's (2010) study of blending by adult US Codas, where ASL base language blends are reported to be 7% of total blending, with the majority (59%) English base language. The one reported exception is one of the Deaf mothers in the study by van den Bogaerde and Baker (2008), who produced a majority of NGT base language blends to her 6-year-old Koda son. Thus the general pattern for base language choice tends to lean towards the spoken language, but this tendency is subject to personal preference.

# 6 Results and discussion – Syntax (Ben and his interlocutors only)

As a first step toward understanding how code-blended utterances are derived, we evaluated the syntax of each utterance in sign and speech separately, for all of the bimodal utterances with at least two spoken words and at least two signs produced by Ben and his interlocutors, as summarized in Table 3. The table shows the number of utterances of each type produced by Ben and his interlocutors (comparable analysis of Igor's data have not yet been performed).

**Table 3.** Syntactic distribution of bimodal utterances for Ben's sessions (✓=grammatical for target language; *=ungrammatical for target language; each row corresponds to one possible type)

| Type | Sign | Speech | Ben | Adults to Ben |
|---|---|---|---|---|
| Congruent | ✓ | ✓ | 18 | 11 |
|  | ✓ | * | 40 | 0 |
|  | * | ✓ | 0 | 10 |
|  | * | * | 0 | 0 |
| Not congruent |  |  | 1 | 0 |

Our first observation is that virtually all of the bimodal utterances produced by Ben, and all of those produced by adults, display the same word order when signs and spoken words are near translation-equivalents. For example, when Ben (2;06) signs PLAY GAME and speaks "play game", the signs and spoken words occur in the same order. Note that Complementary types (as in (9)) may display different word orders for sign and speech, but because they involve different parts of the sentence, they are excluded from the Not Congruent category here.

(9)  ASL:        MOTHER IX(out-window)           (Ben 2;00)
     Eng:   I want    Mommy
     'I want Mommy (who is over there)'

As for the syntactic grammaticality of speech and sign in blends produced by adults, blends were always grammatical in speech, but not always in sign. That is, the blends follow English syntax; when ASL grammar is not compatible, English dominates. However, it is important to note that in the data analyzed for this part of the study, all but one of the code-blends came from speech-target sessions, so it is not surprising that English grammar should dominate for adult production.

In contrast, we see that for Ben, most of his bimodal productions are considered grammatical in ASL, but many are not grammatical in English. However, many of these cases of ungrammatical English are due to common developmental errors such as missing articles, possessive markers, and copulas, or uninflected verbs, as in example (10). In such utterances, the speech is typical for 2-year-old child English.

(10) ASL:  HORSE    FALL                          (Ben 2;00)
    Eng:  horsie   fall down
          'The horsie fell down'

However, there are cases in Ben's blending where English follows an ASL-like word order along with accompanying signs, as illustrated by the WH-final word order in (11).

(11) ASL:  MOTHER   WHERE                         (Ben 2;00)
    Eng:  Mommy    where
          'Where's Mommy?'

Monolingual English-speaking children are not known to produce utterances with non-target word order such as these. Such cases could be interpreted as evidence that knowledge of ASL negatively effects development of English syntax. However, we have argued (Lillo-Martin et al. 2012, 2016) that such examples, like code-switching in unimodal bilingual adults, are more accurately regarded as what we call *Language Synthesis*, reflecting the fact that the mental linguistic computational system can incorporate elements from both of a bilingual's languages into a single derivation. We detail our analysis of language synthesis in the next section.

# 7 Language synthesis

We have proposed a model of *Language Synthesis* designed to capture the range of possibilities by which multiple languages can interact in all multilinguals, including bimodal bilinguals (Koulidobrova 2012, 2016; Lillo-Martin et al. 2012, 2016). Consistent with the view of language competence assumed by generative theories of grammar, particularly Minimalism (Chomsky 1995), the Language Synthesis model describes how sentences are generated; it is not a production model, attempting to capture real-time aspects of sentence construction from 'left to right' online. Finally, the model also incorporates aspects of the theory of Distributed Morphology (Halle and Marantz 1993), in particular, the idea that abstract roots enter into the computation of a sentence before they are specified for a particular language, and that insertion of particular phonological forms occurs relatively late in the derivation. A simplified version of the Language Synthesis model is shown in Figure 5.

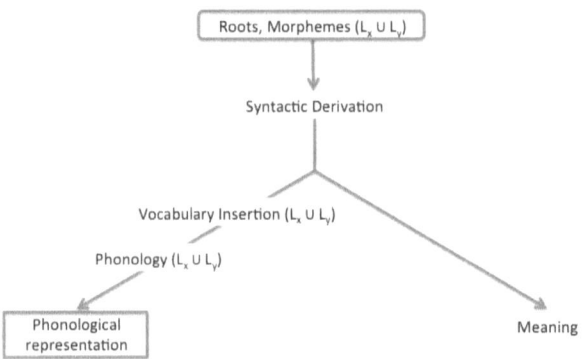

**Figure 5.** Language Synthesis model

Following MacSwan (2000), we assume that no special machinery should be added to our conception of the linguistic system to account for bilingual effects; rather, these should fall out from the design of the system when more than one grammar is included. Thus, according to the Language Synthesis model, a monolingual speaker will build up a sentence using abstract roots and morphemes from their single language. A bilingual speaker can also use just those elements that come from a single language, but also has the option of selecting elements from both languages in constructing a single sentence. If at the point of Vocabulary Insertion some elements are inserted from one language and others are inserted from the other language, the result will be code-switching. In some cases, a speaker might use null functional elements from one language even if all the phonological elements come from the other language. This will often result in utterances of the type variously known as transfer, calquing, or cross-linguistic influence. These processes will be constrained by the requirements of the elements chosen from each language: they must be mutually compatible for feature-checking to succeed.

For bimodal bilinguals, there exists an additional possibility. At the point of vocabulary insertion, the bilingual might choose elements from *both* sign and speech, resulting in code-blending. For the children whose productions we focus on here, they may have additional factors influencing their production, such as potentially incomplete knowledge of the target grammar morpho-syntax. However, as long as the pieces chosen for the syntactic computation are not in conflict, nothing will prohibit production of both speech and sign simultaneously (see Lillo-Martin, Quadros, and Chen Pichler 2016).

The Language Synthesis model takes as its starting point the observation that code-blended utterances express a single proposition (Emmorey et al.

2008). Although it may be physically possible to simultaneously produce sign and speech, bimodal bilinguals have not been observed to produce code-blended utterances in which the sign and a speech encode completely different content. There may be various reasons one could posit for such a restriction, including memory or processing limitations that would not be directly represented in a model of linguistic competence. Under the Language Synthesis model, this restriction follows from the fact that the computational system only generates one proposition at a time, even in bimodal cases.

A more controversial aspect of the Language Synthesis model is the proposal that bilingual utterances including code-blending make use of a single derivation. That is, the Synthesis model rejects simultaneous distinct derivations for sign and speech, even if both are based on the same underlying proposition. Instead, the signed and spoken elements are combined in a single computation that includes two output modalities. The need for two separate simultaneous computations in the derivation of code-blending between Italian and Italian Sign Language has been argued for by Branchini and Donati (2016).

Our basic assumptions of one proposition and one derivation are supported by the results we reported from our coding of child and adult blending in sections 4–6. We will expand on this claim first regarding the one proposition assumption, and then turn to the question of derivation.

Fully bimodal, Sign-base, and Speech-base utterances are 'Redundant' in the sense that whatever is produced in each modality has a match in the other modality. Such cases are clearly instances where speech and sign contribute to one proposition. For Complementary cases, each modality has something different to contribute, but we were able to readily see how an interpretation combining the pieces from speech and sign could be assigned and would fit the context in nearly all the code-blended utterances we analyzed.

There were three possible exceptions to the generalization that speech and sign contribute to a single proposition. All three instances clearly involved lexical issues. The first was produced by the adult interacting with Ben in his speech-target session at 2;06 when she said, "We don't have a trashcan" with the word 'trashcan' aligned with the sign SHEEP. In the previous utterances this adult had been discussing sheep, and the ASL signs TRASH(CAN) and SHEEP are both two handed signs produced on the non-dominant forearm. This is thus likely to be a lexical error, influenced by both priming of sheep and phonological overlap. The other two instances were produced by Igor, and both involved the use of the sign PRETO ('black') along with different spoken color terms (*branco* 'white', and *rosa* 'pink'). Again, these are likely cases of lexical error, as it appears Igor substituted the color sign PRETO for other color signs that he had not yet acquired.

The one-proposition proposal also entails that when sign and speech are produced together, they result in a single utterance. Then, an example like (12) might come as a surprise. This example comes from Igor at (2;10) (Quadros et al. 2013), a session not otherwise included in the current analysis.

(12) [NOVE | nove | nove | nove g(aplausos-mãos)] (Igor, 2;10)

The ELAN screenshot in (12) shows what appears to be a single utterance in the sign modality co-occurring with more than one utterance in the speech modality. The sign NOVE ('nine') is held during three iterations of the spoken word *nove*. Rather than attesting different numbers of propositions in the two modalities, the example shows that sign and speech can use different means of 'lengthening' an utterance, a technique that may be used as a conversational strategy for emphasis, holding attention, maintaining the topic, etc. (Bennett-Kastor 1994).

Recall also example (4b) above, in which repetition was used for a timing repair. Ben's first spoken utterance of 'snake' doesn't match up temporally with his sign SNAKE, so he repeats the spoken word, but again it is misaligned. Finally, in the last repetition for both, the sign starts slightly before the spoken word so that the primary movement of the sign can be aligned with the stressed syllable nucleus of the word. As mentioned earlier, young bimodal bilingual children need time to develop the tight temporal coordination between sign and speech observed for adult Codas. The examples above thus reflect developmental errors or discourse strategies and are not counter-evidence to the 'one proposition' assertion of the Language Synthesis model.

What about the 'one derivation' proposal? All of the examples from children and adults presented in the current study are quite consistent with this proposal, since the word order for signed and spoken production analyzed separately are virtually always Congruent, as shown in Table 3 above. The one Not congruent example for Ben is rather unclear, because his speech is whispered and one crucial sign is marked with the notation [?], indicating uncertainty in the assigned gloss. The uncertainty in both the spoken and signed portions of this example prevents us from analyzing it completely.

It is important to note that a difference in word order between sign and speech is not automatically counter-evidence for the 'one derivation' proposal, but rather, an indication that these utterances warrant more detailed analysis to determine how they can be derived. Relevant examples are attested for various language pairs studied by previous research. Petitto et al. (2001) report six examples (out of 320 code-blended examples) in which the speech and sign follow different orders, each appropriate for the target (monolingual) grammar, such as spoken French *mon chien* ('my dog') signed together with LSQ CHIEN MON. Likewise, Donati and Branchini (2013) report examples of different word orders for spoken Italian and Italian Sign Language (LIS) bimodal bilinguals. Whether such examples are compatible with the one derivation proposal is discussed in Lillo-Martin et al. (2016).

One intriguing question that can be raised about code-blending in young Kodas is whether they use this type of language mixing primarily as a reflection of code-blended input in their environment, or as a natural combination of their knowledge of two languages that would be produced even in the absence of such input. Of course, this question cannot be answered here, given that we have only observed less than four hours of interactions between Ben and a variety of adults, and one hour of interaction between Igor and his mother. Based on our observations of both Kodas in these and other sessions, they clearly have experience with adults using code-blending. However, they do not use blending types in the same way as their interlocutors do, and Ben even uses Sign-base blending in speech-target sessions where this type is not observed for his adult interlocutors. This hints that the Kodas may be combining their languages in ways that they have not observed in their input, or have observed only infrequently. In any case, they are clearly not simply mimicking the code-blending patterns used by their interlocutors, but generating their own patterns. At the same time, Kodas display awareness of the appropriate contexts for different language choices by adjusting their output to the different adults with whom they interact (see Lillo-Martin et al. 2014 for more discussion of this last point).

# 8 Conclusion

We have shown that even very young bimodal bilingual children are able to combine their developing languages in rule-governed and creative ways. They produce code-blending in which some part of an utterance is produced in both sign and speech simultaneously, an option only afforded to bimodal bilinguals. Yet, their code-blends express a single proposition, and are compatible with our proposal that only one syntactic derivation is involved.

Theories of bilingualism have largely been based on data from unimodal bilinguals alone. While it is widely acknowledged that bilinguals creatively 'mix' their languages, the possibility of simultaneous code-blending would not even be considered without data from bimodal bilinguals. Thus, continued, detailed study of the language combinations produced by bimodal bilinguals of a wide range of sign+spoken language pairs, both children and adults, will be eagerly anticipated.

## References

Bennett-Kastor, Tina. 1994. Repetition in language development: From interaction to cohesion. In Barbara Johnstone (ed.), *Repetition in discourse: Interdisciplinary perspectives*, 155–171. Norwood, New Jersey: Ablex.

Bishop, Michelle. 2006. *Bimodal bilingualism in hearing, native users of American Sign Language*. Washington, DC: Gallaudet University PhD thesis.

Bishop, Michelle. 2010. Happen can't hear: An analysis of code-blends in hearing, native signers of American Sign Language. *Sign Language Studies* 11(2). 205–240.

Bishop, Michelle & Sherry Hicks. 2005. Orange eyes: Bimodal bilingualism in hearing adult users of American Sign Language. *Sign Language Studies* 5(2). 188–230.

Branchini, Chiara & Caterina Donati. 2016. Assessing lexicalism through bimodal eyes. *Glossa: A Journal of General Linguistics* 1(1). 48. 1–30.

Cantone, Katja F. 2007. *Code-switching in bilingual children*. Dordrecht: Springer.

Chen Pichler, Deborah, Julie Hochgesang, Diane Lillo-Martin, & Ronice Müller de Quadros. 2010. Conventions for sign and speech transcription in child bimodal bilingual corpora. *Language, interaction and acquisition* 1. 11–40.

Chen Pichler, Deborah, Julie Hochgesang, Diane Lillo-Martin, Ronice Müller de Quadros & Wanette Reynolds. 2016. Best practices for building a bi-modal bi-lingual bi-national child corpus. *Sign Language Studies* 16(3). 361–388.

Chen Pichler, Deborah, Wanette Reynolds, Jeffrey Levi Palmer, Ronice Müller de Quadros, Laura Viola Kozak & Diane Lillo-Martin. 2017. Heritage signers: Bimodal bilingual children from deaf families. In Jiyoung Choi, Hamida Demirdache, Oana Lungu & Laurence Voeltzel (eds.), *Language acquisition at the interfaces: Proceedings of GALA 2015*, 247–269. Newcastle upon Tyne: Cambridge Scholars Publishing.

Chomsky, Noam. 1995. The minimalist program. Cambridge, MA: MIT Press.

Crasborn, Onno & Hans Sloetjes. 2008. Enhanced ELAN functionality for sign language corpora. *Proceedings of LREC 2008, Sixth International Conference on Language Resources and Evaluation*, 39–43. Paris: European Language Resources Association.

Davidson, Kathryn, Diane Lillo-Martin & Deborah Chen Pichler. 2014. Spoken English language development among native signing children with cochlear implants. *Journal of Deaf Studies and Deaf Education* 19(2). 238–250.

Donati, Caterina & Chiara Branchini. 2013 Challenging linearization: Simultaneous mixing in the production of bimodal bilinguals. In Theresa Biberauer & Ian Roberts (eds.), *Challenges to linearization,* 93–128. Berlin: Mouton De Gruyter.

Emmorey, Karen, Helsa B. Borinstein, Robin Thompson & Tamar H. Gollan. 2008. Bimodal bilingualism. *Bilingualism: Language and Cognition* 11(1). 43–61.

Foster, Pauline, Alan Tonkyn & Gillian Wigglesworth. 2000. Measuring spoken language: A unit for all reasons. *Applied Linguistics* 21. 354–375.

Gökgöz, Kadir, Ronice Müller de Quadros, Deborah Chen Pichler & Diane Lillo-Martin. Under revision. Syntactic constraints on code-blending: Evidence from distributions of subject points and object points.

González-Vilbazo, Kay & Luis López. 2011. Some properties of light verbs in code-switching. *Lingua* 121. 832–850.

Goodwin, Corina. 2016. *English morphological development in bimodal bilingual children: Deaf children with cochlear implants and hearing children of Deaf adults*. Storrs, CT: University of Connecticut PhD thesis.

Halle, Morris & Alec Marantz. 1993. Distributed morphology and the pieces of inflection. In Ken Hale & Samuel J. Keyser (eds.), *The view from building 20: Essays in honor of Sylvain Bromberger*, 111–176. Cambridge, MA: MIT Press.

Hulk, Aafke & Natascha Müller. 2000 Bilingual first language acquisition at the interface between syntax and pragmatics. *Bilingualism: Language and Cognition* 3(3). 227–244.

Johnson, Robert, Scott K. Liddell & Carol Erting. 1989. *Unlocking the curriculum: Principles for achieving access in deaf education (Gallaudet Research Institute Working Paper 89–3)*. Washington, DC: Gallaudet University.

Johnston, Trevor. 1991 Transcription and glossing of sign language texts: Examples from Auslan (Australian Sign Language). *International Journal of Sign Linguistics* 2. 3–28.

Kanto, Laura, Marja-Leena Laakso & Kerttu Huttunen. 2015. Differentiation in language and gesture use during early bilingual development of hearing children of Deaf parents. *Bilingualism: Language and Cognition* 18. 769–788.

Kanto, Laura, Marja-Leena Laakso & Kerttu Huttunen. 2016. Use of code-mixing by young hearing children of Deaf parents. *Bilingualism: Language and Cognition*, FirstView.

Kupisch, Tanja. 2007. Determiners in bilingual German-Italian children: What they tell us about the relation between language influence and language dominance. *Bilingualism: Language and Cognition* 10. 57–78.

Koulidobrova, Elena V. 2012. *When the quiet surfaces: 'Transfer' of argument omission in the English of ASL-English bilinguals*. Storrs, CT: University of Connecticut PhD thesis.

Koulidobrova, Elena V. 2016. Language interaction effects in bimodal bilingualism: Argument omission in the languages of hearing ASL-English bilinguals. *Linguistic Approaches to Bilingualism*, online first. doi:10.1075/lab.13047.kou

Lillo-Martin, Diane, Elena V. Koulidobrova, Ronice Müller de Quadros & Deborah Chen Pichler. 2012. Bilingual language synthesis: Evidence from WH-questions in bimodal bilinguals. In Alia K. Biller, Esther Y. Chung & Amelia E. Kimball (eds.), *Proceedings of the 36th Annual Boston University Conference on Language Development*, 302–314. Somerville, MA: Cascadilla Press.

Lillo-Martin, Diane, Ronice Müller de Quadros, Deborah Chen Pichler & Zoe Fieldsteel. 2014. Language choice in bimodal bilingual development. *Frontiers in Psychology* 5(1163).

Lillo-Martin, Diane, Ronice Müller de Quadros & Deborah Chen Pichler. 2016. The development of bimodal bilingualism: Implications for linguistic theory. Invited keynote paper for epistemological issue, *Linguistic Approaches to Bilingualism* 6(6). 719–755.

MacSwan, Jeff. 2000. The architecture of the bilingual language faculty: Evidence from code-switching. *Bilingualism: Language & Cognition* 3. 37–54.

Niparko, John K., Emily A. Tobey, Donna J. Thal, Laurie S. Eisenberg, Nae-Yuh Wang, Alexandra L. Quittner & Nancy E. Fink. 2010. Spoken language development in children following cochlear implantation. *JAMA: The Journal of the American Medical Association* 303. 1498–1506.

Palmer, Jeffrey. 2015. *Bimodal bilingual L1 word order development*. Washington, DC: Gallaudet University PhD thesis.

Petitto, Laura A., Marina Katerelos, Bronna G. Levy, Kristine Gauna, Karine Tétrault & Vittoria Ferraro. 2001. Bilingual signed and spoken language acquisition from birth: Implications for mechanisms underlying bilingual language acquisition. *Journal of Child Language* 28. 453–496.

Quadros, Ronice Müller de, Diane Lillo-Martin & Deborah Chen Pichler. 2013. O que bilíngues bimodais tem a nos dizer sobre o desenvolvimento bilíngue? [What do bimodal bilinguals have to tell us about bilingual development?] *Letras de Hoje* 48(3). 380–388.

Quadros, Ronice Müller de, Diane Lillo-Martin & Deborah Chen Pichler. 2014. Methodological considerations for the development and use of sign language acquisition data. In Tomasso Raso & Heliana Mello (eds.), *Spoken corpora and linguistic studies*, 84–102. Amsterdam & Philadelphia: John Benjamins.

Quadros, Ronice Müller de, Diane Lillo-Martin, Maria Polinsky & Karen Emmorey. 2016. Heritage signers: Bimodal bilingual structures. Manuscript.

Serratrice, Ludovica. 2013. Cross-linguistic influence in bilingual development: Determinants and mechanisms. *Linguistic Approaches to Bilingualism* 3(1). 3–25.

Tevenal, Stephanie & Miako Villanueva. 2009. Are you getting the message? The effects of SimCom on the message received by deaf, hard of hearing, and hearing students. *Sign Language Studies* 9(3). 266–86.

Unsworth, Sharon. 2013. Current issues in multilingual first language acquisition. *Annual Review of Applied Linguistics* 33. 21–50.

van den Bogaerde, Beppie & Anne E. Baker. 2002. Are young deaf children bilingual? In Gary Morgan & Bencie Woll (eds.), *Directions in sign language acquisition*, 183–206. Amsterdam & Philadelphia: John Benjamins.

van den Bogaerde, Beppie & Anne E. Baker. 2005. Code mixing in mother-child interaction in Deaf families. *Sign Language & Linguistics* 8. 153–176.

van den Bogaerde, Beppie & Anne E. Baker. 2008. Bimodal language acquisition in kodas. In Michelle Bishop & Sherry L. Hicks (eds.), *HEARING, MOTHER FATHER DEAF: Hearing people in Deaf families*, 99–131. Washington, DC: Gallaudet University Press.

# Methodological innovations in sign multilingualism research

Jenny Webster, Kang-Suk Byun, Sibaji Panda and Tashi Bradford

This chapter focuses on methodological innovations in the MULTISIGN project, a three-part study that examined a range of complex multilingual behaviours in sign language users, including "cross-signing", "sign-speaking", and "sign-switching" (see Chapter 1). Two main innovative features are explored in this chapter: the post-hoc interviews in the cross-signing strand (1), and the elicitation materials and procedures used in all three strands (2), including cultural adaptations to the local environment. However, this does not encompass all of the innovations inherent in MULTISIGN, and some of these further aspects are covered in other chapters in this volume.

MULTISIGN was the first large-scale study in the field of sign multilingualism, and investigated behaviours that had never been empirically researched before. It therefore posed challenging methodological questions that required creative solutions and adjustments throughout the project cycle. This process of trial and error enabled the research team to develop a set of innovations that may aid further work in sign multilingualism and inform methodologies in other studies that examine incipient communication between people who do not have a shared language.

The methodological innovations explored here were necessary and beneficial for this project because a major aim was to apply extant techniques innovatively in novel contexts. This included adapting experiments in the field for use in local contexts (see section 2); using a "director-matcher" task with cross-signers who have no shared language; and exploiting "reverse fieldwork" for which participants came to the UK in 2012 and India in 2014 for a period of five to six weeks each time (cf. the "data collection fairs" for bimodal bilingual children in Quadros et al. 2015: 253–254). This gave rise to methodological and logistical challenges for the researchers and personal and intellectual challenges for the participants. After the initial video recordings between the cross-signing pairs (each pair being comprised of two signers who do not share a sign language), post-hoc interviews were carried out in which they commented on the interaction, and ultimately provided the team with interesting insights into their meta-linguistic reasoning and levels of comprehension (see section 1). To allow the participants to draw maximal benefit from their involvement in the study, the data collection

https://doi.org/10.1515/9781501503528-007

process ran in parallel with capacity building activities: in the UK, they participated in university events, received research training, and enjoyed external visits to deaf organisations; in India, they took part in a bespoke two-week training programme.

The methodological innovations also connect the three strands, as there are serendipitous and strategic overlaps that permit the results to be triangulated within, and compared more easily across, the three strands.

# 1 Post-hoc introspective interviews

This section focuses on methodological innovation stemming from a series of post-hoc introspective interviews conducted under the cross-signing study. These interviews resulted in a number of key discoveries regarding the types of meta-linguistic reasoning that participants utilised when selecting communicative strategies (please see Chapters 2 and 4 for further details on the cross-signing study).

First, it is useful to consider the wider empirical value of interviews as a technique in linguistics research. This is a common method in sociolinguistics, as it facilitates "structured conversation" that can target specific phenomena (Hill 2015: 201). The use of interviews is dynamic because they can be conducted in the signed language or visual-gestural system, which is often more accessible to deaf participants compared to text-based interviews (e.g. open-ended questions or Likert-scale items). Interviews can supplement other methods for more robust datasets and corpora. Interviewing was one of four methods[1] used to gather data in the British Sign Language Corpus Project (Fenlon, Schembri, Johnston and Cormier 2015: 164). A deaf interviewer asked participants about their language attitudes and awareness for 15 minutes, and the resulting data became part of the BSL corpus. Small-group interviews are sometimes helpful in generating a larger number of forms or signs in a particular target domain; for example, Nyst (2015: 117) suggests that informants find it easier to think of many lexical signs if they are interviewed in a group, and guided through various semantic fields, e.g. animals, colours and food. However, interviews are not only used to collect primary data in linguistic studies, but are also exploited as ancillary data (Edley and Litosseliti 2010: 169). They can be useful for capturing different views on one topic, i.e. providing "multivocality" (Litosseliti 2003: 18; Edley and Litosseliti 2010: 170). Researchers have also relied on interviews to

---

[1] The others were spontaneous conversations, personal anecdotes, and elicitation using a word list.

query the extent of participants' comprehension, similar to the purpose of the interviews here. For example, Noble et al. (2014) interviewed language learners after a test to clarify what linguistic content they understood, what they found difficult, and how they tackled the test questions. The interview method was the only way to determine whether the students had trouble with two particular English discourse features that are common in tests (instructions requiring learners to choose the "best" answer, and refer back to the previous sentence). The researchers would not be able to glean this information by simply viewing their answers and scores. This way of using interviews may contribute to more thoughtful and empowered perspectives among the participants, perhaps enabling them to feel more ownership of the research and enjoy a greater benefit from their involvement, which is especially desirable when participants are from a traditionally disadvantaged minority group (Edley and Litosseliti 2010: 169–170).

Of course, it is worth keeping in mind that the interview method also carries risks and limitations, including the interviewer asking "leading" questions or being directive or influential over the responses; aiming for "neutrality" and "generalisability"; and failing to account appropriately for the specific discourse context or dynamics (Edley and Litosseliti 2010: 173–174). However, such risks are more problematic if the research takes place within a positivist framework, where there is assumed to be some objective truth that the scholar is aiming to uncover. The use of a constructionist framework, on the other hand, addresses these limitations by acknowledging that interviews generate indicative, illustrative, reconstituted data, instead of assuming that the data represents faithful reporting of authentic, objectively verifiable accounts (Edley and Litosseliti 2010: 173). For the present study, a constructionist perspective was adopted, as the post-hoc interviews were intended as a supplementary method to provide insight into the conversational data.

The conversational data were gathered by filming a corpus of 8–10 dyads at least three times each over 4–6 weeks, so that these recordings could then be analysed for linguistic patterns and communicative strategies. The conversational data collection, in contrast to the experimental data collection described in 2, targets the production and output side of the communication. Following the filming sessions, post-hoc introspective interviews were conducted with the participants to gain insight into the rationales behind their strategies and assess their level of mutual comprehension, as this cannot be determined from the recordings alone. These interviews were devised when a pilot study, conducted with a conversational dyad from Turkey and South Korea, showed that substantial misunderstandings often occur, most notably at the lexical level, without the participants being aware of it.

Such interviews formed a vital component of this incipient method, as no previous project had attempted to track a series of interactions between signers who do not know each other's languages. As well as contributing to the robustness of this new method, the post-hoc interviews are an innovative method in and of themselves. They were carried out with each participant on an individual basis, by research team members who were known to them and who had experience of their home country and native sign language.[2] The interviews consisted of sitting with the participant and watching the recording of the free conversation together, with the interviewer and interviewee both encouraged to stop the film at any time to discuss any particular sign, facial expression, disruption in dialogue, successful communication strategy, etc, that they wanted to clarify or highlight. Participants would explain what they were trying to say, or what they understood their conversational partner to be saying. The signers explored the reasons behind the linguistic choices they made and the content from their interlocutor that they did and did not comprehend during the free conversation, as illustrated in 1.1, 1.2 and 1.3 below.

The research team found these interviews extremely useful for clarifying what was said when necessary; for explaining the mental processes that were used, including choice/source of sign(s); and for verifying relevant background information. As exemplified below, the interviews allowed researchers to surmise that "all participants continuously entertain multiple simultaneous hypotheses, both about what their interlocutor is likely to understand (which then in turn influences the choices in their own signed output), and about the likely meaning of what their interlocutor is signing to them" (Zeshan 2015: 248).

---

[2] Because of the requirement for the cross-signers to have no shared language, it was necessary to use deaf intermediaries, one of whom was fluent in each participant's national sign language. Each intermediary was involved in interviews with their respective participant. This was part of the research team's ethical protocol, which emphasised creating opportunities for deaf signers (a typically disadvantaged and marginalised group) to take on active project roles whenever possible. This consideration superseded the empirical risk that the intermediaries' presence may influence the participants' communication strategies. The sign-switching team was also organised with this innovation in mind (see Chapter 3 by Panda and Zeshan, and Chapter 8 by Panda), by engaging the Burundian signers to annotate their own data, and inviting one of them to co-present at a conference (SIGN6 in Goa, India, in 2013).

**Table 1.** Interviewer-participant pairs and their languages and interpreters

| Interviewer | Interpreter | Participant | Language |
|---|---|---|---|
| UZ | KS (iSLanDS staff) | MH | Japanese Sign Language |
| UZ and NP | NP (iSLanDS associate) | MI | Indonesian Sign Language |
| UZ | PS (iSLanDS associate) | MS | Jordanian Sign Language |
| UZ | No interpretation needed | CP | British Sign Language |
| AB | MI (2012 participant) | AM | Indonesian Sign Language |
| AB | MS (2012 participant) | BF | Jordanian Sign Language |
| AB | AJ (facilitator) | AS | Nepali Sign Language |

The interviews took place as soon as possible after each conversation was recorded, and the interviewer conducted them in International Sign (and BSL in one case). Interpretation during the interviews was provided by the intermediaries, research team members who were fluent in participants' native sign languages (see Table 1). The requisite information about participants' multifaceted language backgrounds had already been collected prior to the filming, both to save time on the day of filming (cf. Quadros et al. 2015: 251–252) and to permit plenty of time to arrange the interpreters. In 2012 the interpreters were the iSLanDS staff members who recruited the participants, and in 2014 the interpreters were the facilitators, including two former participants (see Chapters 10 and 11). Extensive notes were taken of each interview to be used when analysing the data; though the signers expressed their feedback in the first person, the notes were written in third person for clarity (Zeshan 2015). The team did not film the interviews (which would have been ideal), because this would have necessitated a very lengthy and costly transcription process. The notes for the 2012 data were combined into one contiguous Excel file as two columns of text (one for each interlocutor's comments) with the relevant times from the video clip in a middle column to reflect how each pair's dialogue developed. The aim in creating these combined files was for researchers to be able to refer to them for insights into the awareness and perceptions of each pair during their communicative encounter (see Figure 1).

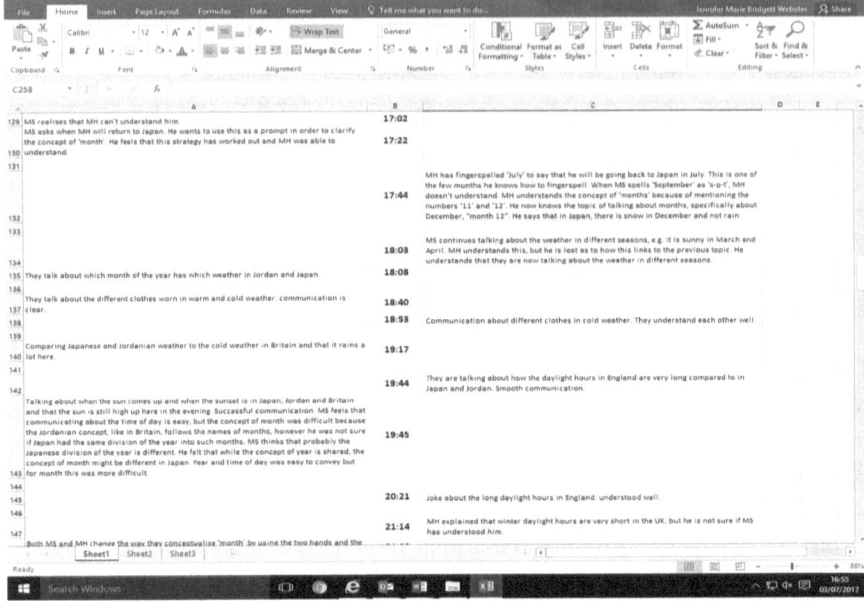

**Figure 1.** Combined Excel file for post-hoc interviews with MS and MH

A major rationale behind the addition of the post-hoc feedback interviews to the overall cross-signing methodology is that this type of communication tends to involve metalinguistic reasoning and experimentation. The most effective technique for investigating these mental processes is a dedicated discussion guided by an attentive interviewer.

This assumption seemed to be borne out gradually as a number of thought processes and strategies become apparent during the post-hoc interviews, including multimodal interaction, the exploitation of metalinguistic reasoning and skills, the active learning of signs, and the maximisation of opportunities to learn signs. Most of these processes rely on metalinguistic awareness, which is broadly defined as "conscious knowledge of the formal aspects of a language" (Rathmann, Mann and Morgan 2007: 192). It involves attending to the form of an expression, whether produced or received, and encompasses various levels of language use such as lexical, phrasal, syntactic, pragmatic and semantic (e.g. Tunmer and Bowey 1984). An additional aspect of the definition for the purposes of cross-signing is "the participants' awareness of their *interaction* and modification thereof, depending on the interlocutor and their respective perceived needs" (Byun, Bradford, Zeshan, Levinson and de Vos 2018). Being bi- and multi-lingual, perhaps unsurprisingly the participants seem able "to see a language as one particular system among many, to view its phenomena under more general categories, and [to be aware of] linguistic operations" (Vygotsky 1962: 196). For the most part, the interviewers eschewed technical linguistic terminology, as this was unnecessary for the purposes of discussion and could have complicated the communication during the interview. In teaching contexts, even intermediate learners tend to use non-technical metalanguage, which has no adverse effect on the smooth operation of communicative activities (Basturkmen, Loewen and Ellis 2002).

Naturally, there are limitations in these post-hoc interviews, including the general weaknesses of the interview method that were mentioned earlier, as well as the more specific risks of memory decay and possible embarrassment from admitting to communicative "errors" or revealing that something was not understood. The former limitation was ameliorated by carrying out the interviews as soon as possible after the free conversations, to maximally reduce any memory attrition or misremembering by participants. The latter, potential embarrassment causing discomfort, was minimised by the research team's attention to participants' comfort and familiarity with the team members. This is one key reason why each participant was matched with an intermediary who had an in-depth knowledge of their country and language (e.g. the Japanese participant was matched with a team member who comes from Japan and is fluent in Japanese Sign Language; see Table 1 above). This is also part of the team's rationale for not filming the interviews, to reduce the anxiety that the camera would likely generate.

In the following three sub-sections, examples of metalinguistic reasoning (1.1), multimodal interaction (1.2) and other metalinguistic skills (1.3) that arose in the post-hoc interviews are highlighted, and the contributions they make to knowledge on these topics are discussed. The unprecedented method of MULTISIGN's cross-signing strand involved tracking participants' emerging communication in free conversations across a number of weeks. To glean as much information as possible about each conversation, post-hoc feedback interviews were carried out with an intermediary who interpreted and clarified certain aspects of the interview. This was done as soon as possible after each cross-signing interaction took place. It allowed the researchers firstly to eliminate ambiguities in the data, secondly to clarify what was understood by the participants, thirdly to give the participants the opportunity to discuss any frustration or confusion they experienced, and fourthly to consolidate any incidental language learning.

## 1.1 Metalinguistic reasoning

Firstly, evidence of metalinguistic reasoning and tracking what has been communicated to a particular person is abundant within the text of the post-hoc interviews. For example, in one dialogue, Indonesian signer MI asks about Japanese signer MH's deaf organisation in Tokyo, but MH does not understand MI's sign for 'organisation', so MI fingerspells O-R-G-A-N-I-Z-A-T-I-O-N, using the international/ASL alphabet for all letters, except 'R' and 'Z' which are from the Indonesian alphabet. MH identifies this when he sees the unfamiliar form for 'Z'. MH asks MI to repeat the word, and in the interview, MI reported that he was considering whether to sign 'G' using the index finger, or the index finger and thumb. MI thinks that MH must be familiar with these forms, because when they introduced each other earlier in the conversation, they were using the international alphabet. MI further explained in the post-hoc interview that he believes the ASL alphabet is international, so surmised that MH must surely know it. This example conveys perhaps how complex cross-signing can be, with the nuance of thoughts and assumptions very difficult to capture without post-hoc interviews. It appears that MI was engaged in careful tracking of what forms his interlocutor might already know, based on whether he had already seen MH use them and to what extent he believed that they were used internationally.

Another instance where the post-hoc interviews "provide explicit evidence that signers keep track of both the current conversation and previous conversations with other participants" (Zeshan 2015) is when MH stated that he had decided to sign the number '12' in the two-handed digital way, i.e. "signing the numerals as a sequence of individual digits, following the sequence of written numbers" (Zeshan 2015: 218). The two-handed way of doing this means that one hand articulates '1' while the other articulates '2'. MH signed '12' this way because he felt it was easier for CP to understand since they had signed '10' previously using this method. Another example is when MI reports that he used the Japanese sign for 'England' because he did not know the British sign for it, but he knew that CP had already met the Japanese signer so he surmised that she may know the Japanese sign for it.

In a further example from the data, a signer chose the ASL sign WHY because he guessed his interlocutor would understand ASL, based on what the signer knew about his background. Other occurrences of this phenomenon involve a signer remembering what signs they had used on prior occasions with their interlocutor, as occurs here with the Japanese participant MH and Jordanian participant MS (also see Figure 2):

*[from MH's interview] MH talks about going to the pub by bus. He used the Japanese sign for 'bus' and thinks MS should know it because MH had previously showed this sign to MS when they went to Blackpool together.*

**Figure 2.** MH articulates the JSL sign for 'bus'

In a few cases, signers had piecemeal knowledge of others' languages. The British participant CP, after producing the international sign for 'England', attempted the Jordanian sign, as she remembered it from a visit to Jordan.

## 1.2 Multimodal interaction

The post-hoc interviews show many occurrences of multimodal interaction, which refers to fingerspelling, mouthing, writing and tracing in addition to signing. These are all representations of spoken language that are accessible to deaf interlocutors, and tend to be especially useful for content that does not easily lend itself to articulation through iconically-motivated signs, characterisation, or spatial arrangement. In a paper on the cross-signing participants' use of numerals, Zeshan (2015: 247) asserts that "signers actively monitor intersubjective multilingual-multimodal repertoires" that are shared and "built up 'on the fly' for all kinds of semantic and grammatical domains, including more abstract domains such as colour".

For example, specific food items can be ambiguous when conveyed through iconic means. When communicating about rice with the Jordanian participant MS, Indonesian participant MI attempts a lexical sign as well as fingerspelling the English word R-I-C-E with three different alphabets, the third of which is understood by his conversational partner:

*[from MI's interview] MI wants to ask if MS if Jordanian people also eat rice. He starts to use the Indonesian fingerspelling to spell R-I-C-E (the English word). Then he tries to use the BSL fingerspelling alphabet. He has already found this alphabet on the internet. Then he uses the ASL fingerspelling alphabet, and MS then understands, and uses the Jordanian sign for 'rice'.*

*[from MS's interview] MS does not understand either the sign or the fingerspelling attempts with the Indonesian and British two-handed alphabets for 'rice', but he understands the third attempt using one-handed international fingerspelling. He knows the word* rice *from learning English at deaf school in Jordan.*

Other interesting forms of multimodal strategies occur when a participant traces a calendar on the wall, and Japanese kanji on his leg. Mouthing is also seen, as when a participant fingerspells his surname and adds a lip pattern, because he had previously seen his interlocutor use a speech gesture to signify a hard /g/ at the throat, and surmised that he was familiar with spoken forms of communication.

A key way in which the post-hoc interviews "illustrate the kinds of reasoning and trial-and-error that can be involved in the choice of lexical signs" (Zeshan 2015: 248) is in exploring the numerous mistakes, miscommunication and corrections that seem to be inherent in the experimental exploitation of multimodal skills in the data, which gradually give rise to the construction of a shared repertoire. Some examples of mistakes and failed attempts are discussed in the interviews:

*MS uses an unfamiliar sign with the thumb on the palm, together with some fingerspelling. He is trying to fingerspell 'Tokyo' but he misspells it. MH initially thinks he is asking about oil.*

*CP mimes to explain the concept of 'busy', but MH still does not understand. He thinks CP wants to talk about doing a lot of work at the same time. He thinks the focus is on the time.*

This suggests that post-hoc interviews are a useful learning and reflection tool for the participants, allowing them to recall their thought processes and, in discussing specific instances of miscommunication, develop their use of metalanguage. Jessner (2005: 66) finds that using metalanguage has a "control function" when people are producing their weaker language(s), as it often comes before a switch between languages and may constitute "a kind of intermediate step towards the retrieval of the target language item" (see also Zeshan and Panda 2015).

## 1.3 Other metalinguistic skills

Apart from multimodal skills, the participants demonstrated an aptitude for creating and acquiring new signs, and for using features of sign languages that cut across individual languages, such as iconic motivations, spatial arrangement, and role shift or characterisation. Such signing-related metalinguistic awareness may also improve the reading and writing skills of signers; Rathmann et al. (2007: 195) note that "meta-linguistic awareness of how signed narratives are constructed [and] how to encode shifts in perspective and character motives can feed into the development of the same literacy skills in the written form".

Firstly, the post-hoc interviews reveal many instances of the participants' engagement in active learning, as they frequently take opportunities to perform and practise new signs. Lennon (1989) highlights the association among language learning, introspection and metalinguistic awareness, which has been shown to "enrich cognitive processes and go hand-in-hand with enhanced introspective powers" (ibid: 378) as well as contributing to language learners being "highly manipulative both of their environment so as to promote learning and of their production so as to promote communication" (ibid: 393). For example, the British participant CP saw the Indonesian participant MI use a mime for 'month'. Later in the same conversation, CP signed 'eight months' using this new mime. MI then wanted to check that CP did indeed intend to use the mime to mean 'month', and that he had understood her meaning correctly, so he asked, 'eight years?' When she responded negatively, he realised that she did mean 'eight months'. In this way, the post-hoc interviews with MI and CP demonstrate that both interlocutors ultimately played a role in CP's learning of a new form for 'month'. Similarly, in another conversation, MI asked the Jordanian participant MS what sports he likes. The post-hoc interview confirmed that MS did not understand MI's sign for 'sport'; MI then attempted to use the Jordanian sign for 'football', which he produced slightly incorrectly, prompting a correction from MS.

Sometimes participants resorted to creating novel signs, an option afforded by the myriad iconic possibilities open to users of sign languages, including "polymorphemic productive forms" (Brennan 1992) and "the cross-domain mapping that is present in conceptual metaphors" (Russo 2005: 344). For example, in MS's post-hoc interview, he reveals that he created his own idiomatic sign to try to convey a concept to MI:

*MS uses a sign for 'keeping things secret' that he invented, thinking that the Jordanian sign would not be intelligible to MI.*

In taking such opportunities for exploiting iconicity, the signers also repeatedly demonstrated visual memory skills in conveying concepts through visual imagery, as exemplified by Jordanian participant MS:

*MS recognises that MH does not understand his sign for 'football', so he tries the sign for 'stadium' and the sign for 'devil', referring to the logo [of the team in question].*

However, the post-hoc interviews also show that what seem to be universal iconic motivations are often particular only to certain cultures and languages, and unknown in others. For example, MS assumed that the sign for 'hope', articulated with crossed fingers, would be understood as a common gesture by the Indonesian participant MI, but Indonesia has no such gesture:

*MS has said he hopes to run a deaf association in Jordan. MI does not recognise the sign for 'hope' with crossed fingers. There is also no gesture in Indonesia for crossing your fingers to mean 'hope'.*

Dedicated utilisation of the sign space is another metalinguistic skill that the participants report drawing on. In CP's post-hoc interview, it is explained that she manipulated the sign space to communicate the concept of 'months':

*CP tries to explain that she used to live with a roommate. MS does not understand CP's sign for 'month', thinking she had meant 'four years' or 'four days'. CP used the signing space to indicate the months, e.g. June, July, etc… MS then understood the concept of 'month' from this.*

Further skills that the signers appear adept at taking advantage of are role shift and characterisation. The Japanese participant, MH, resorts to these strategies after trying signs from British Sign Language (see Figure 3) and Japanese Sign Language to impart the concept of 'game' to MI:

*MH attempts to ask about the game, first using the British sign, slightly mispronounced, and then the Japanese sign for 'toy', followed by the sign for 'game'. MH explains the details of the game [using role shift to convey the perspectives of the players] and MI now recognises it from the fact that two pictures cannot be seen by the players. At this point MI has not played the game but knows about it.*

**Figure 3.** The Japanese signer articulates the BSL sign for 'game'

The complex introspection that such interviews require of participants gives them opportunities to build their critical awareness of language, as noted by Ogulnick (1999) with respect to applied linguistics studies. Because of this, the post-hoc introspective interviews can be seen as a facet of ethically robust and sustainable research that provides its participants and their communities with increased knowledge and skills. Studies that deliberately investigate the precise nature of this benefit and the degree to which informants' skills are enhanced would be useful in terms of establishing this as a standard protocol in research with deaf individuals and communities.

# 2 Elicitation materials and procedures in the sign-switching, sign-speaking and cross-signing strands

This section describes the rationales and procedures for the games that the research team used to elicit utterances for all three strands of MULTISIGN: sign-switching (2.1), sign-speaking (2.2), and cross-signing (2.3). For ease of reference, all of these elicitation activities are also listed in Table 2. The team adjusted the experiments to local contexts, and most materials were prepared in the field, addressing the observation of Morford et al. (2015: 212) that "developing materials for empirical investigations of signed languages is an area of methodology that is ripe for innovation". Harnessing the skills of deaf team members was a priority for this component of the methodology as well. For the Indian sign-speaking study (2.2), pictorial materials were drawn live on site by a local deaf artist, while in Turkey, the sign-switching researcher led a game of Monopoly to elicit fingerspelling and numerals. The map activities for sign-switchers (2.1) were based on culturally well-known locations.

**Table 2.** Elicitation activities for all three strands of MULTISIGN

| Strand | Game | Setting | Target(s) |
| --- | --- | --- | --- |
| Sign-switching | Map game | India | Numerals, fingerspelling, WH questions and negation |
| Sign-speaking | Popular games, e.g. UNO, chess, Monopoly | India | Subordination and 'if' clauses |
| | | Turkey | |
| | Picture matching | India | WH questions |
| | Questions about pictures | | |
| Cross-signing | Colour game | Netherlands | Colour signs |
| | | India | |
| | Picture matching | UK | Emotions, entities and actions |
| | | India | Animate beings and inanimate objects |

## 2.1 Sign-switching elicitation

In India, the innovative data collection and methods for the sign-switching strand involved participants from two different populations (see also Chapter 8). The first group was participants who were bilingual in Burundi Sign Language (BuSL) and Indian Sign Language (ISL), and the second set were bilingual in ISL and American Sign Language (ASL). For elicitation experiments with these bilinguals, the research team used maps which were discussed by the participants in pairs, and observed how much of each language they used, e.g. structures from BuSL versus ISL. One map had questions (e.g. ___km?) and the other had the answers to these (see Figure 4). The participants had to ask each other questions to find out the answers. Annotation on the maps, such as blanks, arrows and "km" for kilometres, presupposes (written) literacy. Because the questions and answers involved the topics of time, transport, and locations, the signers had to exploit a variety of forms including fingerspelling and number signs, which were target structures for this part of the research on unimodal sign bilinguals (see Chapter 3).

It was recognised by the researchers that the location represented on the map may be likely to affect language choice. Thus, another rationale for this activity was to prompt switching between BuSL and ISL by using maps from both Burundi and India, and from a third location abroad. The BuSL-ISL bilinguals had a map of Burundi and a map of their university campus in India, while the ISL-ASL signers had a map of south India and a picture of the London Eye, to represent a "foreign" place that was thought to have the potential to trigger ASL in the same way that the south India map may trigger ISL, because the participants had learned ASL from foreigners. In fact, most of the participants did not even recognise the London Eye, so it was indeed "foreign".

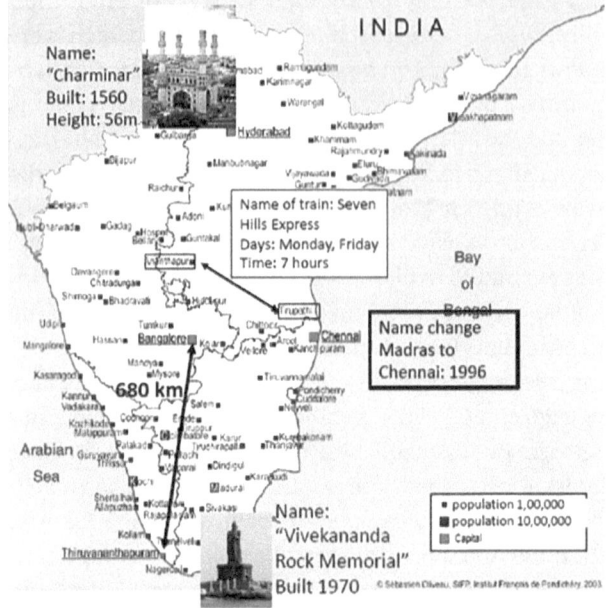

Name of wheel:
Other name:
Time to build it: _____ years
How far you can see from top:
Who built it:
How many visitors per year:
How many passengers can sit same time:
Height:
Name of other older wheel in London:
When built:

Name: The London Eye
Other name: Millennium Wheel
Time to build it: 7 years
How far you can see from top: 28 km
Who built it: Mark Sparrowhawk
Visitors per year: 3.9 million
How many passengers can sit same time: 800
Height: 137m
Name of older wheel in London: The Great Wheel
When built: 1895

**Figure 4.** Materials for the map game

By the time of the Indian sign-switching experiments, innovative methods for this strand had already been utilised by the Turkish research team. The lead researcher in India determined that different elicitation materials were required to ensure participants' comfort and familiarity during the experiments, and thus maximise the quality and quantity of the data. The BuSL-ISL bilinguals were known to be familiar with their home region of East Africa, including Burundi, Uganda, and Rwanda, so a map of this area was used, including deaf schools, churches, and governmental institutions. An Indian map was also required, but as overseas students, they did not know the country as a whole very well. Therefore the research team designed a map of just the immediate vicinity of their campus in New Delhi, including university buildings, the metro station, shops, and restaurants. The relevance of this area to their daily lives enabled them to have discussions about the distances and travel time between locations, modes of transport, the costs of meals and supplies at various establishments, and the names of places on campus. In addition to numerals and fingerspelling, the question-and-answer format of this map experiment was also intended to encourage the production of negative and (WH) interrogative signs (see Zeshan and Panda 2015). The research team's cultural understanding and careful use of the participants' local knowledge was innovative and generated plentiful data.

During the experiments, the participants appeared quite engaged and answered their partners' questions in detail, reflecting their familiarity with the context. The innovative map experiments thus facilitated a natural ecosystem of interaction where the bilingual participants could take full advantage of their linguistic skills, whilst allowing the research team to isolate specific target structures like numeral signs and fingerspelling. A key aspect of this innovation was that it was an experimental setting, but at the same time, it was a "natural" situation generating relative fluency and spontaneity of utterances. Combining the strengths of both methods makes the sign-switching strand inventive in its approach to data collection (Zeshan and Panda 2015; Panda 2016).

In summary, the sign-switching data collection featured a bespoke activity that was expressly designed to prompt code-switching in a targeted yet relatively comfortable and spontaneous manner. This methodological approach differs from that of many studies on code-switching in spoken languages, which rely instead on settings where code-switching is common, such as a call centre (e.g. Lam and Yu 2013) or a chat room frequented by bilingual or bidialectal people (e.g. Siebenhaar 2006), or on instructing participants to switch to their other language by alerting them with randomly-generated signals or tones (e.g. Azuma 1996).

The sign-switching method also allowed the team to gather specific data on multiple constructions using materials that they produced themselves within the field. This unusual combination of features has been rarely seen in other work, even in the related field of sign language typology, where games have been adapted to become culturally appropriate but are generated outside the field and often unable to target the full required range of structures. For example, for the "bargaining game" to elicit numerals (Sagara and Zeshan 2015), the researcher can select merchandise that is commonplace in that particular culture for participants to "haggle" over, but the game itself was not produced in or for a particular setting and it does not enable the researcher to pinpoint any specific numeral forms or structures.

## 2.2 Sign-speaking elicitation

The sign speakers also participated in elicitation sessions that made use of innovative methodologies. The aim of the sign-speaking elicitation was to encourage participants to produce the same utterance in the two different target languages, keeping the individual structures in the two target languages intact. These experiments were carried out in India, with participants who are bilingual in Hindi and ISL. It was originally intended to also execute these with a group of bilingual users of Turkish Sign Language (TİD) and Turkish; however, these individuals participated in 20 free conversations which indicated that they were not frequently using two different structures simultaneously, and therefore were not engaging in sign speaking (see Chapter 5), so performing the experiments with this Turkish group was deemed unnecessary.

In India, the methodology involved three different experiments making use of popular games, picture matching, and questions about pictures. In some research with bilingual bimodal individuals, precedence has been given to ensuring that stimuli are as comparable as possible across modalities and languages (Quadros et al. 2015: 253). However, the method here emphasises the use of stimuli that are authentic and locally-embedded, with comparability being of lesser concern. As per the innovation that has prevailed across the MULTISIGN study, the experiments emerged chiefly in the field, instead of being determined and prepared at the research institute.

The setting for the experiments was a large deaf school with about 500 students. The Indian field researcher had already visited this school many times before and knew its culture and the way people communicated there. Prior to the experiments, he observed the sign speakers by following them and taking note of when they simultaneously signed and spoke in a naturally-occurring situation. For example, families often visit and talk with the staff, so there are deaf youngsters there with hearing family members who cannot sign, and staff sometimes act as interpreters to give access to everyone in the interaction.

Sign speaking is a highly unusual and difficult skill. Therefore, for this research, it was thought to be inadequate to simply display written sentences or pictures as fixed stimuli, because this might result in a somewhat forced, stilted combination of signing and speaking. After discussing this problem with the research team, the team devised some innovative means of elicitation that would facilitate more spontaneous sign-speaking. One of these was the picture matching game for which the materials were already prepared, as they had been used in an earlier sign language typology project (Zeshan and Perniss 2008). A map activity was also considered, but the Indian field researcher was aware that Indian people use maps in a limited way, so it was felt that games would be more culturally appropriate. The field researcher made a list of games that are popular in India and that could be used in this kind of school setting, and gathered a set of game materials. Some games were discounted, because they required one hand to be occupied, e.g. to hold cards, and both hands needed to be free for signing in the sign-speaking experiments.

These locally-known games were bought at a local market, and targeted subordination and 'if' clauses. The sign speaker gave explanations about and directed the game. The time allotted for these game-based experiments was limited to three days and therefore many drawings and photocopies had to be produced very rapidly.

In selecting the hearing and deaf interlocutors who were needed to engage in the experiments with the sign speakers, two things were important. First, they should be well-known and friendly with the sign speakers, in order to facilitate lively interaction, with minimal embarrassment and hesitation on the part of the sign speaker. Secondly, they needed to have had experience in situations where sign speaking was occurring. The hearing interlocutor, who needed to be fluent in Hindi but not in any sign language, required enough exposure to signing so as to be comfortable in the sign-speaking scenario, and such individuals fortunately could be commonly found in the vicinity of the school; the deaf person had to be a fluent signer who was unable to communicate in spoken Hindi. School children were not suitable; the interlocutors needed to be adults who had been educated to college level, to ensure they were of a similar intellectual background and could interact meaningfully. It was also essential that neither the hearing nor the deaf participant was familiar with the games that were being explained to them. This allowed the sign speaker to deliver a meaningful explanation, being genuinely more familiar with the games. The games were UNO, chess, and "Happy Hour". Not all sign speakers were equally au fait with all three games, so the person most familiar with chess was selected to explain the rules of chess, and similarly for the two other games.

In fact, the participants' psychological connection to the activity was an important and potentially innovative consideration; they did not seem to characterise the game as a research activity. All of the individuals involved were known to each other at least superficially; the hearing and deaf interlocutors had some actual interest in learning the game; and the sign speakers were adept at explaining directions as they were all teaching staff. Therefore, these experiments were enacted in a fashion very similar to a real teaching situation, enhancing the validity of the data.

In addition to the games, they took part in the picture matching activity. For this "director-matcher" task (cf. Perniss 2007; Gullberg 2009; Zeshan 2015), the sign speaker had one set of about 18 different pictures, and the hearing and deaf interlocutors had two sets of similar pictures with some small differences between them. Taking each picture in turn, the sign speaker described what was shown, including the colours, positions, and directions of objects and people. Participants were also allowed to ask questions before choosing the correct target picture from their sets. For example, they might ask if there is a cap on the person's head in the picture. The researchers were pleased with the high level of interaction prompted by this activity.

As mentioned above, these pictures were already available from a prior study; however, because there were two "matchers" in this experiment instead of one, a second slightly different picture for each pair was produced. This was done in the field by a local artist (as was the next activity described below), who altered each picture by painting small modifications on it. Some of these pictures were odd for Indians; for example a house with a European-style smoking chimney was thought by the deaf participants to possibly be a factory because they did not conceptualise normal houses as having chimneys.

The next activity, designed in the field, required each sign speaker to ask a series of WH questions to one deaf and one hearing person at the same time, thereby compelling the sign speaker to use both Hindi and ISL. The two interlocutors then had to answer the questions by selecting one of three pictures on an A4 card, of which there were around 23 in total. The sign speaker had the same A4 card, but for the second round of these experiments, a hint was written on the sign speaker's card in English, to prompt them to ask a particular question (see Figure 5). In the first round, the sign speakers had sometimes asked a different, originally unintended question, as the question was not always clear from the three pictures themselves. This was not detrimental to data quality, as sign speaking was occurring in any case, but the activity, analysis and precise targeting of WH questions were easier when sign speakers asked the envisaged question.

Methodological innovations in sign multilingualism research — 247

**Figure 5.** A selection of the elicitation cards used in the sign-speaking activity targeting WH questions

For each picture, the sign speaker tended to start by explaining what was depicted (e.g. a schoolteacher, farmer, and bank manager), and then asking, for example, "Who works in the bank?" Then the deaf and hearing interlocutors ticked the correct picture. Unlike the drawings used in the picture matching activity explained above, the 23 sets of pictures for this question task were all based on the Indian context, tailor made and produced on site by a local deaf artist in Indore, who was a college student employed at the deaf school. This represents an innovation in that the knowledge of local people in the field was utilised to take advantage of their ability to relate culturally to the communicative intent, rather than having the materials created by non-locals outside the field. Local artists tend to be able to devise materials that appear more familiar to the participants and lead to greater comfort in the elicitation setting, and this seems to have been achieved here. For example, in India, when someone is wearing Western clothes it is not always clear to a culturally Indian person whether that individual is male or female; therefore, in the drawings, gendered clothing was made more explicit such that the Indian participants could confidently identify each individual in the drawings as either a man or woman. This innovation of employing local expertise in generating elicitation materials was made possible by the lead field researcher's knowledge as a deaf education professional in India, which enabled him to select from among a number of talented deaf art graduates in the area.

Another benefit to the innovative methodology used in the sign-speaking strand was that the research team were given guidance from local deaf assistants that was invaluable and could be useful in planning improved procedures for future projects. These individuals, who the team met after arriving on site, accompanied the lead researcher as he gathered elicitation materials and offered suggestions for data collection tasks involving engaging game activities which would make participants comfortable and able to have relatively natural conversations.

However, selecting participants and preparing them for these game activities was challenging. It was possible that the complexity of the game reduced the participants' willingness to engage with it. Moreover, as alluded to above, it was difficult to select participants who were already somewhat familiar with each other. This minimises the deaf person's nervousness, which helps make the ethical standards optimal and ensures the data is as valid as possible. Ideally, the sign speaker might, for example, have a hearing cousin who knows deaf people well because they play cricket together or they have seen each other at weddings. So the sign speakers identified several deaf and hearing people who fell within their network and booked them to come in and see the research team. Some hearing individuals were not suitable as participants for this study because they did not appear to be comfortable engaging in such a situation with deaf people; they seemed reticent to interact, which would have lessened the data. The researchers thanked and apologised to them and advised that they might be contacted later. The people that were ultimately selected were the more talkative hearing individuals who also demonstrated ease when in communication with deaf people, as it was felt that they would be most likely to facilitate ample numbers of utterances.

As for the actual procedure of the experiments, before starting on a game sequence, several deaf and hearing participants waited together in another room, where an interpreter was present but none of the sign speakers. They tended to chat and joke with each other whilst waiting. When they came into the activity room, the sign speakers themselves explained the project to the deaf and hearing person; this was not videotaped. The sign speakers were already familiar with the project because there had been a previous sequence of fieldwork which was not based on elicitation activities, and they had in fact already given their consent. The sign speaker explained to the other participants the aim of the project and why they would be signing and speaking simultaneously, and then distributed consent forms. This not only permitted informed consent to be obtained, but it helped the participants to get used to the situation of someone signing and speaking at the same time.

It is important to point out that risks and benefits were both associated with certain aspects of the setting and procedure. Firstly, the researcher was familiar with the field site and the people there, who knew him as an adviser to the school board. This gave him much greater access and willing cooperation than perhaps another researcher might have received. Requests were fulfilled promptly on the whole. This could possibly have made participants feel more compelled to take part than otherwise, and the researcher was aware of his influence in the setting and attempted to ameliorate it through careful explanation of the project's ethical procedures including the complete acceptability of any disinclination to participate for any reason. Being known to others at the site was undoubtedly advantageous in terms of the logistics of the data collection. Plans and ideas had been devised to some extent prior to the researcher's arrival on site, but he needed to improvise on the spot as well. This made the logistics tricky and necessitated the simultaneous organisation of many things such as buying and making materials and finding illustrators. For a researcher heretofore unknown in this setting, such improvisation would have been impossible. In addition, certain practical and environmental challenges such as excessive noise arose which were perhaps easier to deal with given the researcher's familiarity with the context. The environment at the school is quite loud, with dogs barking, cars and people passing by, and many disturbances.

Another issue is that electricity cuts are frequent in this region. There is also a difficulty caused by the high humidity that is typical in this region, because when the ceiling fan was on, its noise reduced the quality of the audio, but when it was turned off, the room became too hot. Finally, as mentioned above, it was decided that the participants should be somewhat familiar with each other, but they were not really close friends and sometimes did not appear to be sufficiently at ease with one another. In particular, in mixed-gender groups, a female may not feel that she can be open and might not participate fully, as shyness in females is expected in the culture. On the other hand, it was not desirable that all participants should be from one gender only, because both males and females engage in cross-signing and to exclude one gender would make the findings less reliable.

## 2.3 Cross-signing elicitation

In addition to the free conversations and post-hoc introspective interviews (see section 1 above), the methodology for the cross-signing strand involved elicitation experiments carried out in the UK in 2012, and India in 2014. Both rounds of elicitation made use of picture pairs, in games played in dyads (two signers at a time). Player B would hold three pictures, while player A had one of these pictures. Player B was expected to find out from player A which picture s/he held. Player B was permitted to ask any question to determine this, but player A had to give answers and descriptions without seeing B's pictures. The signers alternated turns so that every other turn, they held three pictures. The researchers leading each of these rounds briefed the participants by explaining the game and giving a short demonstration as both signer and receiver. These pictures were associated with different target items in each of the two rounds. The first round elicited signs for emotions, entities, and actions; the second round targeted animate beings and inanimate objects (see Chapter 4).

In the first round, carried out in the UK in 2012, there were three targeted categories: actions, emotions, and entities (i.e. objects and persons such as a policeman, soldier, or referee as shown in Figure 6). A picture in the 'action' category might show a man fixing a vehicle. 'Emotion' pictures showed faces, e.g. yellow smiley faces and other typical emoji. However, this proved not to be ideal, as the participants tended not to sign e.g. 'happy', but rather just described the structure of the face (e.g. tracing a smile). Thus, these pictures were not useful for eliciting actual signs for emotions, so instead, participants were explicitly asked, "What is the sign for this in your sign language?"

**Figure 6.** Some of the images used in the cross-signing elicitation experiments for the 'person entities' category, targeting the entities 'policeman', 'soldier' and 'referee'

This data collection procedure was reasonably simple to prepare, and enabled the team to elicit data on a desired topic through relatively natural, spontaneous discussion of the images. The participants appeared to enjoy the game as well.

Participants were prepared for the game through an explanation from the research assistant, who showed an example of another researcher playing the game, and encouraged them to talk freely about the pictures without feeling that they had to choose the correct picture right away. The setup required four chairs: two for the participants, and two for the pictures, so that each player could hide them from his/her partner's view, using the back of the chair.

In retrospect, some of the pictures were inadequate for certain signers; for example, one or two depicted something foreign to a participant's culture (e.g. a tuk-tuk), which caused difficulty as they were not sure how to interpret the picture. If the team were to carry out this experiment again, improved procedures would include carefully recording who used which pictures, and ensuring that each picture is clearly visible to the camera for greater ease in working with the video data subsequently.

Of course the key innovative feature of this elicitation activity is the fact that the participants did not share any language; this caused many challenges for the participants as they had to exploit other strategies for communication. When one or more of these strategies was made unavailable to them (e.g. when the topic was colours and there was not a pertinently-coloured object nearby to point to), the communication task became even more difficult. While the team did not try this activity with non-signers, they were able to observe some hearing BSL students playing the game. It was difficult for these individuals not to use BSL (whereas this was less problematic for the deaf participants), and their progress through the game was slower, perhaps due to their less-developed signing fluency.

Because the same game was repeated at different times across a four-week period, the team was able to surmise that processing times were shorter during the second meetings (i.e. participants took less time to determine the content and match the pictures). They also noticed that there was an increase in the use of lexical signs, as well as more borrowing from Indian Sign Language and the participants' own respective sign languages.

For the second round, performed in 2014 in India, it was decided to use the same task, but with slightly different categories: inanimate objects and animate beings. The previous pictures were included in this round, and further pictures were also sourced. In addition, the 'emotions' category was dropped because the first round had shown that these picture stimuli do not tend to elicit signs for emotions.

The colour game was carried out in India under the supervision of the project's research assistant, with the same four participants as the picture matching game, who were from Nepal, India, Indonesia, and Jordan. The game was repeated at different times over four weeks, targeting signs for colours. It was a director-matcher task (like that described in section 2.2) that required 24 colour chips and 10 line drawings. Unlike the picture matching game described above, which was carried out twice for each round, this colour game was played three times. The first time was followed by a second opportunity one week later, and a third time two weeks after that. The participants were filmed in pairs, two pairs at the same time, and switched partners for further permutations.

Using the 10 pairs of line drawings (see examples in Figure 7), the participants had to communicate to find out which objects were in different colours and which were the same. The director had a picture with several items coloured (e.g. blue shirt, brown desk), unseen by the matcher. The director described each colour to the matcher, who asked questions as needed and tried to select the appropriate colour chip and place it on the relevant object in her/his drawing. Eight different colours were involved in each interaction, so with 24 colours in total, each pair of participants played the game three times to cover all the colours.

Methodological innovations in sign multilingualism research — 253

**Figure 7.** Materials used for the game eliciting colour signs, with rectangles where the matcher had to place the appropriate colour chip

Prior to the coding, each participant was asked explicitly for their signs for each of the 24 colours, so that the researcher would know how to transcribe each sign.

The colour game was ideal for ensuring a substantial contribution from each participant. With elicitation, it can of course be quite problematic if one person does not contribute, or just nods, as the researcher cannot be sure that they have understood. The active choosing of colours required by the colour game demonstrates understanding. Because there were 24 colours involved in the game, they had to be described quite intricately and specifically, and it was interesting to manage this communication. It was sometimes difficult for participants to convey slight variations in shades, e.g. brighter red and darker red, and often they used the same sign for both.

The researchers' hypothesis was that the participants would use their own lexical signs at first but at each meeting understand more and more of the other person's signs. They also thought that there would be more pointing at the beginning and less as time went on. However, they were not investigating pointing, which is primarily gestural and cross-modal (e.g. Barbarà and Zwets 2013), so to reduce its frequency, the researcher ensured that objects and papers were removed from the filming area. Participants may also be tempted to point at their own clothes, so they were given a black covering to put over their clothing to try to further reduce occurrences of pointing.

The number of colour chips to use was a thorny issue for the researchers. The original plan was to use 39 colours, but 24 were selected to make the elicitation more manageable. However, it was problematic to select individual colours out of only 24 in total, as there are so many possible colours. For data collection in the future, worthwhile adjustments might include the use of this wider range of colours; drawing on literature about the signification of different colours in different cultures; and taking note of differences between hues as they appear on the computer screen and on paper, as this caused some anomalies.

As mentioned above, this experiment was done three times instead of only two, because this allowed the researcher to identify a middle point in participants' communicative development. If it is done just twice, this only provides a picture of the beginning and end; what has happened in the middle is then unclear. Having more information about their linguistic evolution permitted the researchers to examine the development of variation, selection, and imitation, over more than just one period of time (see Byun et al. 2018).

## 3 Conclusion

The methodological innovations involved in all three strands of the MULTI-SIGN project prioritised authenticity, local embedding, and an ethical perspective that promotes capacity-building, rather than prioritising the generation of data that is highly comparable and standardised. The post-hoc interviews, in which participants engaged in metalinguistic reasoning and multimodal interaction, have facilitated several important contributions to wider knowledge about cross-cultural signed communication. Though interviews are a common method in linguistic research on both spoken and signed languages (e.g. Lam and Yu 2013; Hill 2015), they are rarely carried out in this manner, i.e. asking the participant about the actual data while viewing it together. These interviews encouraged and exploited introspection, which was essential because this was the first time that cross-signing data had been gathered from individuals with no shared language, and cross-signers' perceptions of their communicative decisions and strategies were the first necessary step in an inductive enquiry into this complex phenomenon.

During the interviews, the participants drew a great deal on their metacognition and metalinguistic skills. Further implementation of this method may enable future research to explore the extent to which building a metalinguistic vocabulary boosts cross-signers' multilingual capacity and facility. This kind of method might also be utilised with hearing non-signers using gestures, for comparative purposes. It is interesting to consider how comparable the gesturing abilities of hearing people are in this context. Looking more closely at the gesturing of hearing people who do not share a language would be a fascinating future project, enabling an investigation of the effects from culture and confidence, for example (cf. Cartmill, Hunsicker, and Goldin-Meadow 2014; Sekine and Kita 2015).

Although it is not always desirable to aim primarily at data comparability, standardising methods would be beneficial to the field of sign language research, as suggested by Morford et al. (2015: 219–221). This might include a uniform way of selecting stimuli; measuring onset of reaction time (e.g. at what physical point an utterance can be said to commence); and listing details about informants' backgrounds, e.g. gender, age at sign language acquisition, and level of education (Morford et al. 2015). Furthermore, sign language researchers are only just beginning to explore the innovation angle in their field, so this is very much an emerging area of work with great scope for developing and refining standardised methodologies. However, it is worth pointing out that while such standardisation could be beneficial, this should not be the ultimate goal, because it is far more valuable for sign language linguists to continue exploring innovative ways to improve research design.

## References

Azuma, Shoji. 1996. Speech production units among bilinguals. *Journal of Psycholinguistic Research* 25(3). 397–416.

Barberà, Gemma & Martine Zwets. 2013. Pointing and reference in sign language and spoken language: Anchoring vs. identifying. *Sign Language Studies* 13(4). 491–515.

Basturkmen, Helen, Shawn Loewen & Rod Ellis. 2002. Metalanguage in focus on form in the communicative classroom. *Language Awareness* 11(1). 1–13.

Brennan, Mary. 1992. The visual world of British Sign Language: An introduction. In David Brien (ed.), *Dictionary of British Sign Language/English*, 1–118. London: Faber and Faber.

Byun, Kang-Suk. 2016. *Cross-signing*. Ishara Signed Publications No. 3. Nijmegen: Ishara Press.

Byun, Kang-Suk, Connie de Vos, Ulrike Zeshan, Anastasia Bradford & Stephen C. Levinson. 2018. First encounters: Repair sequences in cross-signing. *Topics in Cognitive Science* 10(2). 314–334.

Cartmill, Erica A., Dea Hunsicker & Susan Goldin-Meadow. 2014. Pointing and naming are not redundant: Children use gesture to modify nouns before they modify nouns in speech. *Developmental Psychology* 50(6). 1660–1666.

Edley, Nigel & Lia Litosseliti. 2010. Contemplating interviews and focus groups. In Lia Litosseliti (ed.), *Research methods in linguistics*, 155–179. London: Continuum.

Fenlon, Jordan, Adam Schembri, Trevor Johnston & Kearsy Cormier. 2015. Documentary and corpus approaches to sign language research. In Eleni Orfanidou, Bencie Woll & Gary Morgan (eds.), *Research methods in sign language studies: A practical guide*, 156–172. Chichester: John Wiley & Sons.

Gullberg, Marianne. 2009. Reconstructing verb meaning in a second language: How English speakers of L2 Dutch talk and gesture about placement. *Annual Review of Cognitive Linguistics* 7(1). 221–244.

Hill, Joseph C. 2015. Data collection in sociolinguistics. In Eleni Orfanidou, Bencie Woll & Gary Morgan (eds.), *Research methods in sign language studies: A practical guide*, 193–205. Chichester: John Wiley & Sons.

Jessner, Ulrike. 2005. Multilingual metalanguage, or the way multilinguals talk about their languages. *Language Awareness* 14(1). 56–68.

Lam, Marvin & Carol Yu. 2013. English and Cantonese in a bilingual call centre in Hong Kong. *World Englishes* 32(4). 521–535.

Lennon, Paul. 1989. Introspection and intentionality in advanced second-language acquisition. *Language Learning* 39(3). 375–396.

Litosseliti, Lia. 2003. *Using focus groups in research*. London: Continuum.

Morford, Jill P., Brenda Nicodemus & Erin Wilkinson. 2015. Research methods in psycholinguistic investigations of sign language processing. In Eleni Orfanidou, Bencie Woll & Gary Morgan (eds.), *Research methods in sign language studies: A practical guide*, 209–249. Chichester: John Wiley & Sons.

Noble, Tracy, Rachel Kachchaf, Ann Rosebery, Beth Warren, Mary Catherine O'Connor & Yang Wang. 2014. Do linguistic features of science test items prevent English language learners from demonstrating their knowledge? Paper presented at the Annual Meeting of the National Association of Research on Science Teaching, April, Pittsburgh, PA, USA.

Nyst, Victoria. 2015. Sign language fieldwork. In Eleni Orfanidou, Bencie Woll & Gary Morgan (eds.), *Research methods in sign language studies: A practical guide*, 107–122. Chichester: John Wiley & Sons.

Ogulnick, Karen L. 1999. Introspection as a method of raising critical language awareness. *Journal of Humanistic Education and Development* 37(3). 145–159.

Panda, Sibaji. 2016. *Sign-switching: Indian Sign Language and Burundi Sign Language*. Ishara Signed Publications No. 4. Nijmegen: Ishara Press.

Perniss, Pamela. 2007. *Space and iconicity in German Sign Language* (DGS). Nijmegen: Max Planck Institute for Psycholinguistics PhD thesis.

Quadros, Ronice Müller de, Deborah Chen Pichler, Diane Lillo-Martin, Carina Rebello Cruz, Laura Kozak, Jeffrey Levi Palmer, Aline Lemos Pizzio & Wanette Reynolds. 2015. Methods in bimodal bilingualism research: Experimental studies. In Eleni Orfanidou, Bencie Woll & Gary Morgan (eds.), *Research methods in sign language studies: A practical guide*, 250–280. Chichester: John Wiley & Sons.

Rathmann, Christian, Wolfgang Mann & Gary Morgan. 2007. Narrative structure and narrative development in deaf children. *Deafness and Education International* 9(4). 187–196.

Russo, Tommaso. 2005. A crosslinguistic, cross-cultural analysis of metaphors in two Italian Sign Language (LIS) registers. *Sign Language Studies* 5(3). 333–359.

Sagara, Keiko & Ulrike Zeshan. 2015. Semantic fields in sign languages: A comparative typological study. In Ulrike Zeshan & Keiko Sagara (eds.), *Semantic fields in sign languages: Colour, kinship and quantification*, 3–38. Berlin: Mouton de Gruyter and Nijmegen: Ishara Press.

Sekine, Kazuki & Sotaro Kita. 2015. Development of multimodal discourse comprehension: cohesive use of space by gestures. *Language, Cognition and Neuroscience* 30(10). 1245–1258.

Siebenhaar, Beat. 2006. Code choice and code-switching in Swiss-German internet relay chat rooms. *Journal of Sociolinguistics* 10(4). 481–506.

Tunmer, William E. & Judith A. Bowey. 1984. Metalinguistic awareness and reading acquisition. In William E. Tunmer, Chris Pratt & M.L. Herriman (eds.), *Metalinguistic awareness in children: Theory, research and implications*, 144–168. Berlin: Springer.

Vygotsky, Lev S. 1962. *Thought and language*. Cambridge, MA: MIT Press.

Zeshan, Ulrike. 2015. "Making meaning" – Communication between sign language users without a shared language. *Cognitive Linguistics* 26(2). 211–260.

Zeshan, Ulrike & Pamela Perniss (eds.). 2008. Possessive and existential constructions in sign languages. Nijmegen: Ishara Press.

Zeshan, Ulrike & Sibaji Panda. 2015. Two languages at hand: Code-switching in bilingual signers. *Sign Language & Linguistics* 18(1). 90–131.

# Part II

# Burundi Sign Language-Indian Sign Language bilinguals' community of practice

Sibaji Panda

## 1 Introduction

In 2009, a unique bachelor's degree course commenced in India[1], aimed at deaf signers. This programme, the BA in Applied Sign Language Studies (BAASLS), attracted many deaf students both within India and from abroad. The course became a fertile ground for acquiring sign languages, most notably Indian Sign Language (ISL), as a majority of the intake consisted of domestic students from various part of India. The non-Indian, international students were from a variety of different places, including Nepal, Mexico, Uganda, and Burundi.

This chapter focuses on a sub-group of international students, who joined the BAASLS programme from Burundi. Their developing bilingual competence in Indian Sign Language and Burundi Sign Language has been the subject of research by Zeshan and Panda (2015); see also chapter 3. The present chapter is intended to provide some insights into the setting and characteristics of this group of bilingual sign language users.

## 2 The linguistic context

Within the group of deaf BA students, the foreign sign languages were each represented by small groups of 2-5 students, which were of course dwarfed by the Indian group. In addition to some single individuals from other countries, small groups of non-Indian students included the following:
- Two students from Uganda
- Four students from Nepal
- Six students from Burundi

---

[1] The programme was a collaborative venture between Indira Gandhi National Open University, New Delhi and University of Central Lancashire. Deaf sign language users from various countries attended the programme. In total, 22 deaf foreigners and 48 Indians were enrolled in the programme.

This made ISL effectively the dominant language of this university environment, even though the other sign languages had their own minority communities. International Sign was also used by many of the students for cross-cultural communication and social mixing. Within this diverse contact situation, one group was of particular interest: the Burundi signers. This is because their group was comparatively large, being comprised of six people, which enabled them to not only acquire ISL, but continue to use Burundi Sign Language (BuSL) on a regular basis, as well as being exposed to the other sign languages within the university environment. Such an unusual and linguistically versatile situation gives rise to numerous phenomena (see chapter 3), but the present text looks specifically at their language behaviour as a "community of practice" (Wenger 1999), and the factors that prompted them to use each language.

At the beginning of the BAASLS course in 2009, one deaf Burundian arrived, who was a strong BuSL signer. This individual learned ISL very gradually, having the challenge of culture shock to surmount in addition to the novel linguistic environment, and no compatriots to use BuSL with or assist with acclimatisation. In the second year, 2010, two further deaf Burundians joined the programme, allowing this group of three to sign together in BuSL. The following year, 2011, saw the arrival of three new BuSL signers, completing the group of six in total. This enabled all of them to learn ISL at a faster pace, and enriched their communication with each other at the same time. The progressive growth of this community and their distribution in different households over the three years is represented schematically in Figure 1.

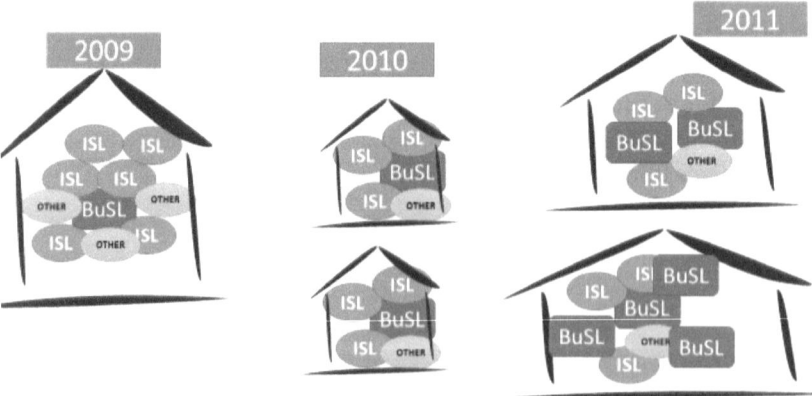

**Figure 1.** Distribution of the BuSL signers over the three years in signing households, indicative of what language contact they were party to.

This community of practice was characterised by different modes of signing for the different permutations of signers at home, in class, and when travelling. The students rented accommodation outside the university, with typically six to eight students sharing a house. The four Burundian women shared a house with two Indian and two Nepalese women, making a house of eight. The BuSL signers' linguistic behaviour was different depending on whether the others were present. At dinner, all eight would tend to eat together and use ISL, in solidarity with the general environment and ISL's status as the dominant language in their host country. After dinner, the Burundi signers would tend to socialise amongst themselves, using BuSL, and their two Nepalese housemates also went off by themselves to use their own native sign language, while their Indian peers talked together in ISL.

The situation was much the same in the men's accommodation, which encompassed two Burundians, four Indians, and two Ugandans. Here again, the Burundians would communicate with each other using BuSL, for example when discussing difficulties in understanding some of the academic material and explaining concepts from the course to each other. In such cases they used little if any ISL. When an Indian peer joined the conversation, they changed to ISL, as they did in a mixed-group situation such as dinnertime.

Their linguistic backgrounds were slightly different as some had knowledge of other East African sign languages, notably Kenyan Sign Language (KSL) and Ugandan Sign Language (UgSL). This is largely because travel in East Africa is frequent and unfettered by border controls, so that many deaf people gain exposure to neighbouring sign languages quite easily. Table 1 conveys the language backgrounds and time spent in India for the BuSL/ISL bilinguals, four of whom who provided the data discussed in chapter 3. All of them grew up using written French due to its dominant language status in Burundi, and they are also familiar with English because it is used quite prevalently in the country's high schools.

**Table 1.** The signers' language backgrounds and time spent in India

|  | CN | AB | NC | WK | MB | SN |
|---|---|---|---|---|---|---|
| Time spent in India | 2009–2015 6 years | 2010–2014 4 years | 2010–2014 4 years | 2011–2015 4 years | 2011–2015 4 years | 2011–2015 4 years |
| Sign languages | BuSL, KSL, UgSL, ISL | BuSL, KSL, ISL | BuSL, ISL | BuSL, KSL, ISL | BuSL, KSL, ISL | BuSL, KSL, ISL |
| Written languages | French, English | French, English | French, English | French, English | French, English | French, English |

## 3 Social life and communication on-campus and off-campus

The students spent considerable time travelling and engaged in off-campus day to day activities such as shopping. When a BuSL signer needed to go to the store or the doctor etc., an ISL signer would often accompany them, or several Burundians and Indians would go together as a group, with the latter of course being able to share their greater knowledge of the logistics and the cultural context. When engaged in such errands or sightseeing, the Indian students commonly acted as tour guides, giving descriptions and explanations, and telling stories illustrative of Indian deaf culture. This facilitated the cultural acclimatisation of the Burundians, as well as enhancing their acquisition of ISL.

Students could avail themselves of opportunities for extensive travel during university holidays, which took place across two months during the summer as well as in two-week or three-week semester breaks. With no course activities to attend to, some of them opted to stay with their new friends in their home villages. Some of the Burundians visited fellow students in this way as a group, enjoying considerable contact with ISL signers whilst travelling and touring. However, one Burundian stayed with an Indian family alone, and was able to experience perhaps a more extensive cultural and linguistic immersion during this visit. Upon returning to their accommodation, this person shared this learning with the other Burundians, through signing in BuSL.

The BuSL-ISL community of practice developed a distinctive bilingual variety (Zeshan and Panda 2015) including strategies such as reiterative code-switching (i.e. repeating the same concept expressed with signs from the two different sign languages; see Quinto-Pozos and Adam 2013), and idiosyncratic ways of articulating certain ISL signs, due to the modelling they provided to each other combined with their emerging acquisition of the language.

Roommates appeared to form signs in ways that were alike, perhaps through the habit of imitating each other. One example was seen with the ISL sign DIFFICULT (Zeshan and Panda 2015). This sign, comprised of two fists, features a brief vertical movement and is accompanied by particular non-manual features such as lowered eyebrows; however, the Burundi signers articulated it with a horizontal movement, and without the requisite non-manual features. This could stem from differences between the phonology of BuSL versus ISL non-manual features, which was seen in connection with other signs as well, and from the tendency for the Burundians to emulate the articulation of the two strongest signers within their group. In line with the argument in Croft (2000), that the propagation of linguistic variants during language change is influenced by social factors, the modus operandi within this community of practice appeared to be that if one of these leading individuals produced a sign in an unusual manner, the rest of the group imitated this, giving secondary or lesser recognition to the citation ISL version. This can in fact be seen as producing ISL with a BuSL 'accent' popularised within the group by influential individuals.

Equally interesting is the students' linguistic behaviour in the classroom environment. Importantly, at the university, some of the tutors had minimal knowledge of International Sign. This was especially the case among the hearing tutors, whose non-native signing skills and reduced use of gesture and non-manual features sometimes made it challenging for an international deaf student to follow the lesson. These hearing tutors in the main were sign monolingual in ISL, and they relied solely on the two-handed ISL alphabet, being unacquainted with the one-handed International Sign alphabet. In contrast, the Burundians on arrival were only familiar with one-handed alphabets, including from International Sign and BuSL. Communication with deaf tutors was somewhat smoother because of their greater native fluency, sign multilingualism, and experience with cross-cultural signed interaction.

Though their comprehension in class was problematic in the beginning, the BuSL signers progressively found it easier to engage with ISL. After the difficult first year, their understanding became easier and they played an increasingly active role in ISL discussions. Interestingly, in mixed small group work, for example where there might be four Indian students and two Burundians, they all used ISL as the first language of the classroom, but when a difficult topic arose, the two Burundians would have a brief separate conversation in BuSL to clarify the matter, and then re-join the group using ISL. Of the six BuSL signers, the two most skilled and knowledgeable individuals (see above) were often asked by the other four for help in class, and sometimes all six would have a discussion amongst themselves. In such cases, the exchange would take place in BuSL, with the signers reverting to ISL when resuming their communication with other classmates.

Thus it would seem that this particular community of practice developed its own distinctive way of life and linguistic behaviours whilst in the university context, as well as when house-sharing and engaging in the wider culture. More research is needed to closely examine these behaviours, the factors that contribute to them, the consequences of their adoption and how the group members view them.

## References

Croft, William. 2000. *Explaining Language Change: An evolutionary approach*. London: Longman.
Quinto-Pozos, David & Robert Adam. 2013. Sign language contact. In Robert Bailey, Richard Cameron & Ceil Lucas (eds.), *The Oxford handbook of sociolinguistics*, 379–403. USA: Oxford University Press.
Wenger, Etienne. 1999. *Communities of practice: Learning, meaning, and identity*. Cambridge: CUP.
Zeshan, Ulrike & Sibaji Panda. 2015. Two languages at hand – Code-switching in bilingual deaf signers. *Sign Language and Linguistics* 18(1). 90–131.

# A community profile of "sign-speakers" at the Indore Deaf Bilingual Academy

Sibaji Panda

## 1 Introduction

This chapter gives an account of a unique group of practitioners in India, who use a sign language and spoken language simultaneously, a behaviour that is called "sign-speaking" here. "Sign-speaking" is defined as speaking and signing at the same time with a considerable level of mismatch between the simultaneously produced structures in both languages because the structure of each language is largely intact, that is, not greatly influenced by interference from the other language (Zeshan and Panda 2017). These "sign-speakers", participants in the Multisign research project (see chapter 1, this volume), are trilingual in Hindi, English, and Indian Sign Language (ISL).

Individuals in this group mainly use spoken language as their first and preferred language and sign language as their second language and/or chiefly a workplace language for teaching, interpreting, and personal communication with deaf people. Given the unique ways in which they use Hindi and ISL, often at the same time, the "sign-speakers" can be seen as forming a "community of practice" (Wenger 1999) at their place of employment, the Indore Deaf Bilingual Academy (IDBA). This chapter describes a micro-community at IDBA consisting of four individuals.

## 2 The setting

The Indore Deaf Bilingual Academy is one of the largest bilingual schools in the country, with approximately 550 deaf students, all of whom use ISL, along with their teachers, as the medium of teaching and learning. The school also has a dedicated sign language department which offers an ISL training programme for interpreters and sign language teachers. Trainee interpreters have opportunities to interact with the students of the school from the very beginning of the training programme; this seems to equip them very quickly with ISL communication skills.

Figure 1 shows a schematic representation of the IDBA campus with its various departments and facilities.

**Figure 1.** The IDBA campus

Some of the hearing practitioners within this specialist environment are skilled at sign-speaking because of their natural daily exposure to this practice. Signing on campus is ubiquitous, and therefore, the hearing people can be seen to engage in the following types of bilingual behaviours when both hearing and deaf people are present:
– Signing and speaking consecutively.
– Signing and speaking simultaneously, with one language (often Hindi) being clearly dominant and influencing the structures of the second language.
– Sign-speaking (as defined in Section 1).

While many hearing people are capable of using the first two behaviours, sign-speaking is less common, and the micro-community investigated here consists of only four individuals who are competent sign-speakers.

The field site offers a comfortable conversational setting for the sign-speaking community, facilitating relatively spontaneous language production. The site was also suitable due to the author's longstanding involvement there, which helped to put participants at ease. The author had served as Chief Advisor of the school and conducted several training events and workshops there. During this span of engagement, the author had been able to informally observe staff members' unusual bilingual capabilities, including both teachers and interpreters, in the classroom as well as in day-to-day interactions.

## 3 Individual backgrounds of sign-speakers and their roles at IDBA

While all of the sign-speakers are fluent in Hindi, their background can be differentiated in terms of their ISL experience. One the one hand, a person may be currently progressing through, or have just completed, the interpreter or teacher training at the school; in other words, their signing skills are non-native and more recently acquired. One the other hand, the individual may have deaf parents or siblings and be a fluent signer before joining the institute, being considered a native sign language user. Despite this difference in background, both types of individuals might be seen to have attained a fluency level sufficient to comfortably communicate with deaf pupils and staff about familiar everyday matters at the school. Since the bulk of the sign-speaking was related to such routine topics, their experiential variance did not tend to impinge upon communication, though it is worthwhile to note that there might be an impact on scenarios where formal interpreting is taking place and/or the demands of the subject matter are high.

Sign-speaking may happen in a number of natural circumstances, so it was interesting to explore this with the sign-speakers and conduct observations to determine how often, when, and with whom they exploit this behaviour. It was noted that, for instance, when there are visitors in the family home, hearing individuals in families with deaf family members often find themselves in a situation that obliges them to sign-speak to enable both the hearing guests and deaf family members to follow the conversation. This is in fact a common practice at home when a hearing signer in the family such as a CODA (Child of Deaf Adults) is engaged in spoken communication with a visitor; they also sign simultaneously when the deaf parents or family members are present.

Sometimes, there are both signing and non-signing individuals within the family itself, and a sign-speaker may make efforts to include everyone in the communication. Interestingly, one such person in the field setting was the sister of a deaf pupil. Because their parents did not learn to sign, she kept her deaf brother included in all conversations at home by signing and speaking simultaneously, feeling that both modes should be used in his family environment. Functioning as a mediator in mixed deaf-hearing family communication tends to help them gradually build skills in signing and speaking at the same time. A person from this kind of background may also engage in sign-speaking outside the home, for example if they are shopping with a deaf parent and there is a necessity to communicate with a non-signing shopkeeper. Such a role diverges from the traditional 'interpreter' role, which usually involves one language being translated consecutively into another; in contrast, for this kind of situation, the individual in question produces translations using simultaneous utterances in both the spoken and the signed language.

On the other hand, individuals from non-signing home environments will not have had such frequent chances to acquire this skill, and sign-speaking behaviour may come to them less 'automatically'. While in training, some of the interpreters who are less used to this skill might start to pick it up because of the plentiful opportunities afforded by the unusual setting they find themselves in, a large school with a round-the-clock signing environment due to the attached boarding facility.

Table 1 below indicates the roles that each participant performed in this community of practice. The first three individuals (A, B and C) all have deaf family members including deaf parents, while the fourth sign-speaker (D) does not have any deaf family members and is an interpreter trainee at the time of the research.

**Table 1.** Roles carried out by the four members of the micro-community

| Role | Person A | Person B | Person C | Person D |
|---|---|---|---|---|
| Informal interpreter inside the school | × | × | × | × |
| Formal interpreter outside the school | × | × | × | × |
| Teacher | × | | | |
| School management | × | × | | |
| Interpreter trainer | × | | | |
| Parent counselling | × | × | × | × |

Despite the frequency of (mostly non-signing) visitors in the form of parents, businesspeople, medical professionals and volunteers, the school's working procedures and requirements do not stipulate an in-house or staff interpreter because almost everybody at the school signs. Interpreting is utilised on an informal basis, by asking whoever is available in the immediate vicinity to provide this service for any meetings or discussions requiring it, for example when parents want to ask specific questions about their child's future career path. In such instances, when a deaf person is present, the interpreter switches to sign-speaking; indeed, many of the ad-hoc interactions and involvement in communication support within the school require those acting as interpreters to sign and speak at the same time. The casual nature of calling on whoever happens to be close by arises from there being no option of a dedicated qualified interpreter; though this may not be viewed as ideal from some vantage points, it allows some of the trainee interpreters regular opportunities to engage in sign-speaking situations. Furthermore, it often permits the newer interpreters, if they are nearby when the mediated communication is occurring, to take advantage of observing as their more experienced peers model the sign-speaking skill.

# 4 Conclusion

In sum, the capacity to perform sign-speaking in discussion, i.e. to fluently produce simultaneous utterances in two different languages, is a complex mental task that seems to be absorbed with regular practice by some individuals. The character and quantity of this practice depends very much on the environment in which the sign-speaking takes place; in particular, the more the sign-speaker's daily environment is comprised of both deaf and hearing people, the more the use of this particular skill is somewhat 'forced', that is, the more the individual feels obligated to facilitate both visual and aural access so that all present may understand the conversation.

The four members of this micro-community of practice appear adept at this skill. However, such groups are little-described in the linguistics literature, and need to be empirically examined further with reference to their development over time and the environmental factors that influence them. In particular, it would be desirable to carry out further research with a larger number of people in each of the two sub-groups discussed in Section 3, namely those with and without deaf family members.

## References

Wenger, Etienne. 1999. *Communities of practice: learning, meaning, and identity*. Cambridge: CUP.

Zeshan, Ulrike & Sibaji Panda. 2017. Sign-speaking: The structure of simultaneous bimodal utterances. *Applied Linguistics Review* 9(1). 1–34.

# Micro-communities of practice: A case study of cross-signing participants in the UK

Tashi Bradford

## 1 Introduction

This chapter focuses on a micro-community of signers that developed during data collection activities for one strand of the research project on multilingual behaviours in sign language users – Multisign (see chapter 1). This was the first of two groups of individuals (see chapter 11 for the second group) who participated in a study on emergent cross-cultural signed communication ("cross-signing" – see chapters 4 and 7 for more detailed descriptions of the study). The study highlighted cross-linguistic phenomena, involving communication across language barriers and bridging cultural differences (Zeshan 2015; Byun et al 2017).

This micro-community, which gathered in Preston, UK, in summer 2012, formed itself around four core research participants from Indonesia, Jordan, Japan and the UK. The international participants travelled to the UK for data collection for the study, which took place at the International Institute for Sign Languages and Deaf Studies (iSLanDS) at the University of Central Lancashire (UCLan).

The contents of this chapter aim to convey a brief picture of the group, their experiences in the research environment, and how they were constituted as a small group. The chapter describes the composition of this micro-community; their activities, associations and interactions in Preston; and the linguistic forms and structures that emerged from their contact with each other.

## 2 Composition of the group

The four core participants gathered for six weeks in Preston during the summer of 2012. One participant (female) was local, while the other three (male) were from abroad and had very limited knowledge of Britain. They were all skilled in at least one sign language and had varying degrees of fluency in written language (see Table 1). All had hearing parents apart from the Japanese participant, whose parents were deaf. They had been chosen by iSLanDS staff members who were familiar with their deaf communities. Participants shared no common language, and all were selected using the following criteria in order to minimise reliance on fingerspelling and common signs:

- Fluency in their native sign languages
- Minimal international travel and contact with users of other sign languages
- Minimal knowledge of English (apart from one British participant)

The Indonesian and Jordanian participants lodged with local Deaf men who were fluent in their guests' sign languages, having lived in those countries for extended periods. The Japanese participant stayed with two British Sign Language (BSL)/English bilinguals, and received daytime interpreting and support from a Japanese deaf postgraduate student who knew Japanese Sign Language (JSL), BSL, Japanese, and English. These arrangements facilitated minimal exposure to BSL upon arrival in Preston, so as not to affect the initial data. The iSLanDS staff who knew the participants' respective sign languages also interpreted during initial briefings, interviews on research data, and initial capacity building activities that ran parallel to the research process.

Throughout their stay, exposure to BSL at home was not the same for all participants. The Indonesian participant MI and his host communicated primarily in Indonesian Sign Language, and there were few BSL users who visited the home. In contrast, the host of Jordanian participant MS regularly received visitors and had an active social life with other BSL users, giving MS frequent exposure to this language.

Table 1. Participants in the 2012 data collection, their linguistic backgrounds and guides

| Participant | Country of origin | Fluent | Intermediate | Minimal | Compatriot guide[1] |
|---|---|---|---|---|---|
| MS | Jordan | Jordanian SL | Written Arabic | Written English, BSL | PS (iSLanDS student) |
| MI | Indonesia | Indonesian SL | Written Bahasa Indonesia | Written English | NP (iSLanDS staff member) |
| CP | UK | British SL, written English, International Sign | | | None |
| HM | Japan | Japanese SL, written Japanese | | Written English | KS (iSLanDS student) |

---

[1] PS and NP acted as guides as well as hosts. KS was a guide during the day but HM had different hosts.

Besides daily contact with their hosts and members of the local community, participants also interacted with the research team at iSLanDS, including the compatriot guides in Table 1, two further staff members, and one more postgraduate student. Most of the participants' time was spent with each other and with their local guides, which promoted inside humour, in-group communication and a distinct group identity (cf. Sutton-Spence and Napoli 2012). Elements of a community of practice emerged such as in-group jokes; for example, participants made a joke that anyone who got all of the answers right in the experimental games would win a lollipop. This gave rise to a new sign used exclusively among group members, depicting a lollipop, to signify 100% correct responses in an elicitation game:

**Figure 1.** The group's constructed sign meaning 'lollipop prize for 100% score'

# 3 Activities and interactions

Aside from research sessions, there were various outings and activities, many geared towards socialising with the local deaf community. The group attended weekly social gatherings and badminton games; visited the Manchester Deaf centre and a deaf-run cafe in Blackburn; went on a day trip to the nearby seaside town of Blackpool; and spent three days in London where they visited Remark (a deaf-led BSL training organisation), the headquarters of the British Deaf Association, a Deaf mosque, the Frank Barnes (deaf) school, and the National Deaf Children's Society. Some also went to Stonehenge and the Arsenal football stadium; the participants from Jordan and Indonesia shared a love of sports and were both Muslim, which provided some common ground for interaction and activities.

In addition to socialising, the group had opportunities to share their skills, acquire new ones, and raise awareness of their home sign languages. At the iSLanDS five-year anniversary celebration event that was held during their visit, each participant had an information stall about their home country. The iSLanDS Institute also held a two-day workshop on Leadership and Development including British and international speakers, and the three participants from overseas presented on their respective countries as well as meeting CODAs (Children of Deaf Adults) and BSL/English interpreters, to learn about their experiences and training. In addition, two participants engaged in research and teaching whilst in Preston: MI helped transcribe data collected in Indonesia for a PhD thesis, and taught Indonesian Sign Language for three hours on a *Jummah* visit for Friday prayers at a Lancaster mosque with hearing members of the local Indonesian community; and HM annotated Japanese Sign Language numeral and kinship terms for a typology project, and delivered a session on teaching sign language.

These opportunities afforded to the participants can also be seen as associated benefits of the research project, but more importantly, they comprised a springboard from which these individuals formed a community of practice (cf. Trowler and Turner 2002) in pursuit of common goals, especially that of building the skills of the three group members from overseas. Thus it is contended that this group can be characterised as a micro-community formed through taking active advantage of capacity building opportunities and engagement with local deaf people, which prompted in-group behaviour such as the production of bespoke sign constructs. The researchers, guides, and participants undertook activities for the common purpose of enabling the three participants from overseas to become culturally acclimatised and build language, metalinguistic and research-based knowledge.

## References

Byun, Kang-Suk, Anastasia Bradford, Ulrike Zeshan, Stephen C. Levinson & Connie de Vos. 2018. First encounters: Repair sequences in cross-signing. *Topics in Cognitive Science* (Special Issue on Miscommunication) 10. 314–334.
Sutton-Spence, Rachel & Donna Jo Napoli. 2012. Deaf jokes and sign language humour. *Humor: International Journal of Humor Research* 25(3). 311–337.
Trowler, Paul R. & Graham H. Turner. 2002. Exploring the hermeneutic foundations of university life: Deaf academics in a hybrid 'community of practice'. *Higher Education* 43. 227–256.
Zeshan, Ulrike. 2015. "Making meaning" – Communication between sign language users without a shared language. *Cognitive Linguistics* 26(2). 211–260.

# Micro-communities of practice: A case study of cross-signing participants in India

Tashi Bradford

## 1 Introduction

This chapter focuses on a micro-community of signers that was formed in 2014 during data collection activities for the cross-signing strand of the Multisign project (see chapter 1 about this project). This was the second of two groups (see chapter 10 for the first group from 2012) who were brought together to participate in incipient cross-cultural signed communication; thus none of the core participants had fluency in any shared language with the others (see chapters 4 and 7 for more detailed descriptions of the cross-signing study). These types of interactions are called 'cross-signing' to give salience to the cross-linguistic aspect of this situation, with associated cultural differences and language barriers (Zeshan 2015: 212).

This micro-community, which gathered for elicitation tasks in Lucknow, India, in late 2014, included four core participants from Indonesia, Jordan, Nepal and India, and members of the research group. The data collection activities took place at Dr Shakuntala Misra National Rehabilitation University (DSMNRU), which in 2014 was the site of the Bachelor of Arts in Applied Sign Language Studies (BAASLS) programme[1] with 20 deaf students from all over India as well as Burundi and Nepal.

What is presented in this chapter concerns the makeup and emergence of common purpose among this group in the Multisign project, which became a community of practice (cf. Trowler and Turner 2002). With assistance from some of the 2012 participants, the 2014 group took advantage of capacity building activities, engagement with local deaf students, and the opportunity of producing their own unique sign constructs. Briefly, this chapter describes the makeup of this micro-community; their activities, associations and interactions in Lucknow; and the linguistic constructs that emerged from their contact with each other.

---

[1] Modules on this programme cover bilingualism, deaf culture and community, language acquisition, linguistics, language planning, and teaching. Students have a foundation entry preparatory year where they hone skills for university study such as ICT, English, and personal development planning.

https://doi.org/10.1515/9781501503528-011

## 2 The makeup of the micro-community

The four participants were selected by research team members[2] familiar with these countries' deaf communities, in consultation with participants from 2012 (see chapter 10 about this group), some of whom served as compatriot guides and interpreters for research interactions such as filmed consent sessions and interviews about collected data.

Table 1. Participants in the 2014 data collection, their linguistic backgrounds and guides

| Participant | Country of origin | Fluent | Intermediate | Minimal | Compatriot guide |
|---|---|---|---|---|---|
| BF | Jordan | Jordanian SL | Written Arabic | Written English | MS (Jordanian participant from 2012 group) |
| AM | Indonesia | Indonesian SL | Written Bahasa Indonesia | | MI (Indonesian participant from 2012 group) |
| AS | Nepal | Nepali SL | Written Nepalese | Written English | AG, a former BAASLS student (deaf Nepali with knowledge of English) |
| NG (experiment phase only) | India | Indian SL | Written English | Written Hindi | None |

By the time this micro-community was brought together, the research team and collaborators were more experienced, having worked with the 2012 group already. Communication amongst the researchers was primarily in British Sign Language and International Sign; additionally, one member was fluent in Indonesian Sign Language, another knew Jordanian Sign Language, and two had skills in Indian Sign Language. A recent graduate from the BAASLS programme was available to act as compatriot guide for the Nepali participant.

This setting can be seen as having a hierarchy or layers of group members, including the researchers, the surrounding local students and the indigenous deaf

---

[2] The research team was an international group in itself, with members from the UK, Germany, USA, India, and Korea.

community, as well as the core participants and the experienced individuals from the 2012 group acting as their compatriot guides (see Figure 1).

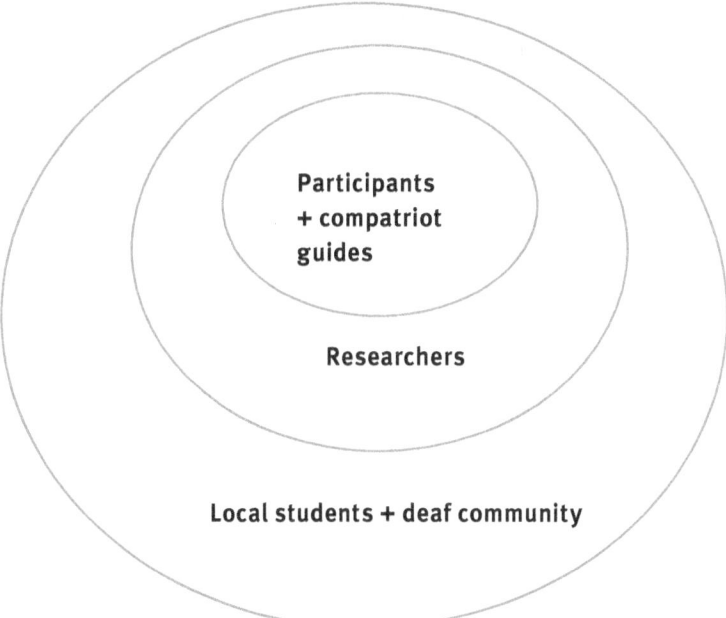

**Figure 1.** Layers of the 2014 community in Lucknow

# 3 Activities, associations and interactions

All participants and their guides stayed in university dormitories, as did the researchers. The two Nepalis shared a room as did the two Jordanians and the two from Indonesia. Upon arrival, contact with the local deaf students was avoided in order to minimise exposure to Indian Sign Language and International Sign, in keeping with the remit that the participants should have no language in common. Therefore, meals were taken apart from the Indian students, and for the brief period until the initial data sessions, participants were encouraged to only speak with their compatriots and research staff who knew their home sign languages. After the initial filming sessions, they were free to mingle amongst each other, with the students, and in the wider community, and had extensive daily contact as a group. They also were given six days of classroom instruction in Indian Sign Language, as well as three weeks of capacity building training alongside 14 other deaf Indians, which was conducted in Indian Sign

Language, International Sign, and basic written English. This training focussed on personal skills, human rights campaigning, sign language linguistics, and organisational development.

The daily schedule began with breakfast for participants and researchers in a hostel kitchen and guest room, where International Sign was used along with the participants' respective languages amongst themselves. Most days were spent with Indian deaf students in the training sessions, where lunch would be catered to a nearby classroom, and in the evening, participants dined with both deaf and hearing students in the main dining hall. Travel off campus was limited, as the university is fairly isolated from the city. Non-Indian participants would leave the campus by taxi or rickshaw only in the company of Indian students. There were a few group outings, including a one-day trip to local sites of interest in Lucknow, an evening at a local mela,[3] and a weekend trip to Agra by train. While this restricted the variety of experiences, it did give the group ample daily exposure to the local sign language. Another noteworthy characteristic of this group is that the Jordanians and Indonesians shared a common religion, Islam, which afforded them some mutual cultural understanding, as well as some shared signs/gestures. The Nepali and Indian participants were both Hindu, but no reference to their faith was observed in the setting or the data.

## 4 Linguistic constructs in the group

As the research group gradually formed, their intra-group communication became more effective, including the innovation of bespoke sign constructions. They generated a community of practice with invented signing constructs and inside jokes (cf. Sutton-Spence and Napoli 2012). One example is the use of a sign depicting 'unshackling' to indicate 'freedom' from not interacting with people from other language backgrounds initially (see Figure 2). Putting that time behind them was cause for celebration, and the sign was seen frequently.

---

[3] A *mela* is a festival or fair, which may be organised for cultural, religious, entertainment, or sports purposes and is a popular part of social life in India. In this case, it was a fun fair with stalls and rides.

**Figure 2.** Construct signifying freedom to interact outside the participant group

Another of their constructs had to do with the pairing by nationality; it began in reference to the two Nepalis, who went practically everywhere together, and whose sign names exploited the same handshape (see Figure 3). The other participants started to refer to them using their names simultaneously (see Figure 4):

ANITA　　　　　　　　　　　　　　ANJU

**Figure 3.** Sign names of Anita (Nepali participant) and Anju (Nepali compatriot guide)

ANITA+ANJU

**Figure 4.** Construct signifying 'Anita and Anju, the pair'

This construct was then extended to indicate the other pairs, such as Baha and Mohammed of Jordan (see Figure 5):

BAHA    MOHAMMED    BAHA & MOHAMMED

**Figure 5.** Sign names of Baha (Jordanian participant) and Mohammed (Jordanian compatriot guide), and construct signifying 'Baha and Mohammed, the pair'

# 5 Conclusion

In a community of practice, having a common endeavour and purpose is a key notion. The group members' learning opportunities described here can be perceived as associated benefits of the Multisign project. As they engaged in the same intensive training activity for three weeks, they developed fervour and single-mindedness as a team dedicated to the joint aim of increasing the knowledge and abilities of the newest group members. Their activities were pursued not only in the interest of research but with a common endeavour of ensuring that the international group enjoyed a productive three weeks of training. Therefore, the group essentially formed a community of practice (cf. Trowler and Turner 2002), aiming to equip its members with improved scholarly, linguistic and communicative capacities.

## References

Sutton-Spence, Rachel & Donna Jo Napoli. 2012. Deaf jokes and sign language humour. *Humor: International Journal of Humor Research* 25(3). 311–337.
Trowler, Paul R. & Graham H. Turner. 2002. Exploring the hermeneutic foundations of university life: Deaf academics in a hybrid 'community of practice'. *Higher Education* 43. 227–256.
Zeshan, Ulrike. 2015. "Making meaning" – Communication between sign language users without a shared language. *Cognitive Linguistics* 26(2). 211–260.

# Community profile of an international group of sign language users: Linguistic and social aspects

Kang-Suk Byun

## 1 Introduction

Between 2003 and 2006, an international group of signers was established at the Max Planck Institute (MPI) for Psycholinguistics in Nijmegen, the Netherlands. The group came together as a consequence of the research project on sign language typology, the systematic comparison of structures across sign languages with respect to semantic-grammatical domains, such as negation and possession (Zeshan 2004a, 2004b, 2006, Zeshan and Perniss 2008). This research involved work with research assistants and visitors from a deliberately wide variety of sign language backgrounds, especially from "non-Western" countries. Apart from three hearing group members from Indonesia and the Netherlands, a local hearing project assistant, some short-term visitors, and the head of the group, all other members were deaf sign language users.

Within the group, staff members were employed approximately for durations between six months and 18 months. In most cases, they worked on sign language data from their home countries. The international ad hoc signed communication between group members was not itself an object of research at the time. However, the significance of this unique situation was recognised, and a plan was implemented for filming signed interactions between group members in order to document this communication, with a view to potential later research. The video recordings that were made in this environment are detailed in chapter 2 (see also Byun et al. 2018). A total of seven deaf signers and one hearing signer were involved in these video recordings. This also included two local deaf signers of NGT (Sign Language of the Netherlands). Figure 1 shows all members of the group, with the inner circle representing those who took part in filming, and the outer circle representing additional members. In the figure, each person is labelled according to the country of origin, with the preceding D or H showing the hearing status.

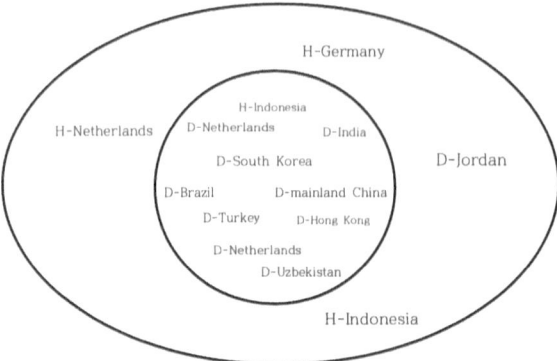

**Figure 1.** Sign language typology group members 2003 – 2006

The aim of this chapter is to document the language contact and social situation in which this group was functioning during the time when video recordings took place.

## 2 The setting

At the time of the sign language typology group, the MPI consisted of ca. 120 staff, research students, and visitors at any one time. Due to a shortage of office space, the sign language typology group was accommodated in a temporary building separately from the main building, just across from the main entrance. A few people from other research groups shared this building, but the majority was taken over by the sign language group. With its own casual meeting space in the middle of the building, and its own kitchen, this setting was conducive to the coherence of the research group.

All members of the sign language group participated in the regular all-staff meetings, and also often attended presentations by other MPI members or visitors, as well as giving presentations at the Institute themselves from time to time. There were daily opportunities to meet other Institute members in shared areas in the main building, particularly the cafeteria. However, for the deaf members of the group the communication barriers were considerable, given that no full-time interpreters were available. Instead, interpreters attended on specific occasions only. The deaf staff members benefited from the standard provision in the Netherlands at the time, which meant the provision of sign language interpreting to the extent of 15 % of working hours for each person, which was paid for by the Dutch government.

Of particular importance to the constitution of the group is the fact that its composition changed constantly, due to the varying and sometimes relatively short length of people's work contracts or visits. This means that any new project member would join the group of the current international signers, would overlap with the other group members to a greater or lesser extent, and leave upon conclusion of the work contract. No two team members had exactly the same duration of stay at the Institute.

Therefore, with the exception of the very first members of the group, each new project member arrived into a situation where the other signers had been communicating with each other for some time, with some group-internal norms of signed communication potentially already developed. Video filming concentrated on each new staff member as they arrived, and this person would meet separately with each of the other participants who had already established themselves at the Institute. As detailed in chapter 3, filming of the same pairs of signers was done repeatedly over time. Most of this video data consists of conversations in pairs, although group interactions, such as dinner conversations, were also filmed a few times. Group interactions have not been analysed though. The participants from Turkey and South Korea are exceptional in that they arrived on the same day, while all other group members arrived individually at separate times.

Most of the signers joined the group directly from their home countries, with two exceptions. The signer from Uzbekistan had been living in Germany for a number of years and joined the group from Germany. The signer from mainland China had studied in the US for several years. Therefore, these two signers were bilingual in the Russian and German sign languages, and in the Chinese and American sign languages respectively.

Figure 2 shows a timeline between 2003 and 2006, plotting the month of arrival and the month of departure for each of the group members who participated in the video filming.

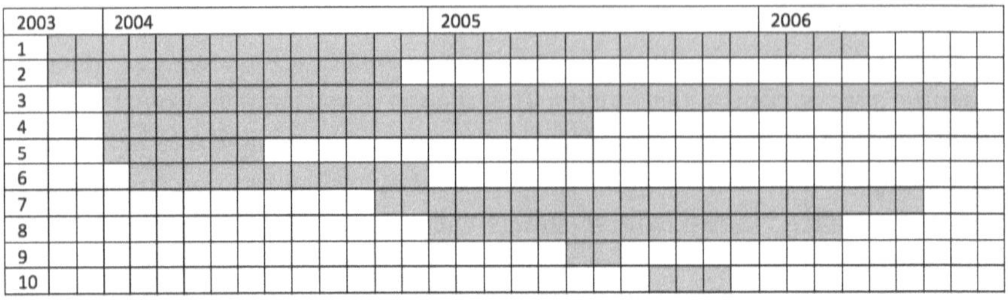

**Figure 2.** Timeline of group composition

1. D-Netherlands (female)
2. D-Netherlands (male)
3. D-Uzbekistan
4. D-South Korea
5. D-Turkey
6. D-mainland China
7. D-India
8. H-Indonesia
9. D-Hong Kong
10. D-Brazil

# 3 Communication

## 3.1 Communication between signers and non-signers

The integration of a group of sign language users with the rest of the Institute was a matter of concern from the beginning. Members of the sign language typology group were peculiar in several ways. First of all, as a non-teaching research institute, the MPI did not have any academic members below the level of PhD student. The sign language typology group, on the other hand, only had two members at post-doctoral level. All the other researchers had lower academic qualifications, and several joined the group with undergraduate levels of education. Moreover, most group members did not have qualifications in linguistics, although all of the international members did have some first-hand experience with sign language research. Thus the common ground in terms of academic background knowledge between members of the sign language group and other members of the MPI was often quite limited.

As mentioned above, sign language interpreting provision was available for the deaf signers. However, International Sign interpreters at the time were not available locally in Nijmegen, and most of the time, they had to travel to the Institute from Amsterdam. This meant that for shorter meetings and interactions, hearing members of the group often undertook interpreting for communication with hearing non-signers outside the group.

In principle, all written communication both within the group and with the wider Institute was in English, the working language of the MPI. However, several deaf members of the group had no or minimal competence in English when they arrived (see Section 3.2 on this issue). Obviously, communication in the wider Institute, given its very international composition, could also include a wide range of other languages, particularly in spoken interactions for non-official purposes. However, deaf signers had by far the most contact with written English during their stay, compared to any other written languages.

In order to encourage more interaction between deaf signers and hearing non-signers at the Institute, the sign language group organised a series of "sign survival" meetings. In these meetings, groups of around 10 hearing non-signers participated in a two-part session for two hours, along with two or three deaf signers. In the first part of the session, the hearing project director gave a presentation that introduced basic information about deaf people's visual communication. This was similar to the communication-related part of "deaf awareness" training that is now commonly available in many European countries. However, at the time, more experienced deaf awareness trainers were not an available resource at the MPI, and the format of the training was invented by the sign language group itself.

After the introductory presentation, the deaf signers would take turns having an improvised gestural communication with one of the hearing non-signers. For instance, they might ask one of the administrative staff how much it costs to send a private fax message, or ask an academic staff member how the password access worked on the computers in the library. The aim of the session was explicitly not to teach any conventional sign language. Rather, hearing non-signers were encouraged to use their gestural repertoire, and their inventiveness in multimodal interactions, also including other ways of communication such as drawing on paper. As a result, communication barriers were lowered, and non-signers could gain some confidence in interacting with deaf signers as well as some basic awareness of visual communication.

These meetings clearly had an influence on the culture at the Institute and within the sign language group. The "sign survival" sessions were also reported on by a regional German newspaper. Sometimes, the proceedings of the sessions had an influence on the sign language group's communication. For example, in one session a hearing staff member with a specialisation in gesture research invented the visually motivated sign for (WORKING-)WEEK shown in Figure 3.

This sign was immediately adopted as an innovation by the sign language typology group, but as the group consisted of skilled signers, the basic gesture was extended to constitute a new family of signs. Figure 4 shows the related sign WEEKEND.

**Figure 3.** (WORKING-)WEEK

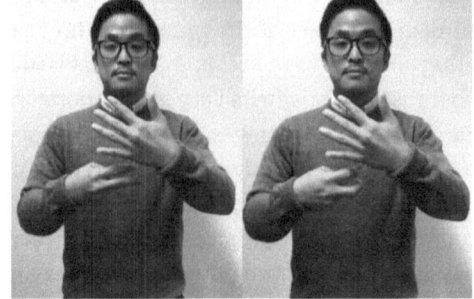

**Figure 4.** WEEKEND

Later on, when the group had a more established system of international signed communication, a more systematic course in international signing was also offered to hearing MPI members, and some took up this opportunity.

The MPI staff category that had most contact with the deaf signers was probably the group of technicians (TG or technical Group). They attended regularly whenever anyone had a technical issue. Interestingly, while they might have no shared language with a deaf staff member beyond some minimal English, communication could still be successful due to shared context. For instance, the deaf signer could point to something on the computer screen and write a couple of words in English, or add a few gestures, for the communication to be successful.

A good measure of the deaf signers' perception in terms of which MPI staff were most important to their work environment is the use of sign names. Within the deaf community, every individual has a sign name which is similar to a nickname in speech communities and consists of a sign that may be based on physical characteristics, a characteristic behaviour, or a combination with a fingerspelled letter (see Meadow 1977, Shun-Chiu and Jingxian 1989, Kourbetis and Hoffmeister 2002 on sign names). A group of deaf people will also develop sign names for new hearing people who they come in contact with, but only if they are sufficiently important to warrant deciding on a sign name; otherwise, hearing people without sign names can be referred to by fingerspelling their name, or by describing them in any ad hoc fashion. The first hearing MPI members who received conventional sign names were some members of the Technical Group, as well as one of the four MPI directors, who was the direct line manager of the group.

## 3.2 Communication within the sign language typology group

Within the sign language typology group, all communication was heavily dominated by signing. All group meetings took place in the signed modality, usually without any voice interpreting. Informal lunchtime conversations and 1:1 meetings, including formal progress monitoring meetings, were also signed. Predominantly, group and individual interactions used the group's own international ad hoc pidgin. Usually there would be well below 10 people in group meetings, so that communication could be constantly adjusted, for example including strategies such as reiterative code-switching, that is, repeating signs with the same meaning from different sign languages one after the other (Quinto-Pozos and Adam 2013). However, signers who knew the same sign language also used their common language when meeting individually. Because most people came from different countries and had limited exposure to and skills in sign languages other than their own (see details in Chapter 3), signers fluent in the same sign language were limited to the following pairs, who did not undertake any filming sessions together:

- Indian Sign Language (hearing German project director and deaf Indian research assistant)
- Turkish Sign Language (hearing German project director and deaf Turkish research assistant)
- Sign Language of the Netherlands (two Dutch deaf project assistants)
- The group members from Hong Kong and mainland China did not overlap during their stay.

Due to the changing composition of the group, at times different sign languages were more dominant than others. For example, for several months in 2004, the deaf research assistant from Uzbekistan, who was bilingual in Russian and German sign languages and was undertaking an MA in linguistics at Amsterdam University concurrently with his job, regularly taught sign language linguistics to other group members. Therefore, German Sign Language became more prominent at the time in some respects, particular in relation to technical terms in linguistics. Later on in the project, American Sign Language became more prominent for a while because one of the deaf research assistants and a hearing linguist visiting the group had strong skills in this language.

During their stay at the Institute, several group members actively worked at improving their English skills. The Turkish and South Korean deaf signers were taught beginners' level English by the project director for several months. The Russian-German signer was using academic English as part of his MA course.

Perhaps most strikingly, Sign Language of the Netherlands never became a strong influence on the communication of the sign language typology group. First and foremost, this was due to the lack of a strong local deaf community in Nijmegen. Nijmegen being quite a small town, there were very few sign language users in the local community, no local deaf club or deaf school, and very few younger deaf people who might have had compatible interests. The two Dutch project assistants both worked on a part-time basis and adjusted to the majority communication rather than exerting an NGT influence, and as mentioned above, the group used International Sign interpreters rather than NGT interpreters.

Occasions where larger groups of deaf Dutch signers gathered locally were very few and far between. Once a month, a "Gebarencafe" ("sign café") was held in Nijmegen, and sometimes attended by group members (though there were few younger deaf people with compatible interests there). Occasionally, the deaf group members would travel to larger cities, usually Arnhem or Amsterdam, and meet deaf Dutch signers there, but this was not at all frequent. Thus to all intents and purposes, the international group of signers was itself the most important deaf community in Nijmegen, and everyone learned a very limited amount of NGT. This is a very unusual setting, especially compared with other groups of cross-signers as described in chapters 10 and 11. In the other cases, the surrounding sign languages, Indian Sign Language and British Sign Language respectively, were a major input into the signed communication of the international group, but this was not the case for the group at the MPI in Nijmegen.

## 4 Social life

In comparison with the other groups of cross-signers, the MPI group as a whole was the most long-standing, albeit with a continually changing composition. In the absence of a large local deaf community, the group's members also had a very active social life with each other outside of working hours. The social life also fully included the two hearing Indonesians, who were equally isolated from their compatriots because there were very few other Indonesians living locally.

To the extent that their stay in the Netherlands overlapped, the deaf signers from India, Turkey, South Korea and Uzbekistan, all of them male, shared a house together, as did the two male hearing Indonesians. Deaf signers from Hong Kong, Brazil, and Jordan were visitors for shorter periods of time and had other living arrangements. The deaf Dutch group members did not live locally, but travelled into Nijmegen on their working days.

Social gatherings, in particular for cooking and eating together, were frequent, both at the Institute and at private homes. For some of the time, an active table tennis group formed, using the table tennis table in the Institute's basement. In addition to the sign language group members, the table tennis group also included several regular hearing non-signing members of the Institute. The mainland Chinese deaf signer also met socially with hearing Chinese MPI members, while other members did not seek out people from their home countries specifically, or there were no other people from their home countries at the MPI.

It is also worth pointing out that for several of the non-Europeans, a clear distinction between working hours and spare time was not a well-established concept in their cultures, and the premise of work-life balance was not familiar. Thus the distinction between work roles and social roles outside of work was also often blurred.

Moreover, some members of the group had a strong sense of joint purpose in terms of promoting sign language research in their home countries and in other countries, particularly in the Global South. Access to university education for deaf sign language users in group members' home countries and elsewhere was also a much-discussed issue. Consequently, four members of the sign language typology group co-founded the Deaf Empowerment Foundation in 2004 as a registered charity ("Stichting" in Dutch law). The DEF organised several events in the Netherlands during the time of the sign language typology group at the MPI, and opened a subsidiary publishing press (Ishara Press) as a social enterprise in 2006, before being dissolved and then re-established in the UK.

## References

Byun, Kang-suk, Connie De Vos, Anastasia Bradford, Ulrike Zeshan & Stephen C. Levinson. 2018. First encounters: Repair sequences in cross-signing. *Topics in Cognitive Science* 10(2). 314–334. doi:10.1111/tops.12303

Kourbetis, Vassilis & Robert J. Hoffmeister. 2002. Name signs in Greek sign language. *American Annals of the Deaf* 147(3). 35–43.

Meadow, Kathryn P. 1977. Name signs as identity symbols in the deaf community. *Sign Language Studies* 16(1). 237–246.

Quinto-Pozos, David & Robert Adam. 2013. Sign language contact. In Robert Bayley, Richard Cameron & Ceil Lucas (eds.), *The Oxford handbook of sociolinguistics*, 379–403. New York: Oxford University Press.

Shun-Chiu, Yau & He Jingxian. 1989. How deaf children in a Chinese school get their name signs. *Sign Language Studies* 65(1). 305–322.

Zeshan, Ulrike. 2004a. Hand, head and face: Negative constructions in sign languages. *Linguistic Typology* 8(1). 1–58.

Zeshan, Ulrike. 2004b. Interrogative constructions in signed languages: Cross-linguistic perspectives. *Language* 80(1). 7–39.

Zeshan, Ulrike (ed.). 2006. *Interrogative and negative constructions in sign languages (Sign Language Typology Series No. 1)*. Nijmegen: Ishara Press.

Zeshan, Ulrike & Pamela Perniss (eds.). 2008. *Possessive and existential constructions in sign languages (Sign Language Typology Series No. 2)*. Nijmegen: Ishara Press.

# Language Index

American Sign Language  5–6, 9–10, 26, 33, 40–43, 46–48, 58, 62, 70, 74, 81, 83, 90–91, 93, 95–99, 101–102, 106, 116, 123, 173, 175, 186–187, 197, 202–203, 207–208, 211, 213–215, 217–219, 221, 234, 236, 240–241, 289
Arabic  14, 34, 58, 134, 274, 278
Argentinean Sign Language  26, 45, 48
Auslan  9, 58–59, 82
Bahasa Indonesia  14, 34, 134, 274, 278
Brazilian Portuguese  5, 202, 207–208, 210, 216–217
Brazilian Sign Language  5, 202, 207–208, 216–217
British Sign Language  16, 81–82, 134, 153, 156–157, 159–160, 163, 228, 231, 236, 238–239, 251, 274–275, 278, 290
Burundi Sign Language  7, 15, 83–91, 93–121, 123, 240–241, 261–265
Chinese  34, 291
Chinese Pidgin English  128, 130
Chinese Sign Language  62, 83, 285
Chinuk Wawa  129
Dutch  34, 42, 94, 102, 109, 175–176, 204–206, 217, 284, 289–291
English  1, 5–6, 8, 13, 26, 30, 32–34, 40, 42, 45, 57–59, 73, 76, 81, 83–85, 90, 94, 102–103, 109, 111, 113, 116, 128, 130–131, 133–134, 173, 175, 178, 186–187, 197, 202–204, 207–208, 211, 214, 217–219, 229, 236, 246, 263, 267, 274–275, 277–278, 280, 287–289
Eskimo Pidgin  128–129
Fanakalo  130–131
Fijian  131
Finnish Sign Language  205
French  4, 84–85, 90, 204, 206, 222, 263
German  34, 131, 203, 206, 287
German Sign Language  32–34, 289
Hindi  5–6, 8, 13–14, 103, 121, 134, 244–246, 267–269, 278
Hiri Motu  131
Hong Kong Sign Language  28, 32, 34, 58, 62
Indian Sign Language  5–8, 13–16, 83–89, 91–122, 133–134, 140, 145–146, 149, 153, 155–158, 160, 162–164, 240–241, 244, 246, 252, 261–265, 267, 269, 278–279, 289–290
Indonesian Sign Language  32, 34, 41, 43, 134, 143–146, 153, 155–157, 159–160, 231, 274, 276, 278
International Sign  16–17, 24–25, 32, 34, 62, 76, 83, 129, 131, 133–134, 136, 153, 231, 235, 262, 265, 274, 278–280, 285–286, 288, 290
Israeli Sign Language  81
Italian  13, 81, 176, 179, 182–184, 206, 221, 223
Italian Sign Language  13, 81, 176, 179, 182–184, 189, 191–193, 196, 221, 223
Japanese  14, 134, 236, 274
Japanese Sign Language  13, 16, 93, 134, 148, 153, 156, 158, 160, 163, 231, 233, 235, 238, 274, 276
Jordanian Sign Language  32, 34, 43, 58, 134, 143, 153, 155–156, 163, 231, 278
Kenyan Sign Language  263
Korean  34, 58
Korean Sign Language  28, 32, 34, 41, 46–47, 58, 62, 74, 263
Mexican Sign Language  81, 93, 102
Ndjuka-Trio Pidgin  130
Nepali  34, 134
Nepali Sign Language  32, 34, 58, 67, 134, 153, 155, 157–158, 160, 162, 164, 231
Portuguese  5, 202, 207
Quechua  119
Russian  32, 34, 81, 125, 285, 289
Russian Sign Language  34
Sign Language of the Netherlands  3, 9, 32, 41–43, 55, 175–176, 204–205, 217, 283, 289–290
Spanish  119, 203
Swahili  90
Turkish  4, 6, 8, 12–13, 15, 171, 173–175, 177–185, 191–197, 244
Turkish Sign Language  4, 6, 12–13, 99, 171, 173–175, 177–185, 191–197, 244, 289
Ugandan Sign Language  96, 99, 263
Yimas-Arafundi Pidgin  130
Zulu  130

https://doi.org/10.1515/9781501503528-013

# Subject Index

alternation 5, 95
articulatory effort 142
base language 175, 205, 217
bilingualism 1–5, 12, 16, 81, 85, 87, 120, 122, 171–173, 175, 185–186, 188–189, 197, 207–208, 223, 277
– bilingual signer 81, 88, 92, 121–122, 261
bimodal bilingualism 4–8, 17, 173–175, 196, 202, 206–208, 222–227
candidate understanding 47
classifier 10, 101, 137–140, 144, 146, 150, 162, 164
Codas (see also kodas) 1, 4, 81, 173–174, 201, 203, 269, 275
code-blending 176, 186–187, 197
code-switching (see also sign-switching) 5, 86, 157
communicative success 12–14, 23, 25, 30, 50–51, 53, 58, 72–74, 129, 144, 149, 160, 230
community of practice (see also micro-community of practice) 12, 14, 17, 82, 120–121, 261–267, 270, 272, 275–277, 280, 282
compound 97, 108, 116, 121, 145, 158, 163
constructed action 10, 137, 140, 146
corpus-driven research 5, 7, 9, 31, 34, 50, 73, 86, 88, 119, 184, 209, 228–229
creole 90
cross-signing 132
distributed morphology 171, 174, 189, 192–195, 219
elicitation 87, 209, 239–240, 244, 251–252
elicitation materials (see also game) 86, 133, 137, 141–142, 146, 150, 152–156, 158–159, 163–164, 189, 227, 239–241, 243–251, 253, 255, 275
Embedded Language 13, 95
experiment 150, 164, 243, 246, 251, 254, 278
facial expression 45, 47, 49, 55, 70, 142, 230
feature pool 15, 130, 132, 142, 152, 158, 160, 162–164
fieldwork 77, 82, 101, 103, 227, 249, 269

fingerspelling (see also literacy) 14, 33, 38, 57–58, 236
first encounter 32, 51, 58–59, 132
first language 41, 84, 127, 129, 157, 159, 162, 174, 265
frequency 39, 51, 54, 57–58, 96, 102–104, 106–108, 150, 152–153, 160, 162–163, 205, 254, 271
game (see also elicitation materials) 10, 86, 134–137, 141–142, 146–147, 149–152, 154, 156–160, 162, 218, 238–240, 242, 244–246, 248–254, 275
gestures, communicative 95, 137, 141, 158
grammatical structure 113, 128–129, 131, 182, 194
heritage signer 208
hesitation phenomenon 30, 112–113, 156
iconicity 43–44, 59, 67–68, 93, 101, 128, 138, 140, 150, 152–154, 162, 164, 236–238
inflectional morphology 129
insertion 7, 95, 119, 189, 191–196, 219–220
interaction 8, 24–25, 27, 128, 130, 201–202, 206, 219, 223, 245, 249, 267, 281
interactive model 171, 173, 186, 190, 196–197
interview 41, 46, 102, 136–137, 229, 231, 233–238
jargon 76, 127–132, 146, 164
kodas (see also codas) 205–208, 217
language acquisition 206–207, 255, 277
language choice 205, 217, 241
language contact 1–3, 8, 11, 26, 81–82, 127, 130, 262, 284
language synthesis 6–7, 174, 189–191, 195–197, 201, 207, 219–222
lexicon 41–42, 83, 93, 127–132, 152, 189
lexifier language 132, 163
linguistic repertoire 24, 29
literacy (see also fingerspelling) 14, 16, 38–39, 50, 53, 57–58, 60, 71–72, 75, 81, 84, 149, 237, 241
Matrix Language 7, 95, 172, 185
Matrix Language Frame model 7, 95, 172, 185

https://doi.org/10.1515/9781501503528-014

metalinguistic  2, 12, 77, 232–234, 237–238, 255, 276
micro-community of practice (see also community of practice)  14–16, 267, 269, 271–273, 276–278
minimalist model  171, 173–174, 185–186, 188–189, 191, 196–197
minimalist program  172, 185, 188
mismatch (between sign and speech)  211, 214–216, 267
mixed languages  6
mouthing  46, 55, 57, 235–236
multilingual setting  12, 15
multimodality  1–9, 11–17, 81, 171–175, 177, 182, 184–186, 191, 193, 196–197, 201–202, 204, 206–227, 232–233, 235–237, 244, 255, 272, 287
Multisign project  1, 4, 16–17, 31–36, 41, 50, 70, 73, 75, 77, 171, 227, 233, 239–240, 244, 255, 267, 273, 277, 282
non-native  128–129, 154, 156–157, 159–160, 162, 208, 265, 267–269
other-initiated repair (see also repair)  28, 30, 39–41, 45–46, 67
pidgin  24, 76, 127–131, 289
referent, human  138, 157
repair  10, 14, 23–31, 36–42, 45, 48–55, 57–59, 64, 67, 70–76, 142, 144, 222
– open repair  40, 42, 45
– repair sequence  28, 37, 39, 41, 49, 51, 71

– repair solution  29
– restricted repair  45
response time  141, 146–149, 160
secondary language  8
selection of variants  15–16, 72, 108, 153, 158, 160, 247
self-initiated repair (see also repair)  28, 30
sign multilingualism  1, 3, 7, 16–17, 227, 265
sign-speaking  269
sign type  150, 152
Simultaneous Communication  4, 203–204
size and shape specifier  51, 68, 101–102, 137–140, 142–145, 149–152, 154, 156–158, 162–163
social learning  2, 12, 14–15
sociolinguistic norms  2, 12, 14–15
syntactic calque  6, 176–177, 179–181, 183, 192
translanguaging  2
trouble sources  23–24, 26–30, 32, 36, 38–49, 51, 54–55, 58–59, 61–62, 64, 67, 70–71, 75–76, 229
unimodal  4, 6–7, 81–82, 100, 122, 172–174, 188, 193, 196–197, 202, 204, 206–207, 219, 223, 241
unimodal bilingual  4, 7, 81, 100, 174, 196, 204, 206, 219
word order  6–7, 13, 90–91, 113–115, 118, 179, 181–182, 184, 193, 211, 218–219, 222

www.ingramcontent.com/pod-product-compliance
Lightning Source LLC
Chambersburg PA
CBHW031326230426
43670CB00006B/251